CYBER SECURITY AND IT INFRASTRUCTURE PROTECTION

CYBER SECURITY AND IT INFRASTRUCTURE PROTECTION

Edited by

JOHN R. VACCA

ELSEVIER

AMSTERDAM • BOSTON • HEIDELBERG • LONDON
NEW YORK • OXFORD • PARIS • SAN DIEGO
SAN FRANCISCO • SYDNEY • TOKYO
Syngress is an imprint of Elsevier

SYNGRESS.

Publisher: Steven Elliot
Senior Developmental Editor: Nathaniel McFadden
Editorial Project Manager: Lindsay Lawrence
Project Manager: Mohanambal Natarajan
Designer: Matthew Limbert

Syngress is an imprint of Elsevier
225 Wyman Street, Waltham, MA 02451, USA

First edition 2014

Library of Congress Cataloging-in-Publication Data
A catalog record for this book is available from the Library of Congress

British Library Cataloguing in Publication Data
A catalogue record for this book is available from the British Library

For information on all **Syngress** publications,
visit our website at store.elsevier.com/Syngress

ISBN: 978-0-12-416681-3

Printed and bound in USA

14 15 16 17 18   10 9 8 7 6 5 4 3 2 1

Working together
to grow libraries in
developing countries

www.elsevier.com • www.bookaid.org

This book is dedicated to my wife Bee.

Contents

Acknowledgements

There are many people whose efforts on this book have contributed to its successful completion. I owe each a debt of gratitude and want to take this opportunity to offer my sincere thanks.

A very special thanks to my publisher, Steve Elliot, without whose continued interest and support this book would not have been possible. Senior development editor Nate McFadden provided staunch support and encouragement when it was most needed. Thanks to my production project manager, Mohanambal Natarajan, whose fine work and attention to detail has been invaluable. Thanks also to my marketing manager, Todd Conly, whose efforts on this book have been greatly appreciated. Finally, thanks to all the other people at Morgan Kaufmann Publishers/Elsevier Science & Technology Books, whose many talents and skills are essential to a finished book.

Thanks to my wife, Bee Vacca, for her love, her help, and her understanding of my long work hours. Finally, I wish to thank all the following authors who contributed chapters that were necessary for the completion of this book: Jeffrey S. Bardin, Rahul Bhaskar, Lauren Collins, Scott R. Ellis, Anna Granova, Ravi Jhawar, Bhushan Kapoor, Luther Martin, Pramod Pandya, Vincenzo Piuri, Marco Santambrogio Marco Slaviero, Terence Spies, William Stallings.

About the Editor

John Vacca is an information technology consultant, professional writer, editor, reviewer and internationally-known, best-selling author based in Pomeroy, Ohio. Since 1982, John has authored 73 books (some of his most recent books include):

- **Computer and Information Security Handbook, 2E** (*Publisher:* Morgan Kaufmann (an imprint of Elsevier Inc.) (June 7, 2013))
- **Identity Theft (Cybersafety)** (*Publisher:* Chelsea House Pub (April 1, 2012)
- **System Forensics, Investigation, And Response** (*Publisher:* Jones & Bartlett Learning (September 24, 2010)
- **Managing Information Security** (*Publisher:* Syngress (an imprint of Elsevier Inc.) (March 29, 2010))
- **Network and Systems Security** (*Publisher:* Syngress (an imprint of Elsevier Inc.) (March 29, 2010))
- **Computer and Information Security Handbook, 1E** (*Publisher:* Morgan Kaufmann (an imprint of Elsevier Inc.) (June 2, 2009))
- **Biometric Technologies and Verification Systems** (*Publisher:* Elsevier Science & Technology Books (March 16, 2007))
- **Practical Internet Security** (Hardcover): (*Publisher:* Springer (October 18, 2006))
- **Optical Networking Best Practices Handbook** (Hardcover): (*Publisher:* Wiley-Interscience (November 28, 2006))
- **Guide to Wireless Network Security** (*Publisher:* Springer (August 19, 2006)
- **Computer Forensics: Computer Crime Scene Investigation (With CD-ROM), 2nd Edition** (*Publisher:* Charles River Media (May 26, 2005)

and, more than 600 articles in the areas of advanced storage, computer security and aerospace technology (copies of articles and books are available upon request). John was also a configuration management specialist, computer specialist, and the computer security official (CSO) for NASA's space station program (Freedom) and the International Space Station Program, from 1988 until his retirement from NASA in 1995. In addition, John is also an independent online book reviewer. Finally, John was one of the security consultants for the MGM movie titled: "AntiTrust," which was released on January 12, 2001. A detailed copy of my author bio can be viewed at URL: http://www.johnvacca.com. John can be reached at: john2164@windstream.net.

Contributors

Jeffrey S. Bardin (Chapter 14), Chief Intelligence Strategist, Treadstone 71 LLC, Barre, MA 01005

Rahul Bhaskar (Chapter 7), Professor, Department of Information Systems and DecisionSciences, California State University, Fullerton, California 92834

Lauren Collins (Chapters 5, 9, 10, 11, 12), Senior Systems Engineer, kCura Corporation, Chicago, IL 60604

Scott R. Ellis, EnCE, RCA (Chapters 5, 13), Manager, Infrastructure Engineering Team, kCura, Chicago, IL 60604

Anna Granova (Chapter 8), Advocate of the High Court of South Africa, Member of the Pretoria Society of Advocates, University of Pretoria, Computer Science Department, Hillcrest, Pretoria, South Africa, 0002

Ravi Jhawar (Chapter 1), Professor, Universita' degli Studi di Milano, Crema (CR), Italy

Bhushan Kapoor (Chapters 2, 7), Chair, Department of Information Systems and Decision Sciences, California State University, Fullerton, California 92834

Luther Martin (Chapter 6), Chief Security Architect, Voltage Security, Palo Alto, California 94304

Pramod Pandya (Chapters 2, 15), Professor, Department of Information Systems and Decision Sciences, California State University, Fullerton, California 92834

Vincenzo Piuri (Chapter 1), Professor, Universita' degli Studi di Milano, Crema (CR), Italy

Marco Santambrogio (Chapter 1), Professor, Universita' degli Studi di Milano, Crema (CR), Italy

Marco Slaviero (Chapter 8), Security Analyst, SensePost Pty Ltd, Pretoria, South Africa

Terence Spies (Chapter 3), Chief Technology Officer// vice president of engineering, Voltage Security, Inc., Palo Alto, California 94304

William Stallings (Chapter 4), Independent consultant, Brewster Massachusetts 02631

Introduction

This Cyber Security And IT Infrastructure Protection derivative book serves as a security practitioner's guide to today's most crucial issues in cyber security and IT infrastructure protection. It offers in-depth coverage of theory, technology, and practice as they relate to established technologies as well as recent advancements in the field. It explores practical solutions to a wide range of cyber-physical and IT infrastructure protection issues with individual chapters authored by leading experts in the field addressing the immediate and long-term challenges in the authors' respective areas of expertise.

Furthermore, this comprehensive book serves as a professional reference to provide the most complete and concise view of how to manage cyber attacks on the critical IT infrastructure computer networks, which are aimed at significantly disrupting or permanently wiping out the functioning of government and business alike. The cyber attacks would produce cascading effects far beyond the targeted sector and physical location of the incident. Thus, this book provides a very detailed comprehensive step-by-step guide on how to defend the communications and information technology infrastructure, which is designed to improve resilience versus attacks; and, to reduce the overall cyber threat.

The book also provides very vital detailed information for practitioners and IT professionals, who are taking IT infrastructure protection to a new level and are creating the latest tools, techniques and solutions for protecting resources from internal and external cyber terrorism. The book is therefore useful to any manager who is currently developing risk management practices. In addition, in this book, you will also learn how to:

1. Develop a new level of technical expertise in the field of theory and practice of cyber security and IT infrastructure protection
2. Remain current and fully informed from multiple viewpoints by comprehensive and up-to-date coverage of cyber security issues
3. Grasp the material, in order to implement practical solutions, and present methods of analysis and problem-solving techniques.
4. Provide a consultative process to assess the cyber security-related risks to organizational missions and business functions
5. Provide a menu of management, operational, and technical security controls, including policies and processes, available to address a range of threats and protect privacy
6. Provide a consultative process to identify the security controls that would adequately address risks that have been assessed and to protect data and information being processed, stored, and transmitted by organizational information systems
7. Provide metrics, methods, and procedures that can be used to assess and monitor, on an ongoing or

continuous basis, the effectiveness of security controls that are selected and deployed in organizational information systems and environments in which those systems operate and available processes that can be used to facilitate continuous improvement in such controls

8. Provide a comprehensive risk management approach that provides the ability to assess, respond to, and monitor information security-related risks and provide senior leaders/executives with the kinds of necessary information sets that help them to make ongoing risk-based decisions

9. Provide a menu of privacy controls necessary to protect privacy

You will also learn the latest strategies and initiatives for protecting the IT infrastructure against cyber attacks. You will learn what the latest threats are; and, how the threat environment is evolving.

Cyber security must address not only deliberate attacks, such as from disgruntled employees, industrial espionage, and terrorists, but also inadvertent compromises of the information infrastructure due to user errors, equipment failures, and natural disasters. You will also acquire knowledge on how organizations assess risk; how cyber security factors into that risk assessment; the current usage of existing cyber security frameworks, standards, and guidelines; and, other management practices related to cyber security.

In addition, an understanding of whether particular frameworks, standards, guidelines, and/or best practices are mandated by legal or regulatory requirements and the challenges organizations perceive in meeting such requirements is vital. This will assist in developing a framework that includes and identifies common practices across sectors.

National and economic security depends on the reliable functioning of the critical infrastructure, which has become increasingly dependent on information technology. Recent trends demonstrate the need for improved capabilities for defending against malicious cyber activity. Such activity is increasing and its consequences can range from theft through disruption to destruction. Steps must be taken to enhance existing efforts to increase the protection and resilience of this IT infrastructure, while maintaining a cyber environment that encourages efficiency, innovation, and economic prosperity, while protecting privacy. Throughout this book, you will gain practical skills through a adoption of the following practices as they pertain to critical IT infrastructure components:

1. Separation of business from operational systems
2. Use of encryption and key management
3. Identification and authorization of users accessing systems
4. Asset identification and management
5. Monitoring and incident detection tools and capabilities
6. Incident handling policies and procedures
7. Mission/system resiliency practices
8. Security engineering practices
9. Privacy protection

Finally, this book is valuable for information security practitioners at the managerial, operational and technical levels. Job titles include IT Manager, Information Security Officer, IT Security Analyst, Security Auditor, etc. This book will also be of value to students in upper-level courses in information security management. For example, the reader should have general familiarity with- and have knowledge equivalent in the following areas:

- Disaster recovery
- Biometrics
- Homeland security
- Cyber warfare
- Cyber security
- National infrastructure security
- Access controls
- Vulnerability assessments and audits
- Cryptography
- Operational and organizational security

The preceding compilation is ideally suited as a standalone product in this high-growth subject area.

ORGANIZATION OF THIS BOOK

The book is composed of 15 contributed chapters by leading experts in their fields. This book is formatted to include methods of analysis and problem-solving techniques through hands-on exercises, worked examples, and case studies. For example, the new format includes the following elements:

- Checklists throughout each chapter to gauge understanding
- Chapter Summaries/ Review Questions/ Exercises/Case Studies

Contributors Ravi Jhawar, Vincenzo Piuri and Marco Santambrogio (Chapter 1, "Fault Tolerance and Resilience in Cloud Computing Environments") focus on characterizing the recurrent failures in a typical Cloud computing environment, analyzing the effects of failures on user's applications, and surveying fault tolerance solutions corresponding to each class of failures.

The increasing demand for flexibility and scalability in dynamically obtaining and releasing computing resources in a cost-effective and device-independent manner, and easiness in hosting applications without the burden of installation and maintenance, has resulted in a wide adoption of the cloud computing paradigm. While the benefits are immense, this computing paradigm is still vulnerable to a large number of system failures; as a consequence, users have become increasingly concerned about the reliability and availability of cloud computing services.

Finally, fault tolerance and resilience serve as an effective means to address users' reliability and availability concerns. In this chapter, the focus is on characterizing the recurrent failures in a typical cloud computing environment, analyzing the effects of failures on users' applications and surveying fault tolerance solutions corresponding to each class of failures. The authors also discuss the perspective of offering fault tolerance as a service to users' applications as one of the effective means of addressing users' reliability and availability concerns.

Next, contributors **Bhushan Kapoor and Pramod Pandya** (Chapter 2, "Data Encryption") discuss the role played by cryptographic technology in data security. In other words, the Internet evolved over the years as a means for users to access information and exchange emails. Later, once the bandwidth became available, businesses exploited the Internet's popularity to reach customers online. In the past few years it has been reported that organizations that store and maintain customers' private and confidential records were compromised on many occasions by hackers breaking into the data networks and stealing the records from storage media. More recently we have come across headline-grabbing security breaches regarding laptops with sensitive data being lost or stolen, and most recently the Feds have encrypted around 1 million laptops with encryption software loaded to secure data such as names and Social Security numbers.

Finally, this chapter is about security and the role played by cryptographic technology in data security. Securing data while it is in storage or in transition from an unauthorized access is a critical function of information technology. All forms of ecommerce activities such as online credit card processing, purchasing stocks, and banking data processing would, if compromised, lead to businesses losing billions of dollars in revenues, as well as customer confidence lost in ecommerce.

Then, contributor **Terence Spies** (Chapter 3, "Public Key Infrastructure") explains the cryptographic background that forms the foundation of PKI systems; the mechanics of the X.509 PKI system (as elaborated by the Internet Engineering Task Force); the practical issues surrounding the implementation of PKI systems; a number of alternative PKI standards; and alternative cryptographic strategies for solving the problem of secure public key distribution. PKI systems are complex objects that have proven to be difficult to implement properly. This chapter aims to survey the basic architecture of PKI systems, and some of the mechanisms used to implement them.

Finally, this chapter does not aim to be a comprehensive guide to all PKI standards or to contain sufficient technical detail to allow implementation of a PKI system. These systems are continually evolving, and the reader interested in building or operating a PKI is advised to consult the current work of standards bodies referenced in this chapter.

Contributor **William Stallings** (Chapter 4, "Physical Security Essentials")

is concerned with physical security and some overlapping areas of premises security. He also looks at physical security threats and then considers physical security prevention measures.

Most people think about locks, bars, alarms, and uniformed guards when they think about security. While these countermeasures are by no means the only precautions that need to be considered when trying to secure an information system, they are a perfectly logical place to begin.

This chapter discusses physical security and with some overlapping areas of premises security. Physical security is a vital part of any security plan and is fundamental to all security efforts with out it, cyber security, software security, user access security, and network security are considerably more difficult, if not impossible, to initiate.

Finally, pPhysical security refers to the protection of building sites and equipment (and all information and software contained therein) from theft, vandalism, natural disaster, man made catastrophes, and accidental damage (from electrical surges, extreme temperatures, and spilled coffee). It requires solid building construction, suitable emergency preparedness, reliable power supplies, adequate climate control, and appropriate protection from intruders.

Next, contributors Lauren Collins and Scott R. Ellis (Chapter 5, "Disaster Recovery") provide insight to the job of DR, and provide a framework of what is necessary to achieve a successful Disaster Recovery plan. Since the environment is ever changing in an organization, the disaster recovery (DR) environment must also be continuously replicated and tested at a pace determined by the team who works on the DR plan. It must be periodically audited. Roles must be revised and reassigned as needed.

Finally, the science of a DR plan, the exact nuts and bolts of the many technologies used and approaches to take, is beyond the scope of this chapter. For example, just the DR options for SQL server applications represent a very large body of work. Failover technologies, software for IP and phone rerouting, and other data synchronization technologies do exist.

Then, contributor Luther Martin (Chapter 6, "Biometrics") discusses the different types of biometrics technology and verification systems and how the following work: biometrics eye analysis technology; biometrics facial recognition technology; facial thermal imaging; biometrics finger-scanning analysis technology; biometrics geometry analysis technology; biometrics verification technology; and privacy-enhanced, biometrics-based verification/ authentication as well as biometrics solutions and future directions. This chapter explains why designing biometric systems is actually a very difficult problem. The problem has been made to look easier than it actually is by the way that the technology has been portrayed in movies and on television.

Finally, biometric systems are typically depicted as being easy to use and secure, whereas encryption that would actually take billions of years of supercomputer time to defeat is often depicted as being easily bypassed with minimal effort. This portrayal of biometric systems may have increased expectations well past what current technologies can actually deliver, and it is important to understand the limitations of existing biometric technologies and to have realistic expectations of the security that such systems can provide in the real world.

Then, contributor Rahul Bhaskar (Chapter 7, "Homeland Security") describes some principle provisions of U.S. homeland security-related laws and Presidential directives. He gives the organizational changes that were initiated to support homeland security in the United States.

The chapter highlights the 9/11 account of the circumstances surrounding the 2001 terrorist attacks and develops recommendations for corrective measures that could be taken to prevent future acts of terrorism. The author also details the Intelligence Reform and Terrorism Prevention Act of 2004 and the Implementation of the 9/11 Commission Recommendations Act of 2007.

The September 11, 2001, terrorist attacks, permanently changed the way the United States and the world's other most developed countries perceived the threat from terrorism. Massive amounts of resources were mobilized in a very short time to counter the perceived and actual threats from terrorists and terrorist organizations. In the United States, this refocus was pushed as a necessity for what was called *homeland security*. The homeland security threats were anticipated for the IT infrastructure as well.

It was expected that not only was the IT at the federal level vulnerable to disruptions due to terrorism-related attacks but, due to the ubiquity of the availability of IT, any organization was vulnerable. Soon after the terrorist attacks, the U.S. Congress passed various new laws and enhanced some existing ones that introduced sweeping changes to homeland security provisions and to the existing security organizations.

The executive branch of the government also issued a series of Homeland Security Presidential Directives to maintain domestic security. These laws and directives are comprehensive and contain detailed provisions to make the U.S. secure from its vulnerabilities.

Later in the chapter, the author describes some principle provisions of these homeland security-related laws and presidential directives. Next, he discusses the organizational changes that were initiated to support homeland security in the United States.

Finally, he highlights the 9-11 Commission that Congress charted to provide a full account of the circumstances surrounding the attacks and to develop recommendations for corrective measures that could be taken to prevent future acts of terrorism. The author also details the Intelligence Reform and Terrorism Prevention Act of 2004 and the Implementation of the 9-11 Commission Recommendations Act of 2007. Finally, he summarizes the chapter's discussion.

Next, contributors Anna Granova and Marco Slaviero (Chapter 8, "Cyber Warfare") define cyber warfare (CW) and discuss its most common tactics, weapons, and tools; as well as, comparing CW terrorism with conventional warfare and addressing the issues of liability and the available legal remedies under international law. The times we live in are called the Information Age for very good reasons: Today information is probably worth much more than any other commodity.

Globalization, the other important phenomenon of the times we live in, has taken the value of information to new heights. On one hand, citizens of a country may now feel entitled to know exactly what is happening in other countries around the globe. On the other, the same people can use the Internet to mobilize forces to overthrow the government in their own country. To this end, the capabilities of the Internet have been put to use and people have become accustomed to receiving information about everyone and everything as soon as it becomes available.

Finally, the purpose of this chapter is to define the concept of cyber warfare (CW), discuss their most common tactics, weapons, and tools, compare CW terrorism with conventional warfare, and address the issues of liability and the avail- able legal remedies under international law. To have this discussion, a proper model and definition of CW first needs to be established.

Then, contributor Lauren Collins (Chapter 9, "System Security") shows you how to protect your information from harm, and also ways to make your data readily available for access to an intended audience of users. Computer security is one division of technology; it is often referred to as information security and is applied to the systems we work on; as well as, the networks that transmit the data.

The term computer security often necessitates cooperative procedures and appliances by which such sensitive and confidential information and services are secure from an attack by unauthorized activities, usually achieved by treacherous individuals. Hackers plan events to take place on systems unexpectedly and usually target an audience or targeted data set that was well thought out and carefully planned.

Finally, this chapter objective includes familiarizing yourself with how to protect your information from harm, and also presents ways to make your data readily available for access to an intended audience of users. The author believes a real world perspective of hardware security is crucial to building secure systems in practice, but it has not been sufficiently addressed in the security research community. Many of the sections in this chapter strive to cover this gap.

In addition, contributor Lauren Collins (Chapter 10, "Securing the Infrastructure"), focuses on how security is presented to protect the infrastructure. Smart grid cyber security in this chapter, also addresses not only deliberate attacks, such as from disgruntled employees, industrial espionage, and terrorists; but, also inadvertent compromises of the information infrastructure due to user errors, equipment failures, and natural disasters.

Collectively, an infrastructure consists of circuits, cabinets, cages, cabling, power, cooling, hardware, data, and traffic. Devices are placed meticulously to transmit data, to secure data, and to allow an organization to conduct business efficiently and effectively.

Finally, security is presented to protect the infrastructure, especially critical applications, and custom rules strive to restrict the susceptibilities of such structures and systems. Incidental occurrences may severely impact the business, and potentially the economy, which is the prime reason engineers architect an infrastructure to manage information securely. The nature of the business that is conducted should be considered when designing the layout of an infrastructure, where security may not always be the top priority and speed is.

Furthermore, contributor Lauren Collins (Chapter 11, "Access Controls,") endeavors to inform the reader about the different types of access controls that are being used, and describes the pros and cons they might have. Thus, the application of security policies for computers and their systems and procedures leads into the mechanism of access control.

The fundamental goal of any access control instrument is to provide a verifiable system for assuring the protection of information from unauthorized or inappropriate access, as outlined in one or more security policies. Generally, this translation from security policy to access control implementation is dependent on the nature of the policy and involves the inclusion of confidentiality and integrity.

Finally, systems are responsible for verifying the authenticity of an individual to gain access to a space, or to detect and exclude a computer program failing a spoof test as an access control. Two-factor authentication occurs when elements representing two factors are required for identification. The ways in which someone may be authenticated fall into three categories, based on what are known as the factors of authentication: something the user knows, something the user has, and something the user is.

Contributor Lauren Collins (Chapter 12, "Assessments and Audits,") continues by presenting the basic technical aspects of conducting information security assessments and audits. She presents technical testing and examination methods and techniques that an organization might use as part of an assessment and audit, and offers insights to assessors on their execution and the potential impact they may have on systems and networks.

Risk Management is a discipline that exists in every professional environment. Having the ability to gauge and measure exposure within an environment effectively prepares the organization to proactively implement workflows and assessments.

Defining security holes in an organization is the delineation of risk that may exist. It is necessary to architect a framework to analyze exclusive incidents, potential outcomes that may arise from such incidents, and the impending consequences.

Managing vulnerability where a team can identify, classify, remediate, and mitigate potential situations is critical to keeping a business up and running. Additionally, tools can be utilized to identify and classify possible vulnerabilities.

Information security needs to be in line with the business objectives, and decisions must be made based on metrics and indicators of vulnerabilities. Regularly combining assessments and audits offers executives a clear, prioritized, and comprehensive view of risks and vulnerabilities, while integrating IT assets, resources, environment and processes into a single platform.

Finally, just as IP addresses had to advance from IPv4 to IPv6, password lengths will have to increase, as will their complexity. Standardization and open collaboration benefit both vendors and consumers; as well as, advance the industry as a whole. Security professionals benefit from the portability and ease of customization of assessing content; as well as, assessing the impact of the latest vulnerability.

Contributor Scott R. Ellis (Chapter 13, "Fundamentals of Cryptography,") discusses how information security is the discipline that provides protection of information from intrusion and accidental or incidental loss. He also provides a framework for the protection of information from unauthorized use, copying, distribution, or destruction of data.

Finally, cryptography plays a key role in supporting the protection of captured data from prying eyes. It does nothing to actually protect the encrypted data from being intercepted.

Next, contributor Jeffrey S. Bardin (Chapter 14, "Satellite Cyber Attack Search and Destroy,") discusses satellite cyber attacks with regards to hacking, interference and jamming. For the last several years, we have been notified that sunspot activity could disrupt Earth's communications. In fact, there have been numerous cell phone outages due to sunspots. This disruption has a significant impact on the daily life of humans on this planet. Nearly all disruptions we have experienced have been the result of natural acts.

Finally, imagine if someone had the capability to hack a satellite. This type of activity appears in movies: Hackers release malware installed on a system that modifies the geographic positioning system of oceangoing oil tankers. Although this potentiality may be unrealistic, the effect should it occur would be extremely high. Whether environmental disaster, or total disruption of command-and-control of a military operation, or massive outages during the Super Bowl of satellite connectivity, the impacts would be significant relative to sunspots.

Finally, contributor **Pramod Pandya** (Chapter 15, "Advanced Data Encryption,") explores advanced data encryption algorithms. Every engineered system has a flaw, and it is only a matter of time before someone compromises it, thus demanding new innovations by exploring applications from algebraic structures such as groups and rings, elliptic curves, hyperelliptic curves, lattice-based and quantum physics.

Over the last 20 years, we have witnessed the evolution of classical cryptography into quantum cryptography, a branch of quantum information theory. Quantum cryptography is based on the framework of quantum physics, and it is meant to solve the problem of key distribution, which is an essential component of cryptography that enables securing the data.

A key allows the data to be so coded that to decode the data one would need to know the key that was used to code the data. This coding of the given data using the key is known as the encryption; and, decoding of the encryption data, which is the reverse step-by-step process, is known as the decryption. Data encryption prevents data from being exposed to unauthorized access and makes it unusable.

John R. Vacca
Editor-in-Chief

Fault Tolerance and Resilience in Cloud Computing Environments

Ravi Jhawar and Vincenzo Piuri

Universita' degli Studi di Milano

1. INTRODUCTION

Cloud computing is gaining an increasing popularity over traditional information processing systems. Service providers have been building massive data centers that are distributed over several geographical regions to efficiently meet the demand for their Cloud-based services [1–3]. In general, these data centers are built using hundreds of thousands of commodity servers, and virtualization technology is used to provision computing resources (by delivering Virtual Machines—VMs—with a given amount of CPU, memory, and storage capacity) over the Internet by following the pay-per-use business model [4]. Leveraging the economies of scale, a single physical host is often used as a set of several virtual hosts by the service provider, and benefits such as the semblance of an inexhaustible set of available computing resources are provided to the users. As a consequence, an increasing number of users are moving to cloud-based services for realizing their applications and business processes.

The use of commodity components, however, exposes the hardware to conditions for which it was not originally designed [5,6]. Moreover, due to the highly complex nature of the underlying infrastructure, even carefully engineered data centers are subject to a large number of failures [7]. These failures evidently reduce the overall reliability and availability of the cloud computing service. As a result, fault tolerance becomes of paramount importance to the users as well as the service providers to ensure correct and continuous system operation even in the presence of an unknown and unpredictable number of failures.

The dimension of risks in the user's applications deployed in the virtual machine instances in a cloud has also changed since the failures in data centers are normally outside the scope of the user's organization. Moreover, traditional ways of achieving fault tolerance require users to have an in-depth knowledge of the underlying mechanisms, whereas, due to the abstraction layers and business model of cloud computing, a system's architectural details are not widely available to the users. This implies that traditional methods of introducing fault tolerance may not be very effective in the cloud computing context, and there is an increasing need to address users' reliability and availability concerns.

The goal of this chapter is to develop an understanding of the nature, numbers, and kind of faults that appear in typical cloud computing infrastructures, how these faults impact users' applications, and how faults can be handled in an efficient and cost-effective manner. To this aim, we first describe the fault model of typical cloud computing environments on the basis of system architecture, failure characteristics of widely used server and network components, and analytical models. An overall understanding of the fault model may help researchers and developers to build more reliable cloud computing services. In this chapter, we also introduce some basic and general concepts on fault tolerance and summarize the parameters that must be taken into account when building a fault tolerant system. This discussion is followed by a scheme in which different levels of fault tolerance can be achieved by users' applications by exploiting the properties of the cloud computing architecture.

In this chapter, we discuss a solution that can function in users' applications in a general and transparent manner to tolerate one of the two most frequent classes of faults that appear in the cloud computing environment. We also present a scheme that can tolerate the other class of frequent faults while reducing the overall resource costs by half when compared to existing solutions in the literature. These two techniques, along with the concept of different fault tolerance levels, are used as the basis for developing a methodology and framework that offers fault tolerance as an additional service to the user's applications. We believe that the notion of offering fault tolerance as a service may serve as an efficient alternative to traditional approaches in addressing user's reliability and availability concerns.

2. CLOUD COMPUTING FAULT MODEL

In general, a failure represents the condition in which the system deviates from fulfilling its intended functionality or the expected behavior. A failure happens due to an error, that is, due to reaching an invalid system state. The hypothesized cause for an error is a fault, which represents a fundamental impairment in the system. The notion of faults, errors, and failures can be represented using the following chain [8,9]:

$$\ldots \text{Fault} \rightarrow \text{Error} \rightarrow \text{Failure} \rightarrow \text{Fault} \rightarrow \text{Error} \rightarrow \text{Failure} \ldots$$

Fault tolerance is the ability of the system to perform its function even in the presence of failures. This implies that it is utmost important to clearly understand and define what constitutes the correct system behavior so that specifications on its failure characteristics can be provided and consequently a fault tolerant system can be developed. In this section, we discuss the fault model of typical cloud computing environments to develop an understanding of the numbers as well as the causes behind recurrent system failures. In order to analyze the distribution and impact of faults, we first describe the generic cloud computing architecture.

Cloud Computing Architecture

Cloud computing architecture comprises four distinct layers as illustrated in Figure 1.1 [10]. Physical resources (blade servers and network switches) are considered the lowest-layer in the stack, on top of which virtualization and system management tools are embedded to form the infrastructure-as-a-service (IaaS) layer. Note that the infrastructure supporting large-scale cloud deployments is typically the data centers, and virtualization technology is used to maximize the use of physical resources, application isolation, and quality of service. Services offered by IaaS are normally accessed through a set of user-level middleware services that provide an environment to simplify application development and deployment (Web 2.0 or higher interfaces, libraries, and programming languages). The layer above the IaaS that binds all user-level middleware tools is referred to as platform-as-a-service (PaaS). User-level applications (social networks and scientific models) that are built and hosted on top of the PaaS layer comprise the software-as-a-service (SaaS) layer.

Failure in a given layer normally has an impact on the services offered by the layers above it. For example, failure in a user-level middleware (PaaS) may produce errors in the software services built on top of it (SaaS applications). Similarly, failures in the physical hardware or the IaaS layer will have an impact on most PaaS and SaaS services. This implies that the impact of failures in the IaaS layer or the physical hardware is significantly high; hence, it is important to characterize typical hardware faults and develop corresponding fault tolerance techniques.

We describe the failure behavior of various server components based on the statistical information obtained from large-scale studies on data center failures using data mining techniques [6,11] and analyze the impact of component failures on users' applications by means of analytical models such as fault trees and Markov chains [12]. Similar to server components, we also present the failure behavior of network component failures.

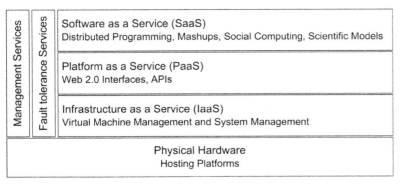

FIGURE 1.1 Layered architecture of cloud computing.

Failure Behavior of Servers

Each server in the data center typically contains multiple processors, storage disks, memory modules, and network interfaces. The study about server failure and hardware repair behavior is to be performed using a large collection of servers (approximately 100,000 servers) and corresponding data on part replacement such as details about server configuration, when a hard disk was issued a ticked for replacement, and when it was actually replaced. Such a data repository, which included server collection spanning multiple data centers distributed across different countries, is gathered [6]. Key observations derived from this study are as follows:

- 92 percent of the machines do not see any repair events, but the average number of repairs for the remaining 8 percent is 2 per machine (20 repair/replacement events contained in nine machines were identified over a 14-month period). The annual failure rate (AFR) is therefore around 8 percent.
- For an 8 percent AFR, repair costs that amounted to $2.5 million are approximately spent for 100,000 servers.
- About 78 percent of total faults/replacements were detected on hard disks, 5 percent on RAID controllers, and 3 percent due to memory failures. Thirteen percent of replacements were due to a collection of components (not particularly dominated by a single component failure). Hard disks are clearly the most failure-prone hardware components and the most significant reason behind server failures.
- About 5 percent of servers experience a disk failure in less than one year from the date when it is commissioned (young servers), 12 percent when the machines are one year old, and 25 percent when they are two years old.
- Interestingly, based on the chi-squared automatic interaction detector methodology, none of the following factors—age of the server, its configuration, location within the rack, and workload run on the machine—were found to be a significant indicator for failures.
- Comparison between the number of repairs per machine (RPM) to the number of disks per server in a group of servers (clusters) indicates that (i) there is a relationship in the failure characteristics of servers that have already experienced a failure, and (ii) the number of RPM has a correspondence to the total number of disks on that machine.

Based on these statistics, it can be inferred that robust fault tolerance mechanisms must be applied to improve the reliability of hard disks (assuming independent component failures) to substantially reduce the number of failures. Furthermore, to meet the high availability and reliability requirements, applications must reduce utilization of hard disks that have already experienced a failure (since the probability of seeing another failure on that hard disk is higher).

The failure behavior of servers can also be analyzed based on the models defined using fault trees and Markov chains [12,13]. The rationale behind the modeling is twofold: (1) to capture the user's perspective on component failures, that is, to understand the behavior of users' applications that are deployed in the VM instances under server component failures and (2) to define the correlation between individual component failures and the boundaries on the impact of each failure. An application may have an impact when there

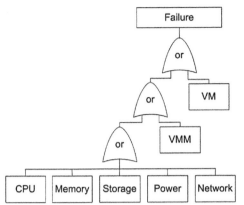

FIGURE 1.2A Fault tree characterizing server failures [12].

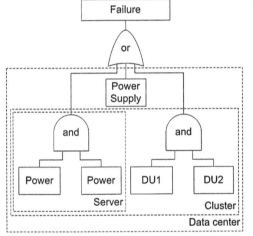

FIGURE 1.2B Fault tree characterizing power failures [12].

is a failure/error either in the processor, memory modules, storage disks, power supply (see Figure 1.2b) or network interfaces of the server, or the hypervisor, or the VM instance itself. Figure 1.2a illustrates this behavior as a fault tree where the top-event represents a failure in the user's application. The reliability and availability of each server component must be derived using Markov models that are populated using long-term failure behavior information [6].

Failure Behavior of the Network

It is important to understand the overall network topology and various network components involved in constructing a data center so as to characterize the network failure behavior (see Figure 1.3b). Figure 1.3a illustrates an example of partial data center network architecture [11,14]. Servers are connected using a set of network switches and routers. In

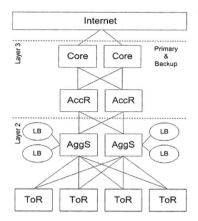

FIGURE 1.3A   Partial network architecture of a data center [11].

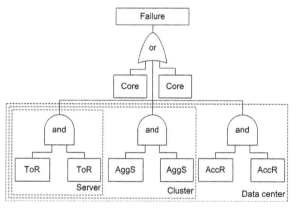

FIGURE 1.3B   Fault tree characterizing network failures [12].

particular, all rack-mounted servers are first connected via a 1 Gbps link to a top-of-rack switch (ToR), which is in turn connected to two (primary and backup) aggregation switches (AggS). An AggS connects tens of switches (ToR) to redundant access routers (AccR). This implies that each AccR handles traffic from thousands of servers and routes it to core routers that connect different data centers to the Internet [11,12]. All links in the data centers commonly use Ethernet as the link layer protocol, and redundancy is applied to all network components at each layer in the network topology (except for ToRs). In addition, redundant pairs of load balancers (LBs) are connected to each AggS, and mapping between static IP address presented to the users and dynamic IP addresses of internal servers that process user's requests is performed. Similar to the study on failure behavior of servers, a large-scale study on network failures in data centers is performed [11]. A link failure happens when the connection between two devices on a specific interface is down, and a device failure happens when the device is not routing/forwarding packets correctly (due to power outage or hardware crash). Key observations derived from this study are as follows:

- Among all the network devices, load balancers are least reliable (with failure probability of 1 in 5) and ToRs are most reliable (with a failure rate of less than

5 percent). The root causes for failures in LBs are mainly the software bugs and configuration errors (as opposed to the hardware errors for other devices). Moreover, LBs tend to experience short but frequent failures. This observation indicates that low-cost commodity switches (ToRs and AggS) provide sufficient reliability.

- The links forwarding traffic from LBs have the highest failure rates; links higher in the topology (connecting AccRs) and links connecting redundant devices have the second highest failure rates.
- The estimated median number of packets lost during a failure is 59 K, and the median number of bytes is 25 MB (the average size of lost packets is 423 Bytes). Based on prior measurement studies (that observe packet sizes to be bimodal with modes around 200 Bytes and 1400 Bytes), it is estimated that most lost packets belong to the lower part (ping messages or ACKs).
- Network redundancy reduces the median impact of failures (in terms of number of lost bytes) by only 40 percent. This observation is against the common belief that network redundancy completely masks failures from applications.

Therefore, the overall data center network reliability is about 99.99 percent for 80 percent of the links and 60 percent of the devices. Similar to servers, Figure 1.3b represents the fault tree for the user's application failure with respect to network failures in the data center. A failure occurs when there is an error in all redundant switches ToRs, AggS, AccR, or core routers, or the network links connecting physical hosts. Since the model is designed in the user's perspective, a failure in this context implies that the application is not connected to the rest of the network or gives errors during data transmission. Through use of this modeling technique, the boundaries on the impact of each network failure can be represented (using server, cluster, and data center level blocks) and can further be used to increase the fault tolerance of the user's application (by placing replicas of an application in different failure zones).

3. BASIC CONCEPTS ON FAULT TOLERANCE

In general, the faults we analyzed in the last section can be classified in different ways depending on the nature of the system. Since, in this chapter, we are interested in typical cloud computing environment faults that appear as failures to the end users, we classify the faults into two types similarly to other distributed systems:

- *Crash faults* that cause the system components to completely stop functioning or remain inactive during failures (power outage, hard disk crash).
- *Byzantine faults* that lead the system components to behave arbitrarily or maliciously during failure, causing the system to behave unpredictably incorrect.

As observed previously, fault tolerance is the ability of the system to perform its function even in the presence of failures. It serves as one of the means to improve the overall system's dependability. In particular, it contributes significantly to increasing the system's reliability and availability.

The most widely adopted methods to achieve fault tolerance against crash faults and byzantine faults are as follows:

- *Checking and monitoring*: The system is constantly monitored at runtime to validate, verify, and ensure that correct system specifications are being met. This technique, though very simple, plays a key role in failure detection and subsequent reconfiguration.
- *Checkpoint and restart*: The system state is captured and saved based on predefined parameters (after every 1024 instructions or every 60 seconds). When the system undergoes a failure, it is restored to the previously known correct state using the latest checkpoint information (instead of restarting the system from start).
- *Replication*: Critical system components are duplicated using additional hardware, software, and network resources in such a way that a copy of the critical components is available even after a failure happens. Replication mechanisms are mainly used in two formats: active and passive. In active replication, all the replicas are simultaneously invoked and each replica processes the same request at the same time. This implies that all the replicas have the same system state at any given point of time (unless designed to function in an asynchronous manner) and it can continue to deliver its service even in case of a single replica failure. In passive replication, only one processing unit (the primary replica) processes the requests, while the backup replicas only save the system state during normal execution periods. Backup replicas take over the execution process only when the primary replica fails.

Variants of traditional replication mechanisms (active and passive) are often applied on modern distributed systems. For example, the semiactive replication technique is derived from traditional approaches wherein primary and backup replicas execute all the instructions but only the output generated by the primary replica is made available to the user. Output generated by the backup replicas is logged and suppressed within the system so that it can readily resume the execution process when the primary replica failure happens. Figure 1.4a depicts the Markov model of a system that uses an active/semiactive replication scheme with two replicas [12]. This model serves as an effective means of deriving the reliability and availability of the system because the failure behavior of both replicas can be taken into account. Moreover, as described earlier, the results of the Markov model analysis can be used to support the fault trees in characterizing the impact of failures in the system. Each state in the model is represented by a pair (x, y) where $x = 1$ denotes that the primary replica is working and $x = 0$ implies that it failed. Similarly, y represents the

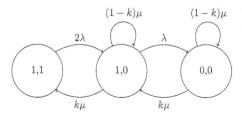

FIGURE 1.4A   Markov model of a system with two replicas in active/semiactive replication scheme [12].

working condition of the backup replica. The system starts and remains in state (1,1) during normal execution, that is, when both the replicas are available and working correctly. A failure either in the primary or the backup replica moves the system to state (0,1) or (1,0) where the other replica takes over the execution process. A single state is sufficient to represent this condition in the model since both replicas are consistent with each other. The system typically initiates its recovery mechanism in state (0,1) or (1,0), and moves to state (1,1) if the recovery of the failed replica is successful; otherwise it transits to state (0,0) and becomes completely unavailable. Similarly, Figure 1.4b illustrates the Markov model of the system for which a passive replication scheme is applied. λ denotes the failure rate, μ denotes the recovery rate, and k is a constant.

Fault tolerance mechanisms are varyingly successful in tolerating faults [15]. For example, a passively replicated system can tolerate only crash faults, whereas actively replicated system using $3f + 1$ replicas are capable of tolerating byzantine faults. In general, mechanisms that handle failures at a finer granularity, offering higher performance guarantees, also consume higher amounts of resources [16]. Therefore, the design of fault tolerance mechanisms must take into account a number of factors such as implementation complexity, resource costs, resilience, and performance metrics, and achieve a fine balance of the following parameters:

- *Fault tolerance model*: Measures the strength of the fault tolerance mechanism in terms of the granularity at which it can handle errors and failures in the system. This factor is characterized by the robustness of failure detection protocols, state synchronization methods, and strength of the fail-over granularity.
- *Resource consumption*: Measures the amount and cost of resources that are required to realize a fault tolerance mechanism. This factor is normally inherent with the granularity of the failure detection and recovery mechanisms in terms of CPU, memory, bandwidth, I/O, and so on.
- *Performance*: Deals with the impact of the fault tolerance procedure on the end-to-end quality of service (QoS) both during failure and failure-free periods. This impact is often characterized using fault detection latency, replica launch latency, failure recovery latency, and other application-dependent metrics such as bandwidth, latency, and loss rate.

We build on the basic concepts discussed in this section to analyze the fault tolerance properties of various schemes designed for cloud computing environment.

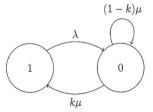

$(1 - k)\mu$ **FIGURE 1.4B** Markov model of a system with two replicas in passive replication scheme [12].

4. DIFFERENT LEVELS OF FAULT TOLERANCE IN CLOUD COMPUTING

As discussed earlier, server components in a cloud computing environment are subject to failures, affecting users' applications, and each failure has an impact within a given boundary in the system. For example, a crash in the pair of aggregate switches may result in the loss of communication among all the servers in a cluster; in this context, the boundary of failure is the cluster since applications in other clusters can continue functioning normally. Therefore, while applying a fault tolerance mechanism such as a replication scheme, at least one replica of the application must be placed in a different cluster to ensure that aggregate switch failure does not result in a complete failure of the application. Furthermore, this implies that deployment scenarios (location of each replica) are critical to correctly realize the fault tolerance mechanisms. In this section, we discuss possible deployment scenarios in a cloud computing infrastructure, and the advantages and limitations of each scenario.

Based on the architecture of the cloud computing infrastructure, different levels of failure independence can be derived for cloud computing services [17,18]. Moreover, assuming that the failures in individual resource components are independent of each other, fault tolerance and resource costs of an application can be balanced based on the location of its replicas. Possible deployment scenarios and their properties are as follows.

- *Multiple machines within the same cluster.* Two replicas of an application can be placed on the hosts that are connected by a ToR switch (within a LAN). Replicas deployed in this configuration can benefit in terms of low latency and high bandwidth but obtain very limited failure independence. A single switch or power distribution failure may result in an outage of the entire application, and both replicas cannot communicate to complete the fault tolerance protocol. Cluster- level blocks in the fault trees of each resource component (network failures as shown in Figure 1.3b) must be combined using a logical AND operator to analyze the overall impact of failures in the system. Note that reliability and availability values for each fault tolerance mechanism with respect to server faults must be calculated using a Markov model.
- *Multiple clusters within a data center.* Two replicas of an application can be placed on the hosts belonging to different clusters in the same data center (on the hosts that are connected via a ToR switch and AggS). Failure independence of the application in this deployment context remains moderate since the replicas are not bound to an outage with a single power distribution or switch failure. The overall availability of an application can be calculated using cluster-level blocks from fault trees combined with a logical OR operator in conjunction with power and network using AND operator.
- *Multiple data centers.* Two replicas of an application can be placed on the hosts belonging to different data centers (connected via a switch), AggS and AccR. This deployment has a drawback with respect to high latency and low bandwidth, but offers a very high level of failure independence. A single power failure has the least effect on

TABLE 1.1 Availability Values (normalized to 1) for Replication Techniques at Different Deployment Scenarios [12].

	Same Cluster	Same Data Center, diff. Clusters	Diff. Data Centers
Semiactive	0.9871	0.9913	0.9985
Semipassive	0.9826	0.9840	0.9912
Passive	0.9542	0.9723	0.9766

the availability of the application. The data center level blocks from the fault trees may be connected with a logical OR operator in conjunction with the network in the AND logic.

As an example [13,19], the overall availability of each representative replication scheme with respect to different deployment levels is obtained as shown in Table 1.1. Availability of the system is highest when the replicas are placed in two different data centers. The value declines when replicas are placed in two different clusters within the same data center, and it is lowest when replicas are placed inside the same LAN. The overall availability obtained by semiactive replication is higher than semipassive replication and lowest for the simple passive replication scheme.

As described earlier, effective implementation of fault tolerance mechanisms requires consideration of the strength of the fault tolerance model, resource costs, and performance. While traditional fault tolerance methods require tailoring of each application having an in-depth knowledge of the underlying infrastructure, in the cloud computing scenario, it would also be beneficial to develop methodologies that can generically function on users' applications so that a large number of applications can be protected using the same protocol. In addition to generality, agility in managing replicas and checkpoints to improve the performance, and reduction in the resource consumption costs while not limiting the strength of fault tolerance mechanisms are required.

Although several fault tolerance approaches are being proposed for cloud computing services, most solutions that achieve at least one of the required properties described above are based on virtualization technology. By using virtualization-based approaches, it is also possible to deal with both classes of faults. In particular, in a later section of this chapter we present a virtualization-based solution that provides fault tolerance against crash failures using a checkpointing mechanism. We discuss this solution because it offers two additional, significantly useful, properties: (1) Fault tolerance is induced independent to the applications and hardware on which it runs. In other words, an increased level of generality is achieved since any application can be protected using the same protocol as long as it is deployed in a VM, and (2) mechanisms such as replication, failure detection, and recovery are applied transparently—not modifying the OS or application's source code. Then, we present a virtualization-based solution that uses typical properties of a cloud computing environment to tolerate byzantine faults using a combination of replication and checkpointing techniques. We discuss this solution because it reduces the resource consumption costs incurred by typical byzantine fault tolerance schemes during fail-free periods nearly by half.

5. FAULT TOLERANCE AGAINST CRASH FAILURES IN CLOUD COMPUTING

A scheme that leverages the virtualization technology to tolerate crash faults in the cloud in a transparent manner is discussed in this section. The system or user application that must be protected from failures is first encapsulated in a VM (say active VM or the primary), and operations are performed at the VM level (in contrast to the traditional approach of operating at the application level) to obtain paired servers that run in active–passive configuration. Since the protocol is applied at the VM level, this scheme can be used independent of the application and underlying hardware, offering an increased level of generality. In particular, we discuss the design of *Remus* as an example system that offers the preceding mentioned properties [20]. Remus aims to provide high availability to the applications, and to achieve this, it works in four phases:

1. Checkpoint the changed memory state at the primary, and continue to the next epoch of network and disk request streams.
2. Replicate system state on the backup.
3. Send checkpoint acknowledgment from the backup when complete memory checkpoint and corresponding disk requests have been received.
4. Release outbound network packets queued during the previous epoch upon receiving the acknowledgment.

Remus achieves high availability by frequently checkpointing and transmitting the state of the active VM on to a backup physical host. The VM image on the backup is resident in the memory and may begin execution immediately after a failure in the active VM is detected. The backup only acts like a receptor since the VM in the backup host is not actually executed during fail-free periods. This allows the backup to concurrently receive checkpoints from VMs running on multiple physical hosts (in an N-to-1 style configuration), providing a higher degree of freedom in balancing resource costs due to redundancy.

In addition to generality and transparency, seamless failure recovery can be achieved; that is, no externally visible state is lost in the event of a single host failure and recovery happens rapidly enough that it appears only like a temporary packet loss. Since the backup is only periodically consistent with the primary replica using the checkpoint-transmission procedure, all network output is buffered until a consistent image of the host is received by the backup, and the buffer is released only when the backup is completely synchronized with the primary. Unlike network traffic, the disk state is not externally visible, but it has to be transmitted to the backup as part of a complete cycle. To address this issue, Remus asynchronously sends the disk state to the backup where it is initially buffered in the RAM. When the corresponding memory state is received, complete checkpoint is acknowledged, output is made visible to the user, and buffered disk state is applied to the backup disk.

Remus is built on Xen hypervisor's live migration machinery [21]. Live migration is a technique through which a complete VM can be relocated onto another physical host in the network (typically a LAN) with a minor interruption to the VM. Xen provides an ability to track guest writes to memory using a technique called shadow page tables. During live migration, memory of the VM is copied to the new location while the VM continues to run normally at the old location. The writes to the memory are then tracked, and the dirtied pages are transferred to the new location periodically. After a sufficient number of iterations, or when no progress in copying the memory is being made (i.e., when the VM is writing to the memory as fast as the migration process), the guest VM is suspended, remaining dirtied memory along with the CPU state is copied, and the VM image in the new location is activated. The total migration time depends on the amount of dirtied memory during guest execution, and total downtime depends on the amount of memory remaining to be copied when the guest is suspended. The protocol design of the system, particularly each checkpoint, can be viewed as the final stop-and-copy phase of live migration. The guest memory in live migration is iteratively copied, incurring several minutes of execution time. The singular stop-and-copy (the final step) operation incurs a very limited overhead—typically in the order of a few milliseconds.

While Remus provides an efficient replication mechanism, it employs a simple failure detection technique that is directly integrated within the checkpoint stream. A timeout of the backup in responding to commit requests made by the primary will result in the primary suspecting a failure (crash and disabled protection) in the backup. Similarly, a timeout of the new checkpoints being transmitted from the primary will result in the backup assuming a failure in the primary. At this point, the backup begins execution from the latest checkpoint. The protocol is evaluated (i) to understand whether or not the overall approach is practically deployable and (ii) to analyze the kind of workloads that are most amenable to this approach.

Correctness evaluation is performed by deliberatively injecting network failures at each phase of the protocol. The application (or the protected system) runs a kernel compilation process to generate CPU, memory, and disk load, and a graphics-intensive client (glxgears) attached to X11 server is simultaneously executed to generate the network traffic. Checkpoint frequency is configured to 25 milliseconds, and each test is performed two times. It is reported that the backup successfully took over the execution for each failure with a network delay of about 1 second when the backup detected the failure and activated the replicated system. The kernel compilation task continued to completion, and glxgears client resumed after a brief pause. The disk image showed no inconsistencies when the VM was gracefully shut down.

Performance evaluation is performed using the SPECweb benchmark that is composed of a Web server, an application server, and one or more Web client simulators. Each tier (server) was deployed in a different VM. The observed scores decrease up to five times the native score (305) when the checkpointing system is active. This behavior is mainly due to network buffering; the observed scores are much higher when network buffering is disabled. Furthermore, it is reported that at configuration rates of 10, 20, 30, and 40 checkpoints per second, the average checkpoint rates achieved are 9.98, 16.38, 20.25, and 23.34, respectively. This behavior can be explained with SPECweb's very fast memory dirtying, resulting in slower checkpoints than desired. The realistic workload therefore illustrates that the amount of network traffic generated by the checkpointing protocol is very large, and as a consequence, this system is not well suited for applications that are very sensitive to network latencies. Therefore, virtualization technology can largely be exploited to develop general-purpose fault tolerance schemes that can be applied to handle crash faults in a transparent manner.

6. FAULT TOLERANCE AGAINST BYZANTINE FAILURES IN CLOUD COMPUTING

Byzantine fault tolerance (BFT) protocols are powerful approaches to obtain highly reliable and available systems. Despite numerous efforts, most BFT systems have been too expensive for practical use; so far, no commercial data centers have employed BFT techniques. For example, the BFT algorithm [22] for asynchronous, distributed, client-server systems requires at least $3f + 1$ replica (one primary and remaining backup) to execute a three-phase protocol that can tolerate f byzantine faults. Note that, as described earlier, systems that tolerate faults at a finer granularity such as the byzantine faults also consume very high amounts of resources, and as already noted, it is critical to consider the resource costs while implementing a fault tolerance solution.

The high resource consumption cost (see Table 1.2) in BFT protocols is most likely due to the way faults are normally handled. BFT approaches typically replicate the server (state machine replication—SMR), and each replica is forced to execute the same request in the same order. This enforcement requirement demands that the server replicas reach an agreement on the ordering of a given set of requests even in the presence of byzantine faulty servers and clients. For this purpose, an agreement protocol that is referred to as the *Byzantine Agreement* is used. When an agreement on the ordering is reached, service execution is performed, and majority voting scheme is devised to choose the correct output (and to detect the faulty server). This implies that two clusters of replicas are necessary to realize BFT protocols.

When realistic data center services implement BFT protocols, the dominant costs are due to the hardware performing service execution and not due to running the agreement protocol [23]. For instance, a toy application running *null* requests with the Zyzzyva BFT approach [24] exhibits a peak throughput of 80 K requests/second, while a database service running the same protocol on comparable hardware exhibits almost three times lower throughput. Based on this observation, ZZ, an execution approach that can be integrated with existing BFT SMR and agreement protocols, is presented [23]. The prototype of ZZ is built on the BASE implementation [22] and guarantees BFT, while significantly reducing resource consumption costs during fail-free periods. Table 1.2 compares the resource costs of well-known BFT techniques. Since ZZ provides an effective balance between resource

TABLE 1.2 Resource Consumption Costs Incurred by Well-Known Byzantine Fault Tolerance Protocols [23].

	PBFT [22]	SEP [25]	Zyzzyva [24]	ZZ [23]
Agreement replicas	$3f + 1$	$3f + 1$	$3f + 1$	$3f + 1$
Execution replicas	$3f + 1$	$2f + 1$	$2f + 1$	$(1 + r)f + 1$

consumption costs and the fault tolerance model, later in this section we discuss its system design in detail.

The design of ZZ is based on the virtualization technology and is targeted to tolerate byzantine faults while reducing the resource provisioning costs incurred by BFT protocols during fail-free periods. The cost reduction benefits of ZZ can be obtained only when BFT is used in the data center running multiple applications, so that sleeping replicas can be distributed across the pool of servers and higher peak throughput can be achieved when execution dominates the request processing cost and resources are constrained. These assumptions make ZZ a suitable scheme to be applied in a cloud computing environment. The system model of ZZ makes the following assumptions similar to most existing BFT systems:

- The service is either deterministic, or nondeterministic operations in the service can be transformed to deterministic ones using an agreement protocol (ZZ assumes a SMR-based BFT system).
- The system involves two kinds of replicas: (1) *agreement replicas* that assign an order to the client's requests and (2) *execution replicas* that execute each client's request in the same order and maintain the application state.
- Each replica fails independently and exhibits byzantine behavior (faulty replicas and clients may behave arbitrarily).
- An adversary can coordinate faulty nodes in an arbitrary manner, but it cannot circumvent standard cryptographic measures (collision-resistant hash functions, encryption scheme, and digital signatures).
An upper bound g on a number of faulty agreement replicas and f execution replicas is assumed for a given window of vulnerability.
- The system can ensure safety in an asynchronous network, but liveness is guaranteed only during periods of synchrony.

Since the system runs replicas inside virtual machines, to maintain failure independence, it requires that a physical host can deploy at most one agreement and one execution replicas of the service simultaneously. The novelty in the system model is that it considers a byzantine hypervisor. Note that, as a consequence of the above replica placement constraint, a malicious hypervisor can be treated by simply considering a single fault in all the replicas deployed on that physical host. Similarly, an upper bound f on the number of faulty hypervisors is assumed. The BFT execution protocol reduces the replication cost from $2f + 1$ to $f + 1$ based on the following principle:

- A system that is designed to function correctly in an asynchronous environment will provide correct results even if some of the replicas are outdated.
- A system that is designed to function correctly in the presence of f byzantine faults will, during a fault-free period, remain unaffected even if up to f replicas are turned off.

The second observation is used to commission only an $f + 1$ replica to actively execute requests. The system is in a correct state if the response obtained from all $f + 1$ replicas is the same. In case of failure (when responses do not match), the first observation is used to continue system operation as if the f standby replicas were slow but correct replicas.

To correctly realize this design, the system requires an agile replica wake-up mechanism. To achieve this mechanism, the system exploits virtualization technology by maintaining additional replicas (VMs) in a "dormant" state, which are either pre-spawned but paused VMs or the VM that is hibernated to a disk. There is a trade-off in adopting either method. Pre-spawned VM can resume execution in a very short span (in the order of few milliseconds) but consumes higher memory resources, whereas VMs hibernated to disks incur greater recovery times but occupy only storage space. This design also raises several interesting challenges such as *how can a restored replica obtain the necessary application state that is required to execute the current request? How can the replication cost be made robust to faulty replica or client behavior? Does the transfer of an entire application state take an unacceptably long time?*

The system builds on the BFT protocol that uses independent agreement and execution clusters [25]). Let A represent the set of replicas in the agreement cluster, $|A| = 2g + 1$, that runs the three-phase agreement protocol [22]. When a client c sends its request Q to the agreement cluster to process an operation o with timestamp t, the agreement cluster assigns a sequence number n to the request. The timestamp is used to ensure that each client request is executed only once and a faulty client behavior does not affect other clients' requests. When an agreement replica j learns of the sequence number n committed to Q, it sends a commit message C to all execution replicas.

Let E represent the set of replicas in the execution cluster where $|E| = f + 1$ during fail-free periods. When an execution replica i receives $2g + 1$ valid and matching commit messages from A, in the form of a commit certificate $\{C_i\}$, $i \in A|2g + 1$, and if it has already processed all the requests with lower sequence than n, it produces a reply R and sends it to the client. The execution cluster also generates an execution report ER for the agreement cluster.

During normal execution, the response certificate $\{R_i\}$, $i \in E|f + 1$ obtained by the client matches replies from all $f + 1$ execution nodes. To avoid unnecessary wake-ups due to a partially faulty execution replica that replies correctly to the agreement cluster but delivers a wrong response to the client, ZZ introduces an additional check as follows: When the replies are not matching, the client resends the same request to the agreement cluster. The agreement cluster sends a reply affirmation RA to the client if it has $f + 1$ valid responses for the retransmitted request. In this context, the client accepts the reply if it receives $g + 1$ messages containing a response digest $\overline{R}$ that matches one of the replies already received. Finally, if the agreement cluster does not generate an affirmation for the client, additional nodes are started.

ZZ uses periodic checkpoints to update the state of newly commissioned replicas and to perform garbage collection on a replica's logs. Execution nodes create checkpoints of the application state and reply logs, generate a checkpoint proof CP, and send it all execution and agreement nodes. The checkpoint proof is in the form of a digest that allows recovering nodes in identifying the checkpoint data they obtain from potentially faulty nodes, and the checkpoint certificate $\{CP_i\}$, $i \in E|f + 1$ is a set of $f + 1$ CP messages with matching digests.

Fault detection in the execution replicas is based on timeouts. Both lower and higher values of timeouts may impact the system's performance. The lower may falsely detect failures, and the higher may provide a window to the faulty replicas to degrade the system's performance. To set appropriate timeouts, ZZ suggests the following procedure: The agreement replica sets the timeout τ_n to Kt_1 upon receiving the first response to the request with sequence number n; t_1 is the response time and K is a preconfigured variance bound. Based on this trivial theory, ZZ proves that a replica faulty with a given probability p can inflate average response time by a factor of:

$$\max\left(1, \sum_{0 \le m \le f} P(m)I(m)\right)$$

where:

$$P(m) = \binom{f}{m} p^m (1-p)^{f-m}$$

$$I(m) = max\left(1, \frac{K.E[MIN_{f+1-m}]}{E[MAX_{f+1}]}\right)$$

$P(m)$ represents the probability of m simultaneous failures, and $I(m)$ is the response time inflation that m faulty nodes can inflict. Assuming identically distributed response times for a given distribution, $E[MIN_{f+1-m}]$ is the expected minimum time for a set of $f+1-m$ replicas, and $E[MAX_{f+1}]$ is the expected maximum response time of all $f+1$ replicas [23]. Replication costs vary from $f+1$ to $2f+1$, depending on the probability of replicas being faulty p and the likelihood of false timeouts π_1. Formally, the expected replication cost is less than $(1+r)f+1$, where $r = 1 - (1-p)^{f+1} + (1-p)^{f+1}\pi_1$. Therefore, virtualization technology can be effectively used to realize byzantine fault tolerance mechanisms at a significantly lower resource consumption costs.

7. FAULT TOLERANCE AS A SERVICE IN CLOUD COMPUTING

The drawback of the solutions discussed earlier is that the user must either tailor its application using a specific protocol (ZZ) by taking into account the system architecture details, or require the service provider to implement a solution for its applications (Remus). Note that the (i) fault tolerance properties of the application remain constant throughout its life cycle using this methodology and (ii) users may not have all the architectural details of the service provider's system. However, the availability of a pool of fault tolerance mechanisms that provide transparency and generality can allow realization of the notion of fault tolerance as a service. The latter perspective on fault tolerance intuitively provides immense benefits.

As a motivating example, consider a user that offers a Web-based e-commerce service to its customers that allows them to pay their bills and manage fund transfers over the Internet. The user implements the e-commerce service as a multitier application that uses the storage service of the service provider to store and retrieve its customer data, and compute service to process its operations and respond to customer queries. In this context, a failure in the service provider's system can impact the reliability and availability of the e-commerce service. The implications of storage server failure may be much higher than a failure in one of the compute nodes. This implies that each tier of the e-commerce application must possess different levels of fault tolerance, and the reliability and availability goals may change over time based on the business demands. Using traditional methods, fault tolerance properties of the e-commerce application remains constant throughout its life cycle, and hence, in the user's perspective, it is complementary to engage with a third party (the fault tolerance service provider—ftSP), specify its requirements based on the business needs, and transparently possess desired fault tolerance properties without studying the low-level fault tolerance mechanisms.

The ftSP must realize a range of fault tolerance techniques as individual modules (separate agreement and execution protocols, and heartbeat-based fault detection technique as an independent module) to benefit from the economies of scale. For example, since the failure detection techniques in Remus and ZZ are based on the same principle, instead of integrating the liveness requests within the checkpointing stream, the heartbeat test module can be reused in both solutions. However, realization of this notion requires a technique for selecting appropriate fault tolerance mechanisms based on users' requirements and a general-purpose framework that can integrate with the cloud computing environment. Without such a framework, individual applications must implement its own solution, resulting in a highly complex system environment. Further in this section, we present a solution that supports ftSP to realize its service effectively.

In order to abstract low-level system procedures from the users, a new dimension to fault tolerance is presented in [26] wherein applications deployed in the VM instances in a cloud computing environment can obtain desired fault tolerance properties from a third party as a service. The new dimension realizes a range of fault tolerance mechanisms that can transparently function on user's applications as independent modules, and a set of metadata is associated with each module to characterize its fault tolerance properties. The metadata is used to select appropriate mechanisms based on users' requirements. A complete fault tolerance solution is then composed using selected fault tolerance modules and delivered to the user's application.

Consider ft_unit to be the fundamental module that applies a coherent fault tolerance mechanism, in a transparent manner, to a recurrent system failure at the granularity of a VM instance. An ft_unit handles the impact of hardware failures by applying fault tolerance mechanisms at the virtualization layer rather than the user's application. Examples of ft_units include the replication scheme for the e-commerce application that uses a checkpointing technique such as Remus (ft_unit1), and the node failures detection technique using the heartbeat test (ft_sol2). Assuming that the ftSP realizes a range of fault tolerance mechanisms as ft_units, a two-stage delivery scheme that can deliver fault tolerance as a service is as follows:

The *design stage* starts when a user requests the ftSP to deliver a solution with a given set of fault tolerance properties to its application. Each ft_unit provides a unique set of properties; the ftSP banks on this observation and defines the fault tolerance property p corresponding to each ft_unit as $p = (u, \hat{p}, A)$, where u represents the ft_unit, $\hat{p}$ denotes the high-level abstract properties such as reliability and availability, and A denotes the set of functional, structural, and operational attributes that characterize the ft_unit u. The set A sufficiently refers to the granularity at which the ft_unit can handle failures, its limitations and advantages, resource consumption costs, and quality of service parameters. Each attribute $a \in A$ takes a value $v(a)$ from a domain D_a, and a partial (or total) ordered relationship is defined on the domain D_a. The values for the abstract properties are derived using the notion of fault trees and the Markov model as described for the availability property in Table 1.1. An example of fault tolerance property for the ft_unit u_1 is $p = (u_1, \hat{p} = \{reliability = 98.9\%, availability = 99.95\%\}, A = \{mechanism = semiactive\_replication, fault\_model = server\_crashes, power\_outage, number\_of\_replicas = 4\})$.

Similar to the domain of attribute values, a hierarchy of fault tolerance properties $\leq_p$ is also defined: If P is the set of properties, and given two properties p_i, $p_j \in P$, $p_i \leq_p p_j$ if $p_i \cdot p = p_j \cdot p$ and for all $a \in A$, $v_i(a) \leq v_j(a)$. This hierarchy suggests that all ft_units that hold the property p_j also satisfy the property p_i. The fault tolerance requirements of the users are assumed to be specified as desired properties p_c, and for each user request, the ftSP first generates a shortlisted set S of ft_units that match p_c. Each ft_unit within the set S is then compared, and an ordered list based on user's requirements is created. An example of the matching, comparison, and selection process is as follows:

As an example, assume that the ftSP realizes three ft_units with properties

$p_1 = (u_1, A = \{mechanism = heartbeat\_test, timeout\_period = 50\,ms,$
number_of_replicas = 3, fault_model = node_crashes\})
$p_2 = (u_2, A = \{mechanism = majority\_voting, fault\_model = programming\_errors\})$
$p_3 = (u_3, A = \{mechanism = heartbeat\_test, timeout\_period = 25\,ms,$
number_of_replicas = 5, fault_model = node_crashes\})

respectively. If the user requests fault tolerance support with a robust crash failure detection scheme, the set $S = (u_1, u_3)$ is first generated (u_2 is not included in the set because it doesn't target server crash failures alone, and its attribute values that contribute to robustness are not defined) and finally after comparing each ft_unit within S, ftSP leverages u_3 since it is more robust than u_1.

Note that each ft_unit serves only as a single fundamental fault tolerance module. This implies that the overall solution ft_sol that must be delivered to the user's application can be obtained by combining a set of ft_units as per specific execution logic. For instance, a heartbeat test-based fault detection module must be applied only after performing replication, and the recovery mechanism must be applied after a failure is detected. In other words, ft_units must be used to realize a process that provides a complete fault tolerance solution, such as:

ft sol[
invoke:ft unit(*VM-instances replication*)
invoke:ft unit(*failure detection*)
do{
execute(*failure detection ft unit*)
}while(*no failures*)
if(*failure detected*)
invoke:ft unit(*recovery mechanism*)
]

By composing ft_sol using a set of modules on the fly, the dimension and intensity of the fault tolerance support can be changed dynamically. For example, the more robust fault detection mechanism can be replaced with a less robust one in the ft_sol based on the user's business demands. Similarly, by realizing each ft_unit as a configurable module, resource consumption costs can also be made limited. For example, a replication scheme using five replicas can be replaced with one having three replicas if desired by the user.

The *runtime stage* starts immediately after ft_sol is delivered to the user. This stage is essential to maintain a high level of service because the context of the cloud computing environment may change at runtime, resulting in mutable behavior of the attributes. To this aim, the ftSP defines a set of rules R over attributes $a \in A$ and their values $v(a)$ such that the validity of all the rules $r \in R$ establishes that the property p is supported by ft_sol (violation of a rule indicates that the property is not satisfied). Therefore, in this stage, the attribute values of each ft_sol delivered to users' applications is continuously monitored at runtime, and a corresponding set of rules are verified using a validation function $f(s, R)$. The function returns true if all the rules are satisfied; otherwise, it returns false. The matching and comparison process defined for the design stage is used to generate a new ft_sol in case of a rule violation. By continuously monitoring and updating the attribute values, note that the fault tolerance service offers support that is valid throughout the life cycle of the application (both initially during design time and runtime).

As an example, for a comprehensive fault tolerance solution ft_sol s_1 with property $p_1 = (s_1, \hat{p} = \{\text{reliability} = 98.9\%, \text{availability} = 99.95\%\}, A = \{\text{mechanism} = \text{active\_replication}, \text{fault\_detection} = \text{heartbeat\_test}, \text{number\_of\_replicas} = 4, \text{recovery\_time} = 25 \text{ ms}\})$, a set of rules R that can sufficiently test the validity of p_1 can be defined as:

r_1: number_of_server_instances ≥ 3
r_2: heartbeat_frequency $= 5$ ms
r_3: recovery_time ≤ 25 ms

These rules ensure that end reliability and availability are always greater than or equal to 98.9 percent and 99.95 percent, respectively.

A conceptual architectural framework, the *Fault Tolerance Manager* (FTM), provides the basis to realize the design stage and runtime stage of the delivery scheme, and serves as the basis for offering fault tolerance as a service (see Figure 1.5). FTM is inserted as a dedicated service layer between the physical hardware and user applications along the virtualization layer. FTM is built using the principles of service-oriented architectures, where each ft_unit is realized as an individual Web service and ft_sol is created by orchestrating a set of ft_units (Web services) using the business process execution language (BPEL) constructs. This allows the ftSP to satisfy its scalability and interoperability goals. The central computing component, denoted as the FTMKernel, has three main components:

- *Service Directory*: It is the registry of all ft_units realized by the service provider in the form of Web services that (i) describes its operations and input/output data structures (WSDL and WSCL), and(ii) allows other ft_units to coordinate and assemble with it. This component also registers the metadata representing the fault tolerance property of each ft_unit. Service Directory matches user's preferences and generates the set S of ft_units that satisfy p_c.
- *Composition Engine*: It receives an ordered set of ft_units from the service directory as input and generates a comprehensive fault tolerance solution ft_sol as output. In terms

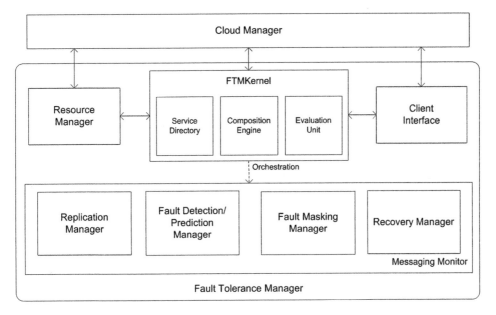

FIGURE 1.5   Architecture of the fault tolerance manager showing all the components.

of service-oriented architectures, the composition engine is a Web service orchestration engine that exploits BPEL constructs to build a fault tolerance solution.
- *Evaluation Unit*: It monitors the composed fault tolerance solutions at runtime using the validation function and the set of rules defined corresponding to each ft_sol. The interface exposed by Web services (WSDL and WSCL) allows the evaluation unit to validate the rules. If a violation is detected, the evaluation unit updates the present attribute values in the metadata; otherwise, the service continues uninterrupted.

Finally, let's take a brief look at a set of components that provide complementary support to fault tolerance mechanisms that are included in the FTM. These components affect the quality of service and support ftSP in satisfying user's requirements and constraints (see checklist: "An Agenda for Action for Satisfying Users' Requirements and Constraints Activities").

AN AGENDA FOR ACTION FOR SATISFYING USERS' REQUIREMENTS AND CONSTRAINTS ACTIVITIES

Figure 1.5 illustrates the overall architecture of the Fault Tolerance Manager (FTM). Satisfying the user's requirements and constraints on the functionality of each component is as follows (check all tasks completed):

_____1. *Client Interface*: This component provides a specification language, which allows clients to specify and define their requirements.

____2. *Resource Manager*: This component maintains a consistent view of all computing resources in the cloud to:

    ____(i) Efficiently perform resource allocation during each user request.

    ____(ii) Avoid over provisioning during failures.

The resource manager monitors the working state of physical and virtual resources, maintains a database of inventory and log information, and a graph representing the topology and working state of all the resources in the cloud.

____3. *Replication Manager*: This component supports the replication mechanisms by invoking the replicas and managing their execution as defined in the ft_unit. The set of replicas that are controlled by a single replication mechanism is denoted as a replica group. The task of the replication manager is to make the user perceive a replica group as a single service and to ensure that each replica exhibits correct behavior in the fail-free periods.

____4. *Fault Detection/Prediction Manager*: This component provides FTM with failure detection support at two different levels. The first level offers failure detection globally, to all the nodes in the cloud (infrastructure-centric), and the second level provides support only to detect failures among individual replicas in each replica group (user application-centric). This component supports several well-known failure detection algorithms (gossip-based protocols, heartbeat protocol) that are configured at runtime according to user's preferences. When a failure is detected in a replica, a notification is sent to the fault masking manager and recovery manager.

____5. *Fault Masking Manager*: The goal of this component is to support ft_units that realize fault masking mechanisms so that the occurrence of faults in the system can be hidden from users. This component applies masking procedures immediately after a failure is detected so as to prevent faults from resulting into errors.

____6. *Recovery Manager*: The goal of this component is to achieve system-level resilience by minimizing the downtime of the system during failures. It supports ft_units that realize recovery mechanisms so that an error-prone node can be resumed back to a normal operational mode. The support offered by this component is complementary to that of the failure detection/prediction manager and fault masking manager, when an error is detected in the system. FTM maximizes the lifetime of the cloud infrastructure by continuously checking for occurrence of faults and by recovering from failures.

____7. *Messaging monitor*: This component extends through all the components of FTM and offers the communication infrastructure in two different forms: message exchange within a replica group and intercomponent communication within the framework. The messaging monitor integrates WS-RM standard with other application protocols to ensure correct messaging infrastructure even in the presence of failures. This component is therefore critical in providing maximum interoperability and serves as a key QoS factor.

For example, consider that at the start of the service, the resource manager generates a profile of all computing resources in the cloud and identifies five processing nodes $\{n_1, \ldots, n_5\} \in N$ with the network topology represented in Figure 1.6a. Further, consider that the FTMKernel, upon gathering the user's requirements from the Client Interface, chooses a passive replication mechanism for the e-commerce service. Based on the chosen fault tolerance mechanism (the set of ft_units that realize the envisioned passive replication scheme), FTMKernel requires that the following conditions be satisfied: (i) the replica group must contain one primary and two backup nodes, (ii) the node on which the primary replica executes must not be shared with any other VM instances, (iii) all the replicas must be located on different nodes at all times, and (iv) node n_5 must not allow any user-level VM instance (rather, it should be used only to run system-level services such as monitoring unit). An overview of the activities performed by each supporting component in the FTM is as follows:

- The replication manager (RM) selects the node n_1 for the primary replica and nodes n_3 and n_4, respectively, for two backup replicas so that a replica group can be formed (see Figure 1.6b). Assume that the replication manager synchronizes the state between the replicas by frequently checkpointing the primary and updating the state of backup replicas.

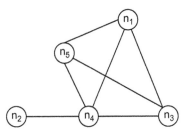

FIGURE 1.6A   Resource graph.

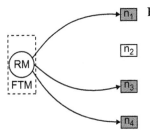

FIGURE 1.6B   Nodes selected by replication manager.

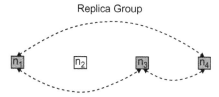

FIGURE 1.6C Messaging Infrastructure created (forms a replica group).

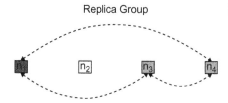

FIGURE 1.6D Failure detected at node n_1.

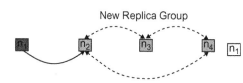

FIGURE 1.6E Fault masking performed – VM instance migrated to node n_2.

- The messaging manager establishes the infrastructure required for carrying out the checkpointing protocol and forms the replica group for the e-commerce service (see Figure 1.6c).
- Assume that the service directory selects a proactive fault tolerance mechanism. As a consequence, the failure detection/prediction manager continuously gathers the state information of nodes n_1, n_3, and n_4, and verifies if all system parameter values satisfy threshold values (physical memory usage of a node allocated to a VM instance must be less than 70 percent of its total capacity).
- When the failure detection/prediction manager predicts a failure in node n_1 (see Figure 1.6d), it invokes the fault masking ft_unit that performs a live migration of the VM instance. The entire OS at node n_1 is moved to another location (node n_2) so that e-commerce customers do not experience any impact of the failure.
- Although the high availability goals are satisfied using the fault masking manager (see Figure 1.6e), the IaaS may be affected since the system now consists of four working nodes only. Therefore, FTM applies robust recovery mechanisms at node n_1 to resume it to a normal working state, increasing the system's overall lifetime (see Figure 1.6f).

Within the FTM framework, the notion of providing fault tolerance as a service can therefore be effectively realized for the cloud computing environment. Based on FTM's delivery scheme, users can achieve high levels of reliability and availability for their applications without having any knowledge about the low-level mechanisms, and dynamically change the fault tolerance properties of its applications (based on the business needs) at runtime.

Replica Group

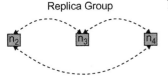

FIGURE 1.6F   Recovery Manager brings back node n_1 to working state.

8. SUMMARY

Fault tolerance and resilience in cloud computing are critical to ensure correct and continuous system operation. We discussed the failure characteristics of typical cloud-based services and analyzed the impact of each failure type on user's applications. Since failures in the cloud computing environment arise mainly due to crash faults and byzantine faults, we discussed two fault tolerance solutions, each corresponding to one of these two classes of faults. The choice of the fault tolerance solutions was also driven by the large set of additional properties that they offer (generality, agility, transparency, and reduced resource consumption costs).

We also presented an innovative delivery scheme that leverages existing solutions and their properties to deliver high levels of fault tolerance based on a given set of desired properties. The delivery scheme was supported by a conceptual framework, which realized the notion of offering fault tolerance as a service to user's applications. Due to the complex nature of cloud computing architecture and difficulties in realizing fault tolerance using traditional methods, we advocate fault tolerance as a service to be an effective alternative to address users' reliability and availability concerns.

Finally, let's move on to the real interactive part of this chapter: review questions/exercises, hands-on projects, case projects, and optional team case project. The answers and/or solutions by chapter can be found in the Online Instructor's Solutions Manual.

CHAPTER REVIEW QUESTIONS/EXERCISES

True/False

1. True or False? Crash faults do not cause the system components to completely stop functioning or remain inactive during failures (power outage, hard disk crash).
2. True or False? Byzantine faults do not lead the system components to behave arbitrarily or maliciously during failure, causing the system to behave unpredictably incorrect.
3. True or False? The system is rarely monitored at runtime to validate, verify, and ensure that correct system specifications are being met.
4. True or False? The system state is captured and saved based on undefined parameters (after every 1024 instructions or every 60 seconds).
5. True or False? Critical system components are duplicated using additional hardware, software, and network resources in such a way that a copy of the critical components is available even before a failure happens.

Multiple Choice

1. What measures the strength of the fault tolerance mechanism in terms of the granularity at which it can handle errors and failures in the system:
   - **A.** Resource consumption
   - **B.** Performance
   - **C.** Fault tolerance model
   - **D.** Multiple machines within the same cluster
   - **E.** All of the above

2. What factor deals with the impact of the fault tolerance procedure on the end-to-end quality of service (QoS) both during failure and failure-free periods?
   - **A.** Resource consumption
   - **B.** Fault tolerance model
   - **C.** Performance
   - **D.** Multiple machines within the same cluster
   - **E.** All of the above

3. How many replicas of an application can be placed on the hosts that are connected by a ToR switch (within a LAN)?
   - **A.** One
   - **B.** Three
   - **C.** Five
   - **D.** Four
   - **E.** Two

4. How many replicas of an application can be placed on the hosts belonging to different clusters in the same data center (on the hosts that are connected via a ToR switch and AggS)?
   - **A.** One
   - **B.** Three
   - **C.** Five
   - **D.** Four
   - **E.** Two

5. How many replicas of an application can be placed on the hosts belonging to different data centers (connected via a switch), AggS and AccR?
   - **A.** Two
   - **B.** Four
   - **C.** One
   - **D.** Three
   - **E.** Five

EXERCISE

Problem

How secure is a cloud-based platform?

Hands-On Projects

Project

What components go into a cloud architecture?

Case Projects

Problem

How does cloud architecture scale?

Optional Team Case Project

Problem

How do you achieve fault tolerance in a cloud?

Acknowledgments

This work was supported in part by the Italian Ministry of Research within the PRIN 2008 project "PEPPER" (2008SY2PH4).

References

[1] Amazon Elastic Compute Cloud, © 2012, Amazon Web Services, Inc. or its affiliates. All rights reserved. <http://aws.amazon.com/ec2>, 2012.

[2] Azure, © 2012 Microsoft. <http://www.windowsazure.com/en-us/>, 2012.

[3] Build your business on Google Cloud Platform. <https://cloud.google.com/>, 2012.

[4] Amazon Elastic Compute Cloud, © 2012, Amazon Web Services, Inc. or its affiliates. All rights reserved. <http://aws.amazon.com/ec2>, 2012.

[5] E. Feller, L. Rilling, C. Morin, Snooze: a scalable and autonomic virtual machine management framework for private clouds, in: Proc. of CCGrid'12, Ottawa, Canada, 2012, pp. 482–489.

[6] K. Vishwanath, N. Nagappan, Characterizing cloud computing hardware reliability, in: Proc. of SoCC'10, Indianapolis, IN, USA, 2010, pp. 193–204.

[7] U. Helzle, L.A. Barroso, The Datacenter as a Computer: An Introduction to the Design of Warehouse-Scale Machines, first ed., Morgan and Claypool Publishers, 2009.

[8] B. Selic, Fault tolerance techniques for distributed systems, <http://www.ibm.com/developerworks/rational/library/114.html>, 2012.

[9] A. Heddaya, A. Helal, Reliability, Availability, Dependability and Performability: A User-Centered View, Boston, MA, USA, Tech. Rep., 1997.

[10] M. Armbrust, A. Fox, R. Griffith, A.D. Joseph, R.H. Katz, A. Konwinski, et al., Tech. Rep. UCB/EECS-2009-28 Above the Clouds: A Berkeley View of Cloud Computing, EECS Department, University of California, Berkeley, 2009

[11] P. Gill, N. Jain, N. Nagappan, Understanding network failures in data centers: measurement, analysis and implications, ACM Comp. Commun. Rev. 41 (4) (2011) 350–361.

[12] R. Jhawar, V. Piuri, Fault tolerance management in IaaS clouds, in: Proc. of ESTEL'12, Rome, Italy, October 20, 2012.

[13] W.E. Smith, K.S. Trivedi, L.A. Tomek, J. Ackaret, Availability analysis of blade server systems, IBM Syst. J. 47 (4) (2008) 621–640.

[14] Load Balancing Data Center Services SRND: Solutions Reference Nework Design, Cisco Systems, Inc., 170 West Tasman Drive, San Jose, CA 95134-1706, Copyright © 2004, Cisco Systems, Inc. All rights reserved.

<https://learningnetwork.cisco.com/servlet/JiveServlet/previewBody/3438-102-1-9467/cdccont_0900aec-d800eb95a.pdf> March 2004.

[15] N. Ayari, D. Barbaron, L. Lefevre, P. Primet, Fault tolerance for highly available internet services: concepts, approaches and issues, IEEE Commun. Surv. Tutor. 10 (2) (2008) 34–46.

[16] R. Jhawar, V. Piuri, M. Santambrogio, A comprehensive conceptual system-level approach to fault tolerance in cloud computing, in: Proc. of IEEE SysCon'12, Vancouver, BA, Canada, 2012, pp. 1–5.

[17] R. Guerraoui, M. Yabandeh, Independent faults in the cloud, in: Proc. of LADIS'10, Zurich, Switzerland, 2010, pp. 12–17.

[18] A. Undheim, A. Chilwan, P. Heegaard, Differentiated availability in cloud computing SLAs, in: Proc. of Grid'11, Lyon, France, 2011, pp. 129–136.

[19] S. Kim, F. Machinda, K. Trivedi, Availability modeling and analysis of virtualized system, in: Proc. of PRDC'09, Shanghai, China, 2009, pp. 365–371.

[20] B. Cully, G. Lefebvre, D. Meyer, M. Feeley, N. Hutchinson, A. Warfield, Remus: high availability via asynchronous virtual machine replication, in: Proc. of NSDI'08, San Francisco, CA, USA, pp. 161–174.

[21] C. Clark, K. Fraser, S. Hand, J.G. Hansen, E. Jul, C. Limpach, et al., Live migration of virtual machines, in: Proc. NSDI'05, Boston, MA, USA, pp. 273–286.

[22] M. Castro, B. Liskov, Practical byzantine fault tolerance, in: Proc. of OSDI'99, New Orleans, LA, USA, 1999, pp. 173–186.

[23] T. Wood, R. Singh, A. Venkataramani, P. Shenoy, E. Cecchet, ZZ and the art of practical BFT execution, in: Proc. of EuroSys'11, Salzburg, Austria, 2011, pp. 123–138.

[24] R. Kotla, L. Alvisi, M. Dahlin, A. Clement, E. Wong, Zyzzyva: speculative byzantine fault tolerance, ACM Trans. Comput. Syst. 27 (4) (2009) 7.1–7.39.

[25] J. Yin, J.P. Martin, A. Venkataramani, L. Alvisi, M. Dahlin, Separating agreement from execution for byzantine fault tolerant services, in: Proc. of SOSP'03, New York, NY, USA, 2003, pp. 253–267.

[26] R. Jhawar, V. Piuri, M. Santambrogio, Fault tolerance management in cloud computing: a system-level perspective, IEEE Syst. J. (2012).

Data Encryption

Dr. Bhushan Kapoor and Dr. Pramod Pandya
California State University

Data security is not limited to wired networks but is equally critical for wireless communications such as in Wi-Fi and cellular. A very recent case was highlighted when the Indian government requested to Research In Motion (RIM) to share the encryption algorithm used in the BlackBerry cellular device. Of course, RIM refused to share the encryption algorithm. This should demonstrate that encryption is an important technology in all forms of communication. It is hard to accept that secured systems could ever remain secured, since they are designed by us and therefore must be breakable by one of us, given enough time. Every human-engineered system must have a flaw, and it is only a matter of time before someone finds it, thus demanding new innovations by exploring applications from algebraic structures such as groups and rings, elliptic curves, and quantum physics.

Over the past 20 years we have seen classical cryptography evolve to quantum cryptography, a branch of quantum information theory. Quantum cryptography is based on the framework of quantum physics, and it is meant to solve the problem of key distribution, which is an essential component of cryptography that enables us to secure data. The key allows the data to be coded so that to decode it, one would need to know the key that was used to code it. This coding of the given data using a key is known as *encryption*, and decoding of the encrypted data, the reverse step-by-step process, is known as *decryption*. At this stage we point out that the encryption algorithm comes in two flavors: symmetric and asymmetric, of which we will get into the details later on. Securing data requires a three-pronged approach: detection, prevention, and response. Data normally resides on storage media that are accessible over a network. This network is designed with a perimeter around it, such that a single access point provides a route for inbound and outbound traffic through a router supplemented with a firewall.

Data encryption prevents data from being exposed to unauthorized access and makes it unusable. Detection enables us to monitor the activities of network users and provides a means to differentiate levels of activities and offers a possible clue to network violations.

Response is equally important, since a network violation must not be allowed to be repeated. Thus the three-pronged approach is evolutionary, and therefore systems analysis and design principles must be taken into account when we design a secured data network.

1. NEED FOR CRYPTOGRAPHY

Data communication normally takes place over an unsecured channel, as is the case when the Internet provides the pathways for the flow of data. In such a case the cryptographic protocols would enable secured communications by addressing the following.

Authentication

Alice sends a message to Bob. How can Bob verify that the message originated from Alice and not from Eve pretending to be Alice? Authentication is critical if Bob is to believe the message—for example, if the bank is trying to verify your Social Security or account number.

Confidentiality

Alice sends a message to Bob. How can Bob be sure that the message was not read by Eve? For example, personal communications need to be maintained as confidential.

Integrity

Alice sends a message to Bob. How does Bob verify that Eve did not intercept the message and change its contents?

Nonrepudiation

Alice could send a message to Bob and later deny that she ever sent a message to Bob. In such a case, how could Bob ever determine who actually sent him the message?

2. MATHEMATICAL PRELUDE TO CRYPTOGRAPHY

We will continue to describe Alice and Bob as two parties exchanging messages and Eve as the eavesdropper. Alice sends either a character string or a binary string that constitutes her message to Bob. In mathematical terms we have the *domain* of the message. The message in question needs to be secured from the eavesdropper Eve—hence it needs to be encrypted.

Mapping or Function

The encryption of the message can be defined as *mapping* the message from the domain to its range such that the inverse mapping should recover the original message. This mapping is a mathematical construct known as the *function*.

So we have a domain, and the range of the function is defined such that the elements of the domain will always map to the range of the function, never outside it. If f represents the function, and the message $m \in$ the domain, then:

$$f(m) = M \in \text{the range}$$

This function can represent, for example, swapping (shifting by k places) the characters positions in the message as defined by the function:

$$f(m,k) = M \in \text{the range}$$

The inverse of this function f must recover the original message, in which case the function is invertible and one-to-one defined. If we were to apply two functions such as f followed by g, the composite function $(g \circ f)$ must be defined and furthermore invertible and one-to-one to recover the original message:

$$(g \circ f)(m) = g(f(m))$$

We will later see that this function is an algorithm that tells the user in a finite number of ways to disguise (encrypt) the given message. The inverse function, if it does exist, would enable us to recover the original message, which is known as the decryption.

Probability

Information security is the goal of the secured data encryption; hence if the encrypted data is truly randomly distributed in the message space (range), to the hacker the encrypted message is equally likely to be in any one of the states (encrypted). This would amount to maximum entropy, so one could reasonably ask as to the likelihood of a hacker breaking the encrypted message, that is, what is the probability of an insecure event taking place? This is conceptually similar to a system being in statistical equilibrium, when it could be equally likely to be in any one of the states. This could lay the foundations of cryptoanalysis in terms of how secure the encryption algorithm is, and can it be broken in polynomial time?

Complexity

Computational complexity deals with problems that could be solved in polynomial time, for a given input. If a given encryption algorithm is known to be difficult to solve and may have a number of solutions, the hacker would have a surmountable task to solve it. Therefore, secured encryption can be examined within the scope of computational complexity to determine whether a solution exists in polynomial time. There is a class of problems that have solutions in polynomial time for a given input, designated as P. By contrast, *NP* is the set of all problems that have solutions in polynomial time but the correctness of the problem cannot be ascertained. Therefore, *NP* is a larger set containing the set *P*. This is useful, for it leads us to NP-completeness, which reduces the solvability of problems in class *P* to class *NP*.

Consider a simple example—a set $S = \{4, 7, 12, 1, 10\}$ of five numbers. We want any three numbers to add to 23. Each of the numbers is either selected once only or not selected. The target is 23. Is there an algorithm for the target 23? If there is one, do we have more than one solution? Let's explore whether we can add three numbers to reach a target of 25. Is there a solution for a target of 25? Does a solution exist, and can we investigate in polynomial time? We could extend this concept of computational complexity to crack encryption algorithm that is public, but the key used to encrypt and decrypt the message is kept private. So, in essence the cryptoanalysis deals with discovering the key.

3. CLASSICAL CRYPTOGRAPHY

The conceptual foundation of cryptography was laid out around 3,000 years ago in India and China. The earlier work in cryptology was centered on messages that were expressed using alphanumeric symbols; hence encryption involved simple algorithms such as shifting characters within the string of the message in a defined manner, which is now known as shift cipher. We will also introduce the necessary mathematics of cryptography: integer and modular arithmetic, linear congruence, Euclidean and Extended Euclidean algorithms, Fermat's theorem, and elliptic curves. We will specify useful notations in context.

Take the set of integers:

$$Z = \{............, -3, -2, -1, 0, 1, 2, 3, ...\}$$

For any integers a and n, we say that n divides a if the remainder is zero after the division, or else we write:

$$a = q \cdot n + r \quad \text{q: quotient, r: remainder}$$

The Euclidean Algorithm

Given two positive integers, a and b, find the greatest common divisors of a and b. Let d be the greatest common divisors (*gcd*) of a and b, then,

$$d = \gcd(a,b)$$

Use the following example:

$$\gcd(36, 10) = \gcd(10, 6) = \gcd(6, 4) = \gcd(4, 2) = \gcd(2, 0) = 2$$

Hence:

$$\gcd(36, 10) = 2$$

The Extended Euclidean Algorithm

Let a and b be two positive integers, then

$$d = \gcd(a, b) = ax + by$$

Use the following example:

$$\gcd(540, 168) = \gcd(168, 36) = \gcd(36, 24)$$
$$= \gcd(24, 12) = \gcd(12, 0) = 12$$

$$540 = 3(168) + 36 \qquad 36 = 540 - 3(168)$$
$$168 = 4(36) + 24 \qquad 24 = 168 - 4(36)$$
$$36 = 1(24) + 12 \qquad 12 = 36 - 1(24)$$
$$12 = 540 - 3(168) - 168 + 4(36)$$
$$= 540 - 4(168) + 4(36)$$
$$= 540 - 4(168) + 4(540) - 12(168)$$
$$= 5(540) - 16(168)$$

Therefore:

$$x = 5 \quad \text{and} \quad y = -16$$

Hence:

$$12 = (5)540 - (16)168$$

Modular Arithmetic

For a given integer a, positive integer m, and the remainder r,

$$r = a \ (\text{mod } m)$$

Consider examples:

$$2 = 27 \bmod 5$$
$$10 = -18 \bmod 14$$

{divide -18 by 14 leaves -4 as a remainder, then add 14 to -4 so that $(-4 + 14) = 10$ so the remainder is nonnegative}

A set of *residues* is a set consisting of remainders obtained by dividing positive integers by a chosen positive number m (modulus).

$Z_m = a \ (\text{mod } m) = \{0, 1, 2, 3, \ldots, m-1\}$

Take $m = 7$, then

$$Z_7 = \{0, 1, 2, 3, 4, 5, 6\}$$

Congruence

In arithmetic we normally use the relational operator, equal (=), to express that the pair of numbers are equal to each other, which is a binary operation. In cryptography we use *congruence* to express that the residue is the same for a set of integers divided by a positive integer. This essentially groups the positive integers into equivalence classes. Let's look at some examples:

$$2 \equiv 2 \bmod 10; \ 2 \equiv 12 \bmod 10; 2 \equiv 22 \bmod 10$$

Hence we say that the set {2, 12, 22} are congruent mod 10.

Residue Class

A residue class is a set of integers congruent mod m, where m is a positive integer. Take $m = 7$:

$$[0] = \{.........., -21, -14, -7, 0, 7, 14, 21, ...\}$$
$$[1] = \{.........., -20, -3, -6, 1, 8, 15, 22, ...\}$$
$$[2] = \{.........., -19, -12, -5, 2, 9, 16, 23, ...\}$$
$$[3] = \{............, -18, -11, -4, 3, 10, 17, 24, ...\}$$
$$[4] = \{............, -17, -10, -3, 4, 11, 18, 25, ...\}$$
$$[5] = \{............., -16, -9, -2, 5, 12, 19, 26, ...\}$$
$$[6] = \{............., -15, -8, -1, 6, 13, 20, 27, ...\}$$

Some more useful operations defined in Z_m:

$$
\begin{aligned}
(a + b)\bmod m &= \{(a \bmod m) + (b \bmod m)\}\bmod m \\
(a - b)\bmod m &= \{(a \bmod m) - (b \bmod m)\}\bmod m \\
(a * b)\bmod m &= \{(a \bmod m) * (b \bmod m)\}\bmod m
\end{aligned}
$$

$$10^n(\bmod x) = \langle 10 \bmod x \rangle^n \bmod m$$

Inverses

In everyday arithmetic, it is quite simple to find the inverse of a given integer if the binary operation is either additive or multiplicative, but such is not the case with modular arithmetic.

We will begin with the additive inverse of two numbers $a, b \in Z_m$

$$(a + b) \equiv 0 \ (\bmod m)$$

That is, the additive inverse of a is $b = (m - a)$.
Given

$$a = 4, \quad \text{and} \quad m = 10$$

then:

$$b = m - a = 10 - 4 = 6$$

Verify:

$$4 + 6 \equiv 0 \ (\mathrm{mod}\ 10)$$

Similarly, the multiplicative inverse of two integers a, $b \in Z_m$ if

$$a * b \equiv 1 \ (\mathrm{mod}\ m)$$

a has a multiplicative inverse $b \in Z_m$ if and only if

$$\gcd(m, a) = 1$$

in which case (m, a) are relative prime.

We remind the reader that a prime number is any number greater than 1 that is divisible (with a remainder 0) only by itself and 1. For example, {2, 3, 5, 7, 11, 13,...} are prime numbers, and we quote the following theorem for the reader.

Fundamental Theorem of Arithmetic

Each positive number is either a prime number or a composite number, in which case it can be expressed as a product of prime numbers.

Let's consider a set of integers mod 10 to find the multiplicative inverse of the numbers in the set:

$$Z_{10} = \{0, 1, 2, 3, 4, 5, 6, 7, 8, 9\}$$
$$(1 * 1)\mathrm{mod}\ 10 = 1$$
$$(3 * 7)\mathrm{mod}\ 10 = 1$$
$$(9 * 9)\mathrm{mod}\ 10 = 1$$

then there are only three pairs (1,1); (3,7); and (9,9):

$$Z_{10*} = \{1, 3, 7, 9\}$$

The numbers {0, 2, 4, 5, 6, 8} have no multiplicative inverse.
Consider a set:

$$Z_6 = \{0, 1, 2, 3, 4, 5\}$$

Then,

$$Z_{6*} = \{1, 5\}$$

You will note that Z_{n*} is a subset of Z_n with unique multiplicative inverse.

Each member of Z_n has a unique additive inverse, whereas each member of Z_{n*} has a unique multiplicative inverse.

Congruence Relation Defined

The a is congruent to b (mod m) if m divides $(a - b)$, that is, the remainder is zero.

$$a \equiv b \bmod m$$

Examples: $87 \equiv 27 \bmod 4$, $67 \equiv 1 \bmod 6$.
Next we quote three theorems:
Theorem 1: Suppose that $a \equiv c \bmod m$ and $b \equiv\, = d \bmod m$, then

$$a + b \equiv c + d (\bmod m)$$
$$a * b \equiv c * d (\bmod m)$$

Theorem 2: Suppose $a*b \equiv a*c$ (mod m)

$$\text{and gcd } (a, m) = 1$$
$$\text{then } b \equiv c \ (\bmod m)$$

Theorem 3: Suppose $a*b \equiv a*c$ (mod m)

$$\text{and } d = \gcd(a, m)$$
$$\text{then } b \equiv c \ (\bmod m/d)$$

Example to illustrate the use of the theorems just stated:

$$6 \equiv 36 \ (\bmod 10)$$

then

$$3 \times 2 \equiv 3 \times 12 \ (\bmod 10)$$

since

$$\gcd(3, \ 10) = 1$$

therefore,

$$2 \equiv 12 \ (\bmod 10)$$

also

$$2 = \gcd(6, 10)$$

therefore,

$$1 \equiv 6 \ (\bmod 5)$$

Given,

$$14x \equiv 12 \ (\bmod 18)$$

find x.

Since

$$gcd(14,\ 18) = 2$$

therefore,

$$7x \equiv 6\ (mod\ 9)$$

you will observe that,

$$gcd(7,\ 9) = 1$$

therefore,

$$x \equiv 6(7^{-1})\ mod\ 9$$

and the multiplicative inverse of 7^{-1} is 4, therefore,

$$x \equiv (6 * 4)\ (mod\ 9) = 6$$

Substitution Cipher

Shift ciphers, also known as *additive ciphers*, are an example of a monoalphabetic character cipher in which each character is mapped to another character, and a repeated character maps to the same character irrespective of its position in the string. We give a simple example of an additive cipher, where the key is 3, and the algorithm is "add." We restrict the mapping to {0, 1, ..., 7} (see Table 2.1)—that is, we use mod 8. This is an example of finite domain and the range for mapping, so the inverse of the function can be determined easily from the ciphertext.

Observations:

- The domain of the function is $x = \{0,1,2,3,4,5,6,7\}$.
- The range of the function is $y = \{0,1,2,3,4,5,6,7\}$.
- The function is 1 to 1.
- The function is invertible.
- The inverse function is $x = (y - 3)\ mod\ 8$.

The affine cipher has two operations, addition and multiplication, with two keys. Once again the arithmetic is mod m, where m is a chosen positive integer.

$$y = (kx + b)\ mod\ m$$

where k and b are chosen from integers {0, 1, 2, 3,........., $(m - 1)$}, and x is the symbol to be encrypted.

TABLE 2.1   Table of values for $y = (x + 3)\ mod\ 8$, given values of $x = \{0,1,... 7\}$.

X	0	1	2	3	4	5	6	7
y	3	4	5	6	7	0	1	2

TABLE 2.2   Monoalphabetic Substitution Cipher.

X	0	1	2	3	4	5	6	7
y	3	0	5	2	7	4	1	6

TABLE 2.3   Transposition Cipher.

1	2	3	4	5
3	1	4	5	2

The decryption is given as:

$$x = [(y - b) * k^{-1}] \bmod m$$

where

$$k^{-1}$$

is the multiplicative inverse of k in Z_{n*}
$(—b)$ is the additive inverse in Z_n
Consider,

$$y = (5 * x + 3) \bmod 8$$

Then,

$$x = (y - 3)5 \bmod 8$$

In this case, the multiplicative inverse of 5 happens to be 5.

Monoalphabetic substitution ciphers are easily broken, since the key size is small (see Table 2.2).

$$Z_8 = \{0, 1, 2, 3, 4, 5, 6, 7, \} Z_{8*} = \{1, 3, 5\}$$

Transposition Cipher

A transposition cipher changes the location of the character by a given set of rules known as *permutation*. A cyclic group defines the permutation with a single key to encrypt, and the same key is used to decrypt the ciphered message. Table 2.3 provides an illustration.

4. MODERN SYMMETRIC CIPHERS

Computers internally represent printable data in binary format as strings of zeros and ones. Therefore any data is represented as a large block of zeros and ones. The processing speed of a computer is used to encrypt the block of zeros and ones. Securing all the data in one go would not be practical, nor would it secure the data; hence the scheme to treat data in chunks of blocks, leading to the concept of block ciphers.

The most common value of a block is 64, 128, 256, or 512 bits. You will observe that these values are powers of 2, since computers process data in binary representation using modular arithmetic with modulus 2. We need an algorithm and a key to encrypt the blocks of binary data such that the ciphered data is confusing and diffusing to the hacker. The algorithm is made public, whereas the key is kept secret from unauthorized users so that hackers could establish the robustness of the cipher by attempting to break the encrypted message. The logic of the block cipher is as follows:

- Each bit of ciphertext should depend on all bits of the key and all bits of the plaintext.
- There should be no evidence of statistical relationship between the plaintext and the ciphertext.

In essence, this is the goal of an encryption algorithm: Confuse the message so that there is no apparent relationship between the ciphertext and the plaintext. This is achieved by the substitution rule (S-boxes) and the key.

If changing one bit in the plaintext has a minimal effect on the encrypted text, it might be possible for the hacker to work backward from the encrypted text to the plaintext by changing the bits. Therefore a minimal change in the plaintext should lead to a maximum change in the ciphertext, resulting in spreading, which is known as *diffusion*. Permutation or P-boxes implement the diffusion.

The symmetric cipher consists of an algorithm and a key. The algorithm is made public, whereas the key is kept secret and is known only to the parties that are exchanging messages. Of course, this does create a huge problem, since every pair that is going to exchange messages will need a secret key, growing indefinitely in number as the number of pairs increases. We also would need a mechanism by which to manage the secret keys. We will address these issues later on.

The symmetric algorithm would consist of finite rounds of S-boxes and P-boxes. Once the plaintext is encrypted using the algorithm and the key, it would need to be decrypted using the same algorithm and key. The decryption algorithm and the key would need to work backward in some sense to revert the encrypted message to its original message.

So you begin to see that the algorithm must consist of a finite number of combinations of S-boxes and P-boxes; encryption is mapping from message space (domain) to another message space (range), that is, mapping should be a closed operation, a "necessary" condition on the encryption algorithm. This implies that message strings get mapped to message strings, and of course these message strings belong to a set of messages. We are not concerned with the semantics of the message; we leave this to the message sender and receiver. The S-boxes and P-boxes would define a set of operations on the messages or bits that represent the string of messages. Therefore we require that this set of operations should also be able to undo the encryption, that is, mapping must be invertible in the mathematical sense. Hence the set of operations must have definite relationships among them, resulting in some structural and logical connection. In mathematics an example of this is an algebraic structure such as group, ring, and field, which we explore in the next section.

S-Box

The reader should note that an S-box can have a 3-bit input binary string, and its output may be a 2-bit. The S-box may use a key or be keyless. Let $S(x)$ be the linear function computed by the following function [1]:

$$S(x_1 x_2 x_3) = [(1 + x_1 + x_2 + x_3 + x_1 \bullet x_2) \bmod 2]$$
$$[(1 + x_3 + x_1 \bullet x_3 + x_1 \bullet x_2) \bmod 2]$$

Such a function is referred to as an *S-box*. For a given 4-bit block of plaintext $x_1 x_2 x_3 x_4$ and the 3-bit key, $k_1 k_2 k_3$, let

$$E(x_1 x_2 x_3 x_4, \ k_1 k_2 k_3) = x_1 x_2 (x_3 x_4 \oplus S(x_2 x_1 x_2 \oplus k_1 k_2 k_3))$$

where $\oplus$ represents exclusive OR

Given ciphertext, $y_1 y_2 y_3 y_4$ computed with E and the key, $k_1 k_2 k_3$, compute

$$D(y_1 y_2 y_3 y_4, \ k_1 k_2 k_3) = (y_1 y_2 \oplus S(y_4 y_3 y_4 \oplus k_1 k_2 k_3)) y_3 y_4$$

S-boxes are classified as linear if the number of output bits is the same as the number of input bits, and they're nonlinear if the number of output bits is different from the number of input bits. Furthermore, S-boxes can be invertible or noninvertible.

P-Boxes

A *P-box* (permutation box) will permute the bits per specification. There are three different types of P-boxes, as shown in Tables 2.4, 2.5, and 2.6.

In the compression P-box, inputs 2 and 4 are blocked.

The expansion P-box maps elements 1, 2, and 3 only.

Let's consider a permutation group with the mapping defined, as shown in Table 2.7.

TABLE 2.4   Straight P-Box.

1	2	3	4	5
4	1	5	3	2

TABLE 2.5   Compression P-Box.

1	2	3	4	5
1		2		3

TABLE 2.6   Expansion P-Box.

1	3	3	1	2
1	2	3	4	5

TABLE 2.7 The Permutation Group.

	1	2	3	4	5	6	7	8
a	2	6	3	1	4	8	5	7
	1	1	1	1	0	0	1	0
	1	0	1	1	1	0	0	1
a^2	6	8	3	2	1	7	4	5
	0	0	1	1	1	1	1	0
a^3	8	7	3	6	2	5	1	4
	0	1	1	0	1	0	1	1
a^4	7	5	3	8	6	4	2	1
	1	0	1	0	0	1	1	1
a^5	5	4	3	7	8	1	6	2
	0	1	1	1	0	1	0	1
a^6	4	1	3	5	7	2	8	6
	1	1	1	0	1	1	0	0
$a^7 = e$	1	2	3	4	5	6	7	8
	1	1	1	1	0	0	1	0

This group is a cyclic group with elements:

$$G = (e, a, a^2, a^3, a^4, a^5, a^6)$$

The identity mapping is given by $a^7 = e$. The inverse element is a^{-1}.
Table 2.7 shows a permutation of an 8-bit string (11110010).

Product Ciphers

Modern block ciphers are divided into two categories. The first category of the cipher uses both invertible and noninvertible components. A Feistel cipher belongs to the first category, and DES is a good example of a Feistel cipher. This cipher uses the combination of S-boxes and P-boxes with compression and expansion (noninvertible).

The second category of cipher only uses invertible components, and Advanced Encryption Standard (AES) is an example of a non-Feistel cipher. AES uses S-boxes with an equal number of inputs and outputs and a straight P-box that is invertible.

Alternation of substitutions and transpositions of appropriate forms when applied to a block of plaintext can have the effect of obscuring statistical relationships between the plaintext and the ciphertext and between the key and the ciphertext (diffusion and confusion).

5. ALGEBRAIC STRUCTURE

Modern encryption algorithms such as DES, AES, RSA, and ElGamal, to name a few, are based on algebraic structures such as group theory and field theory as well as number theory. We will begin with a set S, with a finite number of elements and a binary operation (*) defined between any two elements of the set:

$$*:S \times S \to S$$

that is, if a and $b \in S$, then $a * b \in S$. This is important because it implies that the set is closed under the binary operation. We have seen that the message space is finite, and we want to make sure that any algebraic operation on the message space satisfies the closure property. Hence, we want to treat the message space as a finite set of elements. We remind the reader that messages that get encrypted must be finally decrypted by the received party, so the encryption algorithm must run in polynomial time; furthermore, the algorithm must have the property that it be reversible, to recover the original message. The goal of encryption is to confuse and diffuse the hacker to make it almost impossible for the hacker to break the encrypted message. Therefore, encryption must consist of finite number substitutions and transpositions. The algebraic structure *classical group* facilitates the coding of encryption algorithms.

Next we give some relevant definitions and examples before we proceed to introduce the essential concept of a Galois field, which is central to formulation of a Rijndael algorithm used in the Advanced Encryption Standard.

Definition Group

A definition group $(G, \bullet)$ is a finite set G together with an operation $\bullet$ satisfying the following conditions [2]:

- Closure: $\forall a, b \in G$, then $(a \bullet b) \in G$
- Associativity: $\forall a, b, c \in G$, then $a \bullet (b \bullet c) = (a \bullet b) \bullet c$
- Existence of identity: $\exists a$ unique element $e \in G$ such that $\forall a \in G: a \bullet e = e \bullet a$
- $\forall a \in G: \forall a^{-1}G: a^{-1}a = a^{-1} \bullet a = e$

Definitions of Finite and Infinite Groups (Order of a Group)

A group G is said to be finite if the number of elements in the set G is finite; otherwise the group is infinite.

Definition Abelian Group

A group G is abelian if for all $a, b \in G$, $a \bullet b = b \bullet a$

The reader should note that in a group, the elements in the set do not have to be numbers or objects; they can be mappings, functions, or rules.

Examples of a Group

The set of integers Z is a group under addition $(+)$, that is, $(Z, +)$ is a group with identity $e = 0$, and inverse of an element a is $(-a)$. This is an additive abelian group, but infinite.

Nonzero elements of Q (rationale), R (reals), and C (complex) form a group under multiplication, with the identity element $e = 1$, and a^{-1} being the multiplicative inverse.

For any $n \geq 1$, the set of integers modulo n forms a finite additive group of n elements. $G = <Z_n, + >$ is an abelian group.

The set of Z_{n*} with multiplication operator, $G = <Z_{n*}, x>$ is also an abelian group.

The set Z_{n*}, is a subset of Z_n and includes only integers in Z_n that have a unique multiplicative inverse.

$$Z_{13} = \{0, 1, 2, 3, 4, 5, 6, 7, 8, 9, 10, 11, 12\}$$
$$Z_{13*} = \{1, 2, 3, 4, 5, 6, 7, 8, 9, 10, 11, 12\}$$

Definition: Subgroup

A subgroup of a group G is a non empty subset H of G, which itself is a group under the same operations as that of G. We denote that H is a subgroup of G as $H \subseteq G$, and $H \subset G$ is a proper subgroup of G if the set $H \neq G$ [2]:

Examples of subgroups:

Under addition, $Z \subseteq Q \subseteq R \subseteq C$.

$H = <Z_{10}, + >$ is a proper subgroup of $G = <Z_{12}, + >$

Definition: Cyclic Group

A group G is said to be cyclic if there exists an element $a \in G$ such that for any $b \in G$, and $i \geq 0$, $b = a^i$. Element a is called a generator of G.

The group $G = <Z_{10*}, x>$ is a cyclic group with generators $g = 3$ and $g = 7$.

$$Z_{10*} = \{1, 3, 7, 9\}$$

The group $G = <Z_6, + >$ is a cyclic group with generators g $= 1$ and g $= 5$.

$$Z_6 = \{0, 1, 2, 3, 4, 5\}$$

Rings

Let R be a non-empty set with two binary operations addition $(+)$ and multiplication $(*)$. Then R is called a *ring* if the following axioms are met:

- Under addition, R is an abelian group with zero as the additive identity.
- Under multiplication, R satisfies the closure, the associativity, and the identity axiom; 1 is the multiplicative identity, and that $1 \neq 0$.
- For every a and b that belongs to R, $a \bullet b = b \bullet a$.
- For every a, b, and c that belongs to R, then $a \bullet (b + c) = a \bullet b + a \bullet c$.

Examples

Z, Q, R, and C are all rings under addition and multiplication. For any $n > 0$, Z_n is a ring under addition and multiplication modulo n with 0 as identity under addition, 1 under multiplication.

Definition: Field

If the nonzero elements of a ring form a group under multiplication, the ring is called a *field*.

Examples

Q, R, and C are all fields under addition and multiplication, with 0 and 1 as identity under addition and multiplication.

Note: Z under integer addition and multiplication is not a field because any nonzero element does not have a multiplicative inverse in Z.

Finite Fields $GF(2^n)$

Construction of finite fields and computations in finite fields are based on polynomial computations. Finite fields play a significant role in cryptography and cryptographic protocols such as the Diffie and Hellman key exchange protocol, ElGamal cryptosystems, and AES.

For a prime number p, the quotient Z/p (or F_p) is a finite field with p number of elements. For any positive integer q, $GF(q) = F_q$. We define A to be algebraic structure such as a ring, group, or field.

Definition: A polynomial over A is an expression of the form

$$f(x) = \sum_{i=0}^{n} a_i x^n$$

where n is a nonnegative integer, the coefficient $a_i \in A$, $0 \le i \le n$, and $x \notin A$ [2].

Definition: A polynomial $f \in A[x]$ is said to be irreducible in $A[x]$ if f has a positive degree and $f = gh$ for some g, $h \in A[x]$ implies that either g or h is a constant polynomial [2].

The reader should be aware that a given polynomial can be reducible over one structure but irreducible over another.

Definition: *Let f, g, q, and $r \in A[x]$ with $g \ne 0$. Then we say that r is a remainder of f divided by g:*

$$r \equiv f(mod\ g)$$

The set of remainders of all the polynomials in $A[x](mod\ g)$ denoted as $A[x]_g$.

Theorem: Let F be a field and f be a nonzero polynomial in $F[x]$. Then $F[x]_f$ is a ring and is a field if f is irreducible over F.

Theorem: Let F be a field of p elements, and f be an irreducible polynomial over F. Then the number of elements in the field $F[x]f$ is p^n [2].

For every prime p and every positive integer n there exists a finite field of p^n number of elements.

For any prime number p, Z_p is a finite field under addition and multiplication modulo p with 0 and 1 as the identity under addition and multiplication.

Z_p is an additive ring and the nonzero elements of Z_p, denoted by Z_{p*}, forms a multiplicative group.

Galois field, $GF(p^n)$ is a finite field with number of elements p^n, where p is a prime number and n is a positive integer.

Example: Integer representation of a finite field (Rijndael) element.

Polynomial $f(x) = x^8 + x^4 + x^3 + x + 1$ is irreducible over F_2.

The set of all polynomials(mod f) over F_2 forms a field of 2^8 elements; they are all polynomials over F_2 of degree less than 8. So any element in the field $F_2[x]_f$

$$b_7 x^7 + b_6 x^6 + b_5 x^5 + b_4 x^4 + b_3 x^3 + b_2 x^2 + b_1 x^1 + b_0$$

where $b_7, b_6, b_5, b_4, b_3, b_2, b_1, b_0 \in F_2$ thus any element in this field can represent an 8-bit binary number.

We often use F_{2^8} field with 256 elements because there exists an isomorphism between Rijndael and F_{2^8}.

Data inside a computer is organized in bytes (8 bits) and is processed using Boolean logic, that is, bits are manipulated using binary operations addition and multiplication. These binary operations are implemented using the logical operator XOR, or in the language of finite fields, $GF(2)$. Since the extended ASCII defines 8 bits per byte, an 8-bit byte has a natural representation using a polynomial of degree 8. Polynomial addition would be mod 2, and multiplication would be mod polynomial degree 8. Of course this polynomial degree 8 would have to be irreducible. Hence the Galois field $GF(2^8)$ would be the most natural tool to implement the encryption algorithm. Furthermore, this would provide a close algebraic formulation.

Consider polynomials over $GF(2)$ with $p = 2$ and $n = 1$.

$$1, \ x, \ x + 1, \ x^2 + x + 1, \ x^2 + 1, \ x^3 + 1$$

For polynomials with negative coefficients, -1 is the same as $+1$ in $GF(2)$. Obviously, the number of such polynomials is infinite. Algebraic operations of addition and multiplication in which the coefficients are added and multiplied according to the rules that apply to $GF(2)$ are sets of polynomials that form a ring.

Modular Polynomial Arithmetic Over GF(2)

The Galois field $GF(2^3)$: Construct this field with eight elements that can be represented by polynomials of the form

$$ax^2 + bx + c \text{ where } a, b, c \in GF(2) = \{0, \ 1\}$$

Two choices for a, b, c give $2 \times 2 \times 2 = 8$ polynomials of the form

$$ax^2 + bx + c \in GF_2[x]$$

What is our choice of the irreducible polynomials for this field?

$$(x^3 + x^2 + x + 1), \ (x^3 + x^2 + 1), \ (x^3 + x^2 + x), \ (x^3 + x + 1), \ (x^3 + x^2)$$

These two polynomials have no factors: $(x^3 + x^2 + 1)$, $(x^3 + x + 1)$

So we choose polynomial $(x^3 + x + 1)$. Hence all polynomial arithmetic multiplication and division is carried out with respect to $(x^3 + x + 1)$.

The eight polynomials that belong to $GF(2^3)$:

$$\{0, \ 1, \ x, \ x^2, \ 1 + x, \ 1 + x^2, \ x + x^2, \ 1 + x + x^2\}$$

You will observe that GF(8) = {0,1,2,3,4,5,6,7} is not a field, since every element (excluding zero) does not have a multiplicative inverse such as {2, 4, 6} (mod 8) [2].

Using a Generator to Represent the Elements of $GF(2^n)$

It is particularly convenient to represent the elements of a Galois field with the help of a generator element. If α, is a generator element, then every element of $GF(2^n)$, except for the 0 element, can be written as some power of α. A generator is obtained from the irreducible polynomial that was used to construct the finite field. If $f(\alpha)$ is the irreducible polynomial used, then α, is that element that satisfies the equation $f(\alpha) = 0$. You do not actually solve this equation for its roots, since an irreducible polynomial cannot have actual roots in the field GF(2).

Consider the case of $GF(2^3)$, defined with the irreducible polynomial $x^3 + x + 1$. The generator α, is that element that satisfies $\alpha^3 + \alpha + 1 = 0$. Suppose α is a root in $GF(2^3)$ of the polynomial $p(x) = 1 + x + x^3$, that is, $p(\alpha) = 0$, then

$$\alpha^3 = -\alpha - 1 \ (\text{mod } 2) = \alpha + 1$$
$$\alpha^4 = \alpha(\alpha + 1) = \alpha^2 + \alpha$$
$$\alpha^5 = \alpha^4 \cdot \alpha = (\alpha^2 + \alpha)\alpha = \alpha^3 + \alpha^2 = (\alpha^2 + \alpha + 1)$$
$$\alpha^6 = \alpha^5 \cdot \alpha = \alpha \cdot (\alpha^2 + \alpha + 1) = (\alpha^2 + 1)$$
$$\alpha^7 = (\alpha^2 + 1) \cdot \alpha = (2\alpha + 1)$$

All powers of α generate nonzero elements of GF_8. The polynomials of $GF(2^3)$ represent bit strings, as shown in Table 2.8.

We now consider all polynomials defined over $GF(2)$, modulo the irreducible polynomial $x^3 + x + 1$. When an algebraic operation (polynomial multiplication) results in a polynomial whose degree equals or exceeds that of the irreducible polynomial, we will take for our result the remainder modulo the irreducible polynomial. For example,

$$(x^2 + x + 1) * (x^2 + 1) \ \text{mod} \ (x^3 + x + 1)$$
$$= (x^4 + x^3 + x^2) + (x^2 + x + 1) \ \text{mod} \ (x^3 + x + 1)$$
$$= (x^4 + x^3 + x + 1) \ \text{mod} \ (x^3 + x + 1)$$
$$= -x^2 + x$$
$$= x^2 + x$$

TABLE 2.8   The Polynomials of CF(2^3).

Polynomial	Bit String
0	000
1	001
x	010
$x + 1$	011
x^2	100
$x^2 + 1$	101
$x^2 + x$	110
$x^2 + x + 1$	111

Recall that $1 + 1 = 0$ in GF(2). With multiplications modulo $(x^3 + x + 1)$, we have only the following eight polynomials in the set of polynomials over GF(2):

$$\{0, \ 1, \ x, \ x + 1, \ x^2, \ x^2 + 1, \ x^2 + x, \ x^2 + x + 1\}$$

We refer to this set as $GF(2^3)$, where the power of 2 is the degree of the modulus polynomial. The eight elements of Z_8 are to be integers modulo 8. Similarly, $GF(2^3)$ maps all the polynomials over GF(2) to the eight polynomials shown. But you will note the crucial difference between $GF(2^3)$ and 2^3: $GF(2^3)$ is a field, whereas Z_8 is *not* [2].

$GF(2^3)$ is a Finite Field

We know that $GF(2^3)$ is an abelian group because the operation of polynomial addition satisfies all the requirements of a group operator and because polynomial addition is commutative. $GF(2^3)$ is also a commutative ring because polynomial multiplication is a distributive over polynomial addition. $GF(2^3)$ is a finite field because it is a finite set and because it contains a unique multiplicative inverse for every nonzero element.

$GF(2^n)$ is a finite field for every n. To find all the polynomials in $GF(2^n)$, we need an irreducible polynomial of degree n. AES arithmetic is based on $GF(2^8)$. It uses the following irreducible polynomial:

$$f(x) = x^8 + x^4 + x^3 + x + 1$$

The finite field $GF(2^8)$ used by AES obviously contains 256 distinct polynomials over GF (2). In general, $GF(p^n)$ is a finite field for any prime p. The elements of $GF(p^n)$ are polynomials over GF(p) (which is the same as the set of residues Z_p).

Next we show how the multiplicative inverse of a polynomial is calculated using the Extended Euclidean algorithm:

Multiplicative inverse of $(x^2 + x + 1)$ in $F_2[x]/(x^4 + x + 1)$ is $(x^2 + x)$
$(x^2 + x)(x^2 + x + 1) = 1 \bmod (x^4 + x + 1)$
Multiplicative inverse of $(x^6 + x + 1)$ in $F_2[x]/(x^8 + x^4 + x^3 + x + 1)$ is $(x^6 + x^5 + x^2 + x + 1)$
$(x^6 + x + 1)(x^6 + x^5 + x^2 + x + 1) = 1 \bmod (x^8 + x^4 + x^3x + 1)[2, 3]$

6. THE INTERNAL FUNCTIONS OF RIJNDAEL IN AES IMPLEMENTATION

Rijndael is a block cipher. The messages are broken into blocks of a predetermined length, and each block is encrypted independently of the others. Rijndael operates on blocks that are 128-bits in length. There are actually three variants of the Rijndael cipher, each of which uses a different key length. The permissible key lengths are 128, 192, and 256 bits. The details of Rijndael may be found in Bennett and Gilles (1984), but we give an overview here [2,3].

Mathematical Preliminaries

Within a block, the fundamental unit operated on is a byte, that is, 8 bits. Bytes can be interpreted in two different ways. A byte is given in terms of its bits as $b_7b_6b_5b_4b_3b_2b_1b_0$. We may think of each bit as an element in GF(2), the finite field of two elements (mod 2). First, we may think of a byte as a vector, $b_7b_6b_5b_4b_3b_2b_1b_0$ in $GF(2^8)$. Second, we may think of a byte as an element of $GF(2^8)$, in the following way: Consider the polynomial ring GF $(2)[X]$. We may mod out by any polynomial to produce a factor ring. If this polynomial is irreducible and of degree n, the resulting factor ring is isomorphic to $GF(2^n)$. In Rijndael, we mod out by the irreducible polynomial $X8 + X4 + X3 + X + 1$ and so obtain a representation for $GF(2^8)$. The Rijndael algorithm deals with five units of data in the encryption scheme:

- Bit: A binary digit with a value of 0 or 1
- Byte: A group of 8 bits
- Word: A group of 32 bits
- Block: A block in AES is defined to be 128, 192 or 256 bits
- State: The data block is known as a *state*, and it is made up of a 4×4 matrix of 16 bytes (128 bits)

State

For our discussion purposes, we will consider a data block of 128 bits with a *ky* size of 128 bits. The state is 128 bits long. We think of the state as divided into 16 bytes, a_{ij} where $0 \le i, j \le 3$. We think of these 16 bytes as an array, or matrix, with 4 rows and 4 columns, such that a_{00} is the first byte, b_0 and so on (see Figure 2.1).

$$\begin{bmatrix} a_{00} = b_0 & a_{01} = b_4 & a_{02} = b_8 & a_{03} = b_{12} \\ a_{10} = b_1 & a_{11} = b_5 & a_{12} = b_9 & a_{13} = b_{13} \\ a_{20} = b_2 & a_{21} = b_6 & a_{22} = b_{10} & a_{23} = b_{14} \\ a_{30} = b_3 & a_{31} = b_7 & a_{32} = b_{11} & a_{33} = b_{15} \end{bmatrix}$$

FIGURE 2.1   State.

TABLE 2.9   SubByte Transformation.

	0	1	2	3	4	5	6	7	8	9	A	B	C	D	E	F
0	63	7C	77	7B	F2	6B	6F	C5	30	01	67	2B	FE	D7	AB	76
1	CA	82	C9	7D	FA	59	47	F0	AD	D4	A2	AF	9C	A4	72	C0
2	B7	FD	93	26	36	3F	F7	CC	34	A5	E5	F1	71	D8	31	15
3	04	C7	23	C3	18	96	05	9A	07	12	80	E2	EB	27	B2	75
4	09	83	2C	1A	1B	6E	5A	A0	52	3B	D6	B3	29	E3	2F	84
5	53	D1	00	ED	20	FC	B1	5B	6A	CB	BE	39	4A	4C	58	CF
6	D0	EF	AA	FB	43	4D	33	85	45	F9	02	7F	50	3C	9F	A8
7	51	A3	40	8F	92	9D	38	F5	BC	B6	DA	21	10	FF	F3	D2
8	CD	0C	13	EC	5F	97	44	17	C4	A7	7E	3D	64	5D	19	73
9	60	81	4F	DC	22	2A	90	88	46	EE	B8	14	DE	5E	0B	DB
A	E0	32	3A	0A	49	06	24	5C	C2	D3	AC	62	91	95	E4	79
B	E7	CB	37	6D	8D	D5	4E	A9	6C	56	F4	EA	65	7k	AE	08
C	BA	78	25	2E	1C	A6	B4	C6	E8	DD	74	1F	4B	BD	8B	8A
D	70	3E	B5	66	48	03	F6	0E	61	35	57	B9	86	C1	1D	9E
E	E'I	F8	98	11	69	D9	8E	94	9B	1E	87	E9	CE	55	28	DF
F	8C	A1	89	0D	BF	E6	42	68	41	99	2D	0F	B0	54	BB	16

AES uses several rounds (10, 12, or 14) of transformations, beginning with a 128-bit block. A round is made up of four parts: S-box, permutation, mixing, and subkey addition. We discuss each part here [2,3].

The S-Box (SubByte)

S-boxes, or substitution boxes, are common in block ciphers. These are 1-to-1 and onto functions, and therefore an inverse exists. Furthermore, these maps are nonlinear to make them immune to linear and differential cryptoanalysis. The S-box is the same in every round, and it acts independently on each byte. Each byte belongs to $GF(2^8)$ domain with 256 elements. For a given byte we compute the inverse of that byte in the $GF(2^8)$ field. This sends a byte x to x^{-1} if x is nonzero and sends it to 0 if it is zero. This defines a nonlinear transformation, as shown in Table 2.9.

Next we apply an affine (over GF(2)) transformation. Think of the byte x as a vector in $GF(2^8)$. Consider the invertible matrix A, as shown in Figure 2.2.

The structure of matrix A is relatively simple, successively shifting the prior row by 1. If we define the vector $v \in GF(2^8)$ to be (1, 1, 0, 0, 0, 1, 1, 0), then the second half of the S-box sends byte x to byte y through the affine transformation defined as:

$$y = A \cdot x^{-1} \oplus 1$$

Since the matrix A has an inverse, it is possible to recover x using the following procedure known as the InvSubByte:

$$x = [A^{-1}(y \oplus b)]^{-1}$$

We will demonstrate the action of an S-box by choosing an uppercase letter S, for which the hexadecimal representation is 53_{16} and binary representation is shown in Tables 2.10 and 2.11.

The letter S has a polynomial representation:

$$(x^6 + x^4 + x + 1)$$

The multiplicative inverse of $(x^6 + x^4 + x + 1)$ is $(x^7 + x^6 + x^3 + x)$, which is derived using the Extended Euclidean algorithm.

$$A = \begin{bmatrix} 10001111 \\ 11000111 \\ 11110001 \\ 11110001 \\ 01111100 \\ 00111110 \\ 00011111 \end{bmatrix} \qquad b = \begin{pmatrix} 1 \\ 1 \\ 0 \\ 0 \\ 0 \\ 1 \\ 1 \\ 0 \end{pmatrix}$$

FIGURE 2.2 The invertible matrix.

TABLE 2.10 Hexadecimal and Binary Representation.

a_7	a_6	a_5	a_4	a_3	a_2	a_1	a_0
0	1	0	1	0	0	1	1

TABLE 2.11 Hexadecimal and Binary Representation.

a_7	a_6	a_5	a_4	a_3	a_2	a_1	a_0
1	1	0	0	1	0	1	0

$$\begin{bmatrix} 10001111 \\ 11000111 \\ 11100011 \\ 11110001 \\ 11111000 \\ 01111100 \\ 00111110 \\ 00011111 \end{bmatrix} \begin{pmatrix} 0 \\ 1 \\ 0 \\ 1 \\ 0 \\ 0 \\ 1 \\ 1 \end{pmatrix} + \begin{pmatrix} 1 \\ 1 \\ 0 \\ 0 \\ 0 \\ 1 \\ 1 \\ 0 \end{pmatrix} \ (\text{mod } 2) = \begin{pmatrix} 1 \\ 0 \\ 1 \\ 1 \\ 0 \\ 1 \\ 1 \\ 1 \end{pmatrix}$$

FIGURE 2.3 Multiplying the multiplicative inverse with an invertibile matrix.

TABLE 2.12 Vectory.

Y_7	Y_6	Y_5	Y_4	Y_3	Y_2	Y_1	Y_0
1	1	1	0	1	1	0	1

TABLE 2.13 Illustrating AES.

b_0	b_1	b_2	b_3	b_4	b_5	b_6	b_7	b_8	b_9	b_{10}	b_{11}	b_{12}	b_{13}	b_{14}	b_{15}
Q	U	A	N	T	U	M	C	R	Y	P	T	O	C	O	D
51	55	41	4E	54	55	4D	43	52	59	50	54	4F	47	4F	44

Next we multiply the multiplicative inverse x^{-1} with an invertible matrix A (see Figure 2.3) and add a column vector (b) and get the resulting column vector y (see Table 2.12). This corresponds to SubByte transformation and it is nonlinear [2].

$$y = A * x^{-1} + b$$

The column vector y represents a character ED_{16} in hexadecimal representation.

The reader should note that this transformation using the $GF(2^8)$ field is a pretty tedious computation, so instead we use an AES S-box lookup table (a 17×17 matrix expressed in hexadecimal) to replace the character with a replacement character. This corresponds to the SubByte transformation, and corresponding to the SubByte table there is an InvSubByte table that is the inverse of the SubByte table. The InvSubByte can be found in the references or is readily available on the Internet.

We will work with the following string: QUANTUMCRYPTOGOD, which is 16 bytes long, to illustrate AES (see Table 2.13). The state represents our string as a 4×4 matrix in the given arrangement using a hexadecimal representation of each byte (see Figure 2.4).

We apply SubByte transformation (see Figure 2.5) using the lookup table, which replaces each byte as defined in Table 2.13.

The next two rounds of ShiftRows and Mixing in the encryption lead to a diffusion process. The ShiftRow is a permutation.

$$\text{State} = \begin{bmatrix} 5154524F \\ 55555947 \\ 414D504F \\ 4E435444 \end{bmatrix}$$

FIGURE 2.4 The state represents a string as a 4×4 matrix in the given arrangement using hexadecimal representation of each byte.

$$\text{State} = \begin{bmatrix} D1200084 \\ FCFCCBA0 \\ 83E35384 \\ 2F1A201B \end{bmatrix}$$

FIGURE 2.5 Applying the SubByte transformation.

$$\text{State} = \begin{bmatrix} D1200084 \\ FCCBA0FC \\ 538483E3 \\ 1B2F1A20 \end{bmatrix}$$

FIGURE 2.6 ShiftRows.

ShiftRows

In the first step, we take the state and apply the following logic. The first row is kept as is. The second row is shifted left by one byte. The third row is shifted left by two bytes, and the last row is shifted left by three bytes. The resulting state is shown in Figure 2.6.

InvShiftRows in decryption shift bytes toward the right, similar to ShiftRows.

Mixing

The second step, the MixColumns transformation, mixes the columns. We interpret the bytes of each column as the coefficients of a polynomial in $GF(2^8)[x]/(x^4 + 1)$. Then we multiply each column by the polynomial '03' x^3 + '02' x^2 + '01'x + '02'. Multiplication of the bytes is done in $GF(2^8)$ with mod $(x^4 + 1)$.

The mixing transformation remaps the four bytes to a new four bytes by changing the contents of the individual bytes (see Figure 2.7). The MixColumns transformation is applied to each column of the state, hence each column is multiplied by a constant matrix to obtain a new state, S'_{0i}.

$$S'_{0i} = 2 \circ S_{0i} \oplus 3 \circ S_{1i} \oplus S_{2i} \oplus S_{3i} S'_{00} = 2 \circ S_{00} \oplus 3 \circ S_{10} \oplus S_{20} \oplus S_{30} S_{20} \oplus S_{30} = 53 \oplus 1B$$

$$= (01010011) \oplus (00011011) = (01001000) 2 \circ S_{00} = (00000010) \circ (D1) = (x) \circ (11010001)$$

$$= (x)\,(x^7 + x^6 + x^4 + 1) = (x^8 + x^7 + x^5 + x) \mathrm{mod}(x^8 + x^4 + x^3 + x + 1)$$

$$= (x^7 + x^5 + x^4 + x^3 + 1) = (10111001) 3 \circ S_{10} = (00000011)\,(FC) = (00000011)(11111100)$$

$$= \{(x + 1)\,(x^7 + x^6 + x^5 + x^4 + x^3 + x^2)\} \mathrm{mod}(x^8 + x^4 + x^3 + x + 1) = (00011111) S'_{00}$$

$$= (10111001) \oplus (00011111) \oplus (01001000) = (11101110) = 0 \times EE$$

$$\begin{bmatrix} S'_{0i} \\ S'_{1i} \\ S'_{2i} \\ S'_{3i} \end{bmatrix} = \begin{bmatrix} 2 & 3 & 1 & 1 \\ 1 & 2 & 3 & 1 \\ 1 & 1 & 2 & 3 \\ 3 & 1 & 1 & 2 \end{bmatrix} \begin{bmatrix} S_{0i} \\ S_{1i} \\ S_{2i} \\ S_{3i} \end{bmatrix}$$

FIGURE 2.7   Mixing transformation.

TABLE 2.14   Subkey Addition.

k_0	k_1	k_2	k_3	k_4	k_5	k_6	k_7	k_8	k_9	k_{10}	k_{11}	k_{12}	k_{13}	k_{14}	k_{15}

$$\begin{bmatrix} k_{00}k_{01}k_{02}k_{03} \\ k_{10}k_{11}k_{12}k_{13} \\ k_{20}k_{21}k_{22}k_{23} \\ k_{30}k_{31}k_{32}k_{33} \end{bmatrix}$$

FIGURE 2.8   A 4×4 matrix.

Subkey Addition

From the original key, we produce a succession of 128-bit keys by means of a key schedule. Let's recap that a word is a group of 32 bits. A 128-bit key is labeled as shown in Table 2.14.

word $W_0 = (k_0k_1k_2k_3)$ word $W_1 = (k_4k_5k_6k_7)$
word $W_2 = (k_8k_9k_{10}k_{11})$ word $W_3 = (k_{12}k_{13}k_{14}k_{15})$

which is then written as a 4×4 matrix (see Figure 2.8), where W_0 is the first column, W_1 is the second column, W_2 is the third column, and W_3 is the fourth column.

AES uses a process called *key expansion* that creates $(10 + 1)$ round keys from the given cipher key. We start with four words and end with 44 words—four word per round key. Thus

$$(W_0, ..., W_{42}, W_{43})$$

The algorithm to generate 10 round keys is as follows:
The initial cipher key consists of words: $W_0 W_1 W_2 W_3$
The other 10 round keys are made using the following logic:
If $(j \bmod 4) \neq 0$

$$W_j = W_{j-1} \oplus W_{j-4}$$

else

$$W_j = Z \oplus W_{j-4}$$

where $Z = \text{SubWord}(\text{RotWord}(W_{j-1}) \oplus \text{RCon}_{j/4}$.

RotWord (rotate word) takes a word as an array of four bytes and shifts each byte to the left with wrapping. SubWord (substitute word) uses the SubByte lookup table to

$$\begin{bmatrix} 2B28AB09 \\ 7EAEF7CF \\ 15D2154F \\ 16A6883C \end{bmatrix}$$ **FIGURE 2.9**   RotWord and SubWord.

substitute the byte in the word [2,3]. RCon (round constants) is a four-byte value in which the rightmost three bytes are set to zero [2,3].

Let's work through an example, as shown in Figure 2.9.

Key: 2B 7E 15 16 28 AE D2 A6 AB F7 15 88 09 CF 4F 3C

$W_0 = $ 2B 7E 15 16 $W_1 = $ 28 AE D2 A6 $W_2 = $ AB F7 15 88 $W_3 = $ 09 CF 4F 3C

Compute W_4:

$$W_4 = Z \oplus W_0 \text{RotWord}(W_3) = \text{RotWord}(09 \text{ CF } 4F \text{ } 3C) = (CF4F3C09)\text{SubWord}(CF \text{ } 4F \text{ } 3C \text{ } 09)$$
$$= (8A \text{ } 84 \text{ } EB \text{ } 01)Z = (8A \text{ } 84 \text{ } EB \text{ } 01) \oplus (01 \text{ } 00 \text{ } 00 \text{ } 00)_{16} = 8B \text{ } 84 \text{ } EB \text{ } 01$$

Hence,

$$W_4 = (8B \text{ } 84 \text{ } EB \text{ } 01) \oplus (2B \text{ } 7E1516) = A0 \text{ } FA \text{ } FE \text{ } 17$$

Putting it Together

Put the input into the state: XOR is the state with the 0-th round key. We start with this because any actions before the first (or after the last) use of the key are pointless, since they are publicly known and so can be undone by an attacker. Then apply 10 of the preceding rounds, skipping the column mixing on the last round (but proceeding to a final key XOR in that round). The resulting state is the ciphertext. We use the following labels to describe the encryption procedure (see Table 2.15):

Key 1 : K1 : $W_0W_1W_2W_3$
Key 2 : K2 : $W_4W_5W_6W_7$
Key 11: K11 : $W_{40}W_{41}W_{42}W_{43}$
The Initial State (IS) is the plaintext
The Output State (OSI)
SubByte (SB), ShiftRows (SR), MixColumns (MC)
Round
Pre-round PlainText $\oplus$ K1 $= = = = \rightarrow$OSI

Next we cycle through the decryption procedure:
InvSubByte (ISB), InvShiftRows (ISR), InvMixColumns (IMC)

Round

AES is a non-Feistel cipher, hence each set of transformations such as SubByte, ShiftRows, and MixColumns are invertible so that the decryption must consist of steps to recover the plaintext. You will observe that the round keys are used in the reverse order (see Table 2.16).

TABLE 2.15   The Encryption Procedure.

1.	OS1 →	SB →	SR →	MC ⊕	K2 →	OS2
2.	OS2 →	SB →	SR →	MC ⊕	K3 →	OS3
3.	OS3 →	SB →	SR →	MC ⊕	K4 →	OS4
4.	OS4 →	SB →	SR →	MC ⊕	K5 →	OS5
5.	OS5 →	SB →	SR →	MC ⊕	K6 →	OS6
6.	OS6 →	SB →	SR →	MC ⊕	K7 →	OS7
7.	OS7 →	SB →	SR →	MC ⊕	K8 →	OS8
8.	OS8 →	SB →	SR →	MC ⊕	K9 →	OS9
9.	OS9 →	SB →	SR →	MC ⊕	K10 →	OS10
10.	OS10 →	SB →	SR →	⊕	K11 →	Cipher Text (C)

TABLE 2.16   Round.

	C ⊕	K11 →				OS10
1	OS10 →	ISR →	ISB ⊕	K10 →	IMC →	OS9
2	OS9 →	ISR →	ISB ⊕	K9 →	IMC →	OS8
10	SI →		ISR →	ISB ⊕	K1 →	PlainText

7. USE OF MODERN BLOCK CIPHERS

DES and AES are designed to encrypt and decrypt data blocks of fixed size. Most practical examples have data blocks of fewer than 64 bits or greater than 128 bits, and to address this issue currently, five different modes of operation have been set up. These five modes of operation are known as Electronic Code Book (ECB), Cipher-Block Chaining (CBC), Output Feedback (OFB), Cipher Feedback (CFB), and Counter (CTR) modes.

The Electronic Code Book (ECB)

In this mode, the message is split into blocks, and the blocks are sequentially encrypted. This mode is vulnerable to attack using the frequency analysis, the same sort used in simple substitution. Identical blocks would get encrypted to the same blocks, thus exposing the key [1].

Cipher-Block Chaining (CBC)

A logical operation is performed on the first block with what is known as an *initial vector* using the secret key so as to randomize the first block. The output of this step is logically combined with the second block and the key to generate encrypted text, which is then used with the third block and so on [1].

8. PUBLIC-KEY CRYPTOGRAPHY

In this section we cover what is known as *asymmetric encryption*, which uses a pair of keys rather than one key, as used in symmetric encryption. This single-key encryption between the two parties requires that each party has its secret key, so that as the number of parties increases so does the number of keys. In addition, the distribution of the secret key becomes unmanageable as the number of keys increases. Of course, a longtime use of the same secret key between any pair would make it more vulnerable to cryptoanalysis attack. So, to deal with these inextricable problems, a key distribution facility was born. Symmetric encryption is considered more practical in dealing with vast amounts of data consisting of strings of zeros and ones. Yet another scheme was invented to secure data while in transition, using tools from a branch of mathematics known as number theory. To begin, let's review the necessary number theory concepts [2,3].

Review: Number Theory

Asymmetric-key encryption uses prime numbers, which are a subset of positive integers. Positive integers are all odd and even numbers, including the number 1, such that some of the numbers are composite, that is, products of numbers therein. This critical fact plays a significant role in generating keys. Next we will go through some statements of fact for the sake of completeness.

Coprimes

Two positive integers are said to be coprime or relatively prime if $\gcd(a, b) = 1$.

Cardinality of Primes

The number of primes is infinite. Given a number n, how many prime numbers are smaller than or equal to n? The answer to this question was discovered by Gauss and Lagrange as:

$$\{n/\ln(n) < \Pi(n) < \{n/\ln(n) - 1.08366\}$$

where $\Pi(n)$ is the number of primes smaller than or equal to n.

Check whether a given number 107 is a prime number. We take the square root of 107 to the nearest whole number, which is 10. Then count the number of primes less than 10, which are 2, 3, 5, 7. Next we check whether any one of these numbers will divide 107. In our example none of these numbers can divide 107, so 107 is a prime number.

Euler's Phi-Function $\phi(n)$: Euler's totient function finds the number of integers that are both smaller than n and coprime to n.

- $\phi(1) = 0$
- $\phi(p) = p - 1$ if p is a prime
- $\phi(m \times n) = \phi(n) \times \phi(m)$ if m and n are coprime
- $\phi(p^e) = p^e - p^{e-1}$ if p is a prime

Examples:

$$\phi(2) = 1; \ \phi(3) = 2; \ \phi(4) = 2; \ \phi(5) = 4; \ \phi(6) = 2; \ \phi(7) = 6; \ \phi(8) = 4$$

Factoring

The fundamental theorem of arithmetic states that every positive integer can be written as a product of prime numbers. There are a number of algorithms to factor large composite numbers.

Fermat's Little Theorem

In the 1970s, the creators of digital signatures and public-key cryptography realized that the framework for their research was already laid out in the body of work by Fermat and Euler. Generation of a key in public-key cryptography involves exponentiation modulo of a given modulus.

$$a \equiv b \ (\text{mod } m) \text{ then } a^e \equiv b^e \ (\text{mod } m) \text{ for any positive integer e}$$
$$a^{e+d} \equiv a^e \cdot a^d \ (\text{mod } m)$$
$$(ab)^e \equiv a^e \cdot b^e \ (\text{mod } m)$$
$$(a^d)^e \equiv a^{de} \ (\text{mod } m)$$

Examples:

$2^{13} \ (\text{mod } 33) \equiv 2^{8+4+1} \equiv 25.16.2 \equiv 25.32 \equiv 8(\text{mod } 33)6^{43} \ (\text{mod } 13)2^2 \equiv 4 \quad 3^2 \equiv 92^4 \equiv 4^2 \equiv 16$

$\equiv 33^4 \equiv 32^8 \equiv 3^2 \equiv 93^8 \equiv 92^{16} \equiv 9^2 \equiv 81 \equiv 33^{16} \equiv 32^{32} \equiv 3^2 \equiv 9 \ (\text{mod } 13) \quad 3^{32} \equiv 9 \ (\text{mod } 13)$

Theorem. Let p be a prime number.

1. If a is coprime to p, then $a^{p-1} \equiv 1 \ (\text{mod } p)$
2. $a^p \equiv a \ (\text{mod } p)$ for any integer a

Examples:

$$43^{58} \equiv 1 \ (\text{mod } 59)$$
$$86^{97} \equiv 86 \ (\text{mod } 97)$$

Theorem: Let p and q be distinct primes.

1. If a is coprime to pq, then

$$a^{k(p-1)(q-1)} \equiv 1 \ (\text{mod pq}), k \text{ is any integer}$$

2. For any integer a,

$$a^{k(p-1)(q-1)+1} \equiv a(\bmod\ pq), \text{ k is any positive integer}$$

Example:

$$62^{60} \equiv 62^{(7-1)-(11-1)} \equiv 1\ (\bmod\ 77)$$

Discrete Logarithm

Here we will deal with multiplicative group $G = <Z_{n*}x>$. The order of a finite group is the number of elements in the group G. Let's take an example of a group,

$$G = <Z_{21*},\ x>$$

$$\phi(21) = \phi(3) \times \phi(7) = 2 \times 6 = 12$$

that is, 12 elements in the group, and each is coprime to 21.

$$\{1, 2, 4, 5, 8, 9, 10, 11, 13, 16, 17, 19, 20\}$$

The order of an element, ord(a) is the smallest integer i such that

$$a^i \equiv e\ (\bmod)$$

where $e = 1$.

$$\text{Find the order of all elements in } G = <Z_{10*}x>$$
$$\phi(10) = \phi(2) \times \phi(5) = 1 \times 4 = 4$$
$$\{1, 3, 7, 9\}$$

Lagrange's theorem states that the order of an element divides the order of the group. In our example {1, 2, 4} each of them divide 4, therefore we need to check only these powers to find the order of the element.

$$1^1 \equiv 1\ (\bmod\ 10) \rightarrow \text{ord}(1) = 1$$
$$3^1 \equiv 3\ (\bmod\ 10); 3^2 \equiv 9(\bmod\ 10); 3^4 \equiv 1\ (\bmod\ 10)$$
$$\rightarrow \text{ord}(3) = 4$$
$$7^1 \equiv 7\ (\bmod\ 10); 7^2 \equiv 9\ (\bmod\ 10); 7^4 \equiv 1(\bmod\ 10)$$
$$\rightarrow \text{ord}(7) = 4$$
$$9^1 \equiv 9\ (\bmod\ 10); 9^2 \equiv 1\ (\bmod\ 10) \rightarrow \text{ord}(9) = 2$$

If $a \in G = <Z_{n*},\ x>$, then $a^{\phi(n)} = 1 \bmod n$

Euler's theorem shows that the relationship $a^i \equiv 1\ (\bmod\ n)$ holds whenever the order (*i*) of an element equals $\phi(n)$.

Primitive Roots

In the multiplicative group, if $G = <Z_{n*},\ x>$ when the order of an element is the same as $\phi(n)$, then that element is called the primitive root of the group. This property of primitive root is used in ElGamal cryptosystem.

$G = <Z_{8*}, x>$ has no primitive roots. The order of this group is $\phi(8) = 4$.

$$Z_{8*} = \{1, 3, 5, 7\}$$

1, 2, 4 each divide the order of the group, which is 4.

$$1^1 \equiv 1 \pmod 8 \rightarrow \mathrm{ord}(1) = 1$$
$$3^1 \equiv 3 \pmod 8; \ 3^2 \equiv 1 \pmod 8 \quad \rightarrow \mathrm{ord}(3) = 2$$
$$5^1 \equiv 5 \pmod 8; \ 5^2 \equiv 1 \pmod 8 \quad \rightarrow \mathrm{ord}(5) = 2$$
$$7^1 \equiv 7 \pmod 8; \ 7^2 \equiv 1 \pmod 8 \quad \rightarrow \mathrm{ord}(7) = 2$$

In this example none of the elements has an order of 4, hence this group has no primitive roots. We will rearrange our data as shown in Table 2.17 [2, 3].

Let's take another example: $G = <Z_{7*}, x>$, then $\phi(7) = 6$, hence the order of the group is 6 with these members $\{1, 2, 3, 4, 5, 6\}$, which are all coprime to 7. We note that the order of each of these elements $\{1, 2, 3, 4, 5, 6\}$ is the smallest integer i such that $a^i \equiv 1 \pmod 7$. We note that the order of an element divides the order of the group. Thus the only numbers that divide 6 are $\{1, 2, 3, 6\}$:

A. $1^1 \equiv 1 \pmod 7; \ 1^2 \equiv 1 \pmod 7; \ 1^3 \equiv 1 \pmod 7; \ 1^2 \equiv 1 \pmod 7; 1^5 \equiv 1 \pmod 7;$
$1^6 \equiv 1 \pmod 7; \rightarrow \mathrm{ord}(1) = 1$

B. $2^1 \equiv 2 \pmod 7; \ 2^2 \equiv 4 \pmod 7; \ 2^3 \equiv 1 \pmod 7; \ 2^4 \equiv 2 \pmod 7; 2^5 \equiv 4 \pmod 7;$
$2^6 \equiv 1 \pmod 7; \rightarrow \mathrm{ord}(2) = 3$

C. $3^1 \equiv 3 \pmod 7; \ 3^2 \equiv 2 \pmod 7; \ 3^3 \equiv 6 \pmod 7; \ 3^4 \equiv 4 \pmod 7; 3^5 \equiv 5 \pmod 7;$
$3^6 \equiv 1 \pmod 7; \rightarrow \mathrm{ord}(3) = 6$

D. $4^1 \equiv 4 \pmod 7; \ 4^2 \equiv 2 \pmod 7; \ 4^3 \equiv 1 \pmod 7; \ 4^4 \equiv 4 \pmod 7; 4^5 \equiv 2 \pmod 7;$
$4^6 \equiv 1 \pmod 7; \rightarrow \mathrm{ord}(4) = 3$

E. $5^1 \equiv 5 \pmod 7; \ 5^2 \equiv 4 \pmod 7; \ 5^3 \equiv 6 \pmod 7; \ 5^4 \equiv 2 \pmod 7; 5^5 \equiv 3 \pmod 7;$
$5^6 \equiv 1 \pmod 7; \rightarrow \mathrm{ord}(5) = 6$

F. $6^1 \equiv 6 \pmod 7; \ 6^2 \equiv 1 \pmod 7; \ 6^3 \equiv 6 \pmod 7; \ 6^4 \equiv 1 \pmod 7 6^5 \equiv 6 \pmod 7;$
$6^6 \equiv 1 \pmod 7 \rightarrow \mathrm{ord}(6) = 2$

Since the order of the elements $\{3, 5\}$ is 6, which is the order of the group, therefore the primitive roots of the group are $\{3, 5\}$. In here the smallest integer $i = 6$, $\phi(7) = 6$.

Solve for x in each of the following:

$$5^x \equiv 6 \pmod 7$$

TABLE 2.17 No Primitive Group.

	i = 1	i = 2	i = 3	i = 4	i = 5	i = 6	i = 7
a = 1	x:1	x:1	x:1	x:1	x:1	x:1	x:1
a = 3	x:3	x:1	x:3	x:1	x:3	x:1	x:3
a = 5	x:5	x:1	x:5	x:1	x:5	x:1	x:5
a = 7	x:7	x:1	x:7	x:1	x:7	x:1	x:7

We can rewrite the above as:

$$x = \log_5 6 \pmod 7$$

Using the third term in E). we see that x must be equal to 3.

The group $G = \,<Z_{n*}, x>\,$ has primitive roots only if n is 2, 4, p^t, or $2p^t$, where p is an odd prime not including 2, and t is an integer.

If the group $G = \,<Z_{n*}, x>\,$ has any primitive roots, the number of primitive roots is $\phi(\phi(n))$.

Group $G = \,<Z_{n*}, x>\,$ has primitive roots, then it is cyclic, and each of its primitive roots is a generator of the whole group.

Group $G = \,<Z_{10*}, x>\,$ has two primitive roots because $\phi(10) = 4$, and $\phi(\phi(10)) = 2$. These two primitive roots are $\{3, 7\}$.

$$3^1 \bmod 10 = 3\;\; 3^2 \bmod 10 = 9\;\; 3^3 \bmod 10 = 7\;\; 3^4 \bmod 10 = 1$$
$$7^1 \bmod 10 = 7\;\; 7^2 \bmod 10 = 9\;\; 7^3 \bmod 10 = 3\;\; 7^4 \bmod 10 = 1$$

Group $G = \,<Z_{p*}, x>\,$ is always cyclic.

The group $G = \,<Z_{p*}, x>\,$ has the following properties:

- Its elements are from 1 to $(p - 1)$ inclusive.
- It always has primitive roots.
- It is cyclic, and its elements can be generated using g where x is an integer from 1 to $\phi(n) = p - 1$.
- The primitive roots can be used as the base of a discrete logarithm.

Now that we have reviewed the necessary mathematical preliminaries, we will focus on the subject matter of asymmetric cryptography, which uses a public and a private key to encrypt and decrypt the plaintext. If Alice wants to send plaintext to Bob, she uses Bob's public key, which is advertised by Bob, to encrypt the plaintext and then send it to Bob via an unsecured channel. Bob decrypts the data using his private key, which is known to him only. Of course this would appear to be an ideal replacement for the asymmetric-key cipher, but it is much slower, since it has to encrypt each byte; hence it is useful in message authentication and communicating the secret key (see sidebar, "The RSA Cryptosystem").

THE RSA CRYPTOSYSTEM

Key generation algorithm:

1. Select two prime numbers p and q such that $p \neq q$.
2. Construct $m = p \times q$.
3. Set up a commutative ring $R = \,<Z_{\phi}, +, x>\,$ which is public since m is made public.
4. Set up a multiplicative group $G = \,<Zr_{(m)} *, x>\,$ which is used to generate public and private keys. This group is hidden from the public since $\phi(m)$ is kept hidden.

$$\phi(m) = (p - 1)(q - 1)$$

5. Choose an integer e such that, $1 < e < \phi(m)$ and e is coprime to $\phi(m)$.

6. Compute the secret exponent d such that, $1 < d < \phi$ (m) and that $ed \equiv 1$ (mod ϕ (m)).
7. The public key is "e" and the private key is "d." The value of p, q, and ϕ(m) are kept private.

Encryption:

1. Alice obtains Bob's public key (m, e).
2. The plaintext x is treated as a number to lie in the range $1 < x < m - 1$.
3. The ciphertext corresponding to x is $y = x^e$ (mod m).
4. Send the ciphertext y to Bob.

2. Compute the $x = y^d$ (mod m).
Why RSA works:

$R = <Z_{77}, +, x>$ and $\phi(77) = \phi(7) \phi(11) = 6 \times 10 = 60$
2. The corresponding multiplicative group $G = <Z_{60}^*, x>$.
3. Choose $e = 13$ and $d = 37$ from Z_{60}^* such that $e \times d \equiv 1$ (mod 60). Plaintext $= 5$ $y = x^e$ (mod m) $= 5^{13}$ (mod 77) $= 26 \times = y^d$ (mod m) $= 26^{37}$ (mod 77) $= 5$

Decryption:	Example:
1. Bob uses his private key (m, d).	1. Choose $p = 7$ and $q = 11$, then $m = p \times q = 7 \times 11 = 77$

Note: 384-bit primes or larger are deemed sufficient to use RSA securely. The prime number $e = 2^{16} + 1$ is often used in modern RSA implementations [2,3].

9. CRYPTANALYSIS OF RSA

RSA algorithm relies that p and q, the distinct prime numbers, are kept secret, even though $m = p \times q$ is made public. So if n is an extremely large number, the problem reduces to find the factors that make up the number n, which is known as *the factorization attack.*

Factorization Attack

If the middleman, Eve, can factor n correctly, then she correctly guesses p, q, and $\phi(m)$. Reminding ourselves that the public key e is public, then Eve has to compute the multiplicative inverse of e:

$$d \equiv e^{-1} \ (mod \ m)$$

So if the modulus m is chosen to be 1024 bits long, it would take considerable time to break the RSA system unless an efficient factorization algorithm could be found [2,3] (see sidebars "Chosen-Ciphertext Attack" and "The eth Roots Problem").

Discrete Logarithm Problem

Discrete logarithms are perhaps simplest to understand in the group Z_{p^*}, where p is the prime number. Let g be the generator of Z_{p^*}, then the discrete logarithm problem reduces to computing a, given $(g, p, g^a \bmod p)$ for a randomly chosen $a < (p - 1)$.

CHOSEN-CIPHERTEXT ATTACK

Z_n is a set of all positive integers from 0 to $(n-1)$. Z_{n^*} is a set all integers such that $\gcd(n,a) = 1$, where $a \in Z_{n^*}$

$$Z_n^* \subset Z_n$$

$\Phi(n)$ calculates the number of elements in Z_{n^*} that are smaller than n and coprime to n.

$$\Phi(21) = \Phi(3) \times \Phi(7) = 2 \times 6 = 12$$

Therefore, the number of integers in $\in Z_{21^*}$ is 12.

$$Z_{21}^* = \{1, 2, 4, 5, 8, 10, 11, 13, 16, 17, 19, 20\}$$

Each of which is coprime to 21.

$$Z_{14}^* = \{1, 3, 5, 9, 11, 13\}$$

Each of which is coprime to 14.

$\Phi(14) = \Phi(2) \times \Phi(7) = 1 \times 6 = 6$ number of integers in Z_{14}^*

Example: Choose $p = 3$ and $q = 7$, then $m = 3 \times 7 = 21$.

Encryption and decryption take place in the ring, $R = <Z_{21}, +, x>$

$$\Phi(21) = \Phi(2)\,\Phi(6) = 12$$

Key-Generation Group, $G = <Z_{12}^*, x>$

$\Phi(12) = \Phi(4)\Phi(3) = 2 \times 2 = 4$ number in

$$Z_{12}^* = \{1, 5, 7, 11\}$$

Alice encrypts the message P using the public key e of Bob and sends the encrypted message C to Bob.

$$C = P^e \bmod m$$

Eve, the middleman, intercepts the message and manipulates the message before forwarding to Bob.

1. Eve chooses a random integer $X \in Z_m^*$ (since m is public).
2. Eve calculates $Y = C \times X^e \pmod{m}$.
3. Bob receives Y from Eve, and he decrypts Y using his private key d.
4. $Z = Y^d \pmod{m}$.
5. Eve can easily discover the plaintext P as follows:

$$Z = Y^d \pmod{m} = [C \times X^e]^d \pmod{m}$$
$$= [C^d \times X^{ed}] \pmod{m} = [C^d \times X] \pmod{m}$$

Hence $Z = [P \times X] \pmod{m}$.

Using the Extended Euclidean algorithm, Eve can then compute the multiplicative inverse of X, and thus obtain P:

$$P = Z \times X^{-1} \pmod{m} \ [2,3]$$

If we want to find the kth power of one of the numbers in this group, we can do so by finding its kth power as an integer and then finding the remainder after division by p. This process is called *discrete exponentiation*. For example, consider Z_{23^*}. To compute 3^4 in this group, we first compute $3^4 = 81$, then we divide 81 by 23, obtaining a remainder of 12. Thus $3^4 = 12$ in the group Z_{23^*}

A *discrete logarithm* is just the inverse operation. For example, take the equation $3^k \equiv 12 \pmod{23}$ for k. As shown above $k = 4$ is a solution, but it is not the only solution. Since $3^{22} \equiv 1 \pmod{23}$, it also follows that if n is an integer, then $3^{4+22n} \equiv 12 \times 1^n \equiv 12 \pmod{23}$.

Hence the equation has infinitely many solutions of the form $4 + 22n$. Moreover, since 22 is the smallest positive integer m satisfying $3^m \equiv 1$ (mod 23), that is, 22 is the order of 3 in Z_{23*} these are all solutions. Equivalently, the solution can be expressed as $k \equiv 4$ (mod 22) [2,3].

THE E^{TH} ROOTS PROBLEM

Given:

A composite number n, product of two prime numbers p and q

An integer $e \geq 3$

$\gcd (e, \Phi(n)) = 1$

An integer $c \in Z_{12}*$

Find an integer m such that $m^e \equiv c$ mod n[2,3].

10. DIFFIE-HELLMAN ALGORITHM

The purpose of this protocol is to allow two parties to set up a shared secret key over an insecure communication channel so that they may exchange messages. Alice and Bob agree on a finite cyclic group G and a generating element g in G. We will write the group G multiplicatively [2,3].

1. Alice picks a prime number p, with the base g, exponent a to generate a public key A
2. $A = g^a$ mod p
3. (g, p, A) are made public, and a is kept private.
4. Bob picks a prime number p, base b, and an exponent b to generate a public key B.
5. $B = g^b$ mod p
6. (g, p, B) are made public, and b is kept private,
7. Bob using A generates the shared secret key S.
8. $S = A^b$ mod p
9. Alice using B generates the shared secret key S.
10. $S = B^a$ mod p

Thus the shared secret key S is established between Bob and Alice.
Example:

Alice: p = 53, g = 18, a = 10
  $A = 18^{10}$ mod 53 = 24
Bob: p = 53, g = 18, b = 11
  $B = 18^{11}$ mod 53 = 48
  $S = 24^{11}$ mod 53 = 48^{10} mod 53 = 15

Diffie-Hellman Problem

The middleman Eve would know (g, p, A, B) since these are public. So for Eve to discover the secret key S, she would have to tackle the following two congruences:

$$g^a \equiv A \bmod p \quad \text{and} \quad g^b \equiv B \bmod p$$

If Eve had some way of solving the discrete logarithm problem (DLP) in a time-efficient manner, she could discover the shared secret key S; no probabilistic polynomial-time algorithm exists that solves this problem. The set of values:

$$(g^a \bmod p,\ g^b \bmod p,\ g^a b \bmod p)$$

is called the *Diffie-Hellman problem.*

If the DLP problem can be efficiently solved, then so can the Diffie-Hellman problem.

11. ELLIPTIC CURVE CRYPTOSYSTEMS

For simplicity, we shall restrict our attention to elliptic curves over Zp, where p is a prime greater than 3. We mention, however, that elliptic curves can more generally be defined over any finite field [4]. An *elliptic curve E* over Z_p is defined by an equation of the form

$$y^2 = x^3 + ax + b \qquad\qquad (2.1)$$

where a, $b \in Z_p$, and $4a^3 + 27b^2 \neq 0 \pmod{p}$, together with a special point O called the *point at infinity.* The set $E(Z_p)$ consists of all points (x, y), $x \in Z_p$, $y \in Z_p$, which satisfy the defining equation (1), together with O.

An Example

Let $p = 23$ and consider the elliptic curve E: $y^2 = x^3 + x + 1$, defined over Z_{23}. (In the notation of Equation 24.1, we have $a = 1$ and $b = 1$.) Note that $4a^3 + 27b^2 = 4 + 4 = 8 \neq 0$, so E is indeed an elliptic curve. The points in $E(Z_{23})$ are O and the following are shown in Table 2.18.

TABLE 2.18   Elliptic Curve Cryptosystems.

(0, 1)	(6, 4)	(12, 19)
(0, 22)	(6, 19)	(13, 7)
(1, 7)	(7, 11)	(13, 16)
(1, 16)	(7, 12)	(17, 3)
(3, 10)	(9, 7)	(17, 20)
(3, 13)	(9, 1 6)	(18, 3)
(4, 0)	(11, 3)	(18, 20)
(5, 4)	(11, 20)	(19, 5)
(5, 19)	(12, 4)	(19, 18)

Addition Formula

There is a rule for adding two points on an elliptic curve $E(Zp)$ to give a third elliptic curve point. Together with this addition operation, the set of points $E(Zp)$ forms a group with O serving as its identity. It is this group that is used in the construction of elliptic curve cryptosystems. The addition rule, which can be explained geometrically, is presented here as a sequence of algebraic formula [4].

1. $P + O = O + P = P$ for all $P \in E(Z_p)$
2. If $P = (x, y) \in E(Zp)$ then $(x, y) + (x, -y) = O$ (The point $(x, -y)$ is denoted by $-P$, and is called the *negative* of P; observe that $-P$ is indeed a point on the curve.)
3. Let $P = (x1, y1) \in E(Zp)$ and $Q = (x2, y2) \in E(Zp)$, where $P \neq -Q$. Then $P + Q = (x3, y3)$,

   where:

   $$x_3 = (\lambda^2 - x_1 - x_2) \bmod p \quad y_3 = (\lambda(x_1 - x_3) - y_1) \bmod p$$

   $$\lambda = \frac{y_2 - y_1}{x_2 - x_1} \bmod p \text{ if } P \neq Q \text{ or}$$

   $$\lambda = \frac{3x_1^2 + \alpha}{2y_1} \bmod p \text{ if } P = Q$$

We will digress to modular division: $4/3 \bmod 11$. We are looking for a number, say t, such that $3 * t \bmod 11 = 4$. We need to multiply the left and right sides by 3^{-1}

$$3^{-1} * 3 * t \bmod 11 = 3^{-1} * 4t \bmod 11 = 3^{-1} * 4$$

Next we use the Extended Euclidean algorithm and get (inverse) 3^{-1} is 4 ($3 * 4 = 12$ mod $11 = 1$).

$$4 * 4 \bmod 11 = 5$$

Hence,

$$4/3 \bmod 11 = 5$$

Example of Elliptic Curve Addition

Consider the elliptic curve defined in the previous example. (Also see sidebar, "EC Diffie-Hellman Algorithm.") [4].

1. Let $P = (3, 10)$ and $Q = (9, 7)$. Then $P + Q = (x3, y3)$ is computed as follows:

   $$\lambda = \frac{7 - 10}{9 - 3} = \frac{-3}{6} = \frac{-1}{2} = 11 \in Z_{23}$$

   $x_3 = 11^2 - 3 - 9 = 6 - 3 - 9 = -6 \equiv 17 \pmod{23}$, and $y_3 = 11(3 - (-6)) - 10 = 11(9)$
   $-10 = 89 \equiv 20 \pmod{23}$.
   Hence $P + Q = (17, 20)$.

2. Let $P = (3,10)$. Then $2P = P + P = (x_3, y_3)$ is computed as follows:

$$\lambda = \frac{3(3^2) + 1}{20} = \frac{5}{20} = \frac{1}{4} = 6 \in Z_{23}$$

$x_3 = 6^2 - 6 = 30 \equiv 7 \pmod{23}$, and $y_3 = 6 (3 - 7) - 10 = -24 - 10 = -11 \in 12 \pmod{23}$.

Hence $2P = (7, 12)$.

Consider the following elliptic curve with Z_p^*

$$y^2 \bmod p = (x^3 + ax + b) \bmod p$$

Set $p = 11$ and $a = 1$ and $b = 2$. Take a point $P (4, 2)$ and multiply it by 3; the resulting point will be on the curve with $(4, 9)$.

EC DIFFIE-HELLMAN ALGORITHM

1. Alice has her elliptic curve, and she chooses a secret random number d and computes a number on the curve $Q_A = d_A * P[4]$.
   Alice's public key: (p, a, b, Q_A)
   Alice's private key: d_A
2. Bob has his elliptic curve, and he chooses a secret random number d and computes a number on the curve $Q_B = d_B * P$:
   Bob's public key: (p, a, b, Q_B)
   Bob's private key: d_B

3. Alice computes the shared secret key as

   $$S = d_A * Q_B$$

4. Similarly, Bob computes the shared secret key as

   $$S = d_B * Q_A$$

5. The shared secret key computed by Alice and Bob are the same for:

   $$S = d_B * Q_A = d_B * d_A * P$$

EC Security

Suppose Eve the middleman captures (p, a, b, Q_A, Q_B). Can Eve figure out the shared secret key without knowing either (d_B, d_A)? Eve could use

$$Q_A = P * d_A$$

to compute the unknown d_A, which is known as the Elliptic Curve Discrete Logarithm problem [4].

12. MESSAGE INTEGRITY AND AUTHENTICATION

We live in the Internet age, and a fair number of commercial transactions take place on the Internet. It has often been reported that transactions on the Internet between two parties have been hijacked by a third party, hence data integrity and authentication are critical if ecommerce is to survive and grow.

This section deals with message integrity and authentication. So far we have discussed and shown how to keep a message confidential. But on many occasions we need to make sure that the content of a message has not been changed by a third party, and we need some way of ascertaining whether the message has been tampered with. Since the message is transmitted electronically as a string of ones and zeros, we need a mechanism to make sure that the count of the number of ones and zeros does not become altered, and furthermore, that zeros and ones are not changed in their position within the string.

We create a pair and label it as message and its corresponding message digest. A given block of messages is run through an algorithm hash function, which has its input the message and the output is the compressed message, the message digest, which is a fixed-size block but smaller in length. The receiver, say, Bob, can verify the integrity of the message by running the message through the hash function (the same hash function as used by Alice) and comparing the message digest with the message digest that was sent along with the message by, say, Alice. If the two message digests agree on their block size, the integrity of the message was maintained in the transmission.

Cryptographic Hash Functions

A cryptographic hash function must satisfy three criteria:

- Preimage resistance
- Second preimage resistance (weak collision resistance)
- Strong collision resistance

Preimage Resistance

Given a message m and the hash function hash, if the hash value h = hash(m) is given, it should be hard to find any m such that h = hash(m).

Second Preimage Resistance (Weak Collision Resistance)

Given input m_1, it should be hard to find another message m_2 such that hashing) = hash(m_2) and that $m_1 \neq m_2$

Strong Collision Resistance

It ought to be hard to find two messages $m_1 \neq m_2$ such that hash(m_1) = hash(m_2). A hash function takes a fixed size input n-bit string and produces a fixed size output m-bit string such that m less than n in length. The original hash function was defined by Merkle-Damgard, which is an iterated hash function. This hash function first breaks up the original message into fixed-size blocks of size n. Next an initial vector H_0 (digest) is set up and combined with the message block M_1 to produce message digest H_1, which is then combined with M_2 to produce message digest H_1, and so on until the last message block produces the final message digest.

$$H_i = f(H_{i-1}, M_i) \quad i \geq 1$$

Message digest MD2, MD4, and MD5 were designed by Ron Rivest. MD5 as input block size of 512 bits and produces a message digest of 128 bits [1].

Secure Hash Algorithm (SHA) was developed by the National Institute of Standards and Technology (NIST). SHA-1, SHA-224, SHA-256, SHA-384, and SHA-512 are examples of the secure hash algorithm. SHA-512 produces a message digest of 512 bits.

Message Authentication

Alice sends a message to Bob. How can Bob be sure that the message originated from Alice and not someone else pretending to be Alice? If you are engaged in a transaction on the Internet using a Web client, you need to make sure that you are not engaged with a dummy Web site or else you could submit your sensitive information to an unauthorized party. Alice in this case needs to demonstrate that she is communicating and not an imposter.

Alice creates a message digest using the message (M), then using the shared secret key (known to Bob only) she combines the key with a message digest and creates a message authentication code (MAC). She then sends the MAC and the message (M) to Bob over an insecure channel. Bob uses the message (M) to create a hash value and then recreates a MAC using the secret shared key and the hash value. Next he compares the received MAC from Alice with his MAC. If the two match, Bob is assured that Alice was indeed the originator of the message [1].

Digital Signature

Message authentication is implemented using the sender's private key and verified by the receiver using the sender's public key. Hence if Alice uses her private key, Bob can verify that the message was sent by Alice, since Bob would have to use Alice's public key to verify. Alice's public key cannot verify the signature signed by Eve's private key [1].

Message Integrity Uses a Hash Function in Signing the Message

Nonrepudiation is implemented using a third party that can be trusted by parties that want to exchange messages with one another. For example, Alice creates a signature from her message and sends the message, her identity, Bob's identity, and the signature to the third party, who then verifies the message using Alice's public key that the message came from Alice. Next the third party saves a copy of the message with the sender's and the recipient's identity and the time stamp of the message.

The third party then creates another signature using its private key from the message that Alice left behind. The third party then sends the message, the new signature, and Alice's and Bob's identity to Bob, who then uses the third party's public key to ascertain that the message came from the third party [1].

RSA Digital Signature Scheme

Alice and Bob are the two parties that are going to exchange the messages. So, we begin with Alice, who will generate her public and private key using two distinct prime numbers—say, p and q. Next she calculates $n = p \times q$. Using $\Phi(n) = (p-1)(q-1)$, picks e and computes d such that $e \times d = 1 \bmod (\Phi(n)$. Alice declares (e, n) public, keeping her private key d secret.

Signing: Alice takes the message and computes the signature as:

$$S = M^d (\bmod\ n)$$

She then sends the message M and the signature S to Bob.

Bob receives the message M and the signature S, and then, using Alice's public key e and the signature S, recreates the message $M' = S^e \ (\bmod\ n)$. Next Bob compares M' with M, and if the two values are congruent, Bob accepts the message [1].

RSA Digital Signature and the Message Digest

Alice and Bob agree on a hash function. Alice applies the hash function to the message M and generates the message digest, $D = \text{hash}(M)$. She then signs the message digest using her private key,

$$S = D^d (\bmod\ n)$$

Alice sends the signature S and the message M to Bob. He then uses Alice's public key, and the signature S recreates the message digest $D' = S^e \ (\bmod\ n)$ as well as computes the message digest $D = \text{hash}(M)$ from the received message M. Bob then compares D with D', and if they are congruent modulo n, he accepts the message [1].

Next, let's take a very very brief look at the Triple Data Encryption Algorithm (TDEA), including its primary component cryptographic engine, the Data Encryption Algorithm (DEA). When implemented, TDEA may be used by organizations to protect sensitive unclassified data. Protection of data during transmission or while in storage may be necessary to maintain the confidentiality and integrity of the information represented by the data.

13. TRIPLE DATA ENCRYPTION ALGORITHM (TDEA) BLOCK CIPHER

TDEA is made available for use by organizations and Federal agencies within the context of a total security program consisting of physical security procedures, good information management practices, and computer system/network access controls. The TDEA block cipher includes a Data Encryption Algorithm (DEA) cryptographic engine that is implemented as a component of TDEA. TDEA functions incorporating the DEA cryptographic engine are designed in such a way that they may be used in a computer system, storage facility, or network to provide cryptographic protection to binary coded data. The method of implementation will depend on the application and environment. TDEA implementations are subject to being tested and validated as accurately performing the transformations specified in the TDEA algorithm.

Applications

Cryptography is utilized in various applications and environments. The specific utilization of encryption and the implementation of TDEA is based on many factors particular to the computer system and its associated components. In general, cryptography is used to protect data while it is being communicated between two points or while it is stored in a medium vulnerable to physical theft or technical intrusion (hacker attacks). In the first case, the key must be available by the sender and receiver simultaneously during communication. In the second case, the key must be maintained and accessible for the duration of the storage period. The following checklist (see checklist: "An Agenda For Action Of Conformance Requirements For The Installation, Configuration And Use Of TDEA") lays out an agenda for action for conformance to many of the requirements that are the responsibility of entities installing, configuring or using applications or protocols that incorporate the recommended use of TDEA.

AN AGENDA FOR ACTION OF CONFORMANCE REQUIREMENTS FOR THE INSTALLATION, CONFIGURATION AND USE OF TDEA

These requirements include the following (Check All Tasks Completed):

_____1. TDEA functions incorporating the DEA cryptographic engine shall be designed in such a way that they may be used in a computer system, storage facility, or network to provide cryptographic protection to binary coded data.

_____2. Each 64-bit key shall contain 56 bits that are randomly generated and used directly by the algorithm as key bits.

_____3. A key bundle shall not consist of three identical keys.

_____4. The TDEA block cipher shall be used to provide cryptographic security only when used in an approved mode of operation.

_____5. The following specifications for keys shall be met in implementing the TDEA modes of operation. The bundle and the individual keys shall:

_____a. Be kept secret.

_____b. Be generated using an approved method12 that is based on the output of an approved random bit generator.

_____c. Be independent of other key bundles.

_____d. Have integrity whereby each key in the bundle has not been altered in an unauthorized manner since the time it was generated, transmitted, or stored by an authorized source.

_____e. Be used in the appropriate order as specified by the particular mode.

_____f. Be considered a fixed quantity in which an

---

individual key cannot be manipulated while leaving the other two keys unchanged; and cannot be unbundled except for its designated purpose.

_____6. One key bundle shall not be used to process more than 232 64-bit data blocks when the keys conform to Keying Option 1.

_____7. When Keying Option 2 is used, the keys shall not be used to process more than 220 blocks.

14. SUMMARY

In this chapter we have attempted to cover cryptography from its very simple structure such as substitution ciphers to the complex AES and elliptic curve crypto-systems. There is a subject known as *cryptoanalysis* that attempts to crack the encryption to expose the key, partially or fully. We briefly discussed this in the section on the discrete logarithm problem. Over the past 10 years, we have seen the application of quantum theory to encryption in what is termed *quantum cryptology*, which is used to transmit the secret key securely over a public channel. The reader will observe that we did not cover the Public Key Infrastructure (PKI) due to lack of space in the chapter.

Finally, let's move on to the real interactive part of this Chapter: review questions/exercises, hands-on projects, case projects and optional team case project. The answers and/or solutions by chapter can be found in the Online Instructor's Solutions Manual.

CHAPTER REVIEW QUESTIONS/EXERCISES

True/False

1. True or False? Data security is limited to wired networks but is equally critical for wireless communications such as in Wi-Fi and cellular.
2. True or False? Data communication normally takes place over a secured channel, as is the case when the Internet provides the pathways for the flow of data.
3. True or False? The encryption of the message can be defined as *mapping* the message from the domain to its range such that the inverse mapping should recover the original message.
4. True or False? Information security is the goal of the secured data encryption; hence if the encrypted data is truly randomly distributed in the message space (range), to the hacker the encrypted message is equally unlikely to be in any one of the states (encrypted).
5. True or False? Computational complexity deals with problems that could be solved in polynomial time, for a given input.

Multiple Choice

1. The conceptual foundation of _____ was laid out around 3,000 years ago in India and China.
   A. Cryptography
   B. Botnets
   C. Data retention
   D. Evolution
   E. Security

2. In cryptography we use _____ to express that the residue is the same for a set of integers divided by a positive integer.
   A. Congruence
   B. Traceback
   C. Data retention
   D. Process
   E. Security

3. What is a set of integers congruent mod m, where m is a positive integer?
   A. Evolution
   B. Residue class
   C. Peer-to-peer (P2P)
   D. Process
   E. Security

4. _____ also known as *additive ciphers*, are an example of a monoalphabetic character cipher in which each character is mapped to another character, and a repeated character maps to the same character irrespective of its position in the string:
   A. Security
   B. Data retention
   C. Shift ciphers
   D. Cyber crimes
   E. Evolution

5. A transposition cipher changes the location of the character by a given set of rules known as:
   A. Physical world
   B. Data retention
   C. Standardization
   D. Permutation
   E. All of the above

EXERCISE

Problem

How is the DEA cryptographic engine used by TDEA to cryptographically protect (encrypt) blocks of data consisting of 64 bits under the control of a 64-bit key?

Hands-On Projects

Project

Please expand on a discussion of how each TDEA forward and inverse cipher operation is a compound operation of the DEA forward and inverse transformations.

Case Projects

Problem

For all TDEA modes of operation, three cryptographic keys (*Key*1, *Key*2, *Key*3) define a TDEA key bundle. The bundle and the individual keys should do what?

Optional Team Case Project

Problem

There are a few keys that are considered weak for the DEA cryptographic engine. The use of weak keys can reduce the effective security afforded by TDEA and should be avoided. Give an example of Keys that are considered to be weak (in hexadecimal format).

References

[1] T.H. Barr, Invitation to Cryptology, Prentice Hall, 2002.
[2] W. Mao, Modern Cryptography, Theory & Practice, Prentice Hall, New York, 2004.
[3] B.A. Forouzan, Cryptography and Network Security, McGraw-Hill, 2008.
[4] A. Jurisic, A.J. Menezes, Elliptic curves and cryptograph, Dr. Dobb's Journals (April 01, 1997) http://www.ddj.com/architect/184410167.

3

Public Key Infrastructure

Terence Spies
Voltage Security

The ability to create, manipulate, and share digital documents has created a host of new applications (email, word processing, e-commerce websites), but also created a new set of problems, namely how to protect the privacy and integrity of digital documents when stored and transmitted. The invention of public key cryptography in the 1970s [1] pointed the way to a solution to those problems, most importantly the ability to encrypt data without a shared key, and the ability to "sign" data, insuring its origin and integrity. While these operations are quite conceptually simple, they both rely on the ability to bind a public key (which is typically a large mathematical object) reliably with an identity sensible to the application using the operation (for example, a globally unique name, a legal identifier, or an email address.) Public Key Infrastructure (PKI) is the umbrella term used to refer to the protocols and machinery used to perform this binding.

The most important security protocols used on the Internet rely on PKI to bind names to keys — a crucial function that allows authentication of users and websites. A set of attacks in 2011 called into question the security of the PKI architecture [2,3], especially when governmental entities might be tempted to subvert Internet security assumptions. A number of interesting proposed evolutions of the PKI architecture have been proposed as potential countermeasures to these attacks. Even in the face of these attacks, PKI remains the most important and reliable method of authenticating networked entities.

1. CRYPTOGRAPHIC BACKGROUND

To understand how PKI systems function, it is necessary to grasp the basics of public key cryptography. PKI systems enable the use of public key cryptography, and they also use public key cryptography as the basis for their operation. While there are thousands of varieties of cryptographic algorithms, we can understand PKI operations by looking at only two: signature and encryption.

Digital Signatures

The most important cryptographic operation in PKI systems is the digital signature. If two parties are exchanging some digital document, it may be important to protect that data so that the recipient knows that the document has not been altered since it was sent, and that any document received was indeed created by the sender. Digital signatures provide these guarantees by creating a data item, typically attached to the document in question that is uniquely tied to the data and the sender. The recipient then has some verification operation that confirms that the signature data matches the sender and the document.

Figure 3.1 illustrates the basic security problem that motivates signatures. An attacker controlling communications between the sender and receiver can insert a bogus document, fooling the receiver.

The aim of the digital signature is to block this attack by attaching a signature that can only be created by the sender, as shown in Figure 3.2.

Cryptographic algorithms can be used to construct secure digital signatures. These techniques (for example, the RSA or DSA algorithms) all have the same three basic operations, as shown in Table 3.1.

Public Key Encryption

Variants of the three operations used to construct digital signatures can also be used to encrypt data. Encryption uses a public key to scramble data in such a way that only the holder of the corresponding private key can unscramble it (see Figure 3.3).

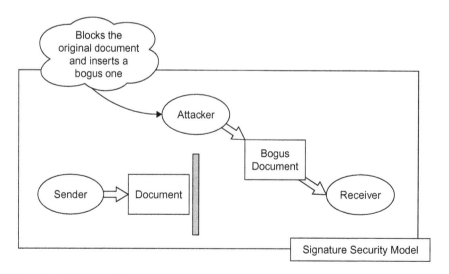

FIGURE 3.1   Block diagram of altering an unsigned document.

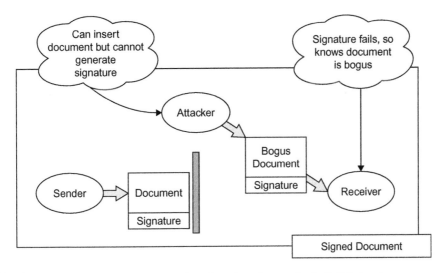

FIGURE 3.2 Block diagram showing prevention of an alteration attack via digital signature.

TABLE 3.1 The Three Fundamental Digital Signature Operations.

Key Generation	Using some random source, the sender creates a public and private key, called Kpublic and Kprivate. Using Kpublic, it is cryptographically difficult to derive Kprivate. The sender then distributes Kpublic, and keeps Kprivate hidden.
Signing	Using a document and Kprivate, the sender generates the signature data.
Verification	Using the document, the signature, and Kpublic, the receiver (or any other entity with these elements) can test that the signature matches the document, and could only be produced with the Kprivate matching Kpublic.

Public key encryption is accomplished with variants of the same three operations used to sign data, as shown in Table 3.2.

The security of signature and encryption operations depends on two factors: first, the ability to keep the private key private and, second, the ability to reliably tie a public key to a sender. If a private key is known to an attacker, they can then perform the signing operation on arbitrary bogus documents, and can also decrypt any document encrypted with the matching public key. The same attacks can be performed if an attacker can convince a sender or receiver to use a bogus public key.

PKI systems are built to securely distribute public keys, thereby preventing attackers from inserting bogus public keys. They do not directly address the security of private keys, which are typically defended by measures at a particular endpoint, such as keeping the private key on a smartcard, encrypting private key data using operating system facilities, or other similar mechanisms. The remainder of this section will detail the design, implementation, and operation of public key distribution systems.

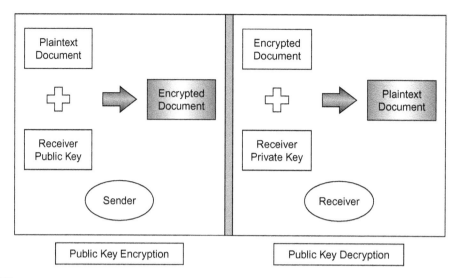

FIGURE 3.3   The public key encryption and decryption process.

TABLE 3.2   The Three Fundamental Public Key Encryption Operations.

Key Generation	Using some random source, the sender creates a public and private key, called Kpublic and Kprivate. Using Kpublic, it is cryptographically difficult to derive Kprivate. The sender then distributes Kpublic, and keeps Kprivate hidden.
Encryption	Using a document and Kpublic, the sender encrypts the document.
Decryption	The receiver uses Kprivate to decrypt the document.

2. OVERVIEW OF PKI

PKI systems solve the problem of associating meaningful names with essentially mean-ingless cryptographic keys. For example, when encrypting an email, the user will typically specify a set of recipients that should be able to decrypt that mail. The user will want to specify these as some kind of name (email address or a name from a directory), not as a set of public keys. In the same way, when signed data is received and verified, the user will want to know what user signed the data, not what public key correctly verified the signature. The design goal of PKI systems is to securely and efficiently connect user identi-ties to the public keys used to encrypt and verify data.

The original Diffie-Hellman paper [1] that outlined public key cryptography proposed that this binding would be done through storing public keys in a trusted directory. Whenever a user wanted to encrypt data to another user, they would consult the "public file" and request the public key corresponding to some user. The same operation would yield the public key needed to verify the signature on signed data. The disadvantage of this approach is that the directory must be online and available for every new encryption and verification operation. (While this older approach was never widely implemented, variants of this approach are now reappearing in newer PKI designs. For more information, see the section on Alternative PKI Architectures.)

PKI systems solve this online problem and accomplish identity binding by distributing "digital certificates", chunks of data that contain an identity and a key, all authenticated by digital signature, and providing a mechanism to validate these certificates. Certificates, first invented by Kohnfelder in 1978, are essentially a digitally signed message from some authority stating "Entity X is associated with public key Y." Communicating parties can then rely on this statement (to the extent they trust the authority signing the certificate) to use the public key Y to validate a signature from X or to send an encrypted message to X. Since time may pass between when the signed certificate is produced and when someone uses that certificate, it may be useful to have a validation mechanism to check that the authority still stands by certificate. We will describe PKI systems in terms of producing and validating certificates.

There are multiple standards that describe how certificates are formatted. The X.509 standard, promulgated by the ITU [4], is the most widely used, and is the certificate format used in the TLS/SSL protocols for secure Internet connections, and the S/MIME standards for secured email. The X.509 certificate format also implies a particular model of how certification works. Other standards have attempted to define alternate models of operation and associated certificate models. Among the other standards that describe certificates are: Pretty Good Privacy (PGP) [pgp], and the Simple Public Key Infrastructure (SPKI) [spki]. In this section, we'll describe the X.509 PKI model, then describe how these other standards attempt to remediate problems with X.509.

3. THE X.509 MODEL

The X.509 model is the most prevalent standard for certificate based PKIs, though the standard has evolved such that PKI-using applications on the Internet are mostly based on the set of IETF standards that have evolved and extended the ideas in X.509. X.509 style certificates are the basis for SSL, TLS, many VPNs, the US Federal Government PKI, and many other widely deployed systems.

The History of X.509

A quick historical preface here is useful to explain some of the properties of X.509. X.509 is part of the X.500 directory standard owned by the International Telecommunications Union Telecommunications Standardization Sector (ITU-T). X.500 specifies a hierarchical directory useful for the X.400 set of messaging standards. As such, it includes naming system (called "distinguished naming") that describes entities by their position in some hierarchy. A sample X.500/X.400 name might look like this:

CN = Joe Davis, OU = Human Resources,
O = WidgetCo, C = US

This name describes a person with a Common Name (CN) of "Joe Davis" that works in an Organizational Unit (OU) called "Human Resources", in an Organization called "WidgetCo", in the United States. These name components were intended to be run by their own directory components (so, for example, there would be "Country" directories that would point to "Organizational" directories, etc.) and this hierarchical description was ultimately reflected in the design of the X.509 system. Many of the changes made by IETF and other bodies that have evolved the X509 standard were made to reconcile this hierarchical naming system with the more distributed nature of the Internet.

The X.509 Certificate Model

The X.509 model specifies a system of Certifying Authorities (CAs) that issue certificates for end entities (users, web sites, or other entities that hold private keys.) A CA issued certificate will contain (among other data) the name of the end entity, the name of the CA, the end entity's public key, a validity period, and a certificate serial number. All of this information is signed with the CA's private key. (Additional details on the information in a certificate and how it is encoded is in Section Z.) To validate a certificate, a relying party uses the CA's public key to verify the signature on the certificate, checks that the time falls within the validity period, and may also perform some other online checks.

This process leaves out on important detail: where did the CA's public key come from? The answer is that another certificate is typically used to certify the public key of the CA. This "chaining" action of validating a certificate by using the public key from another certificate can be performed any number of times, allowing for arbitrarily deep hierarchies of CAs. Of course, this must terminate at some point, typically at a self-signed certificate that is trusted by the relying party. Trusted self-signed certificates are typically referred to as "root" certificates. Once the relying party has verified the chain of signatures from the end-entity certificate to a trusted root certificate, it can conclude that the end-entity certificate is properly signed, and then move onto whatever other validation steps (proper key usage fields, validity dates in some time window, etc.) are required to fully trust the certificate. Figure 3.4 shows the structure of a typical certificate chain.

One other element is required for this system to function securely: CAs much be able "undo" a certification action. While a certificate binds an identity to a key, there are many events that may cause that binding to become invalid. For example, a CA operated by a bank may issue a certificate to a newly hired person that gives that user the ability to sign messages as an employee of the bank. If that person leaves the bank before the certificate expires, the bank needs some way of undoing that certification. The physical compromise of a private key is another circumstance that may require invalidating a certificate. This is accomplished by a validation protocol, where (in the abstract) a user examining a certificate can ask the CA if a certificate is still valid. In practice, revocation protocols are used that simulate this action without actually contacting the CA.

Root certificates are critical to the process of validating public keys through certificates. They must be inherently trusted by the application, since no other certificate signs these certificates. This is most commonly done by installing the certificates as part of the application that will use the certificates under a set of root certificates. For example, Internet

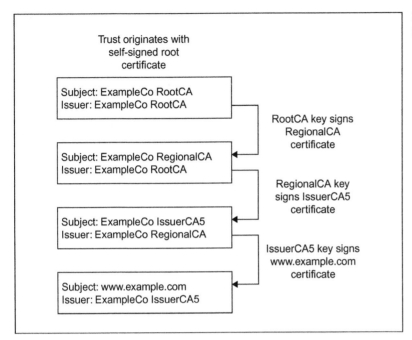

FIGURE 3.4 An example X.509 certificate chain.

Explorer uses X.509 certificates to validate keys used to make Secure Socket Layer (SSL) connections. Internet Explorer has a large set of root certificates installed which can be examined by opening the Internet Options menu item and selecting "Certificates" in the "Content" tab of the Options dialog. A list like the one in Figure 3.5 will appear:

This dialog can also be used to inspect these root certificates. The Microsoft Root certificate details look like the ones shown in Figure 3.6.

The meaning of these fields will be explored in subsequent sections.

4. X.509 IMPLEMENTATION ARCHITECTURES

While, in theory, the Certification Authority is the entity that creates and validates certificates, in practice, it may be desirable or necessary to delegate the actions of user authentication and certificate validation to other servers. The security of the CA's signing key is crucial to the security of a PKI system. By limiting the functions of the server that holds that key, it should be subject to less risk of disclosure or illegitimate use. The X.509 architecture defines a delegated server role, the Registration Authority (RA), which allows delegation of authentication. Subsequent extensions to the core X.509 architecture have created a second delegated role, the Validation Authority (VA), which owns answering queries about the validity of a certificate after creation.

A Registration Authority is typically used to distribute the authentication function needed to issue a certificate without needing to distribute the CA key. The RA's function is to perform the authentication needed to issue a certificate, then send a signed statement

FIGURE 3.5 The Microsoft Internet Explorer trusted root certificates.

containing the fact that it performed the authentication, the identity to be certified, and the key to be certified. The CA validates the RA's message, and issues a certificate in response.

For example, a large multi-national corporation wants to deploy a PKI system using a centralized CA. It wants to issue certificates on the basis of in-person authentication, so needs some way to distribute authentication to multiple locations in different countries. Copying and distributing the CA signing key creates a number of risks, not only due to the fact that the CA key will be present on multiple servers, but also due to the complexities of creating and managing these copies. Sub-CAs could be created for each location, but this requires careful attention to controlling the identities allowed to be certified by each sub-CA (otherwise, an attacker compromising one sub CA could issue a certificate for any identity they liked.) One possible way to solve this problem is to create RAs at each location, and have the CA check that the RA is authorized to authenticate a particular employee when a certificate is requested. If an attacker subverts a given RA signing key, they can request certificates for employees in the purview of that RA, but it is straightforward, once discovered, to deauthorize the RA, solve the security problem, and create a new RA key.

Validation Authorities are given the ability to revoke certificates (the specific methods used to effect revocation are detailed in the X.509 Revocation Protocols section), and offload that function from the CA. Through judicious use of RAs and VAs, it is possible to

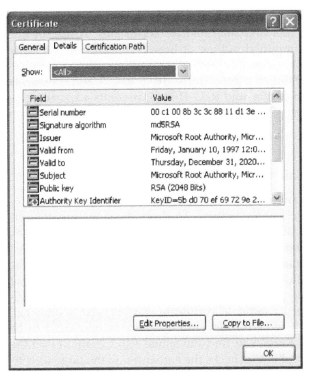

FIGURE 3.6 A view of the fields in an X.509 certificate using Microsoft Internet Explorer.

construct certification architectures where the critical CA server is only accessible to a very small number of other servers, and network security controls can be used to reduce or eliminate threats from outside network entities.

5. X.509 CERTIFICATE VALIDATION

X.509 certificate validation is a complex process, and can be done to several levels of confidence. This section will outline a typical set of steps involved in validating a certificate, but is not an exhaustive catalog of the possible methods that can be used. Different applications will often require different validation techniques, depending on the application's security policy. It is rare for an application to implement certificate validation, as there are several APIs and libraries available to perform this task. Microsoft CryptoAPI, OpenSSL, and the Java JCE all provide certificate validation interfaces. The Server-based Certificate Validity Protocol (SCVP) can also be used to validate a certificate. However, all of these interfaces offer a variety of options, and understanding the validation process is essential to properly using these interfaces.

While a complete specification of the certificate validation process would require hundreds of pages, we supply a sketch of what happens during certificate validation. It is not a complete description, and is purposefully simplified. The certificate validation process typically proceeds in three steps, and typically takes three inputs. The first is the certificate to be validated, the second is any intermediate certificates acquired by the applications, and the third is a store containing the root and intermediate certificates trusted by the application. The following steps are a simplified outline of how certificates are typically validated. In practice, the introduction of bridge CAs and other non-hierarchical certification models have led to more complex validation procedures. IETF RFC 3280 [5] presents a complete specification for certificate validation, and RFC 4158 [6] presents a specification for constructing a certification path in environments where non-hierarchical certification structures are used.

Validation Step 1: Construct the Chain and Validate Signatures

The contents of the target certificate cannot be trusted until the signature on the certificate is validated, so the first step is to check the signature. To check the signature, the certificate for the authority that signed the target certificate must be located. This is done by searching the intermediate certificates and certificate store for a certificate with a Subject field that matches the Issuer field of the target certificate. If multiple certificates match, the validator can search the matching certificates for a Subject Key Identifier extension that matches the Issuer Key Identifier extension in the candidate certificates. If multiple certificates still match, the most recently issued candidate certificate can be used. (Note that, because of potentially revoked intermediate certificates, multiple chains may need to be constructed and examine through steps 2 and 3 to find the actual valid chain.) Once the proper authority certificate is found, the validator checks the signature on the target certificate using the public key in the authority certificate. If the signature check fails, the validation process can be stopped, and the target certificate deemed invalid.

If the signature matches, and the authority certificate is a trusted certfcate, the constructed chain is then subjected to steps 2–4. If not, the authority certificate is treated as a target certificate, and Step 1 is called recursively until it returns a chain to a trusted certificate or fails.

Constructing the complete certificate path requires that the validator is in possession of all the certificates in that path. This requires that the validator keep a database of intermediate certificates or that the protocol using the certificate supplies the needed intermediates. The Server Certificate Validation Protocol (SCVP) provides a mechanism to request a certificate chain from a server, which can eliminate these requirements. The SCVP protocol is described in more detail in a subsequent section.

Step 2: Check Validity Dates, Policy and Key Usage

Once a chain has been constructed, various fields in the certificate are checked to insure that the certificate was issued correctly and that it is currently valid. The following checks should be run on the candidate chain:

The certificate chain times are correct. Each certificate in the chain contains a validity period with a not before and not after time. For applications outside validating the signature on a document, the current time must fall after the not before time and before the not after time. Some applications may require "time nesting", meaning that that the validity period for a certificate must fall entirely within the validity period of the issuer's certificate. It is up to the policy of the application if it treats out-of-date certificates as invalid, or treats it as a warning case that can be overridden by the user. Applications may also treat certificates that are not yet valid differently than certificates that have expired.

Applications that are validating the certificate on a stored document may have to treat validity time as the time that the document was signed as opposed to the time that the signature was checked. There are three cases of interest. The first, and easiest, is where the document signature is checked, and the certificate chain validating the public key contains certificates that are currently within their validity time interval. In this case, the validity times are all good, and verification can proceed. The second case is where the certificate chain validating the public key is currently invalid because one or more certificates are out-of-date, and the document is believed to be signed at a time when the chain was out-of-date. In this case, the validity times are all invalid, and the user should be at least warned.

The ambiguous case arises when the certificate chain is currently out-of-date, but the chain is believed to have been valid with respect to time when the document was signed. Depending on its policy, the application can treat this case in several different ways. It can assume that the certificate Validity times are strict, and fail to validate the document. Alternatively, it can assume that the certificates were good at the time of signing, and validate the document. The application can also take steps to insure that this case does not occur by using a time-stamping mechanism in conjunction with signing the document, or provide some mechanism for resigning documents before certificate chains expire.

Once the certificate chain has been constructed, the verifier must also verify that various X.509 extension fields are valid. Some common extensions that are relevant to the validity of a certificate path are:

- *BasicConstraints*: This extension is required for CAs, and limits the depth of the certificate chain below a specific CA certificate.
- *NameConstraints*: This extension limits the namespace of identities certified underneath the given CA certificate. This extension can be used to limit a specific CA to issuing certificates for a given domain or X.400 namespace.
- *KeyUsage* and *ExtendedKeyUsage*: These extensions limit the purposes a certified key can be used for. CA certificates must have KeyUsage set to allow certificate signing. Various values of ExtendedKeyUsage may be required for some certification tasks.

Step 3: Consult Revocation Authorities

Once the verifier has concluded that it has a suitably signed certificate chain with valid dates and proper keyUsage extensions, it may want to consult the revocation authorities named in each certificate to check that the certificates are currently valid. Certificates may contain extensions that point to Certificate Revocation List (CRL) storage locations or to Online Certificate Status Protocol (OSCP) responders. These methods allow the verifier to check that a CA has not revoked the certificate in question. The next section details these methods in more detail. Note that each certificate in the chain may need to be checked for revocation status. The next section on certificate revocation details the mechanisms used to revoke certificates.

6. X.509 CERTIFICATE REVOCATION

Since certificates are typically valid for a significant period of time, it is possible that during the validity period of the certificate, a key may be lost or stolen, an identity may change, or some other event may occur that causes a certificate's identity binding to become invalid or suspect. To deal with these events, it must be possible for a CA to revoke a certificate, typically by some kind of notification that can be consulted by applications examining the validity of a certificate. Two mechanisms are used to perform this task: Certificate Revocation Lists (CRLs) and the Online Certificate Status Protocol (OCSP).

The original X.509 architecture implemented revocation via a Certificate Revocation List (CRL.) A CRL is a periodically issued document containing a list of certificate serial numbers that are revoked by that CA. X.509 has defined two basic CRL formats, V1 and V2. When CA certificates are revoked by a higher-level CA, the serial number of the CA certificate is placed on an Authority Revocation List (ARL), which is formatted identically to a CRL. CRLs and ARLs, as defined in X.509 and IETF RFC 3280 are ASN.1 encoded objects that contain the following information shown in Table 3.3.

This header is followed by a sequence of revoked certificate records. Each record contains the following information shown in Table 3.4.

The list of revoked certificates is optionally followed by a set of CRL extensions that supply additional information about the CRL and how it should be processed. To process a CRL, the verifying party checks that the CRL has been signed with the key of the named issuer, and that the current date is between the thisUpdate time and the nextUpdate time. This time check is crucial, because if it is not performed, an attacker could use a revoked certificate by supplying an old CRL where the certificate had not yet appeared. Note that expired certificates are typically removed from the CRL, which prevents the CRL from growing unboundedly over time.

TABLE 3.3   Data Fields in an X.509 CRL.

Version	Specifies the format of the CRL. Current version is 2.
Signature Algorithm	Specifies the algorithm used to sign the CRL
Issuer	Name of the CA issuing the CRL
thisUpdate	Time from when this CRL is valid
nextUpdate	Time when the next CRL will be issued

TABLE 3.4   Format of a Revocation Record in an X.509 CRL.

Serial Number	Serial number of a revoked certificate
Revocation Date	Date the revocation is effective
CRL Extensions	[optional] specifies why the certificate is revoked

Note: CRLs can only revoke certificates on time boundaries determined by the nextUpdate time. If a CA publishes a CRL every Monday, for example, a certificate that is compromised on a Wednesday will continue to validate until it's serial number is published in the CRL on the following Monday. Clients validating certificates may have downloaded the CA's CRL on Monday, and are free to cache the CRL until the nextUpdate time occurs. This caching is important, as it means that the CRL is only downloaded once per client per publication period, rather than for every certificate validation. However, it has the unavoidable consequence of having a potential time-lag between a certificate becoming invalid and its appearance on a CRL. The online certificate validation protocols detailed in the next section attempt to solve this problem.

The costs of maintaining and transmitting CRLs to verifying parties has been repeatedly identified as an important component of the cost of running a PKI system [7,8], and several alternative revocation schemes have been proposed to lower this cost. The cost of CRL distribution was also a factor in the emergence of online certificate status checking protocols like OCSP and SCVP.

Delta CRLs

In large systems that issue many certificates, CRLs can potentially become quite lengthy. One approach to reducing the network overhead associated with sending the complete CRL to every verifier is to issue a Delta CRL along with a Base CRL. The base CRL contains the complete set of revoked certificates up to some point in time, and the accompanying Delta CRL contains only the additional certificates added over some time period. Clients that are capable of processing the Delta CRL can then download the Base CRL less frequently, and download the smaller Delta CRL to get recently revoked certificates. Delta CRLs are formatted identically to CRLs, but have a critical extension added in the CRL that denotes that they are a Delta, not Base CRL. IETF RFC 3280 [5] details how Delta CRLs are formatted, and the set of certificate extensions that indicate that a CA issues Delta CRLs.

Online Certificate Status Protocol

The Online Certificate Status Protocol (OSCP) was designed with the goal of reducing the costs of CRL transmission, and eliminating the time-lag between certificate invalidity and certificate revocation inherent in CRL based designs. The idea behind OCSP is straightforward. A CA certificate contains a reference to an OSCP server. A client validating a certificate transmits the certificate serial number, a hash of the issuer name, and a hash of the subject name, to that OSCP server. The OSCP server checks the certificate status and returns an indication as to the current status of the certificate. This removes the need to download the entire list of revoked certificates, and also allows for essentially instantaneous revocation of invalid certificates. It has the design tradeoff of requiring that clients validating certificates have network connectivity to the required OCSP server.

OSCP responses contain the basic information as to the status of the certificate, in the set of "good", "revoked", or "unknown." They also contain a thisUpdate time, similarly to a CRL and are signed. Responses can also contain a nextUpdate time, which indicates how long the client can consider the OSCP response definitive. The reason the certificate was revoked can also be returned in the response. OSCP is defined in IETF RFC 2560 [9].

7. SERVER-BASED CERTIFICATE VALIDITY PROTOCOL

The X.509 certificate path construction and validation process requires a non-trivial amount of code, the ability to fetch and cache CRLs, and, in the case of mesh and bridge CAs, the ability to interpret CA policies. The Server-based Certificate Validity Protocol [10] was designed to reduce the cost of using X.509 certificates by allowing applications to delegate the task of certificate validation to an external server. SCVP offers two levels of functionality: Delegated Path Discovery (DPD), which attempts to locate and construct a complete certificate chain for a given certificate, and Delegated Path Validation (DPV), which performs a complete path validation, including revocation checking, on a certificate chain. The main reason for this division of functionality is that a client can use an untrusted SCVP server for DPD operations, since it will validate the resulting path itself. Only trusted SCVP servers can be used for DPV, since the client must trust the server's assessment of a certificate's validity.

SCVP also allows checking certificates according to some defined certification policy. The can be used to centralize policy management for an organization that wishes all clients to follow some set of rules with respect to what set of CAs are trusted, what certification policies are trusted, etc. To use SCVP, the client sends a query to an SCVP server, which contains the following parameters:

- *QueriedCerts*. This is the set of certificates that the client wants the server to construct (and optionally validate) paths for.
- *Checks*. The Checks parameter specifies what the client wants the server to do. The checks parameter can be used to specify that the server should build a path, should build a path and validate it without checking revocation, or should build and fully validate the path.
- *WantBack*. The WantBack parameter specifies what the server should return from the request. This can range from the public key from the validated certificate path (in which case the client is fully delegating certificate validation to the server), to all certificate chains that the server can locate.
- *ValidationPolicy*. The ValidationPolicy parameter instructs the server how to validate the resultant certification chain. This parameter can be as simple as "use the default RFC 3280 validation algorithm" or can specify a wide range of conditions that must be satisfied. Some of the conditions that can be specified with this parameter are:
  - *KeyUsage and Extended Key Usage*. The client can specify a set of KeyUsage or ExtendedKeyUsage fields that must be present in the end-entity certificate. This allows the client to only accept, for example, certificates that are allowed to perform digital signatures.
  - *UserPolicySet*. The client can specify a set of certification policy OIDs that must be present in the CAs used to construct the chain. CAs can assert that they follow some formally defined policy when issuing certificates, and this parameter allows the

client to only accept certificates issued under some set of these policies. For example, if a client wanted to only accept certificates acceptable under the Medium Assurance Federal Bridge CA policies, it could assert that policy identifier in this parameter. For more information on policy identifiers, see the section on X.509 Extensions.

- *InhibitPolicyMapping*. When issuing bridge or cross-certificates, a CA can assert that a certificate policy identifier in one domain is equivalent to some other policy identifier within it's domain. By using this parameter, the client can state that it does not want to allow these policy equivalences to be used when validating certificates against values in the UserPolicySet parameter.
- *TrustAnchors*. The client can use this parameter to specify some set of certificates that must be at the top of any acceptable certificate chain. By using this parameter a client could, for example, say that only VeriSign Class 3 certificates were acceptable in this context.
- *ResponseFlags*. This specifies various options as to how the server should respond (if it needs to sign or otherwise protect the response) and if a cached response is acceptable to the client.
- *ValidationTime*. The client may want a validation performed as if it was a specific time, so that it can find if a certificate was valid at some point in the past. Note that SCVP does not allow for "speculative" validation, in terms of asking if a certificate will be valid in the future. This parameter allows the client to specify the validation time to be used by the server.
- *IntermediateCerts*. The client can use this parameter to give additional certificates that can potentially be used to construct the certificate chain. The server is not obligated to use these certificates. This parameter is used where the client may have received a set of intermediate certificates from a communicating party, and is not certain that the SCVP server has possession of these certificates.
- *RevInfos*. Like the IntermediateCerts parameter, the RevInfos parameter supplies extra information that may be needed to construct or validate the path. Instead of certificates, the RevInfos parameter supplies revocation information like OSCP responses, CRLs, or Delta CRLs.

8. X.509 BRIDGE CERTIFICATION SYSTEMS

In practice, large scale PKI systems proved to be more complex than could be easily handled under the X.509 hierarchical model. For example, Polk and Hastings [11] identified a number of policy complexities that presented difficulties when attempting to build a PKI system for the United States Federal Government. In this case, certainly one of the largest PKI projects ever undertaken, they found that the traditional model of a hierarchical certification system was simply unworkable. They state:

"The initial designs for a federal PKI were hierarchical in nature because of government's inherent hierarchical organizational structure. However, these initial PKI plans ran into several obstacles. There was no clear organization within the government that could be identified and agreed upon to run a governmental "root" CA. While the search for an appropriate organization dragged on, federal agencies began to deploy autonomous PKIs to enable their electronic processes. The search for a "root" CA for a hierarchical federal PKI was abandoned, due to the difficulties of imposing a hierarchy after the fact."

Their proposed solution to this problem was to use a "mesh CA" system to establish a Federal Bridge Certification Authority. This Bridge architecture has since been adopted in large PKI systems in Europe and the financial services community in the United States. The details of the European Bridge CA can be found at http://www.bridge-ca.org. This part of the chapter will detail the technical design of bridge CAs, and the various X.509 certificate features that enable bridges.

Mesh PKIs and Bridge CAs

Bridge CA architectures are implemented using a non-hierarchical certification structure called a Mesh PKI. The classic X.509 architecture joins together multiple PKI systems by subordinating them under a higher-level CA. All certificates chain up to this CA, and that CA essentially creates trust between the CAs below it. Mesh PKIs join together multiple PKI systems using a process called "cross certification" that does not create this type of hierarchy. To cross certify, the top level CA in a given hierarchy creates a certificate for an external CA called the Bridge CA. This bridge CA then becomes, in a manner of speaking, a sub-CA under the organization's CA. However, the Bridge CA also creates a certificate for the organizational CA, so it can also be viewed as a top level CA certifying that organizational CA.

The end result of this cross-certification process is that if, two organizations, A and B have joined the same bridge CA, the can both create certificate chains from their respective trusted CAs through the other organization's CA to end-entity certificates that it has created. These chains will be longer than traditional hierarchical chains, but have the same basic verifiable properties. Figure 3.7 shows how two organizations might be connected through a bridge CA, and what the resultant certificate chains look like.

In the case illustrated in Figure 3.7, a user that trusts certificates issued by PKI A (that is, PKI A Root is a "trust anchor") can construct a chain to certificates issued by the PKI B SubCA, since it can verify Certificate 2 via its trust of the PKI A Root. Certificate 2 then chains to Certificate 3, which chains to Certificate 6. Certificate 6 then is a trusted issuer certificate for certificates issued by the PKI B SubCA.

Mesh architectures create two significant technical problems: path construction and policy evaluation. In a hierarchical PKI system, there is only one path from the root certificate to an end-entity certificate. Creating a certificate chain is as simple as taking the current certificate, locating the issuer in the subject field of another certificate, and repeating until the root is reached (completing the chain) or no certificate can be found (failing to construct the chain.) In a Mesh system, there are can now be cyclical loops where this process can fail to terminate with a failure or success. This is not a difficult problem to solve, but it is more complex to deal with than the hierarchical case.

Policy evaluation becomes much more complex in the Mesh case. In the hierarchical CA case, the top level CA can establish policies that are followed by Sub CAs, and these policies can be encoded into certificates in an unambiguous way. When multiple PKIs are joined by a bridge CA, these PKIs may have similar policies, but expressed with different

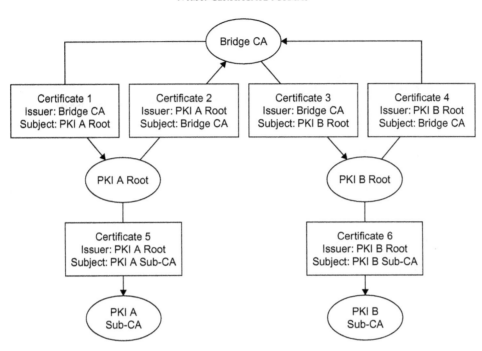

FIGURE 3.7   Showing the structure of two PKIs connected via a bridge CA.

names. PKI A and PKI B may both certify "medium assurance" CAs which perform a certain level of authentication before issuing certificates, but may have different identifiers for these policies. When joined by a bridge CA, clients may reasonably want to validate certificates issued by both CAs, and understand the policies that those certificates are issued under. The PolicyMapping technique allows similar policies under different names from disjoint PKIs to be translated at the bridge CA.

While none of these problems are insurmountable, they increase the complexity of certificate validation code, and helped drive the invention of server-based validation protocols like SCVP. These protocols delegate path discovery and validation to an external server, rather than require that applications integrate this functionality. While this may lower application complexity, the main benefit of this strategy is that questions of acceptable policies and translation can be configured at one central verification server rather than distributed to every application doing certificate validation.

9. X.509 CERTIFICATE FORMAT

The X.509 standard (and the related IETF RFCs) specify a set of data fields that must be present in a properly formatted certificate, a set of optional extension data fields that can be used to supply additional certificate information, how these fields must be signed, and how the signature data is encoded. All of these data fields (mandatory fields, optional fields, and the signature) are specified in Abstract Syntax Notation (aka ASN.1), a formal language that allows for exact definitions of the content of data fields and how those fields are arranged in a data structure. An associated specification, Determined Encoding Rules (DER) is used with specific certificate data and the ASN.1 certificate format to create the actual binary certificate data. The ASN.1 standard is authoritatively defined in ITU Recommendation X.693. (For an introduction to ASN.1 and DER, see [kaliski])

X.509 V1 and V2 Format

The first X.509 certificate standard was published in 1988 as part of the broader X.500 directory standard. X.509 was intended to provide public key based access control to an X.500 directory, and defined a certificate format for that use. This format, now referred to as X.509 v1 defined a static format containing an X.400 Issuer name (the name of the CA), an X.400 Subject name, a validity period, the key to be certified, and the signature of the CA. While this basic format allowed for all the basic PKI operations, the format required that all names be in the X.400 form, and it did not allow for any other information to be added to the certificate. The X.509 v2 format added two more Unique ID fields, but did not fix the primary deficiencies of the v1 format. As it became clear that name formats would have to be more flexible, and certificates would have to accommodate a wider variety of information, work began on a new certificate format.

X.509 V3 Format

The X.509 certificate specification was revised in 1996 to add an optional extension field which allows encoding a set of optional additional data fields into the certificate (see Table 3.5). While this change may seem minor, in fact it allowed certificates to carry a

TABLE 3.5   Data Fields in an X.509 Version3 Certificate.

Version	The version of the standard used to format the certificate
Serial Number	A number, unique relative to the issuer, for this certificate
Signature Algorithm	The specific algorithm used to sign the certificate
Issuer	Name of the authority issuing the certificate
Validity	The time interval this certificate is valid for
Subject	The identity being certified
Subject Public Key	The key being bound to the Subject
Issuer Unique ID	Obsolete field
Subject Unique ID	Obsolete field
Extensions	A list of additional certificate attributes
Signature	A digital signature by the Issuer over the certificate data

wide array of information useful for PKI implementation, and also for the certificate to contain multiple, non-X.400 identities. These extension fields allow for key usage policies, CA policy information, revocation pointers, and other relevant information to live in the certificate. The V3 format is the most widely used X.509 variant and is the basis for the certificate profile in RFC 3280 [5] issued by the Internet Engineering Task Force.

X.509 Certificate Extensions

This section is a partial catalog of common X.509 V3 extensions. There is no existing canonical directory of V3 extensions, so there are undoubtedly extensions in use outside this list. The most common extensions are defined in RFC 3280 [5], which contains the IETF certificate profile, used by S/MIME and many SSL/TLS implementations. These extensions address a number of deficiencies in the base X.509 certificate specification, and, in many cases, are essential for constructing a practical PKI system. In particular, the Certificate Policy, Policy Mapping, and Policy Constraints extensions form the basis for the popular bridge CA architectures.

Authority Key Identifier

The Authority Key Identifier extension identifies which specific private key owned by the certificate issuer was used to sign the certificate. The use of this extension allows a single issuer to use multiple private keys, and unambiguously identifies which key was used. This allows issuer keys to be refreshed without changing the issuer name, and enables handling events such as an issuer key being compromised or lost.

Subject Key Identifier

The Subject Key Identifier extension, like the Authority Key Identifier, indicates which subject key is contained in the certificate. This extension provides a way to quickly identify which certificates belong to a specific key owned by a subject. If the certificate is a CA certificate, the Subject Key Identifier can be used to construct chains by connecting a Subject Key Identifier with a matching Authority Key Identifier.

Key Usage

A CA may wish to issue a certificate that limits the use of a public key. This may lead to an increase in overall system security by segregating encryption keys from signature keys, and even segregating signature keys by utilization. For example, an entity may have a key used for signing documents and a key used for decryption of documents. The signing key may be protected by a smart card mechanism that requires a PIN per signing, while the encryption key is always available when the user is logged in. The use of this extension allows the CA to express that the encryption key cannot be used to generate signatures, and notifies communicating users that they should not encrypt data with the signing public key. The key usage capabilities are defined in a bit field, which allows a single key to have any combination of the defined capabilities ("An Agenda For Action To Define Key Usage Capabilities").

AN AGENDA FOR ACTION TO DEFINE KEY USAGE CAPABILITIES

The extension defines the following capabilities that need to be completed (Check All Tasks Completed):

_____1. *digitalSignature* – The key can be used to generate digital signatures.

_____2. *nonRepudiation* – Signatures generated from this key can be tied back to the signer in such a way that the signer cannot deny generating the signature. This capability is used in electronic transaction scenarios where it is important that signers cannot disavow a transaction.

_____3. *keyEncipherment* – The key can be used to wrap a symmetric key that is then used to bulk encrypt data. This is used in communications protocols, and applications like S/MIME where an algorithm like AES is used to encrypt data, and the public key in the certificate is used to then encipher that AES key. In practice, almost all encryption applications are structured in this manner, as public keys are generally unsuitable for the encryption of bulk data.

_____4. *dataEncipherment* – The key can be used to directly encrypt data. Because of algorithmic limitations of public encryption algorithms,

the keyEncipherment technique is nearly always used instead of directly encrypting data.

_____5. *keyAgreement* – The key can be used to create a communication key between two parties. This capability can be used in conjunction with the encipherOnly and decipherOnly capabilities.

_____6. *keyCertSign* – The key can be used to sign another certificate. This is a crucial key usage capability, as it essentially allows creation of sub-certificates under this certificate, subject to basicConstraints. All CA certificates must have this usage bit set, and all end-entity certificates must NOT have it set.

_____7. *cRLSign* – The key can be used to sign a Certificate Revocation List (CRL). CA certificates may have this bit set, or they may delegate CRL creation to a different key, in which case this bit will be cleared.

_____8. *encipherOnly* – When the key is used for keyAgreement, the resultant key can only be used for encryption.

_____9. *decipherOnly* – When the key is used for keyAgreement, the resultant key can only be used for decryption.

Subject Alternative Name

This extension allows the certificate to define non-X.400 formatted identities for the subject. It supports a variety of name spaces, including email addresses, DNS names for servers, Electronic Document Interchange (EDI) party names, Uniform Resource Identifiers (URIs), and IP addresses, among others.

Policy Extensions

Three important X.509 certificate extensions (Certificate Policy, Policy Mapping, and Policy Constraints) form a complete system for communicating CA policies for how certificates are issued, revoked, and CA security is maintained. They are interesting in that they communicate information that is more relevant to business and policy decision making than the other extensions which are used in the technical processes of certificate chain construction and validation. As an example, a variety of CAs run multiple Sub-CAs that issue certificates according to a variety of issuance policies, ranging from "Low Assurance" to "High Assurance." The CA will typically formally define in a policy document all of it's operating policies, state them in practice statement, define an ASN.1 Object Identifier (OID) that names this policy, and distribute it to parties that will validate those certificates. The policy extensions allow CAs to attach a policy OID to its certificate, translate policy OIDs between PKIs, and limit the policies that can be used by sub CAs.

Certificate Policy

The Certificate Policy extension, if present in an issuer certificate, expresses the policies that are followed by the CA, both in terms of how identities are validated before certificate issuance, but also how certificates are revoked, and the operational practices that are used to insure integrity of the CA. These policies can be expressed in two ways: as an OID, which is a unique number that refers to one given policy, and as a human-readable Certificate Practice Statement (CPS). One Certificate Policy extension can contain both the computer-sensible OID and a printable CPS. One special OID has been set aside for "AnyPolicy", which states that the CA may issue certificates under a free-form policy.

IETF RFC 2527 [12] gives a complete description of what should be present in a CA policy document and CPS. More details on the 2527 guidelines are given in the PKI Policy Description section.

Policy Mapping

The Policy Mapping extension contains two policy OIDs, one for the Issuer domain, the other for the Subject domain. When this extension is present, a validating party can consider the two policies identical, which is to say, the Subject OID, when present in the chain below the given certificate, can be considered to be the same as the policy named in the Issuer OID. This extension is used join together two PKI systems with functionally similar policies that have different policy reference OIDs.

Policy Constraints

The Policy Constraints extension enables a CA to disable policy mapping for CAs farther down in the chain, and also to require explicit policies in all the CAs below a given CA.

10. PKI POLICY DESCRIPTION

In many application contexts, it is important to understand how and when certifying authorities will issue and revoke certificates. Especially when bridge architectures are used, an administrator may need to evaluate a certifying authority's policy to determine how and when to trust certificates issued under that authority. For example, the United States Federal Bridge CA maintains a detailed specification of its operating procedures and requirements for bridged CAs at the US CIO office web site: (http://www.cio.gov/fpkipa/documents/FBCA_CP_RFC3647.pdf). Many other commercial CAs, such as VeriSign, maintain similar documents.

To make policy evaluation easier and more uniform, IETF RFC 2527 [12] specifies a standard format for certifying authorities to communicate their policy for issuing and revoking certificates. This specification divides a policy specification document into the following sections:

- *Introduction*: This section describes the type of certificates that the CA issues, the applications that those certificates can be used in, and the OIDs used to identify CA policies. The Introduction also contains the contact information for the institution operating the CA.
- *General Provisions:*This section details the legal obligations of the CA, any warranties given as to the reliability of the bindings in the certificate, and details as to the legal operation of the CA, including fees and relationship to any relevant laws.
- *Identification and Authentication:*This section details how certificate requests are authenticated at the CA or RA, and how events like name disputes or revocation requests are handled.
- *Operational Requirements:*This section details how the CA will react in case of key compromise, how it renews keys, how it publishes CRLs or other revocation information, how it is audited, and what records are kept during CA operation.
- *Physical, Procedural, and Personnel Security Controls:*This section details how the physical location of the CA is controlled, and how employees are vetted.
- *Technical Security Controls:*This section explains how the CA key is generated and protected though its lifecycle. CA key generation is typically done through an audited, recorded key generation ceremony to assure certificate users that the CA key was not copied or otherwise compromised during generation.
- *Certificate and CRL Profile:*The specific policy OIDs published in certificates generated by the CA are given in this section. The information in this section is sufficient to accomplish the technical evaluation of a certificate chain published by this CA.
- *Specification Administration:*The last section explains the procedures used to maintain and update the certificate policy statement itself.

These policy statements can be substantial documents. The Federal Bridge CA policy statement is at least 93 pages long, and other certificate authorities have similarly exhaustive documents. The aim of these statements is to provide enough legal backing for certificates produced by these CAs so that they can be used to sign legally binding contracts and automate other legally relevant applications.

11. PKI STANDARDS ORGANIZATIONS

The PKIX Working Group was established in the fall of 1995 with the goal of developing Internet standards to support X.509-based Public Key Infrastructures (PKIs). These specifications form the basis for numerous other IETF specifications that use certificates to secure various protocols, such as S/MIME (for secure email), TLS (for secured TCP connections), and IPSEC (for securing internet packets).

IETF PKIX

The PKIX working group has produced a complete set of specifications for an X.509 based PKI system. These specifications span 36 RFCs, and at least eight more RFCs are being considered by the group at the moment. In addition to the basic core of X.509 certificate profiles and verification strategies, the PKIX drafts cover the format of certificate request messages, certificates for arbitrary attributes (rather than for public keys), and a host of other certificate techniques.

Other IETF groups have produced a group of specifications that detail the usage of certificates in various protocols and applications. In particular, the S/MIME group, which details a method for encrypting email messages, and the SSL/TLS group, which details TCP/IP connection security, use X.509 certificates.

SDSI/SPKI

The Simple Distributed Security Infrastructure (SDSI) group was chartered in 1996 to design a mechanism for distributing public keys that would correct some of the perceived complexities inherent in X.509. In particular, the SDSI group aimed at building a PKI architecture [sdsi] that would not rely on a hierarchical naming system, but would instead work with local names that would not have to be enforced to be globally unique. The eventual SDSI design, produced by Ron Rivest and Butler Lampson, has a number of unique features:

- *Public key-centric design.* The SDSI design uses the public key itself (or a hash of the key) as the primary indentifying name. SDSI signature objects can contain naming statements about the holder of a given key, but the names are not intended to be the "durable" name of a entity.
- *Free-form namespaces.* SDSI imposes no restrictions on what form names must take, and imposes no hierarchy that defines a canonical namespace. Instead, any signer may assert identity information about the holder of a key, but no entity is required to the use (or believe) the identity bindings of any other particular signer. This allows each application to create a policy about who can create identities, how those identities are verified, and even what constitutes an identity.
- *Support for groups and roles.* The design of many security constructions (access control lists, for example) often include the ability to refer to groups or roles instead of the

identity of individuals. This allows access control and encryption operations to protect data for groups, which may be more natural in some situations.

The Simple Public Key Infrastructure (SPKI) group was started at nearly the same time, with goals similar to the SDSI effort. In X, the two groups were merged, and the SDSI/SPKI 2.0 specification was produced, incorporating ideas from both architectures.

IETF OpenPGP

The Pretty Good Privacy (PGP) public key system, created by Phillip Zimmermann, is a widely deployed PKI system that allows for the signing and encryption of files and email. Unlike the X.509 PKI architecture, the PGP PKI system uses the notion of a "Web of Trust" to bind identities to keys. The Web of Trust (WoT) [13] replaces the X.509 idea of identity binding via an authoritative server with identity binding via multiple semi-trusted paths.

In a WoT system, the end user maintains a database of matching keys and identities, each of which are given two trust ratings. The first trust rating denotes how trusted the binding between the key and the identity is, and the second denotes how trusted a particular identity is to "introduce" new bindings. Users can create and sign a certificate, and import certificates created by other users. Importing a new certificate is treated as an introduction. When a given identity and key in a database are signed by enough trusted identities, that binding is treated as trusted.

Because PGP identities are not bound by an authoritative server, there is also no authoritative server that can revoke a key. Instead, the PGP model states that the holder of a key can revoke that key by posting a signed revocation message to a public server. Any user seeing a properly signed revocation message then removes that key from their database. Because revocation messages must be signed, only the holder of the key can produce them, so it is impossible to produce a false revocation with out compromising the key. If an attacker does compromise the key, then production of a revocation message from that compromised key actually improves the security of the overall system, because it warns other users to not trust that key.

12. PGP CERTIFICATE FORMATS

To support the unique features of the Web of Trust system, PGP invented a very flexible packetized message format that can encode encrypted messages, signed messages, key database entries, key revocation messages, and certificates. This packetized design, described in IETF RFC 2440, allows a PGP certificate to contain a variable number of names and signatures, as opposed to the single-certification model used in X.509.

A PGP certificate (known as a transferrable public key) contains three main sections of packetized data. The first section contains the main public key itself, potentially followed by some set of relevant revocation packets. The next section contains a set of User ID packets, which ae identities to be bound to the main public key. Each User ID packet is optionally followed by a set of Signature packets, each of which contains an identity and a signature of the User ID packet and the main public key. Each of these Signature packets

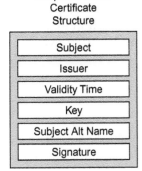

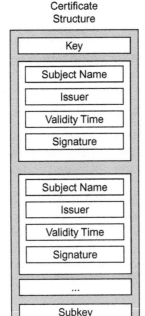

Simplified X.509 Certificate Structure

Simplified PGP Certificate Structure

FIGURE 3.8 Comparing X.509 and PGP certificate structures.

essentially forms an identity binding. Because each PGP certificate can contain any number of these User ID/Signature elements, a single certificate can assert that a public key is bound to multiple identities (for example, multiple email addresses that correspond to a single user), certified by multiple signers. This multiple signer approach enables the Web of Trust model. The last section of the certificate is optional and may contain multiple subkeys, which are single function keys (for example, an encryption only key) also owned by the holder of the main public key. Each of these subkeys must be signed by the main public key.

PGP Signature packets contain all the information needed to perform a certification, including time intervals for which the signature is valid. Figure 3.8 shows how the multiname, multi-signature PGP format differs from the single-name with single-signature X.509 format.

13. PGP PKI IMPLEMENTATIONS

The PGP PKI system is implemented in commercial products sold by the PGP corporation, and several open source projects, including Gnu Privacy Guard (GPG) and

OpenPGP. Thawte offers a Web of Trust service that connects people with "Web of Trust notaries" that can build trusted introductions. PGP Corporation operates a PGP Global Directory that contains PGP keys along with an email confirmation service to make key certification easier. The OpenPGP group (www.openpgp.org) maintains the IETF specification (RFC 2440) for the PGP message and certificate format.

14. W3C

The World Wide Web Consortium (W3C) standards group has published a series of standards on encrypting and signing XML documents. These standards, XML Signature and XML Encryption have a companion PKI specification called XKMS (XML Key Management Specification.)

The XKMS specification describes a meta-PKI that can be used to register, locate, and validate keys that may be certified by an outside X.509 CA, a PGP referrer, a SPKI key signer, or the XKMS infrastructure itself. The specification contains two protocol specifications, X-KISS (XML Key Information Service Specification) and X-KRSS (XML Key Registration Service Specification) X-KISS is used to find and validate a public key referenced in an XML document, and X-KRSS is used to register a public key so that it can be located by X-KISS requests.

15. IS PKI SECURE?

PKI has formed the basis of Internet security protocols like S/MIME for securing email, and the SSL/TLS protocols for securing communications between clients and web servers. The essential job of PKI in these protocols is binding a name, like an email address or domain name to a key that is controlled by that entity. As seen in this chapter, that job boils down to a CA issuing a certificate for an entity. The security of these systems then rests on the trustworthiness of the CAs trusted within an application. If a CA issues a set of bad certificates, the security of the entire system can be called into question.

The issue of a subverted CA was largely theoretical until attacks on the Comodo and DigiNotar CAs [2,3] in 2011. Both of these CAs discovered that an attacker had bypassed their internal controls and obtained certificates for prominent Internet domains (google.com, yahoo.com.) These certificates were revoked, but the incident caused the major browser vendors to revisit their policies about what CA roots are trusted, and the removal of many CAs. In the case of DigiNotar, these attacks ultimately led to the bankruptcy of the company.

By attacking a CA and obtaining a false certificate for a given domain, the attacker can set up a fake version of the domain's web site, and using that certificate, create secure connections to clients that trust that CA's root certificate. This secure connection can be used as a "man-in-the-middle" server that reveals all traffic between the client (or clients) and the legitimate web site.

Can these attacks be prevented? There are research protocols such as "Perspectives" [14] that attempt to detect false certificates that might be signed by a legitimate CA. These protocols use third party repositories to track what certificates and keys are used by individual web sites. A change that is only noticed by some subset of users may indicate an attacker using a certificate to gain access to secured traffic.

Some other products that rely on PKI certification have introduced new features to make these attacks harder to execute. Google's Chrome browser also has recently incorporated security features [15] intended to foil attacks on PKI infrastructure. The Mozilla Foundation, owners of the Firefox browser, have instituted an audit and review system that requires all trusted CAs to attest they have specific kinds of security mechanisms in place to prevent the issuance of illegitimate certificates.

As a general principle, systems built to rely on PKI for security should understand the risks involved in CA compromise, and also understand how critical it is to control exposure to these kinds of attacks. One simple mechanism for doing this is to restrict the number of CAs that are trusted by the application. These large number of roots trusted by the average web browser is quite large, which makes auditing of the complete list of CAs difficult.

16. ALTERNATIVE PKI ARCHITECTURES

PKI systems have proven to be remarkably effective tools for some protocols, most notably SSL, which has emerged as the dominant standard for encrypting internet traffic. Deploying PKI systems for other types of applications or as a general key management system has not been as successful. The differentiating factor seems to be that PKI keys for machine end-entities (like web sites) do not encounter usability hurdles that emerge when issuing PKI keys for human end-entities. Peter Guttman [notdead] has a number of overviews of PKI that present the fundamental difficulties of classic X.509 PKI architectures. Alma Whitten and Doug Tygar [16] published "Why Johnny Can't Encrypt", a study of various users attempting to encrypt email messages using certificates. This study showed substantial user failure rates, due to the complexities of understanding certificate naming and validation practices. A subsequent study [17] showed similar results when using X.509 certificates with S/MIME encryption in Microsoft Outlook Express. The majority of the research on PKI alternatives has focused on making encryption easier to use and deploy.

17. MODIFIED X.509 ARCHITECTURES

Some researchers have proposed modifications or redesigns of the X.509 architecture to make obtaining a certificate easier, and lower the cost of operating applications that depend on certificates. The goal of these systems is often to allow internet based services to use certificate based signature and encryption service without requiring the user to consciously interact with certification services or even understand that certificates are being utilitzed.

Perlman and Kaufman's User-Centric PKI

Perlman and Kaufman proposed the "User-centric PKI" [Perlman], which allows the user to act as their own CA, with authentication provided through individual registration with service providers. It has several features that attempt to protect user privacy through allowing the user to pick what attributes are visible to a specific service provider.

Guttman's Plug and Play PKI

Guttman's proposed "Plug and Play PKI" [gutmann-pnp] provides for similar self-registration with a service provider and adds location protocols to establish how to contact certifying services. The goal is to build a PKI which provides a reasonable level of security and which is essentially transparent to the end user.

Callas' Self-Assembling PKI

In 2003, Jon Callas [18] proposed a PKI system that would use existing, standard PKI elements bound together by a "robot" server that would examine messages sent between users, and attempt to find certificates that could be used to secure the message. In the absence of an available certificate, the robot would create a key on behalf of the user, and send a message requesting authentication. This system has the benefit for speeding deployment of PKI systems for email authentication, but loses many of the strict authentication attributes that drove the development of the X.509 and IETF PKI standards.

18. ALTERNATIVE KEY MANAGEMENT MODELS

While PKI systems can be used for encryption as well as digital signature, these two applications have different operational characteristics. In particular, systems that use PKIs for encryption require that an encrypting party has the ability to locate certificates for its desired set of recipients. In digital signature applications, a signer only requires access to their own private key and certificate. The certificates required to verify the signature can be sent with the signed document, so there is no requirement for verifiers to locate arbitrary certificates. These difficulties have been identified as factors contributing to the difficulty of practical deployment of PKI based encryption systems like S/MIME.

In 1984, Adi Shamir [19] proposed an Identity-Based Encryption (IBE) system for email encryption. In the identity-based model, any string can be mathematically transformed into a public key, typically using some public information from a server. A message can then be encrypted with this key. To decrypt, the message recipient contacts the server and requests a corresponding private key. The server is able to mathematically derive a private key, which is returned to the recipient. Shamir disclosed how to perform a signature operation in this model, but did not give a solution for encryption.

This approach has significant advantages over the traditional PKI model of encryption. The most obvious is the ability to send an encrypted message without locating a certificate for a given recipient. There are other points of differentiation:

- *Key recovery.* In the traditional PKI model, if a recipient loses the private key corresponding to a certificate, all messages encrypted to that certificate's public key cannot be decrypted. In the IBE model, the server can recompute lost private keys. If messages must be recoverable for legal or other business reasons, PKI systems typically add mandatory secondary public keys that senders must encrypt messages to.
- *Group support.* Since any string can be transformed to a public key, a group name can be supplied instead of an individual identity. In the traditional PKI model, groups are either done by expanding a group to a set of individuals at encrypt time, or by issuing group certificates. Group certificates pose serious difficulties with revocation, since individuals can only be removed from a group as often as revocation is updated.

In 2001, Boneh and Franklin gave the first fully described secure and efficient method for IBE [20]. This was followed by a number of variant techniques, including Hierarchical Identity-Based Encryption (HIBE) and Certificateless Encryption. HIBE allows multiple key servers to be used, each of which control part of the namespace used for encryption. Certificateless [21] encryption adds the ability to encrypt to an end user using an identity, but in such a way that the key server cannot read messages. IBE systems have been commercialized, and are the subject of standards under the IETF (RFC 5091) and IEEE (1363.3).

19. SUMMARY

A Public Key Infrastructure (PKI) is the key management environment for public key information of a public key cryptographic system. As discussed in this chapter, there are three basic PKI architectures based on the number of Certificate Authorities (CAs) in the PKI, where users of the PKI place their trust (known as a user's trust point), and the trust relationships between CAs within a multi-CA PKI.

The most basic PKI architecture is one that contains a single CA that provides the PKI services (certificates, certificate status information, etc.) for all the users of the PKI. Multiple CA PKIs can be constructed using one of two architectures based on the trust relationship between the CAs. A PKI constructed with superior-subordinate CA relationships is called a hierarchical PKI architecture. Alternatively, a PKI constructed of peer-to-peer CA relationships is called a mesh PKI architecture.

Directory Architectures

As discussed in this chapter, early PKI development was conducted under the assumption a directory infrastructure (specifically a global X.500 directory) would be used to distribute certificates and certificate revocation lists (CRL). Unfortunately, the global X.500 directory did not emerge resulting in PKIs being deployed using various directory architectures based on how directory requests are serviced. If the initial directory cannot service a request, the directory can forward the request to other known directories using directory chaining. Another way a directory can resolve an unserviceable request is to return a referral to the initiator of the request indicating a different directory that might be able to service the request. If the directories cannot provide directory chaining or referrals, pointers to directory servers can be embedded in a PKI certificate using the Authority Information Access (AIA) and Subject Information Access (SIA) extensions. In general, all PKI users interface to the directory infrastructure using the Lightweight Directory Access Protocol (LDAP) irregardless of how the directory infrastructure is navigated.

Bridge Cas and Revocation Modeling

Bridge Certification Authorities (BCAs) provide the means to leverage the capabilities of existing corporate PKIs as well as Federal PKIs. Public key infrastructures (PKIs) are being fielded in increasing size and numbers, but operational experience to date has been limited to a relatively small number of environments. As a result, there are still many unanswered questions about the ways in which PKIs will be organized and operated in large scale systems. Some of these questions involve the ways in which individual certification authorities (CAs) will be interconnected. Others involve the ways in which revocation information will be distributed.

Most of the proposed revocation distribution mechanisms have involved variations of the original CRL scheme. Examples include the use of segmented CRLs and delta-CRLs. However, some schemes do not involve the use of any type of CRL (on-line certificate status protocols and hash chains).

A model of certificate revocation presents a mathematical model for describing the timings of validations by relying parties. The model is used to determine how request rates for traditional CRLs change over time. This model is then extended to show how request rates are affected when CRLs are segmented. This chapter also presented a technique for distributing revocation information, over-issued CRLs. Over-issued CRLs are identical to traditional CRLs but are issued more frequently. The result of over-issuing CRLs is to spread out requests from relying parties and thus to reduce the peak load on the repository.

A more efficient use of delta-CRLs uses the model described in a model of certificate revocation to analyze various methods of issuing delta-CRLs. It begins with an analysis of the "traditional" method of issuing delta-CRLs and shows that, in some circumstances, issuing delta-CRLs in this manner fails to provide the efficiency gains for which delta-CRLs were designed. A new method of issuing delta-CRLs, sliding window delta-CRLs, was presented. Sliding window delta-CRLs are similar to traditional delta-CRLs, but provide a constant amount of historical information. While this does not affect the request rate for delta-CRLs, it can significantly reduce the peak request rate for base CRLs. The chapter provided an analysis of sliding window delta-CRLs along with advice on how to select the optimal window size to use when issuing delta-CRLs.

Finally, let's move on to the real interactive part of this Chapter: review questions/exercises, hands-on projects, case projects and optional team case project. The answers and/or solutions by chapter can be found in the Online Instructor's Solutions Manual.

CHAPTER REVIEW QUESTIONS/EXERCISES

True/False

1. True or False? The most important security protocols used on the Internet do not rely on PKI to bind names to keys — a crucial function that allows authentication of users and websites.
2. True or False? To understand how PKI systems function, it is not necessary to grasp the basics of public key cryptography.
3. True or False? The most important cryptographic operation in PKI systems is the digital signature.
4. True or False? Variants of the three operations used to construct digital signatures can also be used to encrypt data.
5. True or False? PKI systems solve the problem of associating meaningful names with essentially meaningless cryptographic keys.

Multiple Choice

1. What model is the most prevalent standard for certificate based PKIs, though the standard has evolved such that PKI-using applications on the Internet are mostly based on the set of IETF standards that have evolved and extended the ideas in X.509?
   A. X.510
   B. X.509
   C. X.511
   D. X.512
   E. X.513
2. What model specifies a system of Certifying Authorities (CAs) that issue certificates for end entities (users, web sites, or other entities that hold private keys.)?
   A. X.510
   B. X.509
   C. X.511
   D. X.512
   E. X.513
3. While, in theory, the _____ is the entity that creates and validates certificates, in practice, it may be desirable or necessary to delegate the actions of user authentication and certificate validation to other servers.
   A. Evolution
   B. Residue class
   C. Peer-to-peer (P2P)
   D. Certification Authority
   E. Security
4. What certificate validation is a complex process, and can be done to several levels of confidence?
   A. X.509
   B. X.510

    C. X.511

    D. X.512

    E. X.513

5. The contents of the target certificate cannot be trusted until the signature on the certificate is validated, so the first step is to check the:

    A. Physical world

    B. Data retention

    C. Standardization

    D. Permutation

    E. Signature

EXERCISE

Problem

What are the benefits of PKI?

Hands-On Projects

Project

What are the problems with using PKI?

Case Projects

Problem

How does PKI provide management and control?

Optional Team Case Project

Problem

What are the core components of a PKI?

References

[1] W. Diffie, M.E. Hellman, New directions in cryptography, IEEE Trans. Inform. 6 (1976) 644–654Theory, IT-22.

[2] Fake DigiNotar web certificate risk to Iranians, BBC News, 5 September 2011, Retrieved March 2, 2012. <http://www.bbc.co.uk/news/technology-14789763>.

[3] R. Richmond, An Attack Sheds Light on Internet Security Holes, New York Times, 6 April 2011, Retrieved March 2, 2012. <http://www.nytimes.com/2011/04/07/technology/07hack.html?ref = stuxnet>.

[4] ITU-T Recommendation X.509 (1997 E): Information Technology - Open Systems Interconnection - The Directory: Authentication Framework, June 1997.

[5] R. Housely, W. Ford, W. Polk, D. Solo, Internet X.509 Public Key Infrastructure Certificate and Certificate Revocation List Profile, IETF RFC 3280, April 2002.

[6] M. Cooper, Y. Dzambasow, P. Hesse, S. Joseph, R. Nicholas, Internet X.509 Public Key Infrastructure: Certification Path Building, IETF RFC 4158, September 2005.

[7] S. Berkovits, S. Chokhani, J.A. Furlong, J.A. Geiter, J.C. Guild, Public Key Infrastructure Study: Final Report. Produced by the MITRE Corporation for NIST, April 1994.

[8] S. Micali, Efficient certificate revocation. Technical Report TM-542b, MIT Laboratory for Computer Science, Retrieved March 22, 1996. <http://citeseer.ist.psu.edu/micali96efficient.html>.

[9] M. Myers, R. Ankeny, A. Malpani, S. Galperin, C. Adams, X.509 Internet Public Key Infrastructure: Online Certificate Status Protocol — OCSP, IETF RFC 2560, June 1999.

[10] T. Freeman, R. Housely, A. Malpani, D. Cooper, W. Polk, Server Based Certificate Validation Protocol (SCVP), IETF RFC 5055, December 2007.

[11] W.T. Polk, N.E. Hastings, Bridge Certification Authorities: Connecting B2B Public Key Infrastructures, white paper, US Nat'l Institute of Standards and Technology, 2001. Available at <http://csrc.nist.gov/groups/ST/crypto_apps_infra/documents/B2B-article.pdf>.

[12] S. Chokhani, W. Ford, Internet X.509 Public Key Infrastructure: Certificate Policy and Certification Practices Framework, IETF RFC 2527, March 1999.

[13] A. Abdul-Rahman. The PGP Trust Model. EDI- Forum, April 1997. Available at <http://www.cs.ucl.ac.uk/staff/F.AbdulRahman/docs/>.

[14] D. Wendlandt, D.G. Andersen, Adrian Perrig: Perspectives: Improving SSH-style Host Authentication with Multi-Path Probing. USENIX Annual Technical Conference 2008, pp. 321–334.

[15] New Chromium security features, June 2011, The Chromium Blog, 14 June 2011, Retrieved March 2, 2011. <http://blog.chromium.org/2011/06/new-chromium-security-features-june.html>.

[16] A. Whitten, J.D. Tygar, Why Johnny can't encrypt: a usability evaluation of PGP 5.0, in: Proceedings of the 8th USENIX Security Symposium, August 1999.

[17] S. Garfinkel, R. Miller, Johnny 2: A User Test of Key Continuity Management with S/MIME and Outlook Express, Symposium on Usable Privacy and Security, 2005.

[18] J. Callas, Improving Message Security With a Self-Assembling PKI. In 2nd Annual PKI Research Workshop Pre-Proceedings, Gaithersburg, MD, April 2003. <http://citeseer.ist.psu.edu/callas03improving.html>.

[19] A. Shamir, Identity-based cryptosystems and signature schemes, pp. 47–53 Advances in Cryptology — Crypto '84, Lecture Notes in Computer Science, vol. 196, Spring-Verlag, 1984.

[20] D. Boneh, M. Franklin., Identity-based Encryption from the Weil Pairing, SIAM J. of Computing 32 (3) (2003) 586–615.

[21] S.S. Al-Riyami, K. Paterson, Certificateless public key cryptography, in: C.S. Laih (Ed.), Advances in Cryptology — Asiacrypt 2003, *Lecture Notes in Computer Science*, vol. 2894, Springer-Verlag, 2003.

4

Physical Security Essentials

William Stallings
Independent consultant

Platt[1] distinguishes three elements of information system (IS) security:

- *Logical security.* Protects computer-based data from software-based and communication-based threats.
- *Physical security.* Also called *infrastructure security.* Protects the information systems that house data and the people who use, operate, and maintain the systems. Physical security must also prevent any type of physical access or intrusion that can compromise logical security.
- *Premises security.* Also known as *corporate or facilities security.* Protects the people and property within an entire area, facility, or building(s) and is usually required by laws, regulations, and fiduciary obligations. Premises security provides perimeter security, access control, smoke and fire detection, fire suppression, some environmental protection, and usually surveillance systems, alarms, and guards.

This chapter is concerned with physical security and with some overlapping areas of premises security. We begin by looking at physical security threats and then consider physical security prevention measures.

1. OVERVIEW

For information systems, the role of physical security is to protect the physical assets that support the storage and processing of information. Physical security involves two complementary requirements. First, physical security must prevent damage to the physical

1. F. Platt, "Physical threats to the information infrastructure," in S. Bosworth, and M. Kabay, (eds.), *Computer Security Handbook*, Wiley, 2002.

Cyber Security and IT Infrastructure Protection
DOI: http://dx.doi.org/10.1016/B978-0-12-416681-3.00004-5

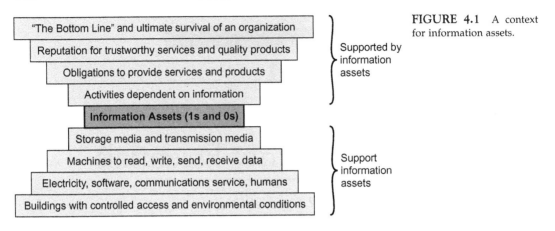

FIGURE 4.1 A context for information assets.

infrastructure that sustains the information system. In broad terms, that infrastructure includes the following:

- *Information system hardware.* Including data processing and storage equipment, transmission and networking facilities, and offline storage media. We can include in this category supporting documentation.
- *Physical facility.* The buildings and other structures housing the system and network components.
- *Supporting facilities.* These facilities underpin the operation of the information system. This category includes electrical power, communication services, and environmental controls (heat, humidity, etc.).
- *Personnel.* Humans involved in the control, maintenance, and use of the information systems.

Second, physical security must prevent misuse of the physical infrastructure that leads to the misuse or damage of the protected information. The misuse of the physical infrastructure can be accidental or malicious. It includes vandalism, theft of equipment, theft by copying, theft of services, and unauthorized entry.

Figure 4.1, based on Bosworth and Kabay[2] , suggests the overall context in which physical security concerns arise. The central concern is the information assets of an organization. These information assets provide value to the organization that possesses them, as indicated by the upper four items in Figure 4.1. In turn, the physical infrastructure is essential to providing for the storage and processing of these assets. The lower four items in Figure 4.1 are the concern of physical security. Not shown is the role of logical security, which consists of software- and protocol-based measures for ensuring data integrity, confidentiality, and so forth.

The role of physical security is affected by the operating location of the information system, which can be characterized as static, mobile, or portable. Our concern in this chapter is primarily with static systems, which are installed at fixed locations. A mobile system is

2. S. Bosworth and M. Kabay (eds.), *Computer Security Handbook*, Wiley, 2002.

installed in a vehicle, which serves the function of a structure for the system. Portable systems have no single installation point but may operate in a variety of locations, including buildings, vehicles, or in the open. The nature of the system's installation determines the nature and severity of the threats of various types, including fire, roof leaks, unauthorized access, and so forth.

2. PHYSICAL SECURITY THREATS

In this pat of the chapter, we first look at the types of physical situations and occurrences that can constitute a threat to information systems. There are a number of ways in which such threats can be categorized. It is important to understand the spectrum of threats to information systems so that responsible administrators can ensure that prevention measures are comprehensive. We organize the threats into the following categories:

- Environmental threats
- Technical threats
- Human-caused threats

We begin with a discussion of natural disasters, which are a prime, but not the only, source of environmental threats. Then we look specifically at environmental threats, followed by technical and human-caused threats.

Natural Disasters

Natural disasters are the source of a wide range of environmental threats to datacenters, other information processing facilities, and their personnel. It is possible to assess the risk of various types of natural disasters and take suitable precautions so that catastrophic loss from natural disaster is prevented.

Table 4.1 lists six categories of natural disasters, the typical warning time for each event, whether or not personnel evacuation is indicated or possible, and the typical duration of each event. We comment briefly on the potential consequences of each type of disaster.

A tornado can generate winds that exceed hurricane strength in a narrow band along the tornado's path. There is substantial potential for structural damage, roof damage, and loss of outside equipment. There may be damage from wind and flying debris. Off site, a tornado may cause a temporary loss of local utility and communications. Offsite damage is typically followed by quick restoration of services. Tornado damage severity is measured by the Fujita Tornado Scale (see Table 4.2).

Hurricanes, tropical storms, and typhoons, collectively know as tropical cyclones, are among the most devastating naturally occurring hazards. Depending on strength, cyclones may also cause significant structural damage and damage to outside equipment at a particular site. Off site, there is the potential for severe regionwide damage to public infrastructure, utilities, and communications. If on-site operation must continue, then

TABLE 4.1　Characteristics of Natural Disasters.

	Warning	Evacuation	Duration
Tornado	Advance warning of potential; not site specific	Remain at site	Brief but intense
Hurricane	Significant advance warning	May require evacuation	Hours to a few days
Earthquake	No warning	May be unable to evacuate	Brief duration; threat of continued aftershocks
Ice storm/ blizzard	Several days warning generally expected	May be unable to evacuate	May last several days
Lightning	Sensors may provide minutes of warning	May require evacuation	Brief but may recur
Flood	Several days warning generally expected	May be unable to evacuate	Site may be isolated for extended period

Source: ComputerSite Engineering, Inc.

TABLE 4.2　Fujita Tornado Intensity Scale.

Category	Wind Speed Range	Description of Damage
F0	40–72 mph 64–116 km/hr	Light damage. Some damage to chimneys; tree branches broken off; shallow-rooted trees pushed over; sign boards damaged.
F1	73–112 mph 117–180 km/hr	Moderate damage. The lower limit is the beginning of hurricane wind speed; roof surfaces peeled off; mobile homes pushed off foundations or overturned; moving autos pushed off the roads.
F2	113–157 mph 181–252 km/hr	Considerable damage. roofs torn off houses; mobile homes demolished; boxcars pushed over; large trees snapped or uprooted; light-object missiles generated.
F3	158–206 mph 253–332 km/hr	Severe damage. Roofs and some walls torn off well-constructed houses; trains overturned; most trees in forest uprooted; heavy cars lifted off ground and thrown.
F4	207–260 mph 333–418 km/hr	Devastating damage. Well-constructed houses leveled; structure with weak foundation blown off some distance; cars thrown and large missiles generated.
F5	261–318 mph 419–512 km/hr	Incredible damage. Strong frame houses lifted off foundations and carried considerable distance to disintegrate; automobile-sized missiles fly through the air in excess of 100 yards; trees debarked.

emergency supplies for personnel as well as a backup generator are needed. Further, the responsible site manager may need to mobilize private poststorm security measures, such as armed guards.

Table 4.3 summarizes the widely used Saffir/Simpson Hurricane Scale. In general, damage rises by about a factor of four for every category increase.

TABLE 4.3 Saffir/Simpson Hurricane Scale.

Category	Wind Speed Range	Storm Surge	Potential Damage
1	74–95 mph 119–153 km/hr	4–5 ft 1–2 m	Minimal
2	96–110 mph 154–177 km/hr	6–8 ft 2–3 m	Moderate
3	111–130 mph 178–209 km/hr	9–12 ft 3–4 m	Extensive
4	131–155 mph 210–249 km/hr	13–18 ft 4–5 m	Extreme
5	155 mph >249 km/hr	>18 ft >5 m	Catastrophic

A major earthquake has the potential for the greatest damage and occurs without warning. A facility near the epicenter may suffer catastrophic, even complete, destruction, with significant and long-lasting damage to datacenters and other IS facilities. Examples of inside damage include the toppling of unbraced computer hardware and site infrastructure equipment, including the collapse of raised floors. Personnel are at risk from broken glass and other flying debris. Off site, near the epicenter of a major earthquake, the damage equals and often exceeds that of a major hurricane. Structures that can withstand a hurricane, such as roads and bridges, may be damaged or destroyed, preventing the movement of fuel and other supplies.

An ice storm or blizzard can cause some disruption of or damage to IS facilities if outside equipment and the building are not designed to survive severe ice and snow accumulation. Off site, there may be widespread disruption of utilities and communications and roads may be dangerous or impassable.

The consequences of lightning strikes can range from no impact to disaster. The effects depend on the proximity of the strike and the efficacy of grounding and surge protector measures in place. Off site, there can be disruption of electrical power and there is the potential for fires.

Flooding is a concern in areas that are subject to flooding and for facilities that are in severe flood areas at low elevation. Damage can be severe, with long-lasting effects and the need for a major cleanup operation.

Environmental Threats

This category encompasses conditions in the environment that can damage or interrupt the service of information systems and the data they house. Off site, there may be severe regionwide damage to the public infrastructure and, in the case of severe hurricanes, it may take days, weeks, or even years to recover from the event.

Inappropriate Temperature and Humidity

Computers and related equipment are designed to operate within a certain temperature range. Most computer systems should be kept between 10 and 32 degrees Celsius (50 and 90 degrees Fahrenheit). Outside this range, resources might continue to operate but produce undesirable results. If the ambient temperature around a computer gets too high, the computer cannot adequately cool itself, and internal components can be damaged. If the temperature gets too cold, the system can undergo thermal shock when it is turned on, causing circuit boards or integrated circuits to crack.

Another temperature-related concern is the internal temperature of equipment, which can be significantly higher than room temperature. Computer-related equipment comes with its own temperature dissipation and cooling mechanisms, but these may rely on, or be affected by, external conditions. Such conditions include excessive ambient temperature, interruption of supply of power or heating, ventilation, and air-conditioning (HVAC) services, and vent blockage.

High humidity also poses a threat to electrical and electronic equipment. Long-term exposure to high humidity can result in corrosion. Condensation can threaten magnetic and optical storage media. Condensation can also cause a short circuit, which in turn can damage circuit boards. High humidity can also cause a galvanic effect that results in electroplating, in which metal from one connector slowly migrates to the mating connector, bonding the two together.

Very low humidity can also be a concern. Under prolonged conditions of low humidity, some materials may change shape and performance may be affected. Static electricity also becomes a concern. A person or object that becomes statically charged can damage electronic equipment by an electric discharge. Static electricity discharges as low as 10 volts can damage particularly sensitive electronic circuits, and discharges in the hundreds of volts can create significant damage to a variety of electronic circuits. Discharges from humans can reach into the thousands of volts, so this is a nontrivial threat. In general, relative humidity should be maintained between 40% and 60% to avoid the threats from both low and high humidity.

Fire and Smoke

Perhaps the most frightening physical threat is fire. It is a threat to human life and property. The threat is not only from the direct flame but also from heat, release of toxic fumes, water damage from fire suppression, and smoke damage. Further, fire can disrupt utilities, especially electricity.

The temperature due to fire increases with time, and in a typical building, fire effects follow the curve shown in Figure 4.2. The scale on the right side of Figure 4.2 shows the temperature at which various items melt or are damaged and therefore indicates how long after the fire is started such damage occurs.

Smoke damage related to fires can also be extensive. Smoke is an abrasive. It collects on the heads of unsealed magnetic disks, optical disks, and tape drives. Electrical fires can produce an acrid smoke that may damage other equipment and may be poisonous or carcinogenic.

The most common fire threat is from fires that originate within a facility, and, as discussed subsequently, there are a number of preventive and mitigating measures that can

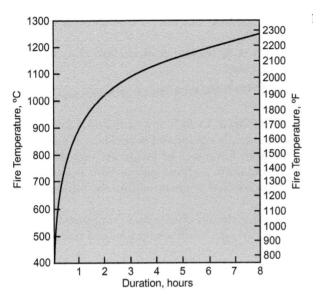

FIGURE 4.2 Fire effects.

be taken. A more uncontrollable threat is faced from wildfires, which are a plausible concern in the western United States, portions of Australia (where the term *bushfire* is used), and a number of other countries.

Water Damage

Water and other stored liquids in proximity to computer equipment pose an obvious threat. The primary danger is an electrical short, which can happen if water bridges between a circuit board trace carrying voltage and a trace carrying ground. Moving water, such as in plumbing, and weather-created water from rain, snow, and ice also pose threats. A pipe may burst from a fault in the line or from freezing. Sprinkler systems, despite their security function, are a major threat to computer equipment and paper and electronic storage media. The system may be set off by a faulty temperature sensor, or a burst pipe may cause water to enter the computer room. For a large computer installation, an effort should be made to avoid any sources of water from one or two floors above. An example of a hazard from this direction is an overflowing toilet.

Less common but more catastrophic is floodwater. Much of the damage comes from the suspended material in the water. Floodwater leaves a muddy residue that is extraordinarily difficult to clean up.

Chemical, Radiological, and Biological Hazards

Chemical, radiological, and biological hazards pose a growing threat, both from intentional attack and from accidental discharge. None of these hazardous agents should be present in an information system environment, but either accidental or intentional intrusion is possible. Nearby discharges (from an overturned truck carrying hazardous materials) can be introduced through the ventilation system or open windows and, in the case of radiation, through perimeter walls. In addition, discharges in the vicinity can disrupt work by causing evacuations to be ordered. Flooding can also introduce biological or chemical contaminants.

In general, the primary risk of these hazards is to personnel. Radiation and chemical agents can also cause damage to electronic equipment.

Dust

Dust is a prevalent concern that is often overlooked. Even fibers from fabric and paper are abrasive and mildly conductive, although generally equipment is resistant to such contaminants. Larger influxes of dust can result from a number of incidents, such as a controlled explosion of a nearby building and a windstorm carrying debris from a wildfire. A more likely source of influx comes from dust surges that originate within the building due to construction or maintenance work.

Equipment with moving parts, such as rotating storage media and computer fans, are the most vulnerable to damage from dust. Dust can also block ventilation and reduce radiational cooling.

Infestation

One of the less pleasant physical threats is infestation, which covers a broad range of living organisms, including mold, insects, and rodents. High-humidity conditions can lead to the growth of mold and mildew, which can be harmful to both personnel and equipment. Insects, particularly those that attack wood and paper, are also a common threat.

Technical Threats

This category encompasses threats related to electrical power and electromagnetic emission.

Electrical Power

Electrical power is essential to the operation of an information system. All the electrical and electronic devices in the system require power, and most require uninterrupted utility power. Power utility problems can be broadly grouped into three categories: undervoltage, overvoltage, and noise.

An *undervoltage* occurs when the IS equipment receives less voltage than is required for normal operation. Undervoltage events range from temporary dips in the voltage supply to brownouts (prolonged undervoltage) and power outages. Most computers are designed to withstand prolonged voltage reductions of about 20% without shutting down and without operational error. Deeper dips or blackouts lasting more than a few milliseconds trigger a system shutdown. Generally, no damage is done, but service is interrupted.

Far more serious is an *overvoltage*. A surge of voltage can be caused by a utility company supply anomaly, by some internal (to the building) wiring fault, or by lightning. Damage is a function of intensity and duration and the effectiveness of any surge protectors between your equipment and the source of the surge. A sufficient surge can destroy silicon-based components, including processors and memories.

Power lines can also be a conduit for *noise*. In many cases, these spurious signals can endure through the filtering circuitry of the power supply and interfere with signals inside electronic devices, causing logical errors.

Electromagnetic Interference

Noise along a power supply line is only one source of electromagnetic interference (EMI). Motors, fans, heavy equipment, and even other computers generate electrical noise that can cause intermittent problems with the computer you are using. This noise can be transmitted through space as well as nearby power lines.

Another source of EMI is high-intensity emissions from nearby commercial radio stations and microwave relay antennas. Even low-intensity devices, such as cellular telephones, can interfere with sensitive electronic equipment.

Human-Caused Physical Threats

Human-caused threats are more difficult to deal with than the environmental and technical threats discussed so far. Human-caused threats are less predictable than other types of physical threats. Worse, human-caused threats are specifically designed to overcome prevention measures and/or seek the most vulnerable point of attack. We can group such threats into the following categories:

- *Unauthorized physical access.* Those who are not employees should not be in the building or building complex at all unless accompanied by an authorized individual. Not counting PCs and workstations, information system assets, such as servers, mainframe computers, network equipment, and storage networks, are generally housed in restricted areas. Access to such areas is usually restricted to only a certain number of employees. Unauthorized physical access can lead to other threats, such as theft, vandalism, or misuse.
- *Theft.* This threat includes theft of equipment and theft of data by copying. Eavesdropping and wiretapping also fall into this category. Theft can be at the hands of an outsider who has gained unauthorized access or by an insider.
- *Vandalism.* This threat includes destruction of equipment and destruction of data.
- *Misuse.* This category includes improper use of resources by those who are authorized to use them, as well as use of resources by individuals not authorized to use the resources at all.

3. PHYSICAL SECURITY PREVENTION AND MITIGATION MEASURES

In this part of the chapter, we look at a range of techniques for preventing, or in some cases simply deterring, physical attacks. We begin with a survey of some of the techniques for dealing with environmental and technical threats and then move on to human-caused threats.

Environmental Threats

We discuss these threats in the same order.

Inappropriate Temperature and Humidity

Dealing with this problem is primarily a matter of having environmental-control equipment of appropriate capacity and appropriate sensors to warn of thresholds being exceeded. Beyond that, the principal requirement is the maintenance of a power supply, discussed subsequently.

Fire and Smoke

Dealing with fire involves a combination of alarms, preventive measures, and fire mitigation. Martin provides the following list of necessary measures[3]:

- Choice of site to minimize likelihood of disaster. Few disastrous fires originate in a well-protected computer room or IS facility. The IS area should be chosen to minimize fire, water, and smoke hazards from adjoining areas. Common walls with other activities should have at least a one-hour fire-protection rating.
- Air conditioning and other ducts designed so as not to spread fire. There are standard guidelines and specifications for such designs.
- Positioning of equipment to minimize damage.
- Good housekeeping. Records and flammables must not be stored in the IS area. Tidy installation of IS equipment is crucial.
- Hand-operated fire extinguishers readily available, clearly marked, and regularly tested.
- Automatic fire extinguishers installed. Installation should be such that the extinguishers are unlikely to cause damage to equipment or danger to personnel.
- Fire detectors. The detectors sound alarms inside the IS room and with external authorities, and start automatic fire extinguishers after a delay to permit human intervention.
- Equipment power-off switch. This switch must be clearly marked and unobstructed. All personnel must be familiar with power-off procedures.
- Emergency procedures posted.
- Personnel safety. Safety must be considered in designing the building layout and emergency procedures.
- Important records stored in fireproof cabinets or vaults.
- Records needed for file reconstruction stored off the premises.
- Up-to-date duplicate of all programs stored off the premises.
- Contingency plan for use of equipment elsewhere should the computers be destroyed.
- Insurance company and local fire department should inspect the facility.

3. J. Martin, *Security, Accuracy, and Privacy in Computer Systems*, Prentice Hall, 1973.

To deal with the threat of smoke, the responsible manager should install smoke detectors in every room that contains computer equipment as well as under raised floors and over suspended ceilings. Smoking should not be permitted in computer rooms.

For wildfires, the available countermeasures are limited. Fire-resistant building techniques are costly and difficult to justify.

Water Damage

Prevention and mitigation measures for water threats must encompass the range of such threats. For plumbing leaks, the cost of relocating threatening lines is generally difficult to justify. With knowledge of the exact layout of water supply lines, measures can be taken to locate equipment sensibly. The location of all shutoff valves should be clearly visible or at least clearly documented, and responsible personnel should know the procedures to follow in case of emergency.

To deal with both plumbing leaks and other sources of water, sensors are vital. Water sensors should be located on the floor of computer rooms as well as under raised floors and should cut off power automatically in the event of a flood.

Other Environmental Threats

For chemical, biological, and radiological threats, specific technical approaches are available, including infrastructure design, sensor design and placement, mitigation procedures, personnel training, and so forth. Standards and techniques in these areas continue to evolve.

As for dust hazards, the obvious prevention method is to limit dust through the use and proper filter maintenance and regular IS room maintenance. For infestations, regular pest control procedures may be needed, starting with maintaining a clean environment.

Technical Threats

To deal with brief power interruptions, an uninterruptible power supply (UPS) should be employed for each piece of critical equipment. The UPS is a battery backup unit that can maintain power to processors, monitors, and other equipment for a period of minutes. UPS units can also function as surge protectors, power noise filters, and automatic shutdown devices when the battery runs low.

For longer blackouts or brownouts, critical equipment should be connected to an emergency power source, such as a generator. For reliable service, a range of issues need to be addressed by management, including product selection, generator placement, personnel training, testing and maintenance schedules, and so forth.

To deal with electromagnetic interference, a combination of filters and shielding can be used. The specific technical details will depend on the infrastructure design and the anticipated sources and nature of the interference.

Human-Caused Physical Threats

The general approach to human-caused physical threats is physical access control. Based on Michael,[4] we can suggest a spectrum of approaches that can be used to restrict access to equipment. These methods can be used in combination:

- Physical contact with a resource is restricted by restricting access to the building in which the resource is housed. This approach is intended to deny access to outsiders but does not address the issue of unauthorized insiders or employees.
- Physical contact with a resource is restricted by putting the resource in a locked cabinet, safe, or room.
- A machine may be accessed, but it is secured (perhaps permanently bolted) to an object that is difficult to move. This will deter theft but not vandalism, unauthorized access, or misuse.
- A security device controls the power switch.
- A movable resource is equipped with a tracking device so that a sensing portal can alert security personnel or trigger an automated barrier to prevent the object from being moved out of its proper security area.
- A portable object is equipped with a tracking device so that its current position can be monitored continually.

The first two of the preceding approaches isolate the equipment. Techniques that can be used for this type of access control include controlled areas patrolled or guarded by personnel, barriers that isolate each area, entry points in the barrier (doors), and locks or screening measures at each entry point. Physical access control should address not just computers and other IS equipment but also locations of wiring used to connect systems, the electrical power service, the HVAC equipment and distribution system, telephone and communications lines, backup media, and documents.

In addition to physical and procedural barriers, an effective physical access control regime includes a variety of sensors and alarms to detect intruders and unauthorized access or movement of equipment. Surveillance systems are frequently an integral part of building security, and special-purpose surveillance systems for the IS area are generally also warranted. Such systems should provide real-time remote viewing as well as recording.

4. RECOVERY FROM PHYSICAL SECURITY BREACHES

The most essential element of recovery from physical security breaches is redundancy. Redundancy does not undo any breaches of confidentiality, such as the theft of data or documents, but it does provide for recovery from loss of data. Ideally, all the important data in the system should be available off site and updated as near to real time as is warranted based on a cost/benefit tradeoff. With broadband connections now almost

4. M. Michael, "Physical security measures," In H. Bidgoli, (ed.), *Handbook of Information Security*, Wiley, 2006.

universally available, batch encrypted backups over private networks or the Internet are warranted and can be carried out on whatever schedule is deemed appropriate by management. At the extreme, a *hotsite* can be created off site that is ready to take over operation instantly and has available to it a near-real-time copy of operational data.

Recovery from physical damage to the equipment or the site depends on the nature of the damage and, importantly, the nature of the residue. Water, smoke, and fire damage may leave behind hazardous materials that must be meticulously removed from the site before normal operations and the normal equipment suite can be reconstituted. In many cases, this requires bringing in disaster recovery specialists from outside the organization to do the cleanup.

5. THREAT ASSESSMENT, PLANNING, AND PLAN IMPLEMENTATION

We have surveyed a number of threats to physical security and a number of approaches to prevention, mitigation, and recovery. To implement a physical security program, an organization must conduct a threat assessment to determine the amount of resources to devote to physical security and the allocation of those resources against the various threats. This process also applies to logical security.

Threat Assessment

In this part of the chapter, we follow Platt[5] in outlining a typical sequence of steps that an organization should take:

1. *Set up a steering committee.* The threat assessment should not be left only to a security officer or to IS management. All those who have a stake in the security of the IS assets, including all of the user communities, should be brought into the process.
2. *Obtain information and assistance.* Historical information concerning external threats, such as flood and fire is the best starting point. This information can often be obtained from government agencies and weather bureaus. In the United States, the Federal Emergency Management Agency (FEMA) can provide much useful information. FEMA has a number of publications available online that provide specific guidance in a wide variety of physical security areas (www.fema.gov/business/index.shtm). The committee should also seek expert advice from vendors, suppliers, neighboring businesses, service and maintenance personnel, consultants, and academics.
3. *Identify all possible threats.* List all possible threats, including those that are specific to IS operations as well as those that are more general, covering the building and the geographic area.

5. F. Platt, "Physical threats to the information infrastructure," in S. Bosworth, and M. Kabay, (eds.), *Computer Security Handbook*, Wiley, 2002.

4. *Determine the likelihood of each threat.* This is clearly a difficult task. One approach is to use a scale of 1 (least likely) to 5 (most likely) so that threats can be grouped to suggest where attention should be directed. All the information from Step 2 can be applied to this task.

5. *Approximate the direct costs.* For each threat, the committee must estimate not only the threat's likelihood but also its severity in terms of consequences. Again a relative scale of 1 (low) to 5 (high) in terms of costs and losses is a reasonable approach. For both Steps 4 and 5, an attempt to use a finer-grained scale, or to assign specific probabilities and specific costs, is likely to produce the impression of greater precision and knowledge about future threats than is possible.

6. *Consider cascading costs.* Some threats can trigger consequential threats that add still more impact costs. For example, a fire can cause direct flame, heat, and smoke damage as well as disrupt utilities and result in water damage.

7. *Prioritize the threats.* The goal here is to determine the relative importance of the threats as a guide to focusing resources on prevention. A simple formula yields a prioritized list:

$$\text{Importance} = \text{Likelihood} \times [\text{Direct Cost} + \text{Secondary Cost}]$$

where the scale values (1 through 5) are used in the formula.

8. *Complete the threat assessment report.* The committee can now prepare a report that includes the prioritized list, with commentary on how the results were achieved. This report serves as the reference source for the planning process that follows.

Planning and Implementation

Once a threat assessment has been done, the steering committee, or another committee, can develop a plan for threat prevention, mitigation, and recovery. The following is a typical sequence of steps an organization could take:

1. *Assess internal and external resources.* These include resources for prevention as well as response. A reasonable approach is again to use a relative scale from 1 (strong ability to prevent and respond) to 5 (weak ability to prevent and respond). This scale can be combined with the threat priority score to focus resource planning.

2. *Identify challenges and prioritize activities.* Determine specific goals and milestones. Make a list of tasks to be performed, by whom and when. Determine how you will address the problem areas and resource shortfalls that were identified in the vulnerability analysis.

3. *Develop a plan.* The plan should include prevention measures and equipment needed and emergency response procedures. The plan should include support documents, such as emergency call lists, building and site maps, and resource lists.

4. *Implement the plan.* Implementation includes acquiring new equipment, assigning responsibilities, conducting training, monitoring plan implementation, and updating the plan regularly.

6. EXAMPLE: A CORPORATE PHYSICAL SECURITY POLICY

To give the reader a feel for how organizations deal with physical security, we provide a real-world example of a physical security policy. The company is a European Union (EU)-based engineering consulting firm that specializes in the provision of planning, design, and management services for infrastructure development worldwide. With interests in transportation, water, maritime, and property, the company is undertaking commissions in over 70 countries from a network of more than 70 offices.

Figure 4.3 is extracted from the company's security standards document. For our purposes, we have changed the name of the company to *Company* wherever it appears in the document. The company's physical security policy relies heavily on ISO 17799 (*Code of Practice for Information Security Management*).

7. INTEGRATION OF PHYSICAL AND LOGICAL SECURITY

Physical security involves numerous detection devices, such as sensors and alarms, and numerous prevention devices and measures, such as locks and physical barriers. It should be clear that there is much scope for automation and for the integration of various computerized and electronic devices. Clearly, physical security can be made more effective if there is a central destination for all alerts and alarms and if there is central control of all automated access control mechanisms, such as smart card entry sites.

From the point of view of both effectiveness and cost, there is increasing interest not only in integrating automated physical security functions but in integrating, to the extent possible, automated physical security and logical security functions. The most promising area is that of access control. Examples of ways to integrate physical and logical access control include the following:

- Use of a single ID card for physical and logical access. This can be a simple magnetic-strip card or a smart card.
- Single-step user/card enrollment and termination across all identity and access control databases.
- A central ID-management system instead of multiple disparate user directories and databases.
- Unified event monitoring and correlation.

As an example of the utility of this integration, suppose that an alert indicates that Bob has logged on to the company's wireless network (an event generated by the logical access control system) but did not enter the building (an event generated from the physical access control system). Combined, these two events suggest that someone is hijacking Bob's wireless account.

For the integration of physical and logical access control to be practical, a wide range of vendors must conform to standards that cover smart card protocols, authentication and access control formats and protocols, database entries, message formats, and so on. An

5. Physical and Environmental security

5.1. *Secure Areas*

    5.1.1. *Physical Security Perimeter* - Company shall use security perimeters to protect all non-public areas, commensurate with the value of the assets therein. Business critical information processing facilities located in unattended buildings shall also be alarmed to a permanently manned remote alarm monitoring station.

    5.1.2. *Physical Entry Controls* - Secure areas shall be segregated and protected by appropriate entry controls to ensure that only authorised personnel are allowed access. Similar controls are also required where the building is shared with, or accessed by, non-Company staff and organisations not acting on behalf of Company.

    5.1.3. *Securing Offices, Rooms and Facilities* - Secure areas shall be created in order to protect office, rooms and facilities with special security requirements.

    5.1.4. *Working in Secure Areas* - Additional controls and guidelines for working in secure areas shall be used to enhance the security provided by the physical control protecting the secure areas.

        Employees of Company should be aware that additional controls and guidelines for working in secure areas to enhance the security provided by the physical control protecting the secure areas might be in force. For further clarification they should contact their Line Manager.

    5.1.5. *Isolated Access Points* - Isolated access points, additional to building main entrances (e.g. Delivery and Loading areas) shall be controlled and, if possible, isolated from secure areas to avoid unauthorised access.

    5.1.6. *Sign Posting Of Computer Installations* - Business critical computer installations sited within a building must not be identified by the use of descriptive sign posts or other displays. Where such sign posts or other displays are used they must be worded in such a way so as not to highlight the business critical nature of the activity taking place within the building.

5.2. *Equipment Security*

    5.2.1. *Equipment Sitting and Protection* - Equipment shall be sited or protected to reduce the risk from environmental threats and hazards, and opportunity for unauthorised access.

    5.2.2. *Power Supply* - The equipment shall be protected from power failure and other electrical anomalies.

    5.2.3. *Cabling Security* - Power and telecommunication cabling carrying data or supporting information services shall be protected from interception or damage commensurate with the business criticality of the operations they serve.

    5.2.4. *Equipment Maintenance* - Equipment shall be maintained in accordance with manufacturer's instruction and/or documented procedures to ensure its continued availability and integrity.

    5.2.5. *Security of Equipment off-premises* - Security procedures and controls shall be used to secure equipment used outside any Company's premises

        Employees are to note that there should be security procedures and controls to secure equipment used outside any Company premises. Advice on these procedures can be sought from the Group Security Manager.

    5.2.6. *Secure Disposal or Re-use of Equipment* - Information shall be erased from equipment prior to disposal or reuse.

        For further guidance contact the Group Security Manager.

    5.2.7. *Security of the Access Network* - Company shall implement access control measures, determined by a risk assessment, to ensure that only authorised people have access to the Access Network (including: cabinets, cabling, nodes etc.).

FIGURE 4.3   The Company's physical security policy.

5.2.8. *Security of PCs* - Every Company owned PC must have an owner who is responsible for its general management and control. Users of PCs are personally responsible for the physical and logical security of any PC they use. Users of Company PCs are personally responsible for the physical and logical security of any PC they use, as defined within the Staff Handbook.

5.2.9. *Removal of "Captured Data"* - Where any device (software or hardware based) has been introduced to the network that captures data for analytical purposes, all data must be wiped off of this device prior to removal from the Company Site. The removal of this data from site for analysis can only be approved by the MIS Technology Manager.

5.3. *General Controls*

5.3.1. *Security Controls* - Security Settings are to be utilised and configurations must be controlled

> *No security settings or software on Company systems are to be changed without authorisation from MIS Support*

5.3.2. *Clear Screen Policy* - Company shall have and implement clear-screen policy in order to reduce the risks of unauthorised access, loss of, and damage to information.

> *This will be implemented when all Users of the Company system have Windows XP operating system.*
>
> *When the User has the Windows XP system they are to carry out the following:*
>
> - *Select the Settings tab within the START area on the desktop screen.*
> - *Select Control Panel.*
> - *Select the icon called DISPLAY.*
> - *Select the Screensaver Tab.*
> - *Set a Screen saver.*
> - *Set the time for 15 Mins.*
> - *Tick the Password Protect box; remember this is the same password that you utilise to log on to the system.*
>
> *Staff are to lock their screens using the Ctrl-Alt-Del when they leave their desk*

5.3.3. *Clear Desk Policy* – Staff shall ensure that they operate a Clear Desk Policy

> *Each member of staff is asked to take personal and active responsibility for maintaining a "clear desk" policy whereby files and papers are filed or otherwise cleared away before leaving the office at the end of each day*

5.3.4. *Removal of Property* - Equipment, information or software belonging to the organisation shall not be removed without authorisation.

> *Equipment, information or software belonging to Company shall not be removed without authorisation from the Project Manager or Line Manager and the MIS Support.*

5.3.5. *People Identification* - All Company staff must have visible the appropriate identification whenever they are in Company premises.

5.3.6. *Visitors* - All Company premises will have a process for dealing with visitors. All Visitors must be sponsored and wear the appropriate identification whenever they are in Company premises.

5.3.7. *Legal Right of Entry* - Entry must be permitted to official bodies when entry is demanded on production of a court order or when the person has other legal rights. Advice must be sought from management or the Group Security Manager as a matter of urgency.

FIGURE 4.3   (Continued)

important step in this direction is FIPS 201-2 *(Personal Identity Verification (PIV) of Federal Employees and Contractors)*, issued in 2011. The standard defines a reliable, government-wide PIV system for use in applications such as access to federally controlled facilities and information systems. The standard specifies a PIV system within which common identification credentials can be created and later used to verify a claimed identity. The standard also identifies federal governmentwide requirements for security levels that are dependent on risks to the facility or information being protected. The standard applies to private-sector contractors as well, and serves as a useful guideline for any organization.

Figure 4.4 illustrates the major components of FIPS 201-2 compliant systems. The PIV front end defines the physical interface to a user who is requesting access to a facility, which could be either physical access to a protected physical area or logical access to an information system. The PIV front-end subsystem supports up to three-factor authentication; the number of factors used depends on the level of security required. The front end makes use of a smart card, known as a *PIV card*, which is a dual-interface contact and contactless card. The card holds a cardholder photograph, X.509 certificates, cryptographic keys, biometric data, and the cardholder unique identifier (CHUID). Certain cardholder information may be read-protected and require a personal identification number (PIN) for read access by the card reader. The biometric reader, in the current version of the standard, is a fingerprint reader.

The standard defines three assurance levels for verification of the card and the encoded data stored on the card, which in turn leads to verifying the authenticity of the person holding the credential. A level of *some confidence* corresponds to use of the card reader and PIN. A level of *high confidence* adds a biometric comparison of a fingerprint captured and encoded on the card during the card-issuing process and a fingerprint scanned at the physical access point. A *very high confidence* level requires that the process just described is completed at a control point attended by an official observer.

The other major component of the PIV system is the *PIV card issuance and management subsystem.* This subsystem includes the components responsible for identity proofing and registration, card and key issuance and management, and the various repositories and services (public key infrastructure [PKI] directory, certificate status servers) required as part of the verification infrastructure.

The PIV system interacts with an *access control subsystem*, which includes components responsible for determining a particular PIV cardholder's access to a physical or logical resource. FIPS 201-1 standardizes data formats and protocols for interaction between the PIV system and the access control system.

Unlike the typical card number/facility code encoded on most access control cards, the FIPS 201 CHUID takes authentication to a new level, through the use of an expiration date (a required CHUID data field) and an optional CHUID digital signature. A digital signature can be checked to ensure that the CHUID recorded on the card was digitally signed by a trusted source and that the CHUID data have not been altered since the card was signed. The CHUID expiration date can be checked to verify that the card has not expired. This is independent of whatever expiration date is associated with cardholder privileges. Reading and verifying the CHUID alone provides only some assurance of identity because it authenticates the card data, not the cardholder. The PIN and biometric factors provide identity verification of the individual.

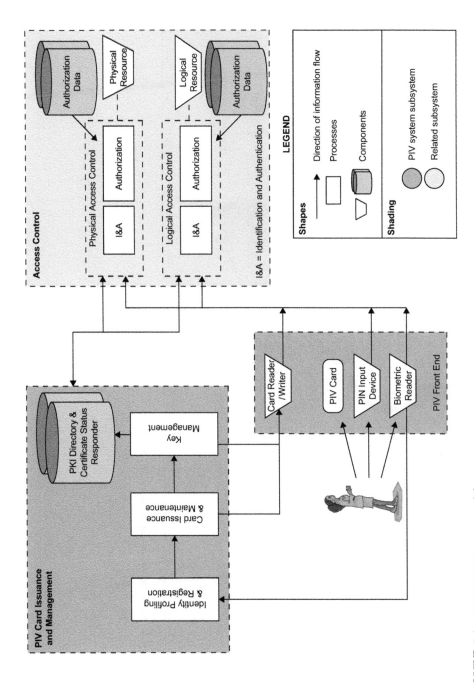

FIGURE 4.4 FIPS 201 PIV system model.

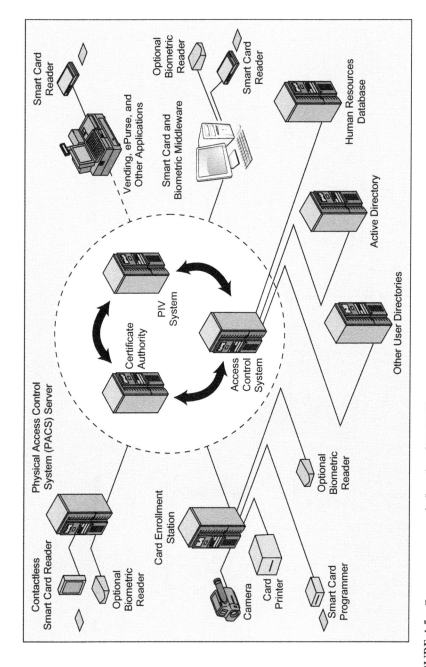

FIGURE 4.5 Convergence example (based on [FORR06]).

Figure 4.5, adapted from Forristal,[6] illustrates the convergence of physical and logical access control using FIPS 201-2. The core of the system includes the PIV and access control system as well as a certificate authority for signing CHUIDs. The other elements of Figure 4.5 provide examples of the use of the system core for integrating physical and logical access control.

If the integration of physical and logical access control extends beyond a unified front end to an integration of system elements, a number of benefits accrue, including the following[7]:

- Employees gain a single, unified access control authentication device; this cuts down on misplaced tokens, reduces training and overhead, and allows seamless access.
- A single logical location for employee ID management reduces duplicate data entry operations and allows for immediate and real-time authorization revocation of all enterprise resources.
- Auditing and forensic groups have a central repository for access control investigations.
- Hardware unification can reduce the number of vendor purchase-and-support contracts.
- Certificate-based access control systems can leverage user ID certificates for other security applications, such as document esigning and data encryption.

Finally, let's briefly look at a physical security checklist. The effectiveness of the recommendations in the physical security checklist is most useful when initiated as part of a larger plan to develop and implement security policy throughout an organization.

8. PHYSICAL SECURITY CHECKLIST

While it may be tempting to simply refer to the following checklist as your security plan, to do so would limit the effectiveness of the recommendations. Some recommendations and considerations are included the following checklist: "An Agenda For Action For Physical Security").

AN AGENDA FOR ACTION FOR PHYSICAL SECURITY

The brevity of a checklist can be helpful, but it in no way makes up for the detail of the text. Thus, the following set of Check Points for Physical Security must be adhered to (check all tasks completed):

---

6. J. Forristal, "Physical/logical convergence," *Network Computing*, November 23, 2006.

7. J. Forristal, "Physical/logical convergence," *Network Computing*, November 23, 2006.

Create a Secure Environment: Building and Room Construction:

_____1. Does each secure room or facility have low visibility (no unnecessary signs)?

_____2. Has the room or facility been constructed with full-height walls?

_____3. Has the room or facility been constructed with a fireproof ceiling?

_____4. Are there two or fewer doorways?

_____5. Are doors solid and fireproof?

_____6. Are doors equipped with locks?

_____7. Are window openings to secure areas kept as small as possible?

_____8. Are windows equipped with locks?

_____9. Are keys and combinations to door and window locks secured responsibly?

_____10. Have alternatives to traditional lock and key security measures (bars, anti-theft cabling, magnetic key cards, and motion detectors) been considered?

_____11. Have both automatic and manual fire equipment been properly installed?

_____12. Are personnel properly trained for fire emergencies?

_____13. Are acceptable room temperatures always maintained (between 50 and 80 degrees Fahrenheit)?

_____14. Are acceptable humidity ranges always maintained (between 20 and 80 percent)?

_____15. Are eating, drinking, and smoking regulations in place and enforced?

_____16. Has all non-essential, potentially flammable, material (curtains and stacks of computer paper) been removed from secure areas?

Guard Equipment:

_____17. Has equipment been identified as critical or general use, and segregated appropriately?

_____18. Is equipment housed out of sight and reach from doors and windows, and away from radiators, heating vents, air conditioners, and other duct work?

_____19. Are plugs, cabling, and other wires protected from foot traffic?

_____20. Are up-to-date records of all equipment brand names, model names, and serial numbers kept in a secure location?

_____21. Have qualified technicians (staff or vendors) been identified to repair critical equipment if and when it fails?

_____22. Has contact information for repair technicians (telephone numbers, customer numbers, maintenance contract numbers) been stored in a secure but accessible place?

_____23. Are repair workers and outside technicians required to adhere to the organization's security policies concerning sensitive information?

Rebuff Theft:

_____24. Has all equipment been labeled in an overt way that clearly and permanently identifies its owner (the school name)?

_____25. Has all equipment been labeled in a covert way that only authorized staff would know to look for (inside the cover)?

_____26. Have steps been taken to make it difficult for unauthorized people

_____27. to tamper with equipment (by replacing case screws with Allen-type screws)?

_____27. Have security staff been provided up-to-date lists of personnel and their respective access authority?

_____28. Are security staff required to verify identification of unknown people before permitting access to facilities?

_____29. Are security staff required to maintain a log of all equipment taken in and out of secure areas?

Attend to Portable Equipment and Computers:

_____30. Do users know not to leave laptops and other portable equipment unattended outside of the office?

_____31. Do users know and follow proper transportation and storage procedures for laptops and other portable equipment?

Regulate Power Supplies:

_____32. Are surge protectors used with all equipment?

_____33. Are Uninterruptible Power Supplies (UPSs) in place for critical systems?

_____34. Have power supplies been "insulated" from environmental threats by a professional electrician?

_____35. Has consideration been given to the use of electrical outlets so as to avoid overloading?

_____36. Are the negative effects of static electricity minimized through the use of anti-static carpeting, pads, and sprays as necessary?

Protect Output:

_____37. Are photocopiers, fax machines, and scanners kept in open view?

_____38. Are printers assigned to users with similar security clearances?

_____39. Is every printed copy of confidential information labeled as "confidential"?

_____40. Are outside delivery services required to adhere to security practices when transporting sensitive information?

_____41. Are all paper copies of sensitive information shredded before being discarded?

9. SUMMARY

Physical security requires that building site(s) be safeguarded in a way that minimizes the risk of resource theft and destruction. To accomplish this, decision-makers must be concerned about building construction, room assignments, emergency procedures, regulations governing equipment placement and use, power supplies, product handling, and relationships with outside contractors and agencies.

The physical plant must be satisfactorily secured to prevent those people who are not authorized to enter the site and use equipment from doing so. A building does not need to feel like a fort to be safe. Well-conceived plans to secure a building can be initiated without adding undue burden on your staff. After all, if they require access, they will receive it—as long as they were aware of, and abide by, the organization's stated security policies and guidelines. The only way to ensure this is to demand that before any person is given access to your system, they have first signed and returned a valid Security Agreement. This necessary security policy is too important to permit exceptions.

Finally, let's move on to the real interactive part of this Chapter: review questions/exercises, hands-on projects, case projects and optional team case project. The answers and/or solutions by chapter can be found in the Online Instructor's Solutions Manual.

CHAPTER REVIEW QUESTIONS/EXERCISES

True/False

1. True or False? Information system hardware includes data processing and storage equipment, transmission and networking facilities, and online storage media.
2. True or False? Physical facility includes the buildings and other structures housing the system and network components.
3. True or False? Supporting facilities under scores the operation of the information system.
4. True or False? Personnel are humans involved in the control, maintenance, and use of the information systems.
5. True or False? It is possible to assess the risk of various types of natural disasters and take suitable precautions so that catastrophic loss from natural disaster is achieved.

Multiple Choice

1. What are the three elements of information system (IS) security?
    A. Logical security
    B. Physical security
    C. Maritime security
    D. Premises security
    E. Wireless security
2. In broad terms, which of the following is not included in the critical infrastructure?
    A. Environmental threats
    B. Information system hardware
    C. Physical facility
    D. Supporting facilities
    E. Personnel
3. Which of the following are threats?
    A. Environmental
    B. Natural
    C. Technical
    D. Access
    E. Human-caused

4. Which of the following is not a human-caused threat?
   A. Unauthorized physical access
   B. Theft
   C. Vandalism
   D. Decryption
   E. Misuse
5. Dealing with fire involves a combination of alarms, preventive measures, and fire mitigation. Which of the following is not a necessary measure?
   A. Choice of site to minimize likelihood of disaster
   B. Positioning of equipment to minimize damage
   C. Good housekeeping
   D. Fire detectors
   E. Physical contact

EXERCISE

Problem

A company's physical security team analyzed physical security threats and vulnerabilities for their systems. What type of vulnerabilities did the company focus on?

Hands-On Projects

Project

An engineering company operating within a highly regulated industry, in which privacy and compliance are of paramount importance, wanted to compare itself relative to its peers in physical security provision and establish a baseline from which to quantify improvement. Please identify the best practices; compare organizational and outsourcing models; compare security technologies utilized; and, calibrate investment in physical security against its peers.

Case Projects

Problem

This case study illustrates how a company uses intelligent video processing (a subsystem of its video surveillance system) to detect intrusions at land ports of entry. Virtual fences are integrated into each facility to compliment both the facility's perimeter physical security system (composed of a combination of fences, gates, and barriers) and the video surveillance system. What should happen if these virtual fences are breached?

Optional Team Case Project

Problem

A company wants to further develop its access control system (ACS) use of video, proximity-based ID cards, biometrics, RFID, VoIP, and remotely controlled gates for manned and unmanned access control. What does the company need to do to further develop its ACS?

Disaster Recovery

Scott R. Ellis and Lauren Collins
kCura Corporation

1. INTRODUCTION

In almost every organization, when a technology-oriented task is at hand, and where no one knows who would handle the request, it typically lands in the information technology department (IT). Whether the task consists of a special, faulty light bulb or a backup for a grease stop in the kitchen sink, organizations rely heavily on the IT department to know the unknown, and to fix anything that breaks.

Disaster recovery (DR), not unlike the plugged sink, is another task that many organizations fail to consider until after much of the technology groundwork has been laid, the corporation is profitable, and suddenly someone realizes that *not* having a DR site is a serious risk to the business. It is at this time that they begin to consider, and they begin to ponder, what a strategy might look like that enables the business to continue to run in the event of Force Majeure or some other disaster, such as if a hacker came in and tore their system down, or somehow seized control of it.

Hardware, physical or virtual, must be acquired and configured to capture the environment as it currently sits—and it must be able to continue with its synchronization. Whether this is by the minute, the hour, the day, or the week is a business decision. In fact, much of the DR strategy is driven by business continuity requirements. In the event of a disaster, there must be a plan in place that considers which individuals will act in the event of a disaster. Those individuals must know what constitutes a disaster, and the roles must be defined for those individuals.

2. MEASURING RISK AND AVOIDING DISASTER

A key component of a disaster recovery (DR) plan is for the committee to assess conceivable risks to the organization that could result in the disasters or emergency situations

Cyber Security and IT Infrastructure Protection
DOI: http://dx.doi.org/10.1016/B978-0-12-416681-3.00005-7

themselves. All events must be considered, and the impact must also be reflected upon so that the organization has the ability to continue and deliver business as usual. Quantitative and qualitative risks are considered separately in a DR plan; however, both come together when determining how an organizations reputation and earnings should be managed in the event of a disaster. Risk is assessed on an inherent and residual basis, allowing an entity to understand the extent to which potential events might impact objectives from two perspectives, likelihood and impact.

Assessing Risk in the Enterprise

Enterprise Risk Management (ERM) is not a template that can be given to every company to meet their needs and fit their business structure. Proper risk assessment identifies the risks throughout the organization and specifies the external and internal sources that the organization may face. The organization engages members from each organizational unit (Executives, HR, Finance, etc.), and asks questions such as "What do you perceive to be the largest risks to the company in terms of significance and likelihood?" and "What do you perceive to be the biggest risks within your control?" After a common understanding is met and all are aware of the risks, such risk assessments should be linked to strategic objectives as shown in Figure 5.1.

Once the company has an understanding of the top risks that can impact the organization, the executive team determines the company's risk appetite and risk tolerance. Risk appetite is the amount of risk, on a comprehensive level, that an entity is willing to accept

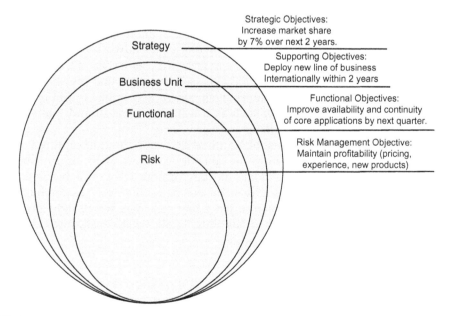

FIGURE 5.1 Risk assessments are linked to strategic objectives in an organization as a whole to allow a company to understand the risks in the organization, the company's risk appetite, and risk tolerance.

in pursuit of value. Risk tolerance, on the other hand, is the range of acceptable variation around the company's objectives. The key is to determine the degree of maturity that meets the needs of your organization.

Steps in the Risk Process

There are five steps to consider for a company to come out ahead when a disaster hits to avoid risk and protect your data. The following checklist (see checklist: An Agenda for Action for Risk Assessment) is a list of these steps, from assessment to planning, architecting, specifying and implementing a full-bodied disaster recovery (DR) solution.

AN AGENDA FOR ACTION FOR RISK ASSESSMENT

Steps in Risk Assessment (check all tasks completed):

_____**1.** Discover the potential threats:

    _____**a.** Environmental (tornado, hurricane, flood, earthquake, fire, landslide, epidemic).

    _____**b.** Organized or deliberate disruption (terrorism, war, arson).

    _____**c.** Loss of utilities or services (electrical power failure, petroleum shortage, communications services breakdown).

    _____**d.** Equipment or system failure (internal power failure, air conditioning failure, production line failure, equipment failure).

    _____**e.** Security threat (leak of sensitive information, loss of records or data, cyber-crime).

    _____**f.** Supplementary emergency situations (workplace violence, public transportation disruption, health and safety hazard).

_____**2.** Determine requirements:

    _____**a.** Prioritize processes

    _____**b.** Determine recovery objectives

    _____**c.** Plan for common incidents

    _____**d.** Communicate the plan

    _____**e.** Choose individuals who will test plan regularly and act in the event of a disaster

_____**3.** Understand DR options:

    _____**a.** Determine how far to get the data out of the data center.

    _____**b.** Will the data center be accessible at the same time as the disaster.

    _____**c.** Determine the process to backup and/or replicate data off-site.

    _____**d.** Determine the process to recreate an environment off-site.

_____**4.** Audit providers:

    _____**a.** Compare list of providers with internal list of requirements.

    _____**b.** Understand range of data protection solutions offered

---

_____c. Assess proximity (power grid/communications and contingencies).

_____d. Data center hardening features and their DR contingencies.

_____5. Record findings, implement/test, and revise if/as necessary:

_____a. Documentation is the heart of your plan.

_____b. Test and adjust plan as necessary, record findings.

_____c. As the environment changes and business needs change, revise the plan and test again.

Downtime presents serious consequences for businesses, no matter what their function may be. It is difficult, if not impossible, to recoup lost revenue and rebuild a corporate reputation that is damaged by an outage. While professionals cannot expect to avoid every downtime event, the majority of system downtime is caused by preventable failures. Distinguishing between planned and unplanned system downtime allocates different procedures as both present vastly diverse paths when bringing systems back up.

While both planned and unplanned downtime can be stressful, planned downtime must be finished on time. Unplanned is the worst. Unplanned can be good for teaching troubleshooting techniques to junior IT staff, but can be very frustrating to the workforce. The authors see fewer and fewer techs with troubleshooting experience, and more and more senior techs launching their own consultancies. The biggest cost is how it affects the customers and the impressions of the company that a severe outage can make on the organization's customers and clients. Planning, having people on staff with good troubleshooting skills, and documenting how the issue was found and fixed will help resolve the issue faster next time.

Matching the Response to the Threat

Separate each of your significant processes into one of three categories: Mission Critical, Business Critical or Organizationally Critical. By classifying processes into categories, you are able to define which parts of the organization would be recovered first in the event of an outage or disaster. How long can your organization or group live without access to a particular system? Should this system fail, how much data can the business realistically handle losing? Define, succinctly, what the organization considers a disastrously disruptive event and set the maximum amount of time you can go without access to your system. Then set the acceptable amount of data loss from the most recent backup, or replication. Repeat this step for each system and you will soon realize which systems have the highest priorities and highest impact. Look back in history and identify types of outages the firm has experienced and how those outages were dealt with. If one is more relevant than another, plan for that incident first.

3. THE BUSINESS IMPACT ASSESSMENT (BIA)

A business impact assessment is a solution that determines critical business processes based on their impact during a disruption. An organization must define resilience requirements, justify business continuity investments, and identify a robust risk mitigation strategy. Unplanned disruptions can be costly, resulting in major losses, customer dissatisfaction, and compliance issues. To counter such risks, developing an effective, end-to-end business resilience plan is a necessary component to business continuity and recovery solutions.

Identifying Business-Critical Activities

An organization must have a thorough understanding of the critical business processes and the tolerance of a business outage to define objectives to succeed in the event of an outage. A successful solution employs a vertical and horizontal, or top/down approach to understand, identify, and map critical business processes, functions, IT systems, resource dependencies, and delivery channels. The organization must analyze the cost of disruptions and place them into resilience tiers to assist in defining operational availability and disaster recovery requirements from a business perspective.

Additionally, Recovery Point Objectives (RPOs) and Recovery Time Objectives (RTOs) are perhaps the most important key metrics when architecting a disaster recovery solution. An RTO is the amount of time it takes to recover from a disaster event, and an RPO is the amount of data, measured in time, that your organization lost from that same event. The two business-driven metrics will set the stage for:

- Media chosen to recover (disk, tape, etc.)
- Location where data is being recovered
- Size of the recovery infrastructure and staff needed

Keep in mind that there are several intricacies to consider when assessing RTOs and RPOs. First, the objective in both stands for "objective" and should be defined as the target. If an RPO is five hours, then the architecture must ensure data loss of five hours or less. Therefore, when testing or recovering from a disaster, document and track actual thresholds achieved, including recovery point and recovery time. In many test cases, the time to recover does not meet the objective due to overhead time. Examples of overhead time are as follows:

- Selection of staff and determination in DR teams
- Declaration of the disaster and logistics to the recovery site
- Consideration of massive chaos is involved in initiating a recovery from a disaster event

When tracking and documenting actual versus objective, especially during testing, you will understand what is being accomplished in a given period of time. Figure 5.2 illustrates a flowchart of conflict resolution in the BIA and shows how time can be calculated when following the flow of the dependencies. Ultimately, this will allow a firm to defend future investment by honing your recovery methodologies and processes to better meet or exceed those objectives. Once the recovered data is made available and back to the

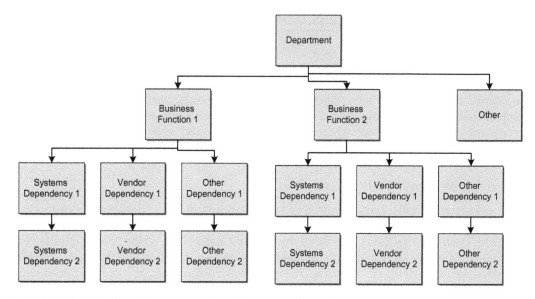

FIGURE 5.2 Flowchart illustrating the formula used to calculate the time a department receives items and performs actions prior to passing onto another department.

application, the end users and owners of the applications only understand the RPO and RTO specific to usability of the application with an understood and acceptable amount of data loss in a specified amount of time.

Specifying Required IT Support from Technical Staff

There are challenges associated with managing a high-density infrastructure coupled with the technology each department integrates into that infrastructure. To meet the continually increasing demand for faster, better, and more powerful technology, IT directors are deploying high-density equipment with great processing powers encompassing a small footprint in the data center.

Incongruent IT teams include storage, server, network, and application teams; all understand their specific roles in recovering from a disaster, which is why tests are so crucial. However, once the infrastructure is recovered with the associated application data, many more tasks are required to make the application usable and available to the end users. Consider, for example, what the DBAs need to do to the databases and what the application and software teams need to do in order to validate functionality. Thus, having these objects defined and metrics in place will help with the testing and checkpoints in the recovery process to ensure that the RTOs and RPOs are met successfully.

Designing Recovery Solutions

Many kinds of "disasters" can occur in business. Typically, one thinks mostly of natural disasters when one thinks of disasters. To do this when planning a disaster recovery solution is a fatal mistake. For example, consider a small company (or possibly even a large company!) where one or a small number of people control access to all data. Perhaps only one person has access to critical systems that, one day, may require reconfiguration or repair. What if that day comes sooner than expected, and what if that person was involved in a fatal car accident on the way to work? This sort of scenario and myriad others plague the information technology industry. The amount of risk tied up in IT director fiefdoms could, if exercised by a wide-scale disaster one day, bring about a nationwide business calamity. Think about the assorted systems that could be affected by the following "disasters:"

- Loss of bidirectional communication
- Loss of Internet connectivity
- Data loss
- Life lost

The final point, while not directly related to information technology and the preservation of business continuity through tragic, business-altering events is included because, at the heart of all the systems exist the human beings who operate and understand them. Recovery solutions should consider the human element. More importantly, a disaster recovery should be able to do just what the name implies—it should allow complete recovery, if not business continuity, through any disaster.

Consider, for example, a software company called Knowledge Inc. that provides critical software services to many of the Fortune 500 companies. On a Friday afternoon, a terrorist attack destroys their one, and only, location. The 400 + people who ran the company, except for those who were out sick or were on the road, are no more. Granted, the owner of the company has nothing to worry about anymore; he was in his office, but those 300 Fortune 500 companies, what about them? From their perspective, they are likely asking themselves why they never asked to see the DR plan for Knowledge Inc. They should have asked about the business recovery plan. Ostensibly, then, a DR plan contains two parts:

- Technology and data redundancy
- Business recovery

No business should ever *close down* due to a disaster. Yes, closing a business's books and winding down after a disaster could be the outcome of a disaster, but that should be a business decision, not a forced event. That is, the disaster itself, followed by a poorly executed or nonexistent DR plan, should not be a business-ending event. Closing the business or selling its assets may be the decision made by survivors and beneficiaries, but by preserving the business through proper DR planning, this should be just one of many options, not the only option after a disaster. As intimated earlier, disasters come in many forms, which can be loosely grouped into three categories:

1. Force Majeure
2. Conditional
3. Human

Force Majeure, or catastrophe, is obvious. Events such as hurricanes, earthquakes, fire, flood, war, volcanic eruptions, and terrorist acts all fall into this category.

Conditional is less obvious and revolves around the circumstances of an unexpected change in infrastructure conditions. For example, on a Monday afternoon, the Internet "goes down." Service doesn't' resume until Wednesday evening because it took that long for the service provider to find the problem. In another example, a construction crew saws through all three trunks that service the city of Chicago. As a result, 99% of the city loses its Internet. The other 1%? They had a recovery plan that included routing phones and Internet through a satellite dish on their roof.

The human category means loss of life and the business impact. For example, what if a strange new virus decimated more than half the organization's staff, and for some strange reason, it wiped out all but the most itinerant staff members, who have little knowledge of operations. A solid DR plan will consider that a disaster can occur, and all infrastructure may remain intact.

Establishing a Disaster Recovery Site

Once a disaster recovery plan has been created that includes both fail and no-fail infrastructure circumstances, a plan must be made that allows for varying degrees of infrastructure failure. For example, consider the conditions that must exist before someone says "Break out the black book!" and the organization *shifts* its mind-set into one of disaster recovery. For example, consider the following course of events:

1. The Internet goes down.
2. IT fails to back up Internet connections (there are three alternative paths to the Internet). Each path fails.
3. A DR link to the data center is powered up and established. This link is a point-to-point optical wireless linkup to the data center. There is no Internet at the data center either.
4. The DR link to the failover data center is powered up and established. This data center is also down.
5. Nobody knows what is happening yet, but one thing is certain: While the plan was okay, because there was even an alternative, nonphysical link to two data centers, one that was a failover site, it didn't help because the DR data center site was only a couple of miles from the primary.

In the event of a disaster, DR sites should be as logically separated from a catastrophe point of view as possible. To establish what makes a good DR site, let's explore disaster a little bit.

Site Choices: Configuration and Acquisition

Since this is a book about computer and information security, and not about business alternative planning, these next sections will focus primarily on force majeure and conditional disasters. The assumption it makes is that the business critical functions have been deemed complex and necessary enough that a geographically disparate location is desirable and necessary. For many, disaster recovery is about backup planning. A distinction between the two must be made. Backup and recovery addresses one thing, and only one thing: For example, a hacker accesses the system and deletes a small but critical table from a database. This is a backup and recovery option. You simply restore from backup, and you are up and running again. Disaster recovery is more severe, and it implies that the recovery of data after an incident that destroys equipment or data in tandem with an event of some sort has rendered equipment and communications at a particular site unusable. In this case the definition of unusable is one of a business nature:

- DR definition of *unusable*: Equipment or data or communications that are not functioning for such a length of time as to render irreparable damage to business revenues or relationships.
- *Unusable*, then, in the business sense, must be taken in the context of this sentence.
- Disaster recovery is a sequence of events that, regardless of extenuating circumstances, will restore the full functionality of data, communications, or equipment, located at some one site or many sites, that has been rendered unusable by some event.

Over time, some piece of equipment may become unserviceable, but in terms of disaster recovery, something is *unusable* only if its unserviceability inflicts damage on the business. Disaster recovery assumes one thing is true: that a major, business critical function has ceased operation due to one of the aforementioned reasons, and that it can no longer continue.

The following list details a number of disasters and chooses alternative locations. In the end, one may consider that the disaster is too unlikely to occur, and that if the disaster were to occur (such as an asteroid strike), there would likely be no point in continuing business anyway—simply surviving will be everyone's concern, and whether or not customers can purchase concert tickets will be moot if nobody is going to be going to concerts any time soon. Table 5.1 provides a sample listing of DR failover locations, the disaster that occurs, and the reason why it is a bad choice. This table seeks to provide a thought experiment framework whereby a planner may base a similar table for her location.

Choosing Suppliers: In-House Versus Third Party

As evidenced by Table 5.1, the complexity of choosing a DR location that is a perfect *ying* to your primary locations *yang* is not an easy task. If one assumes that the third-party provider has been in business for a while, has experience in the field, and is not just an investor who purchased an underground quarry in Kansas City and simply didn't know what to do with it, then the primary reason to contract a DR provider will be one of reliability.

Furthermore, the DR provider will host *other* companies, which means that they will likely be performing the sort of monthly and manual testing of their failover electrical and uplink capabilities that is required. This results in a savings due to the economy of scale. A company that has to test its systems understands that testing takes time, is expensive, and may result in unanticipated damage to equipment should a faulty failover mechanism result in a massive surge through the power grid.

Typically, businesses that aren't savvy or interested in the facts of disasters— that they do happen, and they can happen to them—may make a rather cursory attempt at DR. They may blend some non-DR site functions with the DR site. The mistake they make in doing this relates directly to redundancy—inherent to the DR strategy is that, essentially, both sites require each other to act as backup. If the DR site is being used, and it fails, it

TABLE 5.1 The Portland Example Serves to Illustrate that While a Disaster Recovery Planned Site may Appear to be Perfectly Acceptable, even if Affected by Collateral After-Affects, the type of Infrastructure and the Routing of the Trunks, all May Play a Part. The ENTIRE Infrastructure of the Environment, and all the Unknown Interdependencies should be thoroughly Uncovered, Explored, and Understood.

Primary Site	Disaster	DR Location	Pass/Fail
Quad Cities	Flood	St. Louis	It flooded too.
Chicago	Military strike	New York	Communications in New York were also targeted.
Miami	Hurricane	Chicago	Pass.
San Francisco	Earthquake	San Jose	Fail. San Jose is under water.
Portland	Volcano	Seattle	Fail. The Seattle site depends on optical wireless, which are due to Portland's ash cloud and northerly winds.
New York	Tsunami	San Diego	Pass.
St. Louis	Tornado	Undisclosed location in Nevada	Pass. The use of a hardened, undisclosed location protects against additional threats, such as terrorist or military action, that may strike multiple communication centers simultaneously. With satellite uplinks, this location is ideal against myriad threats.

would need to failover to the primary site. Organizations that are greatly concerned about business continuity will segregate business functions completely. When contracting a vendor to handle DR, the business will drive the requirements. Things like email, database applications, HR, and finance systems may not have the same impact of loss as, for example, a Web site that takes customer orders.

When building a DR plan, the planners must consider the scope of the disaster as well, how the vendor charges, and whether or not multiple vendors are required to fully comply with business needs. For example, for some companies, it is perfectly acceptable that employees could work for home in case the DR triggering event also closed the physical office. Other companies may have differing compliance issues and may require a secure facility. They may even require that employees travel to a distant location and work there. Now, arrangements have to be made for both PC access to network systems and food and lodging. This author recommends a nice resort that has conference center capabilities that could be set up to provide workstations. Do bear in mind that some employees will require family housing. Choosing to provision DR through in-house versus choosing an external vendor requires comparing and determining a number of factors:

• Skills—Decide whether or not the IT team has the skills and the time (or can hire someone.)
• Location—Determine whether or not the location is suitable. For example, a large law firm may already have multiple data centers. It begins to make sense to handle disaster

recovery internally if the company is not segmented in such a way that use of its multiple data centers will cause internal turmoil (this speaks to the IT fiefdoms alluded to earlier.)

- Estimated downtime—The definition of a disaster has already been described as involving the length of the downtime. How much further past the qualifying outage window is tolerable? If the best that internal resources can do is 24 hours to get a remote DR site functional and the requirement is 2 hours, outside help should be sought.

Figure 5.3 diagrams a failover site. Data flows are unidirectional *to* the DR site. It is a common fallacy that the DR site can also provide some functionality to the enterprise and serve as more than just a graveyard for servers, waiting for the day they must spring to life and perform a critical duty.

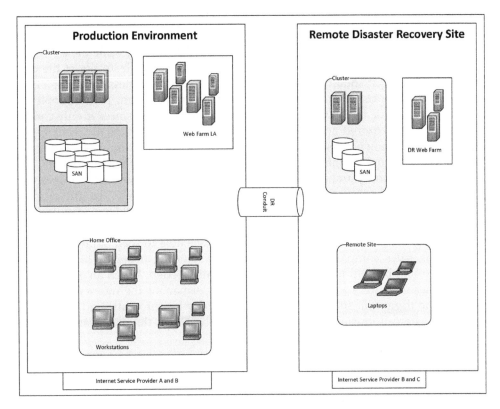

FIGURE 5.3   In a DR site, one can expect to see a slimming down of the amount of equipment needed. Configuring applications to work in such an environment will be a balance between labor costs and estimates of configuration time and the cost of additional servers. Rewriting application code to force a distributed application to work with a reduced server requirement may not be cost effective.

Specifying Equipment

The challenge of a DR site is primarily cost, followed closely by configuration. Setting it up, planning redundancy, creating strategies for rerouting voice, messaging, email, delivery of goods, and so on are things that can be written and kept within arm's reach of all employees. ALL employees should be aware of the DR plan. No single employee should be left wondering what his role is during a disaster.

Configuration and cost are closely related. In just one example (of many similar), consider a complex federated database where many applications and many databases commingle information and exist in harmony on a home-grown system across 30 or 40 SQL servers. Picking up something so complex, and moving it, is not a simple task. It may take many weeks of reconfiguration to get such as system to be functional at the DR site. The complexity of an application and the ease of setting it up in a DR site should always be considered *during the purchasing and application review phase*. Waiting until afterwards to think about the DR site can be a very costly mistake. A DR-ready application will be able to collapse down to just a couple of servers and will be able to provide core functionality, with additional functionality brought online with the addition of more servers as needed.

A DR site is a site that is to be used for a temporary period of time. Typically, the hope is that the DR failover will not be permanent. However, this should be a planned contingency—that it will be permanent and that you may need to rapidly scale the environment. This is not to say that a DR site should be a fully functional, duplicate site of the primary site that failed. Rather, it should be able to support essential business functions. Suppose, for example, an enterprise that hosts a document review platform. Many people would like to access the system, but in the contract with its clients, the business is only committed to support minimal, required activities, and they are listed. Contractually, activity should be restricted. Only known, business-critical activity should be conducted. Users should only be performing activities that are business critical for them or their customers.

From an equipment purchasing standpoint, then, only minimal hardware need be purchased. Some companies may even refer to their DR site as "the graveyard" and the DR plan as a "Dawn of the Dead" plan. However, from a strategic standpoint, rack space MUST be available for rapid growth. Should the disaster become lengthy, or should the outage be permanent, the enterprise must be able to scale rapidly. Many business computing sales companies will configure a "standing order." This is something that, for a price, can be held in a sort of "escrow" until needed. When an outage becomes extensive, or permanent, or is recognized as being permanent the moment it happened, then pulling the trigger on such an order could actually be automatic and scripted in the failover plan. After all, in the event of a Dawn of the Dead, the graveyard will need to be fed more brains.

4. SUMMARY

Creating an effective, risk-biased, deployable DR plan that carefully considers human and technology interests takes time and attention. The solution to just about all DR issues that crop up will be to *spend more money*. This is where the art of it, and the experience of the designers, will either make or break the plan. Inexperienced planners may make assumptions and will overlook critical aspects of how to deploy the plan. They may not take it seriously, but as has been seen in recent history, *expect the worst*. Maintaining a heightened state of awareness is the rule of the day. Experienced IT professionals will be able to design a plan that is effective.

These authors recommend that a disaster recovery team be made up of the most senior people in the company—people who have been with the company for a long time and know its every system inside and out. These are people who should have ten or more years of experience in IT, if not with the company itself. These are the people who can ensure that, should a disaster occur, business will continue—because they are the ones doing this work already— they are the ones who are called when something is broken and nobody else can get it right. They are the ones who can unclog a plugged firewall, who have the part number for that odd LED in the service rack memorized, and they are the ones who could, if needed, rebuild the entire infrastructure from scratch, preferably while they sleep. Essentially, that is what DR is. It is an essential-function rebuilding of the entire company. Asking it to be anything less is simply asking for failure.

Finally, let's move on to the real interactive part of this chapter: review questions/exercises, hands-on projects, case projects, and optional team case project. The answers and/or solutions by chapter can be found in the Online Instructor's Solutions Manual.

CHAPTER REVIEW QUESTIONS/EXERCISES

True/False

1. True or False? Disaster recovery (DR), not unlike the plugged sink, is another task that many organizations fail to consider until after much of the technology groundwork has been laid, the corporation is profitable, and suddenly someone realizes that *not* having a DR site is a serious risk to the business.
2. True or False? A general component of a disaster recovery (DR) plan is for the committee to assess conceivable risks to the organization that could result in the disasters or emergency situations themselves.
3. True or False? Enterprise Risk Management (ERM) is not a template that can be given to every company to meet their needs and fit their business structure.
4. True or False? Downtime presents moderate consequences for businesses, no matter what their function may be.
5. True or False? A business impact assessment is a solution that determines critical business processes based on their impact during a disruption.

Multiple Choice

1. An organization must have a thorough understanding of the _____ and the tolerance of a business outage to define objectives to succeed in the event of an outage.
   A. qualitative analysis
   B. vulnerabilities

   C. critical business processes
   D. malformed request DoS
   E. data controller
2. There are challenges associated with managing a _____, coupled with the
   technology each department integrates into that infrastructure.
   A. network attached storage (NAS)
   B. risk assessment
   C. valid
   D. high-density infrastructure
   E. bait
3. There are many types of _____ that can occur in business.
   A. data minimization
   B. fabric
   C. disasters
   D. risk communication
   E. security
4. Once a disaster recovery plan has been created that includes both fail and no-fail
   infrastructure circumstances, a plan must be made that allows for varying degrees of:
   A. risk management
   B. greedy strategy
   C. infrastructure failure
   D. SAN protocol
   E. taps
5. What are equipment or data or communications that are not functioning for such a
   length of time as to render irreparable damage to business revenues or relationships?
   A. Irrelevant
   B. Tape library
   C. IP storage access
   D. Configuration file
   E. Unusable

EXERCISE

Problem

What are the differences among a Continuity of Operations Plan (COOP), a Business Continuity Plan (BCP), a Critical Infrastructure Protection (CIP) Plan, a Disaster Recovery Plan (DRP), an Information System Contingency Plan (ISCP), a Cyber Incident Response Plan, and an Occupant Emergency Plan (OEP)?

Hands-On Projects

Project

What type of alternate site should an organization choose as a disaster recovery strategy?

Case Projects

Problem

When an event occurs, who should be notified?

Optional Team Case Project

Problem

With what other activities should the ISCP and the recovery solutions be coordinated?

Biometrics

Luther Martin

Voltage Security

Biometrics is the analysis of biological observations and phenomena. People routinely use biometrics to recognize other people, commonly using the shape of a face or the sound of a voice to do so. Biometrics can also be used to create automated ways of recognizing a person based on her physiological or behavioral characteristics. Using biometrics as the basis of technologies that can be used to recognize people is not a new idea; there is evidence that fingerprints were used to sign official contracts in China as early as AD 700 and may have been used by ancient Babylonian scribes to sign cuneiform tablets as early as 2000 BC.[1] In both of these cases, a fingerprint was pressed in clay to form a distinctive mark that could characterize a particular person. It is likely that the sophistication of the techniques used to analyze biometric data has increased over the past 4000 years, but the principles have remained essentially the same.

Using biometrics in security applications is certainly appealing. Determining a person's identity through the presence of a physical object such as a key or access card has the problem that the physical token can be lost or stolen. Shared secrets such as passwords can be forgotten. Determining a person's identity using biometrics seems an attractive alternative. It allows an identity to be determined directly from characteristics of the person. It is generally impossible for people to lose or forget their biometric data, so many of the problems that other means of verifying an identity are essentially eliminated if biometrics can be used in this role.

Not all biometric data is suitable for use in security applications, however. To be useful, such biometric data should be as unique as possible (uniqueness), should occur in as many people as possible (universality), should stay relatively constant over time (permanence), and should be able to be measured easily (measurability) and without causing undue inconvenience or distress to a user (acceptability). Examples of technologies that

1. R. Heindl, *System und Praxis der Daktyloskopie und der sonstigen technischen Methoden der Kriminalopolizei*, De Gruyter, 1922.

TABLE 6.1   Overview of Selected Biometric Technologies.

Biometric	Uniqueness	Universality	Permanence	Measurability	Acceptability
DNA	High	High	High	Low	Low
Face geometry	Low	High	Medium	High	High
Fingerprint	High	Medium	High	Medium	Medium
Hand geometry	Medium	Medium	Medium	High	Medium
Iris	High	High	High	Medium	Low
Retina	High	High	Medium	Low	Low
Signature dynamics	Low	Medium	Low	High	High
Voice	Low	Medium	Low	Medium	High

seem to meet these criteria to varying degrees are those that recognize a person based on his DNA, geometry of his face, fingerprints, hand geometry, iris pattern, retina pattern, handwriting, or voice. Many others are also possible. Not all biometrics are equally suited for use in security applications. Table 6.1 compares the properties of selected biometric technologies, rating each property as high, medium, or low. This table shows that there is no "best" biometric for security applications. Though this is true, each biometric has a set of uses for which its particular properties make it more attractive than the alternatives.

Biometrics systems can be used as a means of authenticating a user. When they are used in this way, a user presents his biometric data along with his identity, and the biometric system decides whether or not the biometric data presented is correct for that identity. Biometrics used as a method of authentication can be very useful, but authentication systems based on biometrics also have very different properties from other authentication technologies, and these differences should be understood before biometrics are used as part of an information security system.

Systems based on biometrics can also be used as a means of identification. When they are used in this way, captured biometric data is compared to entries in a database, and the biometric system determines whether or not the biometric data presented matches any of these existing entries. When biometrics are used for identification, they have a property that many other identification systems do not have. In particular, biometrics do not always require the active participation of a subject. While a user always needs to enter her password when the password is used to authenticate her, it is possible to capture biometric data without the user's active involvement, perhaps even without her knowledge. This lets data be used in ways that other systems cannot. It is possible to automatically capture images of customers in a bank, for example, and to use the images to help identify people who are known to commit check fraud. Or it is possible to automatically capture images of airline passengers in an airport and use the images to help identify suspicious travelers.

The use of biometrics for identification also has the potential to pose serious privacy issues. The interests of governments and individual citizens are often at odds. Law enforcement agencies might want to be able to track the movements of certain people, and the automated use of biometrics for identification can certainly support this goal. On the other hand, it is unlikely that most people would approve of law enforcement having a database that contains detailed information about their travels. Similarly, tax authorities might want to track all business dealings to ensure that they collect all the revenue they are due, but it seems unlikely that most people would approve of government agencies having a database that tracks all merchants they have had dealings with, even if no purchases were made. Using some biometrics may also inherently provide access to much more information that is needed to just identify a person. DNA, for example, can used to identify people, but it can also be used to determine information about genetic conditions that are irrelevant to the identification process. But if a user needs to provide a DNA sample as a means of identification, the same DNA sample could be used to determine genetic information that the user might rather have kept private.

Designing biometric systems has been dubbed a "grand challenge" by researchers,[2] indicating that a significant level of research will be required before it will be possible for real systems to approach the performance that is expected of the technology, but one that also has the possibility for broad scientific and economic impact when technology finally reaches that level. So, although biometric systems are useful today, we should expect to see them become even more useful in the future and for the technology to eventually become fairly commonly used.

1. RELEVANT STANDARDS

The American National Standard (ANS) X9.84, "Biometric Information Management and Security for the Financial Services Industry," is one of the leading standards that provide an overview of biometrics and their use in information security systems. It is a good high-level discussion of biometric systems, and the description of the technology in this chapter roughly follows the framework defined by this standard. This standard is particularly useful to system architects and others concerned with a high-level view of security systems. On the other hand, this standard does not provide many details of how to implement such systems.

There are also several international (ISO/IEC) standards that cover the details of biometric systems with more detail than ANS X9.84 does. These are listed in Table 6.2. These standards provide a good basis for implementing biometric systems and may be useful to both engineers and others who need to build a biometric system, and others who need the additional level of detail that ANS X9.84 does not provide. Many other ISO/IEC standards for biometric systems are currently under development that address other aspects of such systems, and in the next few years it is likely that the number of these standards that have been finalized will at least double from the number that are listed here. The JTC 1/SC 37 technical committee of the ISO is responsible for the development of these standards.

---

2. A. Jain, et al., "Biometrics: A grand challenge," *Proceedings of the 17th International Conference on Pattern Recognition*, Cambridge, UK, August 2004, pp. 935–942.

TABLE 6.2   Current ISO/I EC Standards for Biometric Systems.

Standard	Title
ISO/IEC 19784-1:2006	Information technology – Biometric Application Programming Interface – Part 1: BioAPI Specification
ISO/IEC 19784-2:2007	Information technology – Biometric Application Programming Interface – Part 2: Biometric Archive Function Provider Interface
ISO/IEC 19785-1:2006	Information technology – Common Biometric Exchange Formats Framework (CBEFF) – Part 1: Data Element Specification
ISO/IEC 19785-2:2006	Information technology – Common Biometric Exchange Formats Framework (CBEFF) – Part 2: Procedures for the Operation of the Biometric Registration Authority
ISO/IEC 19794-1:2006	Information technology – Biometric data interchange format – Part 1: Framework
ISO/IEC 19794-2:2005	Information technology – Biometric data interchange format – Part 2: Finger minutiae data
ISO/IEC 19794-3:2006	Information technology – Biometric data interchange format – Part 3: Finger pattern spectral data
ISO/IEC 19794-4:2005	Information technology – Biometric data interchange format – Part 4: Finger image data
ISO/IEC 19794-5:2005	Information technology – Biometric data interchange format – Part 5: Face image data
ISO/IEC 19794-6:2005	Information technology – Biometric data interchange format – Part 6: Iris image data
ISO/IEC 19794-7:2006	Information technology – Biometric data interchange format – Part 7: Signature/sign time series data
ISO/IEC 19794-8:2006	Information technology – Biometric data interchange format – Part 8: Finger pattern skeletal data
ISO/IEC 19794-9:2007	Information technology – Biometric data interchange format – Part 9: Vascular image data
ISO/IEC 19795-1:2006	Information technology – Biometric performance testing and reporting – Part 1: Principles and framework
ISO/IEC 19795-2:2007	Information technology – Biometric performance testing and reporting – Part 2: testing methodologies for technology and scenario evaluation
ISO/IEC 24709.1: 2007	BioAPI Conformance Testing – Part 1: Methods and Procedures
ISO/IEC 24709.2: 2007	BioAPI Conformance Testing – Part 2: Test Assertions for Biometric Service Providers

2. BIOMETRIC SYSTEM ARCHITECTURE

All biometric systems have a number of common subsystems. These are the following:

- A data capture subsystem
- A signal processing subsystem
- A matching subsystem
- A data storage subsystem
- A decision subsystem

An additional subsystem, the adaptation subsystem, may be present in some biometric systems but not others.

Data Capture

A data capture subsystem collects captured biometric data from a user. To do this, it performs a measurement of some sort and creates machine-readable data from it. This could be an image of a fingerprint, a signal from a microphone, or readings from a special pen that takes measurements while it is being used. In each case, the captured biometric data usually needs to be processed in some way before it can be used in a decision algorithm. It is extremely rare for a biometric system to make a decision using an image of a fingerprint, for example. Instead, features that make fingerprints different from other fingerprints are extracted from such an image in the signal processing subsystem, and these features are then used in the matching subsystem. The symbol that is used to indicate a data capture subsystem is shown in Figure 6.1.

The performance of a data capture subsystem is greatly affected by the characteristics of the sensor that it uses. A signal processing subsystem may work very well with one type of sensor, but much less well with another type. Even if identical sensors are used in each data capture subsystem, the calibration of the sensors may need to be consistent to ensure the collection of data that works well in other subsystems.

Environmental conditions can also significantly affect the operation of a data capture subsystem. Dirty sensors can result in images of fingerprints that are distorted or incomplete. Background noise can result in the collection of a data that makes it difficult for the signal processing subsystem to identify the features of a voice signal. Lighting can also affect any biometric data that is collected as an image so that an image collected against a gray background might not work as well as an image collected against a white background.

Because environmental conditions affect the quality and usefulness of captured biometric data, they also affect the performance of all the subsystems that rely on it. This means

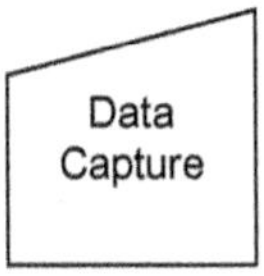

FIGURE 6.1   Symbol used to indicate a data capture subsystem.

that it is essential to carry out all testing of biometric systems under conditions that duplicate the conditions under which the system will normally operate (see checklist, "An Agenda For Action For Biometrics Testing"). Just because a biometric system performs well in a testing laboratory when operated by well-trained users does not mean that it will perform well in real-world conditions. Because the data capture subsystem is typically the only one with which users directly interact, it is also the one that may require training of users to ensure that it provides useful data to the other subsystems.

AN AGENDA FOR ACTION FOR BIOMETRICS TESTING

Steps in technical requirements for biometrics testing accreditation (Check All Tasks Completed):

Personnel:

_____1. The laboratory shall maintain competent administrative and technical staff that are :

  _____a. Knowledgeable of all biometrics standards pertaining to the specific tests found on the laboratory's scope(s) of accreditation.

  _____b. Familiar with the biometrics terminology, biometrics modalities, biometrics systems and sub-systems.

  _____c. Familiar with the "acceptable use" (collection, storage, handling, etc.) of Personally Identifiable Information (PII) as described in federal and state laws.

  _____d. Familiar with the biometrics products testing protocols, procedures and tools, when applicable.

  _____e. Familiar with human-crew interaction and human-crew rights and responsibilities, when applicable.

_____2. The laboratory shall maintain a list of personnel designated to fulfill requirements including:

  _____a. Laboratory's director

  _____b. Authorized Representative

  _____c. Approved Signatories

  _____d. team leaders

  _____e. Key technical persons in the laboratory

_____3. The laboratory shall identify a staff member as quality manager with overall responsibility for quality assurance and for maintenance of the quality manual. An individual may be assigned or appointed to serve in more than one position; however, to the extent possible, the laboratory director and the quality manager positions should be independently staffed.

_____4. The laboratory key technical personnel who conduct biometrics products testing activities shall have at least a Bachelor of Science in Computer Science, Computer

Engineering, Electrical Engineering, Human Factors or similar technical discipline or equivalent experience.

_____5. Laboratory staff collectively shall have knowledge of or experience in the following areas:

    _____a. Biometrics modalities available.

    _____b. Design/analysis of biometrics systems and sub-systems.

    _____c. Database systems.

    _____d. Biometrics products testing protocols and procedures.

    _____e. Biometrics data structures.

    _____f. Biometrics standards and special publications referenced in this handbook.

    _____g. Familiarity with operating systems under which the biometrics systems are operating.

    _____h. Any specific technology upon which testing is conducted.

_____6. The laboratory shall have documented a detailed description of its training program for new and current staff members. Each new staff member shall be trained for assigned duties.

_____7. The training program shall be updated and current staff members shall be retrained when relevant standards or scope of accreditation changes, or when the individuals are assigned new responsibilities. Each staff member may receive training for assigned duties either through on-the-job training, formal classroom study, attendance at conferences, or another appropriate mechanism.

_____8. Training materials that are maintained within the laboratory shall be kept up-to-date.

_____9. The laboratory shall have a competency review program and procedures for the evaluation and maintenance of the competency of each staff member for each test method the staff member is authorized to conduct.

_____10. An evaluation and an observation of performance shall be conducted annually for each staff member by the immediate supervisor or a designee appointed by the laboratory director.

_____11. A record of the annual evaluation of each staff member shall be dated and signed by the supervisor and the employee.

_____12. A description of competency review programs shall be maintained in the management system.

_____13. If the mechanism by which the laboratory employs staff members is through contracting, any key personnel who are contractors shall be identified and listed in the laboratory's application for accreditation.

_____14. If the mechanism by which the laboratory employs staff members is through contracting, any key personnel who are contractors shall be identified and listed in the laboratory's application for accreditation.

_____15. The laboratory personnel who handle PII documents shall obey all laboratory policies and procedures that implement the federal and state privacy laws that stress the "acceptable uses" of PII.

FIGURE 6.2   Symbol used to indicate a signal processing subsystem.

Signal Processing

A signal processing subsystem takes the captured biometric data from a data capture subsystem and transforms the data into a form suitable for use in the matching subsystem. This transformed data is called a *reference*, or a *template* if it is stored in a data storage subsystem. A template is a type of reference, and it represents the average value that we expect to see for a particular user.

A signal processing subsystem may also analyze the quality of captured biometric data and reject data that is not of high enough quality. An image of a fingerprint that is not oriented correctly might be rejected, or a sample of speech that was collected with too much background noise might be rejected. The symbol that is used to indicate a signal processing subsystem is shown in Figure 6.2.

If the captured biometric data is not rejected, the signal processing subsystem then transforms the captured biometric data into a reference. In the case of fingerprints, for example, the signal processing subsystem may extract features such as the locations of branches and endpoints of the ridges that comprise a fingerprint. A biometric system that uses the speech of users to characterize them might convert the speech signal into frequency components using a Fourier transform and then look for patterns in the frequency components that uniquely characterize a particular speaker. A biometric that uses an image of a person's face might first look for large features such as the eyes, nose, and mouth and then look for distinctive features such as eyebrows or parts of the nose relative to the large ones, to uniquely identify a particular user. In any case, the output of the signal processing subsystem is the transformed data that comprises a reference. Although a reference contains information that has been extracted from captured biometric data, it may be possible to recover the captured biometric data, or a good approximation to it, from a template.[3]

3. M. Martinez-Diaz, et al., "Hill-climbing and brute-force attacks on biometric systems: A case study in match-on-card fingerprint verification," *Proceedings of the 40th IEEE International Carahan Conference on Security Technology*, Lexington, October 2006, pp. 151–159.

Note that though several standards exist that define the format of biometric references for many technologies, these standards do not describe how references are obtained from captured biometric data. This means that there is still room for vendor innovation while remaining in compliance with existing standards.

Matching

A matching subsystem receives a reference from a signal processing subsystem and then compares the reference with a template from a data storage subsystem. The output of the matching subsystem is a numeric value called a *comparison score* that indicates how closely the two match.

Random variations occur in a data capture subsystem when it is used. This means that the reference created from the captured data is different each time, even for the same user. This makes the comparison score created for a particular user different each time they use the system, with random variations occurring around some average value. This concept is shown in Figure 6.3, in which the distribution of comparison scores that are calculated from repeated captures of biometric data from a single user are random. Such random data tend to be close to an average value every time that they are calculated from captured biometric data but not exactly the average value.

This is much like the case we get in other situations where observed data has a random component. Suppose that we flip a fair coin 100 times and count how many times the result "heads" appears. We expect to see this result an average of 50 times, but this average value actually occurs fairly rarely; exactly 50 out of 100 flips coming up heads happen less than 8% of the time. On the other hand, the number of heads will usually be not too far from the average value of 50, with the number being between 40 and 60 more than 95% of the time. Similarly, with biometrics, captured data will probably be close, but not identical, to an average value, and it will also not be too different from the average value.

The comparison score calculated by a matching subsystem is passed to a decision subsystem, where it is used to make a decision about the identity of the person who was the source of the biometric data. The symbol that is used to indicate a matching subsystem is shown in Figure 6.4.

FIGURE 6.3   Distribution in comparison scores for a typical user.

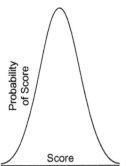

FIGURE 6.4   Symbol used to indicate a matching subsystem.

FIGURE 6.5   Symbol used to indicate a data storage subsystem.

FIGURE 6.6   Symbol used to indicate a decision subsystem.

Data Storage

A data storage subsystem stores templates that are used by the matching subsystem. The symbol that is used to indicate a data storage subsystem is shown in Figure 6.5.

A database is one obvious candidate for a place to store templates, but it is possible to store a template on a portable data storage device such as a chip card or a smart card. The relative strengths and weaknesses of different ways of doing this are discussed in the section on security considerations.

Decision

A decision subsystem takes a comparison score that is the output of a matching subsystem and returns a binary *yes* or *no* decision from it. This decision indicates whether or not the matching subsystem made a comparison which resulted in a match or not. The value *yes* is returned if the comparison was probably a match; the value *no* is returned is the comparison was probably not a match. The symbol that is used to indicate a decision subsystem is shown in Figure 6.6.

To make a *yes* or *no* decision, a decision subsystem compares a comparison score with a parameter called a *threshold*. The threshold value represents a measure of how good a comparison needs to be to be considered a match. If the comparison score is less than or equal to the threshold value then the decision subsystem returns the value *yes*. If the comparison score is greater than the threshold, it returns the value *no*. Comparison scores that will result in a *yes* or *no* response from a decision subsystem are shown in Figure 6.7.

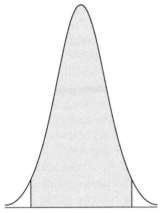

FIGURE 6.7 Comparison scores close to the average that result in a *yes* decision.

Comparison scores in the gray area of this illustration are close to the average value and result in a *yes*, whereas comparison scores that are outside the gray area are too far from the average value and result in a *no*. In Figure 6.7, the threshold value defines how far the gray area extends from the central average value. If the threshold is decreased, the size of the gray area will get narrower and decrease in size so that fewer comparison scores result in a *yes* answer. If the threshold is increased, the gray area will get wider and increase in size so that more comparison scores result in a *yes* answer.

Errors may occur in any decision subsystem. There are two general types of errors that can occur. In one case, a decision subsystem makes the incorrect decision of *no* instead of *yes*. In this case, a user is indeed who she claims to be, but large random errors occur in the data capture subsystem and cause her to be incorrectly rejected. This type of error might result in the legitimate user Alice inaccurately failing to authenticate as herself.

This class of error is known as a *type*-1 error by statisticians,[4] a term that would almost certainly be a contender for an award for the least meaningful terminology ever invented if such an award existed. It was once called *false rejection* by biometrics researchers and vendors, a term that has more recently been replaced by the term *false nonmatch*. One way in which the accuracy of biometric systems is now typically quantified is by their false nonmatch rate (FNMR), a value that estimates the probability of the biometric system making a type-1 error in its decision subsystem.

In the second case, a decision subsystem incorrectly returns a *yes* instead of a no. In this case, random errors occur that let a user be erroneously recognized as a different user. This might happen if the user Alice tries to authenticate as the user Bob, for example. This class of error is known as a *type*-2 error by statisticians.[5] It was once called *false acceptance* by biometrics researchers and vendors, a term that has been more recently been replaced by the term *false match*. This leads to quantifying the accuracy of biometrics by their false

4. J. Neyman and E. Pearson, "On the use and interpretation of certain test criteria for purposes of statistical inference: Part I," *Biometrika*, Vol. 20 A, No. 1–2, pp. 175–240, July 1928.

5. S. King, H. Harrelson and G. Tran, "Testing iris and face recognition in a personnel identification application," 2002 Biometric Consortium Conference, February 2002.

match rate (FMR), a value that estimates the probability of the biometric system making a type-2 error.

For a particular biometric technology, it is impossible to simultaneously reduce both the FNMR and the FMR, although improving the technology does make it possible to do this. If the parameters used in a matching subsystem are changed so that the FNMR decreases, the FMR rate must increase; if the parameters used in a matching subsystem are changed so that the FMR decreases, the FNMR must increase. This relationship follows from the nature of the statistical tests that are performed by the decision subsystem and is not limited to just biometric systems. Any system that makes a decision based on statistical data will have the same property. The reason for this is shown in Figures 6.8 and 6.9.

Suppose that we have two users of a biometric system: Alice and Bob, whose comparison scores are distributed as shown in Figure 6.8. Note that the distributions of these values overlap so that in the area where they overlap, the comparison score could have come from either Alice or Bob, but we cannot tell which. If the average values that we expect for Alice and Bob are far enough apart, the chances of this happening may get extremely low, but even in such cases it is possible to have large enough errors creep into the data capture step to make even the rarest of errors possible.

Figure 6.9 shows how a false match can occur. Suppose that Bob uses our hypothetical biometric system but claims to be Alice when he does this, and the output of the matching subsystem is the point B that is shown in Figure 6.9. Because this point is close enough to the average that we expect from biometric data from Alice, the decision subsystem will

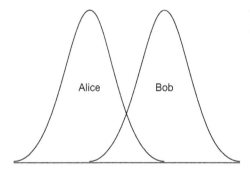

FIGURE 6.8 Overlap in possible comparison scores for Alice and Bob.

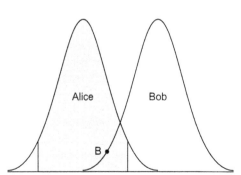

FIGURE 6.9 Type-2 error that causes a false match.

erroneously decide that the biometric data that Bob presented is good enough to authenticate him as Alice. This is a false match, and it contributes to the FMR of the system.

Figure 6.10 shows how a false nonmatch can occur. Suppose that Alice uses our hypothetical biometric system and the output of the matching subsystem is the point A that is shown in Figure 6.10. Because this point is too far from the average that we expect when Alice uses the system, it is more likely to have come from someone else other than from Alice, and the decision subsystem will erroneously decide that the biometric data that Alice presented is probably not hers. This is a false nonmatch, and it contributes to the FNMR of the system.

Because the FNMR and FMR are related, the most meaningful way to represent the accuracy of a biometric system is probably by showing the relationship between the two error rates. The relationship between the two is known by the term *receiver operating characteristic*, or ROC, a term that originated in the study of the sensitivity of radio receivers as their operating parameters change. Figure 6.11 shows an ROC curve for a hypothetical

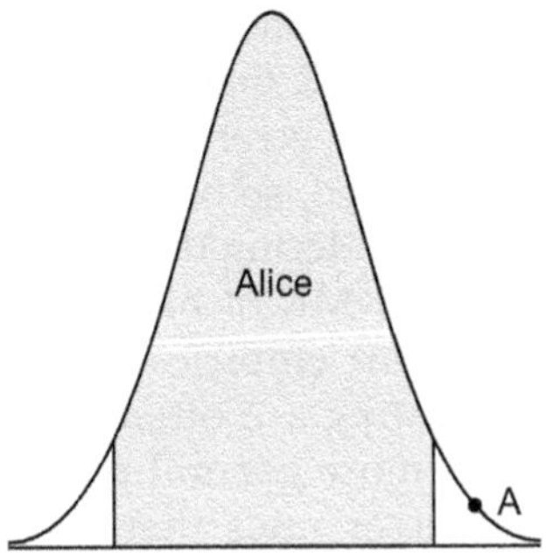

FIGURE 6.10   Type-1 error that causes a false nonmatch.

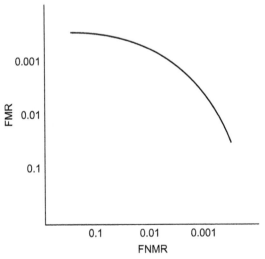

FIGURE 6.11   ROC for a hypothetical biometric system.

biometric. Such an ROC curve assumes that the only way in which the error rates are changed is by changing the threshold value that is used in the decision subsystem. Note that this ROC curve indicates that when the FMR increases the FNMR decreases, and vice versa.

By adjusting the threshold that a decision subsystem uses it is possible to make the FMR very low while allowing the FNMR to get very high or to allow the FMR to get very high while making the FNMR very low. Between these two extreme cases lies the case where the FMR and the FNMR are the same. This point is sometimes the equal error rate (EER) or crossover error rate (CER) and is often used to simplify the discussions of error rates for biometric systems.

Though using a single value does indeed make it easier to compare the performance of different biometric systems, it can also be somewhat misleading. In high-security applications like those used by government or military organizations, keeping unauthorized users out may be much more important than the inconvenience caused by a high FNMR. In consumer applications, like ATMs, it may be more important to keep the FNMR low. This can help avoid the anger and accompanying support costs of dealing with customers who are incorrectly denied access to their accounts. In such situations, a low FNMR may be more important than the higher security that a higher FMR would provide. The error rates that are acceptable are strongly dependent on how the technology is being used, so be wary of trying to understand the performance of a biometric system by only considering the CER.

There is no theoretical way to accurately estimate the FMR and FNMR of biometric systems, so all estimates of these error rates need to be made from empirical data. Because testing can be expensive, the sample sizes used in such testing are often relatively small, so the results may not be representative of larger and more general populations. This is further complicated by the fact that some of the error rates that such testing attempts to estimate are fairly low. This means that human error from mislabeling data or other mistakes that occur during testing may make a bigger contribution to the measured error rates than the errors caused by a decision subsystem. It may be possible to create a biometric system that makes an error roughly only one time in 1 million operations, for example, but it is unrealistic to expect such high accuracy from the people who handle the data in an experiment that tries to estimate such an error rate. And because there are no standardized sample sizes and test conditions for estimating these error rates, there can be a wide range of reliability of error rate estimates. In one study,[5] a biometric system that performed well in a laboratory setting when used by trained users ended up correctly identifying enrolled users only 51% of the time when it was tested in a pilot project under real-world conditions, perhaps inviting an unenviable comparison with a system that recognizes a person by his ability to flip a coin and have it come up heads. Because of these effects, estimates of error rates should be viewed with a healthy amount of skepticism, particularly when extremely low rates are claimed.

Adaptation

Some biometric data changes over time. This may result in matches with a template becoming worse and worse over time, which will increase the FNMR of a biometric system. One way to avoid the potential difficulties associated with having users eventually

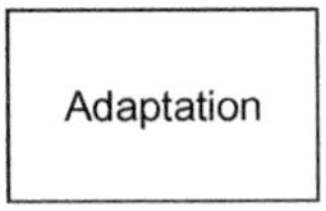

Adaptation

FIGURE 6.12 Symbol used to indicate an adaptation subsystem.

becoming unrecognizable is to update their template after a successful authentication. This process is called *adaptation,* and it is done by an optional part of a biometric system called an adaptation subsystem. If an adaptation subsystem is present, the symbol shown in Figure 6.12 is used to indicate it.

3. USING BIOMETRIC SYSTEMS

There are three main operations that a biometric system can perform. These are the following.

- *Enrollment.* During this operation, a biometric system creates a template that is used in later authentication and identification operations. This template, along with an associated identity, is stored in a data storage subsystem.
- *Authentication.* During this operation, a biometric system collects captured biometric data and a claimed identity and determines whether or not the captured biometric data matches the template stored for that identity. Although the term *authentication* is almost universally used in the information security industry for this operation, the term *verification* is often used by biometrics vendors and researchers to describe this.
- *Identification.* During this operation, a biometric system collects captured biometric data and attempts to find a match against any of the templates stored in a data storage subsystem.

Enrollment

Before a user can use a biometric system for either authentication or identification, a data storage subsystem needs to contain a template for the user. The process of initializing a biometric system with such a template is called *enrollment,* and it is the source of another error rate that can limit the usefulness of biometric systems. The interaction of the subsystems of a biometric system when enrolling a user is shown in Figure 6.13.

In the first step of enrollment, a user presents his biometric data to a data capture subsystem. The captured biometric data is then converted into a reference by a signal processing subsystem. This reference is then stored in a data storage subsystem, at which point it becomes a template. Such a template is typically calculated from several captures of biometric data to ensure that it reflects an accurate average value. An optional step includes using a matching subsystem to ensure that the user is not already enrolled.

The inherent nature of some captured biometric data as well as the randomness of captured biometric data can cause the enrollment process to fail. Some people have biometrics that are far enough outside the normal range of such data that they cause a signal processing subsystem to fail when it attempts to convert their captured data into a

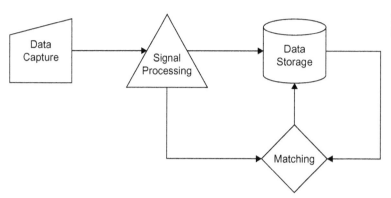

FIGURE 6.13 Enrollment in a biometric system.

reference. The same types of random errors that contribute to the FMR and FNMR are also present in the enrollment process, and can be sometimes be enough to turn captured biometric data that would normally be within the range that the signal processing subsystem can handle into data that is outside this range. In some cases, it may even be impossible to collect some types of biometric data from some users, like the case where missing hands make it impossible to collect data on the geometry of the missing hands.

The probability of a user failing in the enrollment process is used to calculate the failure to enroll rate (FER). Almost any biometric can fail sometimes, either temporarily or permanently. Dry air or sticky fingers can cause fingerprints to temporarily change. A cold can cause a voice to temporarily become hoarse. A broken arm can temporarily change the way a person writes his signature. Cataracts can permanently make retina patterns impossible to capture. Some skin diseases can even permanently change fingerprints.

A useful biometric system should have a low FER, but because all such systems have a nonzero value for this rate, it is likely that there will always be some users that cannot be enrolled in any particular biometric system, and a typical FER for a biometric system may be in the range of 1% to 5%. For this reason, biometric systems are often more useful as an additional means of authentication in multifactor authentication system instead of the single method used.

Authentication

After a user is enrolled in a biometric system, the system can be used to authenticate this user. The interaction of the subsystems of a biometric system when used to authenticate a user is shown in Figure 6.14.

To use a biometric system for authentication, a user first presents both a claimed identity and his biometric data to a data capture subsystem. The captured biometric data is then passed to a signal processing subsystem where features of the captured data are extracted and converted into a reference. A matching subsystem then compares this reference to a template from a data storage subsystem for the claimed identity and produces a comparison score. This comparison score is then passed to a decision subsystem, which produces a *yes* or *no* decision that reflects whether or not the biometric data agrees with

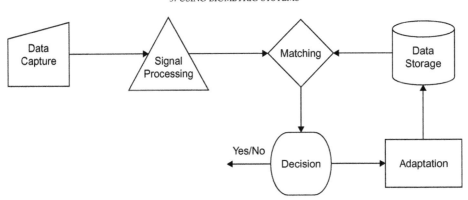

FIGURE 6.14 Authentication with a biometric system.

the template stored for the claimed identity. The result of the authentication operation is the value returned by the decision subsystem.

A false match that occurs during authentication will allow one user to successfully authenticate as another user. So if Bob claims to be Alice and a false match occurs, he will be authenticated as Alice. A false nonmatch during authentication will incorrectly deny a user access. So if Bob attempts to authenticate as himself, he will be incorrectly denied assess if a false nonmatch occurs.

Because biometric data may change over time, an adaptation subsystem may update the stored template for a user after they have authenticated to the biometric system. If this is done, it will reduce the number or times that users will need to go through the enrollment process again when their biometric data changes enough to increase their FNMR rate to an unacceptable level.

Identification

A biometric system can be used to identify a user that has already enrolled in the system. The interaction of the subsystems of a biometric system when used for identification is shown in Figure 6.15.

To use a biometric system for identification, a user presents his biometric data to a data capture subsystem. The captured biometric data is then passed to a signal processing subsystem where features of the captured data are extracted and converted into a reference. A matching subsystem then compares this reference to each of the templates stored in a data storage subsystem and produces a comparison score. Each of these comparison scores are passed to a decision subsystem, which produces a *yes* or *no* decision that reflects whether or not the reference is a good match for each template. If a *yes* decision is reached, then the identity associated with the template is returned for the identification operation. It is possible for this process to return more that one identity. This may or may not be useful, depending on the application. If a *yes* decision is not reached for any of the templates in a data storage subsystem, then a response that indicates that no match was found is returned for the identification operation.

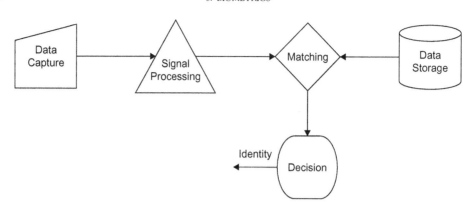

FIGURE 6.15   Identification with a biometric system.

A false match that occurs during identification will incorrectly identify a user as another enrolled user. So if Bob uses a biometric system for identification, he might be incorrectly identified as Alice if a false match occurs. Because there are typically many comparisons done when a biometric system is used for identification, the FMR can increase dramatically because there is an opportunity for a false match with every comparison. Suppose that for a single comparison we have an FMR of ε_1 and that ε_n represents the FMR for n comparisons. These two error rates are related by $\varepsilon_n = 1 - (1 - \varepsilon_1)^n$. If $n \cdot \varepsilon_1 \ll 1$. then we have that $\varepsilon_n \approx n \cdot \varepsilon_1$. This means that for a small FMR, the FMR is increased by a factor equal to the number of enrolled users when a system is used for identification instead of authentication. So an FMR of 10^{-6} when a system is used for authentication will be increased to approximately 10^{-3} if the identification is done by comparing to 1000 templates. A false nonmatch during identification will fail to identify an enrolled user as one who is enrolled in the system. So Bob might be incorrectly rejected, even though he is actually an enrolled user.

4. SECURITY CONSIDERATIONS

Biometric systems differ from most other authentication or identification technologies in several ways, and these differences should be understood by anyone considering using such systems as part of an information security architecture. Biometric data is not secret, or at least it is not very secret. Fingerprints, for example, are not very secret because so-called latent fingerprints are left almost everywhere. On the other hand, reconstructing enough of a fingerprint from latent fingerprints to fool a biometric system is actually very difficult because latent fingerprints are typically of poor quality and incomplete. Because biometric data is not very secret, it may be useful to verify that captured biometric data is fresh instead of being replayed. There are technologies available that make it more difficult for an adversary to present fake biometric data to a biometric system for this very purpose. The technology exists to distinguish between a living finger and a manufactured copy, for example. Such technologies are not foolproof and can themselves be circumvented by clever attackers. This means that they just make it more difficult for an adversary to defeat a biometric system, but not impossible.

It is relatively easy to require users to frequently change their passwords and to enforce the expiration of cryptographic keys after their lifetime has passed, but many types of biometric data last for a long time, and it is essentially impossible to force users to change their biometric data. So when biometric data is compromised in some way, it is not possible to reissue new biometric data to the affected users. For that reason, it may be useful to both plan for alternate forms of authentication or identification in addition to a biometric system and to not rely on a single biometric system being useful for long periods of time.

Biometrics used for authentication may have much lower levels of security than other authentication technologies. This, plus the fact there is usually a non-zero FER for any biometric system, means that biometric systems may be more useful as an additional means of authentication than as a technology that can work alone. Types of authentication technology can be divided into three general categories or "factors":

- Something that a user *knows*, such as a password or PIN
- Something that a user *has*, such as a key or access card
- Something that a user *is* or *does*, which is exactly the definition of a biometric

To be considered a *multifactor* authentication system, a system must use means from more than one of these categories to authenticate a user so that a system that uses two independent password-based systems for authentication does not qualify as a multifactor authentication system, whereas one that uses a password plus a biometric does. There is a commonly held perception that multifactor authentication is inherently more secure than authentication based on only a single factor, but this is not true. The concepts of *strong* authentication, in which an attacker has a small chance of bypassing the means of authentication, and multifactor authentication are totally independent. It is possible to have strong authentication based on only one factor. It is also possible to have weak authentication based on multiple authentication factors. So, including a biometric system as part of a multifactor authentication system should be done for reasons other than to simply use more than a single authentication factor. It may be more secure to use a password plus a PIN for authentication than to use a password plus a biometric, for example, even though both the password and PIN are the same type of authentication factor.

Error Rates

The usual understanding of biometric systems assumes that the FMR and FNMR of a biometric system are due to random errors that occur in a data capture subsystem. In particular, this assumes that the biometrics that are used in these systems are actually essentially unique. The existing market for celebrity lookalikes demonstrates that enough similarities exist in some physical features to justify the concern that similarities also exist in the more subtle characteristics that biometric systems use.

We assume, for example, that fingerprints are unique enough to identify a person without any ambiguity. This may indeed be true,[6] but there has been little careful research that demonstrates that this is actually the case. The largest empirical study of the uniqueness of fingerprints used only 50,000 fingerprints, a sample that could have come from as few as 5000 people, and has been criticized by experts for its careless use of statistics.[7] This is an area that deserves a closer look by researchers, but the expense of large-scale investigations probably means that they will probably never be carried out, leaving the uniqueness of biometrics an assumption that underlies the use of the technology for security applications. Note that other parts of information security also rely on assumptions that may never be proved. The security provided by all public-key cryptographic algorithms, for example, assumes that certain computational problems are intractable, but there are currently no proofs that this is actually the case.

The chances that the biometrics used in security systems will be found to be not unique enough for use in such systems is probably remote, but it certainly could happen. One easy way to prepare for this possibility is to use more than one biometric to characterize users. In such multi-modal systems, if one of the biometrics used is found to be weak, the others can still provide adequate strength. On the other hand, multi-modal systems have the additional drawback of being more expensive that a system that uses a single biometric.

Note that a given error rate can have many different sources. An error rate of 10% could be caused by an entire population having an error rate of 10%, or it could be caused by 90% of a population having an error rate of zero and 10% of the population having an error rate of 100%. The usability of the system is very different in each of these cases. In one case, all users are equally inconvenienced, but in the other case, some users are essentially unable to use the system at all. So understanding how errors are distributed can be important in understanding how biometric systems can be used. If a biometric system is used to control access to a sensitive facility, for example, it may not be very useful in this role if some of the people who need entry to the facility are unlucky enough to have a 100% FNMR. Studies have suggested that error rates are not uniformly distributed in some populations, but they are not quite as bad as the worst case. The nonuniform distribution of error rates that is observed in biometric systems is often called Doddington's Zoo and is named after the researcher who first noticed this phenomenon and the colorful names that he gave to the classes of users who made different contributions to the observed error rates.

Doddington's Zoo

Based on his experience testing biometric systems, George Doddington divided people into four categories: sheep, goats, lambs, and wolves.[8] Sheep are easily recognized by a

6. S. Pankanti, S. Prabhakar and A. Jain, "On the individuality of fingerprints," *IEEE Transactions on Pattern Analysis and Machine Intelligence*, Vol. 24, No. 8, pp. 1010–1025, August 2002.

7. S. Cole, *Suspect Identities: A History of Fingerprinting and Criminal Identification*, Harvard University Press, 2002.

8. G. Doddington, et al., "Sheep, goats, lambs and wolves: A statistical analysis of speaker performance in the NIST 1998 speaker recognition evaluation," *Proceedings of the Fifth International Conference on Spoken Language Processing*, Sydney, Australia, November–December, 1998, pp. 1351–1354.

biometric system and comprise most of the population. Goats are particularly unsuccessful at being recognized. They have chronically high FNMRs, usually because their biometric is outside the range that a particular system recognizes. Goats can be particularly troublesome if a biometric system is used for access control, where it is critical that all users be reliably accepted. Lambs are exceptionally vulnerable to impersonation, so they contribute to the FMR. Wolves are exceptionally good false matchers and they also make a significant contribution to the FMR.

Doddington's goats can also cause another problem. Because their biometric pattern is outside the range that a particular biometric system expects, they may be unable to enroll in such a system and thus be major contributors to the FER of the system.

Note that users that may be sheep for one biometric may turn out to be goats for another, and so on. Because of this it is probably impossible to know in advance how error rates are distributed for a particular biometric system, it is almost always necessary to test such systems thoroughly before deploying them on a wide scale.

Birthday Attacks

Suppose that we have n users enrolled in a biometric system. This biometric system maps arbitrary inputs into $n + 1$ states that represent deciding on a match with one of the n users plus the additional "none of the above" user that represents the option of deciding on a match with none of the n enrolled users. From this point of view, this biometric system acts like a hash function so might try to use well-known facts about hash functions to understand the limits that this property puts on error rates. In particular, errors caused by the FMR of a biometric system look like a collision in this hash function, which happens when two different input values to a hash function result in the same output from the hash function. For this reason, we might think that the same "birthday attack" that can find collisions for a hash function can also increase the FMR of a biometric system. The reason for this is as follows.

For a hash function that maps inputs into m different message digests, the probability of finding at least one collision, a case where different inputs map to the same message digest, after calculating n message digests is approximately $1 - e^{-n^2/2m}$.[9] Considering birthdays as a hash function that maps people into one of 365 possible birthdays, this tells us that the probability of two or more people having the same birthday in a group of only 23 people is approximately $1 - e^{-23^2/2 \cdot 365} \approx 0.52$. This means that there is greater that a 50% chance of finding two people with the same birthday in a group of only 23 people, a result that is often counter to people's intuition. Using a biometric system is much like a hash function in that it maps biometric data into the templates in the data storage subsystem that it has a good match for, and collisions in this hash function cause a false match. Therefore, the FMR may increase as more users are added to the system, and if it does, we might expect the FMR rate to increase in the same way that the chances of a collision in a hash function do. This might cause false matches at a higher rate that we might expect, just like the chances of finding matching birthdays does.

9. D. Knuth, *The Art of Computer Programming, Volume 2: Sorting and Searching*, Addison-Wesley, 1973.

In practice, however, this phenomenon is essentially not observed. This may be due to the nonuniform distribution in error rates of Doddingon's Zoo. If the threshold used in a decision subsystem is adjusted to create a particular FMR, it may be limited by the properties of Doddington's lambs. This may leave the sheep that comprise the majority of the user population with enough room to add additional users without getting too close to other sheep.

ANS X9.84 requires that the FMR for biometric systems provide at least the level of security provided by a four-digit PIN, which equates to an FMR of no greater than 10^{-4} and recommends that they provide an FMR of no more than 10^{-5}. In addition, this standard requires that the corresponding FNMR be no greater than 10^{-2} at the FMR selected for use. These error rates may be too ambitious for some existing technologies, but it is certainly possible to attain these error rates with some technologies.

On the other hand, these error rates compare very unfavorably with other authentication technologies. For example, an FMR of 10^{-4} is roughly the same as the probability of randomly guessing a four-digit PIN, a three-character password, or a 13-bit cryptographic key. And although few people would find three-character passwords or 13-bit cryptographic keys acceptable, they might have to accept an FMR of 10^{-4} from a biometric system because of the limitations of affordable current technologies. Table 6.3 summarizes how the security provided by various FMRs compares to both the security provided by all-numeric PINs and passwords that use only case-independent letters.

Comparing Technologies

There are many different biometrics that are used in currently available biometric systems. Each of these competing technologies tries to be better than the alternatives in some way, perhaps being easier to use, more accurate, or cheaper to operate. Because there are so many technologies available, however, it should come as no surprise that there is no single "best" technology for use in biometric systems. Almost any biometric system that is available is probably the best solution for some problem, and it is impossible to list all of the cases where each technology is the best without a very careful analysis of each authentication or identification problem. So any attempt to make a simple comparison between

TABLE 6.3 Comparison of Security Provided by Biometrics and Other Common Mechanisms.

FMR	PIN Length	Password Length	Key Length
10^{-3}	3 digits	2 letters	10 bits
10^{-4}	4 digits	3 letters	13 bits
10^{-5}	5 digits	4 letters	17 bits
10^{-6}	6 digits	4 letters	20 bits
10^{-7}	7 digits	5 letters	23 bits
10^{-8}	8 digits	6 letters	27 bits

TABLE 6.4 Comparison of Selected Biometric Technologies.

Biometric	Ease of Use	Accuracy	Cost
DNA	Low	High	High
Face geometry	High	Medium	Medium
Fingerprint	High	High	Low
Hand geometry	Medium	Medium	Medium
Iris	High	High	High
Retina	Medium	High	High
Signature dynamics	Low	Medium	Medium
Voice	Medium	Low	Low
(Password)	(Medium)	(Low)	(Low)

the competing technologies will be inherently inaccurate. Despite this, Table 6.4 attempts to make such a high-level comparison. In this table, the ease of use, accuracy and cost are rated as high, medium, or low.

Using DNA as a biometric provides an example of the difficulty involved in making such a rough classification. The accuracy of DNA testing is limited by the fairly large number of identical twins that are present in the overall population, but in cases other than distinguishing identical twins it is very accurate. So if identical twins need to be distinguished, it may not be the best solution. By slightly abusing the usual understanding of what a biometric is, it is even possible to think of passwords as a biometric that is based purely on behavioral characteristics, along with the FMR, FNMR, and FER rates that come with their use, but they are certainly outside the commonly understood meaning of the term. Even if they are not covered by the usual definition of a biometric, passwords are fairly well understood, so they provide a point of reference for comparing against the relative strengths of biometrics that are commonly used in security systems. The accuracy of passwords here is meant to be that of passwords that users select for their own use instead of being randomly generated. Such passwords are typically much weaker than their length indicates because of the structure that people need to make passwords easy to remember. This means that the chances of guessing a typical eight-character case-insensitive password is actually much greater than the 26^{-8} that we would expect for strong passwords. Studies of the randomness in English words have estimated that there is approximately one bit of randomness per letter.[10] If we conservatively double this to estimate that there are approximately two bits of randomness per letter in a typical user-selected password, we get the estimate that an eight-character password probably provides only about 16 bits

10. C. Shannon, "Prediction and entropy of printed english," *Bell System Technical Journal*, Vol. 30, pp. 50−64, January 1951.

of randomness, which is close to the security provided by a biometric system with an FMR of 10^{-5}. This means that the security of passwords as used in practice is often probably comparable to that attainable by biometric systems, perhaps even less if weak passwords are used.

Storage of Templates

One obvious way to store the templates used in a biometric system is in a database. This can be a good solution, and the security provided by the database may be adequate to protect the templates that it stores. In other cases, it may be more useful for a user to carry his template with him on some sort of portable data storage device and to provide that template to a matching subsystem along with his biometric data. Portable, credit-card-sized data storage devices are often used for this purpose. There are three general types of such cards that are used in this way, and each has a different set of security considerations that are relevant to it.

In one case, a memory card with unencrypted data storage can be used to store a template. This is the least expensive option, but also the least secure. Such a memory card can be read by anyone who finds it and can easily be duplicated, although it may be impossible for anyone other that the authorized user to use it. Nonbiometric data stored on such a card may also be compromised when a card is lost.

In principle, a nonauthorized user can use such a card to make a card that lets them authenticate as an authorized user. This can be done as follows. Suppose that Eve, a nonauthorized user, gets the memory card that stores the template for the authorized user Alice. Eve may be able to use Alice's card to make a card that is identical in every way to Alice's card but that has Eve's template in place of Alice's. Then when Eve uses this card to authenticate, she uses her biometric data, which then gets compared to her template on the card and gets her authenticated as the user Alice. Note that doing this relies on a fairly unsecured implementation.

A case that is more secure and also more expensive is a memory card in which data storage is encrypted. The contents of such a card can still be read by anyone who finds it and can easily be duplicated, but it is infeasible for an unauthorized user to decrypt and use the data on the card, which may also include any nonbiometric data on the card. Encrypting the data storage also makes it impractical for an unauthorized user to make a card that will let them authenticate as an authorized user. Though it may be possible to simply replace one template with another if the template is stored unencrypted on a memory card, carrying out the same attack on a memory card that stores data encrypted requires being able to create a valid encrypted template, which is just as difficult as defeating the encryption.

The most secure as well as the most expensive case is where a smart card with cryptographic capabilities is used to store a template. The data stored on such a smart card can only be read and decrypted by trusted applications, so that it is infeasible for anyone who finds a lost smart card to read data from it or to copy it. This makes it infeasible for unauthorized users to use a smart card to create a way to authenticate as an authorized user. It also protects any nonbiometric data that might be stored on the card.

5. SUMMARY

Using biometric systems as the basis for security technologies for authentication or identification is currently feasible. Each biometric has properties that may make it useful in some situations but not others, and security systems based on biometrics have the same property. This means that there is no single "best" biometric for such use and that each biometric technology has an application where it is superior to the alternatives.

There is still a great deal of research that needs to be done in the field, but existing technologies have progressed to the point that security systems based on biometrics are now a viable way to perform authentication or identification of users, although the properties of biometrics also make them more attractive as part of a multifactor authentication system instead of the single means that is used.

Finally, let's move on to the real interactive part of this Chapter: review questions/exercises, hands-on projects, case projects and optional team case project. The answers and/or solutions by chapter can be found in the Online Instructor's Solutions Manual.

CHAPTER REVIEW QUESTIONS/EXERCISES

True/False

1. True or False? *Biometrics* is the analysis of biological observations and phenomena. People routinely use biometrics to recognize other people, commonly using the shape of a face or the sound of a voice to do so.
2. True or False? Not all biometric systems have a number of common subsystems.
3. True or False? A data subsystem collects captured biometric data from a user.
4. True or False? A signal processing subsystem takes the captured biometric data from a data subsystem and transforms the data into a form suitable for use in the matching subsystem.
5. True or False? A matching subsystem receives a reference from a signal processing subsystem and then compares a template from a data storage subsystem.

Multiple Choice

1. What subsystem stores templates that are used by the matching subsystem?
   A. Qualitative analysis
   B. Vulnerabilities
   C. Data storage
   D. Malformed request DoS
   E. Data controller
2. What subsystem takes a comparison score that is the output of a matching subsystem and returns a binary *yes* or *no* decision from it?
   A. Network attached storage (NAS)
   B. Risk assessment
   C. Valid

    D. Decision

    E. Bait

3. One way to avoid the potential difficulties associated with having users eventually becoming unrecognizable is to update their template after a successful authentication. This process is called:

    A. Adaptation

    B. Fabric

    C. Disasters

    D. Risk communication

    E. Security

4. During what operation, does a biometric system create a template that is used in later authentication and identification operations?

    A. Enrollment

    B. Greedy strategy

    C. Infrastructure failure

    D. SAN protocol

    E. Taps

5. During what operation, does a biometric system collect captured biometric data and a claimed identity and determines whether or not the captured biometric data matches the template stored for that identity?

    A. Irrelevant

    B. Authentication

    C. IP storage access

    D. Configuration file

    E. Unusable

EXERCISE

Problem

How are biometrics collected?

Hands-On Projects

Project

What are biometric templates?

Case Projects

Problem

Can one interact with a biometric device without touching something?

Optional Team Case Project

Problem

Why are there so many different biometric modalilties?

7

Homeland Security

Rahul Bhaskar, Ph.D. and Bhushan Kapoor

California State University

1. STATUTORY AUTHORITIES

Here we discuss the important homeland security-related laws passed in the aftermath of the terrorist attacks. These laws are listed in Figure 7.1.

The USA PATRIOT Act of 2001 (PL 107-56)

Just 45 days after the September 11 attacks, Congress passed the USA PATRIOT Act of 2001 (also known as the Uniting and Strengthening America by Providing Appropriate Tools Required to Intercept and Obstruct Terrorism Act of 2001). This Act, divided into 10 titles, expands law enforcement powers of the government and law enforcement authorities.[1] These titles are listed in Figure 7.2. A summary of the titles is shown in the sidebar, "Summary of USA PATRIOT Act Titles."

SUMMARY OF USA PATRIOT ACT TITLES

Title I – Enhancing Domestic Security Against Terrorism

Increased funding for the technical support center at the Federal Bureau of Investigation, allowed military assistance to enforce prohibition in certain emergencies, and expanded National Electronic Crime Task Force Initiative.

---

1. "USA PATRIOT Act of 2001" U.S. Government Printing Office, http://frwebgate.access.gpo.gov/cgi-bin/getdoc.cgi?dbname = 107_cong_public_laws&docid = f:publ056.107.pdf (downloaded 10/20/2008).

Title II – Enhanced Surveillance Procedures

Authorized to intercept wire, oral, and electronic communications relating to terrorism, computer fraud and abuse offenses, to share criminal investigative information. It allowed seizure of voicemail messages pursuant to warrants and subpoenas for records of electronic communications. It provided delaying notice of the execution of a warrant, pen register and trap and trace authority under the Foreign Intelligence Surveillance Act, access to records and other items under FISA, interception of computer trespasser communications, and nationwide service of search warrants for electronic evidence.

Title III – International Money-laundering Abatement and Antiterrorist Financing Act of 2001

Special measures relating to the following three subtitles were created:

A. International Counter Money Laundering and Related Measures
B. Bank Secrecy Act Amendments and Related Improvements
C. Currency Crimes and Protection

Title IV – Protecting the Border

Special measures relating to the following three subtitles were created:

A. Protecting the Northern Border
B. Enhanced Immigration Provisions
C. Preservation of Immigration Benefits for Victims of Terrorism

Title V – Removing Obstacles to Investigating Terrorism

Attorney General and Secretary of State are authorized to pay rewards to combat terrorism. It allowed DNA identification of terrorists and other violent offenders, and allowed disclosure of information from National Center for Education Statistics (NCES) surveys.

Title VI – Providing for Victims of Terrorism, Public Safety Officers, and their Families

Special measures relating to the following subtitles were created:

A. Aid to Families of Public Safety Officers
B. Amendments to the Victims of Crime Act of 1984

Title VII – Increased Information Sharing for Critical Infrastructure Protection

Expansion of regional information sharing systems to facilitate federal, state, and local law enforcement response related to terrorist attacks.

Title VIII – Strengthening the Criminal Laws against Terrorism

Strengthened laws against terrorist attacks and other acts of violence against mass transportation systems and crimes committed at U.S. facilities abroad.

Provided for the development and support of cyber security forensic capabilities and expanded the biological weapons statute.

Title IX — Improved Intelligence

Responsibilities of Director of Central Intelligence regarding foreign intelligence collected under the Foreign Intelligence Surveillance Act of 1978.

Inclusion of international terrorist activities within scope of foreign intelligence under National Security Act of 1947.

Disclosure to Director of Central Intelligence of foreign intelligence-related information with respect to criminal investigations.

Foreign terrorist asset tracking center.

Title X — Miscellaneous

Review of the Department of Justice.

A. Definition of electronic surveillance.
B. Venue in money-laundering cases.
C. Automated fingerprint identification system at overseas consular posts and points of entry to the United States.
D. Critical infrastructures protection.

The USA PATRIOT Act of 2001
The Aviation and Transportation Security Act of 2001
Enhanced Border Security and Visa Entry Reform Act of 2002
Public Health Security, Bioterrorism Preparedness & Response Act of 2002
Homeland Security Act of 2002
E-Government Act of 2002

FIGURE 7.1   Laws passed in the aftermath of the 9/11 terrorist attacks.

The Aviation and Transportation Security Act of 2001 (PL 107-71)

The series of September 11 attacks, perpetrated by 19 hijackers, killed 3000 people and brought commercial aviation to a standstill. It became obvious that enhanced laws and strong measures were needed to tighten aviation security. The Aviation and Transportation Security Act of 2001 transfers authority over civil aviation security from the Federal Aviation Administration (FAA) to the Transportation Security Administration (TSA).[2] With the passage of the Homeland Security Act of 2002, the TSA was later transferred to the Department of Homeland Security.

Key features of the act include the creation of an Undersecretary of Transportation for Security; federalization of airport security screeners; and the assignment of Federal Security Managers to each airport. Also included in the act are these provisions: airports provide for the screening of all checked baggage by explosive detection devices; allowing

2. "Aviation and Transportation Security Act of 2001," National Transportation Library, http://ntl.bts.gov/faq/avtsa.html (downloaded 10/20/2008).

TITLE I	Enhancing Domestic Security Against Terrorism
TITLE II	Enhanced Surveillance Procedures
TITLE III	International Money Laundering Abatement and Antiterrorist Financing Act of 2001
TITLE IV	Protecting the Border
TITLE V	Removing Obstacles to Investigate Terrorism
TITLE VI	Providing for Victims of Terrorism, Public Safety Officers, and their Families
TITLE VII	Increased Information Sharing for Critical Infrastructure Protection
TITLE VIII	Strengthening the Criminal Laws against Terrorism
TITLE IX	Improved Intelligence
TITLE X	Miscellaneous

FIGURE 7.2   USA PATRIOT Act titles.

Creation of an Undersecretary of Transportation for Security
Federalization of Airport Security Screeners
Assignment of Federal Security Managers
Airport Screening by Explosion Detection Devices
Allowing Pilots to Carry Firearms
Electronic Transmission of Passenger Manifests on International Flights

FIGURE 7.3   Key features of the Aviation and Transportation Security Act of 2001.

pilots to carry firearms; requiring the electronic transmission of passenger manifests on international flights prior to landing in the U.S.; requiring background checks, including national security checks, of persons who have access to secure areas at airports; and requiring that all federal security screeners be U.S. citizens.[3] These key features are highlighted in the Figure 7.3.

3. "Aviation and Transportation Security Act of 2001," National Transportation Library, http://ntl.bts.gov/faq/avtsa.html (downloaded 10/20/2008).

CYBER SECURITY AND IT INFRASTRUCTURE PROTECTION

Enhanced Border Security and Visa Entry Reform Act of 2002 (PL 107–173)

This Act, divided into six titles, represents the most comprehensive immigration-related response to the terrorist threat.[4] The titles are listed in Figure 7.4. A summary of these titles is shown in the sidebar, "Summary of the Border Security and Visa Entry Reform Act of 2002."

SUMMARY OF THE BORDER SECURITY AND VISA ENTRY REFORM ACT OF 2002

Title I – Funding

The Act provides for additional staff and training to increase security on both the northern and southern borders.

Title II – Interagency Information Sharing

The Act requires the President to develop and implement an interoperable electronic data system to provide current and immediate access to information contained in the databases of federal law enforcement agencies and the intelligence community that is relevant to visa issuance determinations and determinations of an alien's admissibility or deportability.

Title III – Visa Issuance

This requires consular officers issuing a visa to an alien to transmit an electronic version of the alien's visa file to the INS so that the file is available to immigration inspectors at U.S. ports of entry before the alien's arrival.

This Act requires the Attorney General and the Secretary of State to begin issuing machine-readable, tamper-resistant travel documents with biometric identifiers.

Title IV – Inspection and Admission of Aliens

It requires the President to submit to Congress a report discussing the feasibility of establishing a North American National Security Program to enhance the mutual security and safety of the U.S., Canada, and Mexico.

It also requires that all commercial flights and vessels coming to the U.S. from any place outside the country must provide to manifest information about each passenger, crew member, and other occupant prior to arrival in the U.S. In addition, each vessel or aircraft departing from the U.S. for any destination outside the U.S. must provide manifest information before departure.

Title VI – Foreign Students and Exchange Visitors

It requires the Attorney General, in consultation with the Secretary of State, to establish an electronic means to monitor and verify the various steps involved in the admittance to the U.S. of foreign students, such as: the issuance of documentation of acceptance of a foreign student by an educational institution or exchange visitor program.

---

4. "Enhanced Border Security and Visa Entry Reform Act of 2002 (PL 107-173)," Center for Immigration Studies, www.cis.org/articles/2002/back502.html (downloaded 10/20/2008).

Title VII – Miscellaneous

The Act requires the Comptroller General to conduct a study to determine the feasibility of requiring every nonimmigrant alien in the U.S. to provide the INS, on an annual basis, with a current address, and where applicable, the name and address of an employer.

It requires the Secretary of State and the INS Commissioner, in consultation with the Director of the Office of Homeland Security, to conduct a study on the procedures necessary for encouraging or requiring countries participating in the Visa Waiver Program to develop an intergovernmental network of interoperable electronic data systems.

TITLE I	Funding
TITLE II	Interagency Information Sharing
TITLE III	Visa Issuance
TITLE IV	Inspection and Admission of Aliens
TITLE V	Removing the Obstacles to Investigate Terrorism
TITLE VI	Foreign Students and Exchange Visitors
TITLE VII	Miscellaneous

FIGURE 7.4   Border Security and Visa Entry Reform Act of 2002.

Public Health Security, Bioterrorism Preparedness & Response Act of 2002 (PL 107–188)

The Act authorizes funding for a wide range of public health initiatives.[5] Title I of the Act addresses the national need to combat threats to public health, and to provide grants to state and local governments to help them prepare for public health emergencies, including emergencies resulting from acts of bioterrorism. The Act establishes opportunities for grants and cooperative agreements for states and local governments to conduct evaluations of public health emergency preparedness, and enhance public health infrastructure and the capacity to prepare for and respond to those emergencies. Other grants support efforts to combat antimicrobial resistance, improve public health laboratory capacity, and support collaborative efforts to detect, diagnose, and respond to acts of bioterrorism. The Act also addresses other related public health security issues. Some of these provisions include:

- New controls on biological agents and toxins
- Additional safety and security measures affecting the nation's food and drug supply

5. "Public Health Security, Bioterrorism Preparedness & Response Act of 2002," U.S. Government Printing Office, http://frwebgate.access.gpo.gov/cgi-bin/getdoc.cgi?dbname = 107_cong_public_laws&docid = f: publl88.107 (downloaded 10/20/2008).

- Additional safety and security measures affecting the nation's drinking water
- Measures affecting the Strategic National Stockpile and development of priority countermeasures to bioterrorism

Homeland Security Act of 2002 (PL 107-296)

This landmark Act establishes a new Executive Branch agency, the U.S. Department of Homeland Security (DHS), and consolidates the operations of 22 existing federal agencies.[6] The primary mission of the DHS is given in Figure 7.5. As a part of this act, a directorate (see checklist, "An Agenda For Action For Implementing The Directorate Of Information Analysis And Infrastructure Protection") of information analysis and infrastructure protection was set up.

Prevent Terrorist Attacks
Reduce the Vulnerability of the United States to Terrorism
Minimize the damage, and assist in recovery from terrorist attacks that do occur in the United States

FIGURE 7.5 DHS mission.

AN AGENDA FOR ACTION FOR IMPLEMENTING THE DIRECTORATE OF INFORMATION ANALYSIS AND INFRASTRUCTURE PROTECTION

The primary role of this directorate is to[7] (Check All Tasks Completed):

_____**1.** Access, receive, and analyze law enforcement information, intelligence information, and other information from agencies of the federal government, state and local government agencies (including law enforcement agencies), and private sector entities, and to integrate such information in order to :

_____**a.** Identify and assess the nature and scope of terrorist threats to the homeland.

_____**b.** Detect and identify threats of terrorism against the United States.

_____**c.** Understand such threats in light of actual and potential vulnerabilities of the homeland.

_____**2.** Carry out comprehensive assessments of the vulnerabilities

---

6. "Homeland Security Act of 2002," Homeland Security, www.dhs.gov/xabout/laws/law_regulation_rule_0011.shtm (downloaded 10/20/2008).

7. "Homeland Security Act of 2002," Homeland Security, www.dhs.gov/xabout/laws/law_regulation_rule_0011.shtm (downloaded 10/20/2008).

of the key resources and critical infrastructure of the United States, including the performance of risk assessments to determine the risks posed by particular types of terrorist attacks within the United States (including an assessment of the probability of success of such attacks and the feasibility and potential efficacy of various countermeasures to such attacks).

____3. Integrate relevant information, analyses, and vulnerability assessments (whether such information, analyses, or assessments are provided or produced by the Department or others) in order to identify priorities for protective and support measures by the Department, other agencies of the federal government, state and local government agencies and authorities, the private sector, and other entities.

____4. Ensure, pursuant to section 202, the timely and efficient access by the Department to all information necessary to discharge the responsibilities under this section, including obtaining such information from other agencies of the federal government.

____5. Develop a comprehensive national plan for securing the key resources and critical infrastructure of the United States, including power production, generation, and distribution systems, information technology and telecommunications systems (including satellites), electronic financial and property record storage and transmission systems,

emergency preparedness communications systems, and the physical and technological assets that support such systems

____6. Recommend measures necessary to protect the key resources and critical infrastructure of the United States in coordination with other agencies of the federal government and in cooperation with state and local government agencies and authorities, the private sector, and other entities.

____7. Administer the Homeland Security Advisory System, including:

____a. Exercising primary responsibility for public advisories related to threats to homeland security.

____b. In coordination with other agencies of the federal government, providing specific warning information, and advice about appropriate protective measures and countermeasures, to state and local government agencies and authorities, the private sector, other entities, and the public.

____8. Review, analyze, and make recommendations for improvements in the policies and procedures governing the sharing of law enforcement information, intelligence information, intelligence-related information, and other information relating to homeland security within the federal government and between the federal government and state and local government agencies and authorities.

_____ 9. Disseminate, as appropriate, information analyzed by the Department within the Department, to other agencies of the federal government with responsibilities relating to homeland security, and to agencies of state and local governments and private sector entities with such responsibilities in order to assist in the deterrence, prevention, preemption of, or response to, terrorist attacks against the United States.

_____ 10. Consult with the Director of Central Intelligence and other appropriate intelligence, law enforcement, or other elements of the federal government to establish collection priorities and strategies for information, including law enforcement-related information, relating to threats of terrorism against the United States through such means as the representation of the Department in discussions regarding requirements and priorities in the collection of such information.

_____ 11. Consult with state and local governments and private sector entities to ensure appropriate exchanges of information, including law enforcement-related information, relating to threats of terrorism against the United States.

_____ 12. Ensure that:

_____ a. Any material received pursuant to this Act is protected from unauthorized disclosure

and handled and used only for the performance of official duties.

_____ b. Any intelligence information under this Act is shared, retained, and disseminated consistent with the authority of the Director of Central Intelligence to protect intelligence sources and methods under the National Security Act of 1947 (50 U.S.C. 401 et seq.) and related procedures and, as appropriate, similar authorities of the Attorney General concerning sensitive law enforcement information.

_____ 13. Request additional information from other agencies of the federal government, state and local government agencies, and the private sector relating to threats of terrorism in the United States, or relating to other areas of responsibility assigned by the Secretary, including the entry into cooperative agreements through the Secretary to obtain such information.

_____ 14. Establish and utilize, in conjunction with the chief information officer of the Department, a secure communications and information technology infrastructure, including data mining and other advanced analytical tools, in order to access, receive, and analyze data and information in furtherance of the responsibilities under this section, and to disseminate information acquired and analyzed by the Department, as appropriate.

_____15. Ensure, in conjunction with the chief information officer of the Department, any information databases and analytical tools developed or utilized by the Department:

   _____a. Are compatible with one another and with relevant information databases of other agencies of the federal government.

   _____b. Treat information in such databases in a manner that complies with applicable federal law on privacy.

_____16. Coordinate training and other support to the elements and personnel of the Department, other agencies of the federal government, and state and local governments that provide information to the Department, or are consumers of information provided by the Department, in order to facilitate the identification and sharing of information revealed in their ordinary duties and the optimal utilization of information received from the Department.

_____17. Coordinate with elements of the intelligence community and with federal, state, and local law enforcement agencies, and the private sector, as appropriate.

_____18. Provide intelligence and information analysis and support to other elements of the Department.

_____19. Perform such other duties relating to such responsibilities as the Secretary may provide.

E-Government Act of 2002 (PL 107–347)

The E-Government Act of 2002 establishes a Federal Chief Information Officers Council to oversee government information and services, and creation of a new Office of Electronic Government within the Office of Management and Budget.[8] The purposes of the Act are:

- To provide effective leadership of federal government efforts to develop and promote electronic government services and processes by establishing an Administrator of a new Office of Electronic Government within the Office of Management and Budget.
- To promote use of the Internet and other information technologies to provide increased opportunities for citizen participation in government.
- To promote interagency collaboration in providing electronic government services, where this collaboration would improve the service to citizens by integrating related

8. "E-Government Act of 2002," U.S. Government Printing Office, http://frwebgate.access.gpo.gov/cgi-bin/getdoc.cgi?dbname = 107_cong_public_laws&docid = f:publ347.107.pdf (downloaded 10/20/2008).

functions, and in the use of internal electronic government processes, where this collaboration would improve the efficiency and effectiveness of the processes.

- To improve the ability of the government to achieve agency missions and program performance goals.
- To promote the use of the Internet and emerging technologies within and across government agencies to provide citizen-centric government information and services.
- To reduce costs and burdens for businesses and other government entities.
- To promote better informed decision-making by policy makers.
- To promote access to high quality government information and services across multiple channels.
- To make the federal government more transparent and accountable.
- To transform agency operations by utilizing, where appropriate, best practices from public and private sector organizations.
- To provide enhanced access to government information and services in a manner consistent with laws regarding protection of personal privacy, national security, records retention, access for persons with disabilities, and other relevant laws.

Title III of the Act is known as the Federal Information Security Management Act of 2002. This act applies to the national security systems, that include any information systems used by an agency or a contractor of an agency involved in intelligence activities; cryptology activities related to the nation's security; command and control of military equipment that is an integral part of a weapon or weapons system or is critical to the direct fulfillment of military or intelligence missions. Nevertheless, this definition does not apply to a system that is used for routine administrative and business applications (including payroll, finance, logistics, and personnel management applications). The purposes of this Title are to:

- Provide a comprehensive framework for ensuring the effectiveness of information security controls over information resources that support federal operations and assets.
- Recognize the highly networked nature of the current federal computing environment and provide effective government-wide management and oversight of the related information security risks, including coordination of information security efforts throughout the civilian, national security, and law-enforcement communities.
- Provide for development and maintenance of minimum controls required to protect federal information and information systems.
- Provide a mechanism for improved oversight of federal agency information security programs.
- Acknowledge that commercially developed information security products offer advanced, dynamic, robust, and effective information security solutions, reflecting market solutions for the protection of critical information infrastructures important to the national defense and economic security of the nation that are designed, built, and operated by the private sector.
- Recognize that the selection of specific technical hardware and software information security solutions should be left to individual agencies from among commercially developed products.

2. HOMELAND SECURITY PRESIDENTIAL DIRECTIVES

Presidential directives are issued by the National Security Council and are signed or authorized by the President. A series of Homeland Security Presidential Directives (HSPDs) were issued by President George W. Bush on matters pertaining to Homeland Security[9]:

- HSPD 1: Organization and Operation of the Homeland Security Council. Ensures coordination of all homeland security-related activities among executive departments and agencies and promotes the effective development and implementation of all homeland security policies.
- HSPD 2: Combating Terrorism Through Immigration Policies. Provides for the creation of a task force which will work aggressively to prevent aliens who engage in or support terrorist activity from entering the United States and to detain, prosecute, or deport any such aliens who are within the United States.
- HSPD 3: Homeland Security Advisory System. Establishes a comprehensive and effective means to disseminate information regarding the risk of terrorist acts to federal, state, and local authorities and to the American people.
- HSPD 4: National Strategy to Combat Weapons of Mass Destruction. Applies new technologies, increased emphasis on intelligence collection and analysis, strengthens alliance relationships, and establishes new partnerships with former adversaries to counter this threat in all of its dimensions.
- HSPD 5: Management of Domestic Incidents. Enhances the ability of the United States to manage domestic incidents by establishing a single, comprehensive national incident management system.
- HSPD 6: Integration and Use of Screening Information. Provides for the establishment of the Terrorist Threat Integration Center.
- HSPD 7: Critical Infrastructure Identification, Prioritization, and Protection. Establishes a national policy for federal departments and agencies to identify and prioritize United States critical infrastructure and key resources and to protect them from terrorist attacks.
- HSPD 8: National Preparedness. Identifies steps for improved coordination in response to incidents. This directive describes the way federal departments and agencies will prepare for such a response, including prevention activities during the early stages of a terrorism incident. This directive is a companion to HSPD-5.
- HSPD 8 Annex 1: National Planning. Further enhances the preparedness of the United States by formally establishing a standard and comprehensive approach to national planning.
- HSPD 9: Defense of United States Agriculture and Food. Establishes a national policy to defend the agriculture and food system against terrorist attacks, major disasters, and other emergencies.

9. "Homeland Security presidential directives," Homeland Security, https://www.drii.org/professional_prac/profprac_appendix.html#BUSINESS_CONTINUITY_PLANNING_INFORMATION, 2008 (downloaded 10/24/2008).

- HSPD 10: Biodefense for the 21st Century. Provides a comprehensive framework for our nation's Biodefense.
- HSPD 11: Comprehensive Terrorist-Related Screening Procedures. Implements a coordinated and comprehensive approach to terrorist-related screening that supports homeland security, at home and abroad. This directive builds upon HSPD 6.
- HSPD 12: Policy for a Common Identification Standard for Federal Employees and Contractors. Establishes a mandatory, government-wide standard for secure and reliable forms of identification issued by the federal government to its employees and contractors (including contractor employees).
- HSPD 13: Maritime Security Policy. Establishes policy guidelines to enhance national and homeland security by protecting U.S. maritime interests.
- HSPD 15: U.S. Strategy and Policy in the War on Terror.
- HSPD 16: Aviation Strategy. Details a strategic vision for aviation security while recognizing ongoing efforts, and directs the production of a National Strategy for Aviation Security and supporting plans.
- HSPD 17: Nuclear Materials Information Program.
- HSPD 18: Medical Countermeasures against Weapons of Mass Destruction. Establishes policy guidelines to draw upon the considerable potential of the scientific community in the public and private sectors to address medical countermeasure requirements relating to CBRN threats.
- HSPD 19: Combating Terrorist Use of Explosives in the United States. Establishes a national policy, and calls for the development of a national strategy and implementation plan, on the prevention and detection of, protection against, and response to terrorist use of explosives in the United States.
- HSPD 20: National Continuity Policy. Establishes a comprehensive national policy on the continuity of federal government structures and operations and a single National Continuity Coordinator responsible for coordinating the development and implementation of federal continuity policies.
- HSPD 20 Annex A: Continuity Planning. Assigns executive departments and agencies to a category commensurate with their COOP/COG/ECG responsibilities during an emergency.
- HSPD 21: Public Health and Medical Preparedness. Establishes a national strategy that will enable a level of public health and medical preparedness sufficient to address a range of possible disasters.
- HSPD 23: National Cyber Security Initiative.
- HSPD 24: Biometrics for Identification and Screening to Enhance National Security. Establishes a framework to ensure that federal executive departments use mutually compatible methods and procedures regarding biometric information of individuals, while respecting their information privacy and other legal rights.

3. ORGANIZATIONAL ACTIONS

These laws and homeland security presidential directives called for deep and fundamental organizational changes to the executive branch of the government. The Homeland

Security Act of 2002 established a new Executive Branch agency, the U.S. Department of Homeland Security (DHS), and consolidated the operations of 22 existing federal agencies.[10] This Department's overriding and urgent missions are (1) to lead the unified national effort to secure the country and preserve our freedoms, and (2) to prepare for and respond to all hazards and disasters. The citizens of the United States must have the utmost confidence that the Department can execute both of these missions.

Faced with the challenge of strengthening the components to function as a unified Department, DHS must coordinate centralized, integrated activities across components that are distinct in their missions and operations. Thus, sound and cohesive management is the key to department-wide and component-level strategic goals. We seek to harmonize our efforts as we work diligently to accomplish our mission each and every day.

The Department of Homeland Security is headed by the Secretary of Homeland Security. It has various departments, including management, science and technology, health affairs, intelligence and analysis, citizenship and immigration services, and national cyber security center.

Department of Homeland Security Subcomponents

There are various subcomponents of The Department of Homeland Security that are involved with Information Technology Security.[11] These include the following:

- The Office of Intelligence and Analysis is responsible for using information and intelligence from multiple sources to identify and assess current and future threats to the United States.
- The National Protection and Programs Directorate houses offices of the Cyber Security and Communications Department.
- The Directorate of Science and Technology is responsible for research and development of various technologies, including information technology.
- The Directorate for Management is responsible for department budgets and appropriations, expenditure of funds, accounting and finance, procurement, human resources, information technology systems, facilities and equipment, and the identification and tracking of performance measurements.
- The Office of Operations Coordination works to deter, detect, and prevent terrorist acts by coordinating the work of federal, state, territorial, tribal, local, and private-sector parties and by collecting and turning information from a variety of sources. It oversees the Homeland Security Operations Center (HSOC), which collects and fuses information from more than 35 federal, state, local, tribal, territorial, and private-sector agencies.

10. "Public Health Security, Bioterrorism Preparedness & Response Act of 2002," U.S. Government Printing Office, http://frwebgate.access.gpo.gov/cgi-bin/getdoc.cgi? dbname = 107_cong_public_laws&docid = f:publ188.107 (downloaded 10/20/2008).

11. "Public Health Security, Bioterrorism Preparedness & Response Act of 2002," U.S. Government Printing Office, http://frwebgate.access.gpo.gov/cgi-bin/getdoc.cgi? dbname = 107_cong_public_laws&docid = f:publ188.107 (downloaded 10/20/2008).

State and Federal Organizations

There are various organizations that support information sharing at the state and the federal levels. The Department of Homeland Security through the Office of Intelligence and Analysis provides personnel with operational and intelligence skills. The support to the state agencies is tailored to the unique needs of the locality and serves to:

- Help the classified and unclassified information flow
- Provide expertise
- Coordinate with local law enforcement and other agencies
- Provide local awareness and access

As of March 2008, there were 58 fusion centers around the country. The Department has provided more than $254 million from FY 2004–2007 to state and local governments to support the centers.

The Homeland Security Data Network (HSDN), which allows the federal government to move information and intelligence to the states at the Secret level, is deployed at 19 fusion centers. Through HSDN, fusion center staff can access the National Counterterrorism Center (NCTC), a classified portal of the most current terrorism-related information.

There are various organizations at the state levels that support the homeland security initiatives. These organizations vary in their size and budget from very large independently run departments to a department that is a part of a larger related department. As an example, California has the Office of Management Services that is responsible for any emergencies in the state of California. The Governor's Office of Homeland Security is responsible for the coordination among different departments to secure the state against potential terrorist threats. Very specific to IT security, the California Office of Information Security and Privacy Protection is functional.

The Governor's Office of Homeland Security

The Governor's Office of Homeland Security (OHS) acts as the Cabinet-level state office for the prevention of and preparation for a potential terrorist event.[12] OHS serves a diverse set of federal, state, local, private sector, and tribal entities by taking an "all-hazards" approach to reducing risk and increasing responder capabilities.

Because California is prone to floods, fires, and earthquakes in addition to the potential for an attack using manmade weapons of mass destruction, OHS is committed to contributing to a comprehensive, well-planned all-hazards strategy to prevent, prepare for, respond to, and recover from any possible emergency. OHS is responsible for several key state functions, including[13]:

- Analysis and dissemination of threat-related information
- Protection of California's critical infrastructure

12. "The Governor's Office of Homeland Security (OHS)," www.homeland.ca.gov/(downloaded 10/24/2008).

13. "The Governor's Office of Homeland Security (OHS)," www.homeland.ca.gov/ (downloaded 10/24/2008).

- Management of the state's homeland security grants
- S/B training and exercising of first responders for terrorism events

California Office of Information Security and Privacy Protection

The California Office of Information Security and Privacy Protection (OISPP) unites consumer privacy protection with the oversight of government's responsible management of information. OISPP provides services to consumers, recommends practices to business, and provides policy direction, guidance, and compliance monitoring to state government.[14]

OISPP was established within the State and Consumer Services Agency by Chapter 183 of the Statutes of 2007 (Senate Bill 90), effective January 1, 2008. This legislation merged the Office of Privacy Protection, which opened in 2001 in the Department of Consumer Affairs with a mission of identifying consumer problems in the privacy area and encouraging the development of fair information practices, and the State Information Security Office, established within the Department of Finance with a mission of overseeing information security, risk management, and operational recovery planning within state government.[15]

Private Sector Organizations for Information Sharing

Intelligence sharing and analysis groups have been set up in many private infrastructure industries. As an example, National Electric Reliability Council has such a group, Electricity Sector Information Sharing and Analysis Center (ESISAC), which serves the electricity sector by facilitating communications between sector participants, federal governments, and other critical infrastructure organizations. It is the job of the ESISAC to promptly disseminate threat indications, analyses, and warnings, together with interpretations, to assist electricity sector participants take protective actions. Similarly, many other organizations in other infrastructure sectors are also members of an ISAC.

There are other organizations that share information among the member companies on issues related to incident response (see sidebar, "National Commission on Terrorist Attacks Upon the United States [The 9-11 Commission]"). These organizations include FIRST, the Forum of Incident Response and Security Teams,[16] which has as its members major corporations from all over the world. The FBI encourages organizations from the private sector to become members of InfraGard to encourage exchange of information among the members.[17]

14. "California Office of Information Security and Privacy Protection," www.oispp.ca.gov/ (downloaded 10/20/2008).

15. "California Office of Information Security and Privacy Protection," www.oispp.ca.gov/ (downloaded 10/20/2008).

16. "Forum of incident response and security teams," www.first.org/ downloaded 10/20/2008).

17. InfraGard, www.infragard.net/ (downloaded 10/20/2008).

NATIONAL COMMISSION ON TERRORIST ATTACKS UPON THE UNITED STATES (THE 9-11 COMMISSION)

Congress charted the National Commission on Terrorist Attacks Upon the United States (known as the 9-11 Commission) by Public Law 107-306, signed by the President on November 27, 2002, to provide a "full and complete accounting" of the attacks of September 11, 2001 and recommendations as to how to prevent such attacks in the future.[18] On July 22, 2004, the 9-11 Commission issued its final report, which included 41 wide-ranging recommendations to help prevent future terrorist attacks.[19] Many of these recommendations were put in place with the passage of the Intelligence Reform and Terrorism Prevention Act of 2004 (PL 108-458), which brought about significant reorganization of the intelligence community. Soon after the Democratic Party came into the majority in the House of Representatives, the 110th Congress passed another act, Implementing Recommendations of the 9-11 Commission Act of 2007 (PL 110-53). This section is subdivided into the following four subsections:

1. Creation of the National Commission on Terrorist Attacks Upon the United States (the 9-11 Commission)
2. Final Report of the National Commission on Terrorist Attacks Upon the United States (the 9-11 Commission Report)
3. Intelligence Reform and Terrorism Prevention Act of 2004 (PL 108-458)
4. Implementing Recommendations of the 9-11 Commission Act of 2007 (PL 110-53)

Creation of the National Commission on Terrorist Attacks Upon the United States (The 9-11 Commission)

Congress created the National Commission on Terrorist Attacks Upon the United States (known as the 9-11 Commission) to provide a "full and complete accounting" of the terrorist attacks and recommendations as to how to prevent such attacks in the future.[20] Specifically, the Commission was required to investigate "facts and circumstances relating to the terrorist attacks of September 11, 2001," including those relating to intelligence agencies; law-enforcement agencies; diplomacy; immigration, nonimmigrant visas, and border control; the flow of assets to terrorist organizations; commercial aviation; the role of congressional oversight and resource allocation; and other areas determined relevant by the Commission for its inquiry.

The Commission was composed of 10 members, of whom not more than five members of the Commission were from the same political party.

In response to the requirements under law, the Commission organized work teams

18. "National Commission on Terrorist Attacks upon the United States Act of 2002," www.9-11commission.gov/about/107-306.pdf (downloaded 10/20/2008).

19. "The 9-11 Commission Report," National Commission on Terrorist Attacks upon the United States, http://govinfo.library.unt.edu/911/report/911Report.pdf (downloaded 10/20/2008).

20. "National Commission on Terrorist Attacks upon the United States Act of 2002," www.9-11commission.gov/about/107-306.pdf (downloaded 10/20/2008).

to address each of the following eight topics[21]:

1. Al Qaeda and the organization of the 9-11 attack
2. Intelligence collection, analysis, and management (including oversight and resource allocation)
3. International counterterrorism policy, including states that harbor or harbored terrorists, or offer or offered terrorists safe havens
4. Terrorist financing
5. Border security and foreign visitors
6. Law enforcement and intelligence collection inside the United States
7. Commercial aviation and transportation security, including an Investigation into the circumstances of the four hijackings
8. The immediate response to the attacks at the national, state, and local levels, including issues of continuity of government.

Final Report of the National Commission on Terrorist Attacks Upon the United States (The 9-11 Commission Report)

The 9-11 Commission interviewed more than 1000 individuals in 10 countries and held at least 10 days of public hearings, receiving testimony from more than 110 federal, state, and local officials and experts from the private sector. The Commission issued three subpoenas to government agencies: the Federal Aviation Administration (FAA), the Department of Defense, and the City of New York. On July 22, 2004, the 9-11 Commission issued its final report, which included 41 wide-ranging recommendations to help prevent future terrorist attacks. This report covers both general and specific findings. Here is the summary of their general findings:

Since the plotters were flexible and resourceful, we cannot know whether any single step or series of steps would have defeated them. What we can say with confidence is that none of the measures adopted by the U.S. government from 1998 to 2001 disturbed or even delayed the progress of the al Qaeda plot. Across the government, there were failures of imagination, policy, capabilities, and management.[22]

Imagination

The most important failure was one of imagination. We do not believe leaders understood the gravity of the threat. The terrorist danger from Bin Laden and al Qaeda was not a major topic for policy debate among the public, the media, or in Congress. Indeed, it barely came up during the 2000 presidential campaign.

Al Qaeda's new brand of terrorism presented challenges to U.S. governmental institutions that they were not well-designed to meet. Though top officials all told us that they understood the danger, we believe there was uncertainty among them as to whether this was just a new and especially venomous version of the ordinary terrorist threat the United States had lived with for decades, or it was indeed radically new, posing a threat beyond any yet experienced.

As late as September 4, 2001, Richard Clarke, the White House staffer long

21. "National Commission on Terrorist Attacks upon the United States Act of 2002," http://www.9-11commission.gov/about/107-306.pdf (downloaded 10/20/2008).

22. "The 9-11 Commission Report," National Commission on Terrorist Attacks upon the United States, http://govinfo.library.unt.edu/911/report/911Report.pdf (downloaded 10/20/2008).

responsible for counterterrorism policy coordination, asserted that the government had not yet made up its mind how to answer the question: "Is al Qaeda a big deal?"

A week later came the answer.

Terrorism was not the overriding national security concern for the U.S. government under either the Clinton or the pre-9/11 Bush administration.

The policy challenges were linked to this failure of imagination. Officials in both the Clinton and Bush administrations regarded a full U.S. invasion of Afghanistan as practically inconceivable before 9/11.

Capabilities

Before 9/11, the United States tried to solve the al Qaeda problem with the capabilities it had used in the last stages of the Cold War and its immediate aftermath. These capabilities were insufficient. Little was done to expand or reform them.

The CIA had minimal capacity to conduct paramilitary operations with its own personnel, and it did not seek a large-scale expansion of these capabilities before 9/11. The CIA also needed to improve its capability to collect intelligence from human agents.

At no point before 9/11 was the Department of Defense fully engaged in the mission of countering al Qaeda, even though this was perhaps the most dangerous foreign enemy threatening the United States.

America's homeland defenders faced outward. North American Aerospace Defense Command (NORAD) itself was barely able to retain any alert bases at all. Its planning scenarios occasionally considered the danger of hijacked aircraft being guided to American targets, but only aircraft that were coming from overseas.

The most serious weaknesses in agency capabilities were in the domestic arena. The

FBI did not have the capability to link the collective knowledge of agents in the field to national priorities. Other domestic agencies deferred to the FBI.

FAA capabilities were weak. Any serious examination of the possibility of a suicide hijacking could have suggested changes to fix glaring vulnerabilities—expanding no-fly lists, searching passengers identified by the Computer Assisted Passenger Prescreening System (CAPPS) screening system, deploying federal air marshals domestically, hardening cockpit doors, alerting air crews to a different kind of hijacking possibility than they had been trained to expect. Yet the FAA did not adjust either its own training or training with NORAD to take account of threats other than those experienced in the past.

Management

The missed opportunities to thwart the 9/11 plot were also symptoms of a broader inability to adapt the way government manages problems to the new challenges of the twenty-first century. Action officers should have been able to draw on all available knowledge about al Qaeda in the government. Management should have ensured that information was shared and duties were clearly assigned across agencies, and across the foreign-domestic divide.

There were also broader management issues with respect to how top leaders set priorities and allocated resources.

For instance, on December 4, 1998, Director of Central Intelligence (DCI), Tenet issued a directive to several CIA officials and the Deputy Director of Central Intelligence (DDCI) for Community Management, stating: "We are at war. I want no resources or people spared in this effort, either inside CIA or the Community." The memorandum had little overall effect on mobilizing the CIA or the intelligence community. This episode indicates the limitations of the DCI's authority over the direction of the intelligence community, including agencies within the Department of Defense.

The U.S. government did not find a way of pooling intelligence and using it to guide the planning and assignment of responsibilities for joint operations involving entities as disparate as the CIA, the FBI, the State Department, the military, and the agencies involved in homeland security.

Intelligence Reform and Terrorism Prevention Act of 2004 (PL 108-458)

Many of the recommendations of the Final Report of the National Commission on Terrorist Attacks Upon the United States (The 9-11 Commission Report) were put into the Intelligence Reform and Terrorism Prevention Act of 2004. This Act, divided into 10 titles, brought about significant reorganization of intelligence community and critical infrastructures protection.[23]

Title I—Reform of the Intelligence Community

Special measures relating to the following subtitles were created:

A. Establishment of Director of National Intelligence
B. National Counterterrorism Center, National Counter Proliferation Center, and National Intelligence Centers
C. Joint Intelligence Community Council
D. Improvement of education for the intelligence community
E. Additional improvements of intelligence activities
F. Privacy and civil liberties

G. Conforming and other amendments
H. Transfer, termination, transition, and other provisions
I. Other matters

Title II—Federal Bureau of Investigation

Improvement of intelligence capabilities of the Federal Bureau of Investigation

Title III—Security Clearances

Special measures relating to the security clearances have been created.

Title IV—Transportation Security

Special measures relating to the following subtitles were created:

A. National strategy for transportation security
B. Aviation security
C. Air cargo security
D. Maritime security
E. General provisions

Title V—Border Protection, Immigration, and Visa Matters

Special measures relating to the following subtitles were created:

A. Advanced Technology Northern Border Security Pilot Program
B. Border and immigration enforcement
C. Visa requirements
D. Immigration reform
E. Treatment of aliens who commit acts of torture, extrajudicial killings, or other atrocities abroad

Title VI—Terrorism Prevention

Special measures relating to the following subtitles were created:

A. Individual terrorists as agents of foreign powers

23. "Intelligence Reform and Terrorism Prevention Act of 2004," U.S. Senate Select Committee on Intelligence http://intelligence.senate.gov/laws/pl108-458.pdf (downloaded 10/20/2008).

B. Money laundering and terrorist financing

C. Money laundering abatement and financial antiterrorism technical corrections

D. Additional enforcement tools

E. Criminal history background checks

F. Grand jury information sharing

G. Providing material support to terrorism

H. Stop Terrorist and Military Hoaxes Act of 2004

I. Weapons of Mass Destruction Prohibition Improvement Act of 2004

J. Prevention of Terrorist Access to Destructive Weapons K. Pretrial detention of terrorists

Title VII—Implementation of 9-11 Commission Recommendations

Special measures relating to the following subtitles were created:

A. Diplomacy, foreign aid, and the military in the war on terrorism

B. Terrorist travel and effective screening

C. National preparedness

D. Homeland security

E. Public safety spectrum

F. Presidential transition

G. Improving international standards and cooperation to fight terrorist financing

H. Emergency financial preparedness

Title VIII—Other Matters

Special measures relating to the following subtitles were created:

A. Intelligence matters

B. Department of homeland security matters

C. Homeland security civil rights and civil liberties protection

Implementing Recommendations of the 9-11 Commission Act of 2007 (PL 110-53)

Soon after the Democratic Party came into the majority in the House of Representatives, the 110th Congress passed another act, "Implementing Recommendations of the 9-11 Commission Act of 2007 (PL 110-53, August 3, 2007)."[24] Approximately a year after the passing of this law, the Majority Staffs of the Committees on Homeland and Foreign Affairs put its attention on the extent to which the law was indeed implemented and issued a report on "Wasted Lessons of 9/11: How The Bush Administration Ignored the Law and Squandered Its Opportunities to Make Our Country Safer."[25]

This comprehensive Homeland Security legislation included provisions to strengthen the nation's security against terrorism by requiring screening of all cargo placed on passenger aircraft; securing mass transit, rail and bus systems; assuring the scanning of all U.S.-bound maritime cargo; distributing Homeland Security grants based on risk; creating a dedicated grant program to improve interoperable radio communications; creating a coordinator for U.S. nonproliferation programs and improving international cooperation for interdiction of weapons of mass destruction; developing better mechanisms for modernizing education in Muslim communities and Muslim-

24. "Implementing Recommendations of the 9-11 Commission Act of 2007," The White House, www.whitehouse.gov/news/releases/2007/08/20070803-1.html (downloaded 10/24/2008).

25. "Wasted lessons of 9/11: How the bush administration ignored the law and squandered its opportunities to make our country safer," *The Gavel*, http://speaker.house.gov/blog/?p=1501 (downloaded 10/24/2008).

majority countries, and creating a new forum for reform-minded members of those countries; formulating coherent strategies for key countries; establishing a common coalition approach on the treatment of detainees; and putting resources into making democratic reform an international effort, rather than a unilaterally U.S. one. When President George W. Bush signed H. R. 1 into law on August 3, 2007 without any limiting statement, it seemed that the unfulfilled security recommendations of the 9-11 Commission would finally be implemented. To ensure that they were, over the past year the Majority staffs of the Committees on Homeland Security and Foreign Affairs have conducted extensive oversight to answer the question, *How is the Bush Administration doing on fulfilling the requirements of the "Implementing Recommendations of the 9-11 Commission Act of 2007 (P.L. 110-53)?* The Majority staffs of the two Committees prepared this report to summarize their findings. While the Majority staffs of the Committees found that the Bush Administration has taken some steps to carry out the provisions of the Act, this report focuses on the Administration's

performance with respect to key statutory requirements in the following areas: (1) aviation security; (2) rail and public transportation security; (3) port security; (4) border security; (5) information sharing; (6) privacy and civil liberties; (7) emergency response; (8) biosurveillance; (9) private sector preparedness; and (10) national security. In each of the 25 individual assessments in this report, a status update is provided on the Bush Administration's performance on these key provisions. The status of the key provisions identified in the report, help explain why the report is entitled "Wasted Lessons of 9/11: How the Bush Administration Has Ignored the Law and Squandered Its Opportunities to Make Our Country Safer."[26]

Based on this report, it is clear that the Bush Administration did not deliver on myriad critical homeland and national security mandates set forth in the "Implementing the Recommendations of 9-11 Commission Act of 2007." Members of the Committees were alarmed that the Bush Administration did not make more progress on implementing these key provisions.,

4. SUMMARY

Within about a year after the terrorist attacks, Congress passed various new laws, such as The USA PATRIOT Act, Aviation and Transportation Security Act, Enhanced Border Security and Visa Entry Reform Act, Public Health Security, Bioterrorism Preparedness & Response Act, Homeland Security Act, and E-Government Act, and introduced sweeping changes to homeland security provisions and to the existing security organizations. The executive branch of the government also issued a series of Homeland Security Presidential Directives (HSPDs) to maintain domestic security. These laws and directives are comprehensive and contain detailed provisions to make the United States secure. For example,

26. "Wasted lessons of 9/11: How the bush administration ignored the law and squandered its opportunities to make our country safer," *The Gavel*, http://speaker.house.gov/blog/?p=1501 (downloaded 10/24/2008)

HSPD 5 enhances the ability of the United States to manage domestic incidents by establishing a single, comprehensive national incident management system.

These laws and homeland security presidential directives call for deep and fundamental organizational changes to the executive branch of the government. For example, the Homeland Security Act of 2002 established a new Executive Branch agency, the U.S. Department of Homeland Security (DHS), and consolidated the operations of 22 existing federal agencies. Intelligence-sharing and analysis groups have been set up in many private infrastructure industries as well. For example, the National Electric Reliability Council has such a group, the Electricity Sector Information Sharing and Analysis Center (ESISAC), which serves the electricity sector by facilitating communications between sector participants, federal governments, and other critical infrastructure organizations.

Congress charted the "National Commission on Terrorist Attacks Upon the United States (The 9-11 Commission)" on November 27, 2002, to provide a "full and complete accounting" of the attacks of September 11, 2001, and recommendations as to how to prevent such attacks in the future. On July 22, 2004, the 9-11 Commission issued its final report, which included 41 wide-ranging recommendations to help prevent future terrorist attacks. Many of these recommendations were put in place with the passage of the "Intelligence Reform and Terrorism Prevention Act" and "Implementing Recommendations of the 9-11 Commission Act of 2007."

About a year after the passing of this law, the Majority Staffs of the Committees on Homeland and Foreign Affairs drew its attention on the extent to which the law was indeed implemented and issued a report on "Wasted Lessons of 9/11: How the Bush Administration Ignored the Law and Squandered Its Opportunities to Make Our Country Safer." This report demonstrates that it is clear that the Bush Administration did not deliver on myriad critical homeland and national security mandates set forth in the "Implementing the 9-11 Commission Recommendations Act of 2007." Fulfilling the unfinished business of the 9-11 Commission will most certainly be a major focus of President Obama, as many of the statutory requirements are to be met in stages.

Finally, let's move on to the real interactive part of this Chapter: review questions/exercises, hands-on projects, case projects and optional team case project. The answers and/or solutions by chapter can be found in the Online Instructor's Solutions Manual.

CHAPTER REVIEW QUESTIONS/EXERCISES

True/False

1. True or False? The Public Health Security, Bioterrorism Preparedness & Response Act of 2002, authorizes funding for a wide range of public health initiatives.
2. True or False? The Homeland Security Act of 2002 establishes a new Executive Branch agency, the U.S. Department of Homeland Security (DHS), and consolidates the operations of 33 existing federal agencies.
3. True or False? The E-Government Act of 2012 establishes a Federal Chief Information Officers Council to oversee government information and services, and creation of a new Office of Electronic Government within the Office of Management and Budget.

4. True or False? Presidential directives are issued by the National Security Council and are signed or authorized by the Vice President.

5. True or False? The homeland security presidential directives called for deep and fundamental organizational changes to the executive branch of the government.

Multiple Choice

1. Faced with the challenge of strengthening the components to function as a unified Department, _____ must coordinate centralized, integrated activities across components that are distinct in their missions and operations.
   A. Qualitative analysis
   B. Vulnerabilities
   C. Data storage
   D. Malformed request DoS
   E. DHS

2. There are various _____ of The Department of Homeland Security that are involved with Information Technology Security.
   A. Network attached storage (NAS)
   B. Risk assessment
   C. Valid
   D. Subcomponents
   E. Bait

3. There are various _____that support information sharing at the state and the federal levels.
   A. Organizations
   B. Fabric
   C. Disasters
   D. Risk communication
   E. Security

4. The Governor's Office of Homeland Security (OHS) acts as the _____ for the prevention of and preparation for a potential terrorist event.
   A. Cabinet-level state office
   B. Greedy strategy
   C. Infrastructure failure
   D. SAN protocol
   E. Taps

5. The California Office of Information Security and Privacy Protection (OISPP) unites _____ with the oversight of government's responsible management of information.
   A. Irrelevant
   B. Consumer privacy protection
   C. IP storage access
   D. Configuration file
   E. Unusable

EXERCISE

Problem

How does the new National Terrorism Advisory System (NTAS) work?

Hands-on Projects

Project

How will one find out that an NTAS Alert has been announced?

Case Projects

Problem

What should Americans do when an NTAS Alert is announced?

Optional Team Case Project

Problem

How should one report suspicious activity?

8

Cyber Warfare

Anna Granova* and Marco Slaviero**

*Pretoria Society of Advocates, **SensePost Pty Ltd

The times we live in are called the Information Age for very good reasons: Today information is probably worth much more than any other commodity. Globalization, the other important phenomenon of the times we live in, has taken the value of information to new heights. On one hand, citizens of a country may now feel entitled to know exactly what is happening in other countries around the globe. On the other, the same people can use the Internet to mobilize forces to overthrow the government in their own country.[1] To this end, the capabilities of the Internet have been put to use and people have become accustomed to receiving information about everyone and everything as soon as it becomes available. The purpose of this chapter is to define the concept of cyber warfare (CW), discuss their most common tactics, weapons, and tools, compare CW terrorism with conventional warfare, and address the issues of liability and the available legal remedies under international law. To have this discussion, a proper model and definition of CW first needs to be established.

October 20, 1969, marked the first message sent on the Internet,[2] and more 40 years on we cannot imagine our lives without it. Internet banking, online gaming, and online shopping and social media have become just as important to some as food and sleep. As the world has become more dependent on automated environments, interconnectivity, networks, and the Internet, instances of abuse and misuse of information technology infrastructures have increased proportionately.[3] Such abuse has, unfortunately, not been limited only to the abuse

1. *Egypt: AP Confirms Government has Disrupted Internet Service* (2011), http://pomed.org/blog/2011/01/egypt-ap-confirms-government-has-disrupted-internet-service.html/, accessed on 09 April 2012.

2. *An Internet History* (2008), www.services.ex.ac.uk/cmit/modules/the_internet/webct/ch-history.html, accessed on 19 February 2008.

3. *Symantec Global Internet Security Threat Report Trends for July–December 07* (2008) Vol. 13, published April 2008 available at http://eval.symantec.com/mktginfo/enterprise/white_papers/b-whitepaper_internet_security_threat_report_xiii_04-2008.en-us.pdf, accessed on 21 April 2008.

of business information systems and Web sites but over time has also penetrated the military domain of state security. Today this penetration of governmental IT infrastructures, including, among others, the military domain, is commonly referred to as *cyber warfare*. However, these concepts are not yet clearly defined and understood. Furthermore, this type of warfare is a multidisciplinary field requiring expertise from technical, legal, offensive, and defensive perspectives. Information security professionals are challenged to respond to this type of warfare issues in a professional and knowledgeable way.

1. CYBER WARFARE MODEL

The authors propose a model for CW by mapping important concepts regarding them on a single diagrammatic representation (see Figure 8.1). This aids in simplifying a complex concept as well as providing a holistic view on the phenomenon. To this end, this chapter addresses the four axes of CW: technical, legal, offensive, and defensive, as depicted in Figure 8.1.

The technical side of CW deals with technical exploits on one side and defensive measures on the other. As is apparent from Figure 8.1, these range from the most destructive offensive strategies, such as a distributed denial-of-service (DDoS) attack or stuxnet, to various workstation emergency response teams, such as US-CERT.

Considered from a legal perspective, CW can range from criminal prosecutions in international courts to use of force in retaliation. Therefore, the four axes of CW continuously interact and influence each other, as will become clearer from the discussion that follows.

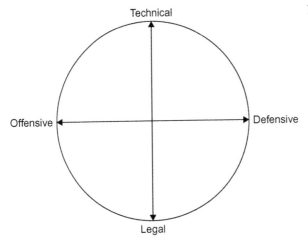

FIGURE 8.1 A perspective on CW.

2. CYBER WARFARE DEFINED

The manner in which war is being conducted has evolved enormously,[4] and CW has not only been accepted as a new direction in military operations,[5] but also been incorporated into some of the top military forces in the world, with China implementing an CW policy as early as 1995,[6] with United States Cyber Command (USCYBERCOM) established in 2009,[7] followed by China in July 2010,[8] US Cyber Warfare Intelligence Center[9] unveiled in November 2010 and the Cyber Warfare Administration in Israel in breathed into life in 2012.[10] A number of definitions are relevant for the purposes of this chapter. Some authors[11] maintain that CW covers "the full range of competitive information operations from destroying IT equipment to subtle perception management, and from industrial espionage to marketing." If one regards the more "military" definition of CW, one could say that CW is "a subset of information operations"—in other words "actions taken to adversely affect information and information systems while defending one's own information and information systems."[12]

The UN Secretary-General's report on *Development in the Field on Information and Telecommunications in the context of International Security* describes CW as "actions aimed at achieving information superiority by executing measures to exploit, corrupt, destroy, destabilise, or damage the enemy's information and its functions."[13] This definition is very similar to one of the more recent and accepted definitions found in literature that states that CW is "actions taken in support of objectives that influence decision-makers by affecting the information and/or information systems of others while protecting your own information and/or information systems."[14] If one, however, looks at CW in purely a military light, the following technical definition seems to be the most appropriate: "The broad

---

4. Schmitt, "Wired Warfare-Workstation Network Attack and *jus in bello*" 2002 *International Review of the Red Cross*, 365.

5. Rogers "Protecting America against Cybeterrorism" 2001 *United States Foreign Policy Agenda*, 15.

6. Ball "Security Challenges", Vol. 7, No. 2 (Winter 2011), pp. 81−103, http://www.securitychallenges.org.au/ArticlePDFs/vol7no2Ball.pdf, accessed on 09 April 2012.

7. *Cyber Command Achieves Full Operational Capability* (2010) http://www.defense.gov/releases/release.aspx?releaseid = 14030 accessed on 09 April 2012.

8. Branigan "Chinese army to target cyber war threat" (2010), http://www.guardian.co.uk/world/2010/jul/22/chinese-army-cyber-war-department accessed on 09 April 2012.

9. *Construction begins on first cyber warfare intelligence center* (2010), http://www.af.mil/news/story.asp?id = 123204543accessed on 09 April 2012.

10. *Israel to Establish Cyber Warfare Administration* (2012), http://www.israelnationalnews.com/News/News.aspx/151713 accessed on 09 April 2012.

11. Hutchinson and Warren, *CW − Corporate Attack and Defence in a Digital World (2001) and XVIIII.*

12. Schmitt, "Wired Warfare-Workstation Network Attack and *jus in bello*" 2002 *International Review of the Red Cross* 365. See also the definition by Goldberg available on line at http://psycom.net/CWar.2.html.

13. UNG.A.Res A/56/164 dated 3 July 2001.

14. Thornton, R, *Asymmetric Warfare − Threat and Response in the 20-First Century* 2007.

class of activities aimed at leveraging data, information and knowledge in support of military goals."[15]

In light of the preceding, it is clear that CW is all about information superiority because "the fundamental weapon and target of CW is information."[16] This being so, some authors[17] outline the basic strategies of CW as follows:

1. Deny access to information
2. Disrupt/destroy data
3. Steal data
4. Manipulate data to change its context or its perception

A slightly different perspective on the aims of CW is perhaps to see it as "an attack on information systems for military advantage using tactics of destruction, denial, exploitation or deception."[18] Since about 2008, however, the CW starting to cross over into the physical realm through one of its forms: cyber warfare, which can be defined as *politically motivated hacking to conduct sabotage and espionage*.

With these definitions in mind, it is now appropriate to consider whether CW is a concept that has been created by enthusiasts such as individual hackers to impress the rest of the world's population or is, in fact, part of daily military operations.

3. CW: MYTH OR REALITY?

Groves once said: "... nowhere it is safe ... no one knows of the scale of the threat, the silent deadly menace that stalks the network."[19] With the growing risk of terrorists and other hostile entities engaging in missions of sabotaging, either temporarily or permanently, important public infrastructures through cyber attacks, the number of articles[20] on the topic has grown significantly. To understand the gravity of CW and its consequences, the following real-life examples need to be considered. At the outset, however, it is important to mention that the reason there is so little regulation (see checklist, "An Agenda For Action For Regulating High Level Cyber Warfare Strategies") of computer-related activities with specific reference to CW both on national and international planes is that lawyers are very reluctant to venture into the unknown. The following examples, however, demonstrate that CW has consistently taken place since at least 1991. One of the first CW incidents was recorded in 1991 during the first Gulf War, where CW was used by the United States against Iraq.[21]

---

15. Vacca, J. R., *Computer Forensics: Computer Crime Scene Investigation (2nd Edition)* Charles River Media, 2005.

16. Hutchinson and Warren, *CW – Corporate Attack and Defence in a Digital World (2001), p. xviiii.*

17. Hutchinson and Warren, *CW – Corporate Attack and Defence in a Digital World (2001) p. xviiii.*

18. Vacca, J. R., *Computer Forensics: Computer Crime Scene Investigation (2nd Edition)* Charles River Media, 2005.

19. Lloyd, I. J., *Information Technology Law* Oxford University Press 181 (5th Edition) 2008.

20. Groves, The War on Terrorism: Cyberterrorist be Ware, *Informational Management Journal*, Jan-Feb 2002.

21. Goodwin "Don't Techno for an Answer: The false promise of CW."

AN AGENDA FOR ACTION FOR REGULATING HIGH LEVEL CYBER WARFARE STRATEGIES

Please see the following recommendations for regulating high level cyber warfare strategies (Check All Tasks Completed):

_____ 1. The President of the United States should task the National Office for Cyberspace (NOC) to work with appropriate regulatory agencies to develop and issue standards and guidance for securing critical cyber infrastructure, which those agencies would then apply in their own regulations.

_____ 2. The NOC should work with the appropriate regulatory agencies and with the National Institute of Standards and Technology (NIST) to develop regulations for industrial control systems (ICS).

_____ 3. The government should reinforce regulations by making the development of secure control systems an element of any economic stimulus package.

_____ 4. The NOC should immediately determine the extent to which government-owned critical infrastructures are secure from cyber attack.

_____ 5. The president should direct the NOC and the federal Chief Information Officers Council, working with industry, to develop and implement security guidelines for the procurement of IT products (with software as the first priority).

_____ 6. The president should task the National Security Agency (NSA) and NIST, working with international partners, to reform the National Information Assurance Partnership (NIAP).

_____ 7. The president should take steps to increase the use of secure Internet protocols.

_____ 8. The president should direct the Office of Management OMB and the NOC to develop mandatory requirements for agencies to contract only with telecommunications carriers that use secure Internet protocols.

In 1998 an Israeli national hacked into the government workstations of the United States.[22] In 1999, a number of cyber attacks took place in Kosovo. During the attacks the Serbian and NATO Web sites were taken down with the aim of interfering with and indirectly influencing the public's perception and opinion of the conflict.[23]

These cyber attacks were executed for different reasons: Russians hacked U.S. and Canadian websites "in protest" against NATO deployment,[24] Chinese joined the online

22. *Israeli citizen arrested in Israel for hacking United States and Israeli Government Workstations* (1998) http://www.usdoj.gov/criminal/cybercrime/ehudpr.hgm(accessed on 13 October 2002).

23. Hutchinson and Warren, *CW — Corporate Attack and Defence in a Digital World (2001).*

24. Skoric (1999), http://amsterdam.nettime.org/Lists-Archives/net-time-1-9906/msg00152.html, (accessed on 03 October 2002).

war because their embassy in Belgrade was bombed by NATO,[25] and U.S. nationals were paralyzing the White House[26] and NATO[27] Web sites "for fun." In 2000, classified information was distributed on the Internet,[28] and attacks were launched on NASA's laboratories,[29] the U.S. Postal Service, and the Canadian Defense Department.[30] As early as 2001, detected intrusions into the U.S. Defense Department's Web site numbered 23,662.[31] Furthermore, there were 1300 pending investigations into activities "ranging from criminal activity to national security intrusions."[32] Hackers also attempted to abuse the U.S. Federal Court's database[33] to compromise the peace process in the Middle East.[34]

In 2002, incidents of cyber terrorism in Morocco, Spain, Moldova, and Georgia[35] proved once again that a "hacker influenced by politics is a terrorist," illustrated by more than 140,000 attacks in less than 48 hours allegedly executed by the "G-Force" (Pakistan)[36]. During this period, a series of convictions on charges of conspiracy, the destruction of energy facilities,[37] the destruction of telecommunications facilities, and the disabling of air navigation facilities,[38] as well as cases of successful international luring and subsequent prosecutions, were recorded.[39]

25. Messmer (1999) http://www.cnn.com/TECH/computing/9905/12/cyberwar.idg/, (accessed on 03 October 2002).

26. *"Web Bandit" Hacker Sentenced to 15 Months Imprisonment, 3 Years of Supervised Release, for Hacking USIA, NATO, Web Sites* (1999), www.usdoj.gov/criminal/cybercrime/burns.htm (accessed on 13 October 2002).

27. *Access to NATO's Web Site Disrupted* (1999), www.cnn.com/WORLD/europe/9903/31/nato.hack/ (accessed on 03 October 2002).

28. Lusher (2000), www.balkanpeace.org/hed/archive/april00/hed30. shtml (accessed on 03 October 2002).

29. *Hacker Pleads Guilty in New York City to Hacking into Two NASA Jet Propulsion Lab Workstations Located in Pasadena, California* (2000), www.usdoj.gov/criminal/cybercrime/rolex.htm (accessed on 13 October 2002).

30. (2000) www.usdoj.gov/criminal/cybercrime/VAhacker2.htm (accessed on 13 October 2002).

31. www.coe.int/T/E/Legal_affairs/Legal_co-operation/Combating_economic_crime/Cybercrime/International_conference/ConfCY(2001) 5E-1.pdf (accessed on 9 October 2002).

32. Rogers, *Protecting America against Cyberterrorism* U.S. Foreign Policy Agenda (2001).

33. (2001) "Hacker Into United States Courts' Information System Pleads Guilty," www.usdoj.gov/criminal/cybercrime/MamichPlea.htm (accessed on 13 October 2002).

34. (2001) "Computer Hacker Intentionally Damages Protected Computer" www.usdoj.gov/criminal/cybercrime/khanindict.htm (accessed on 13 October 2002).

35. *Hacker Influenced by Politics is Also a Terrorist* (2002), www.utro.ru/articles/2002/07/24/91321.shtml (accessed on 24 July 2002).

36. www.echocct.org/main.html (accessed on 20 September 2002).

37. *Hackers Hit Power Companies* (2002) www.cbsnews.com/stories/2002/07/08/tech/main514426.shtml (accessed on 20 September 2002).

38. U.S. v. Konopka (E.D.Wis.), www.usdoj.gov/criminal/cybercrime/konopkaIndict.htm (accessed on 13 October 2002).

39. U.S. v. Gorshkov (W.D.Wash), www.usdoj.gov/criminal/cybercrime/gorshkovSent.htm (accessed on 13 October 2002).

In the second half of 2007, 499,811 new malicious code threats were detected, which represented a 571% increase from the same period in 2006.[40] With two thirds of more than 1 million identified viruses created in 2007,[41] the continued increase in malicious code threats has been linked to the sharp rise in the development of new Trojans and the apparent existence of institutions that employ "professionals" dedicated to creation of new threats.[42] In 2008 it has been reported in the media that "over the past year to 18 months, there has been 'a huge increase in focused attacks on our [United States] national infrastructure networks . . .. and they have been coming from outside the United States.'"[43]

It is common knowledge that over the past 15 years, the United States has tried to save both manpower and costs by establishing a system to remotely control and monitor the electric utilities, pipelines, railroads, and oil companies all across the United States.[44] The reality of the threat of CW has been officially confirmed by the U.S. Federal Energy Regulatory Commission, which approved eight cyber-security standards for electric utilities, which include "identity controls, training, security 'parameters' physical security of critical cyber equipment, incident reporting and recovery."[45] In January 2008, a CIA analyst warned the public that cyber attackers have hacked into the workstation systems of utility companies outside the United States and made demands, which led to at least one instance where, as a direct result, a power outage that affected multiple cities took place.[46]

Furthermore, since 2007, there have been a number of high profile events, which can be categorized as cyber attacks. Estonia was first in line to suffer from this debilitating form of aggression: it unleashed a wave of DdoS attacks, where websites were swamped by tens of thousands of requests, which in turn disabled them by overcrowding the

40. *Symantec Global Internet Security Threat Report Trends for July–December 07* (2008) Vol. 13, published April 2008 available at http://eval.symantec.com/mktginfo/enterprise/white_papers/b-whitepaper_internet_security_threat_report_xiii_04-2008.en-us.pdf accessed on 21 April 2008 at p.45.

41. *Symantec Global Internet Security Threat Report Trends for July–December 07* (2008) Vol. 13, published April 2008 available at http://eval.symantec.com/mktginfo/enterprise/white_papers/b-whitepaper_internet_security_threat_report_xiii_04-2008.en-us.pdf accessed on 21 April 2008 at p. 45.

42. *Symantec Global Internet Security Threat Report Trends for July–December 07* (2008) Vol. 13, published April 2008 available at http://eval.symantec.com/mktginfo/enterprise/white_papers/b-whitepaper_internet_security_threat_report_xiii_04-2008.en-us.pdf accessed on 21 April 2008 at p. 46.

43. Nakashima, E and Mufson, S, "Hackers have attacked foreign utilities, CIA Analysts says," 19 January 2008, available at www.washingtonpost.com/wp/dyn/conmttent/atricle/2008/01/18/AR2008011803277bf.html, accessed on 28 January 2008.

44. Nakashima, E and Mufson, S, "Hackers have attacked foreign utilities, CIA Analysts says," 19 January 2008, available at www.washington-post.com/wp/dyn/conmttent/atricle/2008/01/18/AR2008011803277bf.html, accessed on 28 January 2008.

45. Nakashima, E and Mufson, S, "Hackers have attacked foreign utilities, CIA Analysts says," 19 January 2008, available at www.washington-post.com/wp/dyn/conmttent/atricle/2008/01/18/AR2008011803277bf.html, accessed on 28 January 2008.

46. Nakashima, E and Mufson, S. (2008), "Hackers have attacked foreign utilities, CIA Analysts says," www.washingtonpost.com/wp/dyn/conmttent/atricle/2008/01/18/AR2008011803277bf.html, accessed on 28 January 2008.

bandwidths for the servers running the websites of the Estonian government, political parties, half of media organizations and the top two banks.[47]

Russia was blamed for the Estonian cyber conflict which was caused by the removal of a statue of significant importance to Russian people. The repeat of the showdown, but now with Georgia on the receiving end, was witnessed in 2008 when Georgia was literally blown offline during its military conflict with Russia.[48]

China also appears to be waging a persistent low-profile campaign against many foreign nations, such as Japan,[49] the United States[50] and the United Kingdom.[51] The United States themselves are not above suspicion: some experts hint that it might have been that country[52] that unleashed such a powerful "cyber weapon" as Stuxnet which impacted Iran's ability to conduct nuclear research.

With Duqu worm having been discovered on 01 September 2011, and showing similar capabilities as Stuxnet,[53] it is only a matter of time before one is able to find the country behind the worm by analyzing the motives behind the facility which will suffer its onslaught. The appropriate questions that then arise are: How can CW be brought about and how can one ward against it?

47. Traynor "Russia accused of unleashing cyberwar to disable Estonia" (2007) http://www.guardian.co.uk/world/2007/may/17/topstories3.russia accessed on 19 April 2012.

48. Danchev "Coordinated Russia vs Georgia cyber attack in progress" (2008) http://www.zdnet.com/blog/security/coordinated-russia-vs-georgia-cyber-attack-in-progress/1670 accessed on 09 April 2012, Tikk "Cyber Attacks Against Georgia: Legal Lessons Identified" (2008) http://www.carlisle.army.mil/DIME/documents/Georgia%201%200.pdf accessed on 09 April 2012.

49. "Japan parliament hit by China-based cyber attack" (2011) http://www.telegraph.co.uk/news/worldnews/asia/japan/8848100/Japan-parliament-hit-by-China-based-cyber-attack.html accessed on 09 April 2012.

50. "Identified Massive Global Cyberattack Targeting U.S., U.N. Discovered; Experts Blame China" (2011) http://www.foxnews.com/scitech/2011/08/03/massive-global-cyberattack-targeting-us-un-discovered-experts-blame-china/ accessed on 09 April 2012, Finkle "Cyber attack from China targets chemical firms: Symantec" (2011) http://www.msnbc.msn.com/id/45105397/ns/technology_and_science-security/t/cyber-attack-china-targets-chemical-firms-symantec/ accessed on 09 April 2012, Gorman "U.S. Report to Warn on Cyberattack Threat From China" (2012) http://online.wsj.com/article/SB10001424052970203961204577267923890777392.html accessed on 09 April 2012.

51. Foster "China chief suspect in major cyber attack" (2012) http://www.telegraph.co.uk/technology/news/8679658/China-chief-suspect-in-major-cyber-attack.html accessed on 09 April 2012.

52. Langner "Cracking Stuxnet, a 21st-century cyber weapon" (2011) http://www.ted.com/talks/ralph_langner_cracking_stuxnet_a_21st_century_cyberweapon.html accessed on 09 April 2012, Waug "How the world's first cyber super weapon 'designed by the CIA' attacked Iran - and now threatens the world" (2011) http://www.dailymail.co.uk/sciencetech/article-2070690/How-worlds-cyber-super-weapon-attacked-Iran--threatens-world.html accessed on 09 April 2012.

53. Naraine "Duqu FAQ" http://www.securelist.com/en/blog/208193178/Duqu_FAQ#comments accessed on 09 April 2012.

4. CYBER WARFARE: MAKING CW POSSIBLE

To conduct any form of warfare, one would require an arsenal of weapons combined with an array of defensive technologies as well as laboratories and factories for researching and producing both. As far as CW is concerned, three general strategies need to be considered: preparation, offensive strategies and defensive strategies.

Preparation

Without arms, wars cannot be fought. Weapons are not constructed overnight and so in order to be prepared to enter any war, a state must have stockpiles of weapons ready to be deployed; CW is no different. Preparation will play a major role in CW as hostile acts occur in seconds or minutes, but the acts themselves are the culmination of many man-years worth of work.

In addition to training personnel and producing cyber weapons, the preparation stage also consists of a wide range of information gathering activities. Effective warfare is premised on knowledge of the opponent's weaknesses, and having extensive knowledge of an adversary's technology and networks prior to any hostilities is important for planning.

Preparation thus broadly consists of research, reconnaissance and vulnerability enumeration. The preparation phase never reaches a conclusion; ongoing research produces new tools, vulnerabilities and exploits, reconnaissance must continually discover new targets while removing stale targets, and vulnerability enumeration must keep track of new and old targets, while testing for recent vulnerabilities.

Research

CW does not require the infrastructure investment that physical arms do,[54] however it requires highly trained personnel to develop cyber weapons and the process of training to the required skill levels occupies a significant portion of activities prior to hostilities breaking out. In addition, once personnel have the necessary skills they need time to uncover vulnerabilities and turn those into usable weapons. These are separate jobs; the notion of vulnerability research as a separate discipline to exploit writing is growing especially as the continued fragmentation of applications and hardware forces extreme specialization. In the commercial information security market, vulnerability research and exploit writing are often separate tasks handed to different individuals, especially where memory corruption bugs are concerned.

The bug finders' skills tend towards quickly understanding how an application or system is built, how they often fail using common usage patterns and the ability to reverse engineer protocols quickly. Good bug finders are adept at automating this process. Their task, for example, is to find input that will cause a memory corruption to occur, after which the test case is handed to an exploit writer. Vulnerabilities are found at all layers and are introduced all stages of development, and vulnerability research strives to

---

54. Of the $707.5 billion requested for the U.S. Department of Defense 2012 budget, $159 million was earmarked for the Cyber Command.

understand each component. Software bugs are not the only target; flaws in algorithms are highly valued and common misconfigurations often yield trivial exploits.

The exploit writer has extreme specialist knowledge of the inner working of the operating system on which the application runs, and is able to craft exploits that bypass operating system protections designed to thwart their exploits. With a working exploit in hand, the exploit writer then ensures it runs without crashing across a wide range of possible versions of the target software and operating system. The exploit will also often be obfuscated in some manner, to avoid detection. For the moment it serves to simplify cyber arms by thinking of them as exploits, but as we shall see, cyber weapons consist of further components.

The combined process of finding a bug and writing an exploit for it can take months. While not all vulnerabilities require that level of input, it is by no means extreme. Consider that cyber weapons are not simply just bugs and exploits; superficially, configuration and operational failures are prevalent but deeper issues in protocols and algorithms also exist.

Reconnaissance

This phase of preparation focuses on identifying government organs, industries, infrastructure, companies, organizations and individuals that are potential targets. This is fed by a country's intelligence services, and overlaps with targets for physical warfare. In producing targets, information is gathered on the purpose of the targets, likely data that they store, technologies in use, network presence (on public or private networks) and channels by which the target could be engaged.

A discovery exercise is conducted on targets to determine which network services, if any, are accessible. Access to targets over the Internet is certainly not a requirement for CW but, for those that are, prior knowledge of their presence saves time when hostilities break out.

Vulnerability Enumeration

With reconnaissance complete, the next preparation step is to discover vulnerable systems. Vulnerability scanning is a common activity in the commercial security industry, and numerous scanners exist. A scanner has a large database holding knowledge of tens of thousands of issues, as well as how to test for those issues. The kinds of tests vary; in some instances a test consists of simply checking a software version number extracted from a service banner, but in other tests more complex methods are required such as harmless exploits that confirm the vulnerability but do not take further action. By unleashing the scanner on a wide range of targets, a database of vulnerable machines can be saved prior to an CW.

Vulnerable systems are not the only benefit of wide scale scanning. Even a database of version numbers or technology types will improve targeting, for example when vulnerabilities for a system are discovered in the future.

The problem with scanners is that they are not subtle. They often test for issues unrelated to the technology on which the service runs, and protection mechanisms such as IDS are tuned to detect vulnerability scans. One improvement is scanning for specific issues across the target's networks which reduces the likelihood of detection, as well as masking tests to evade signature-based detection methods.

Offensive Strategies

Scale is an important decision in deciding on an CW strategy. To extend the analogy of physical warfare, the strategic focus in CW could either be on small but highly experienced and trained tactical teams who are able to compromise targets at will, or to deploy an overwhelming number of moderately skilled operators. The analogy has flaws: whereas adding an extra operator in the physical realm increases the capabilities of that unit, adding extra CW operators past some point starts to see diminishing returns. The reason for this is that many CW operations can be automated and parallelized; additional *infrastructure* is often more valuable than additional personnel. Smaller teams decrease personnel and training costs, though they are more vulnerable to physical attacks against the teams.

A second consideration is the type of hostilities that CW covers. It will very likely be employed as a support to a kinetic war in the same way that ground troops value air cover. There is a second set of tactics that are *covert*, and these are akin to espionage. Regardless of whether the strategy is overt or covert, we refer to them a hostilities.

The arsenal of CW includes weapons of psychological and technical nature. Both are significant and a combination of the two can bring about astounding and highly disruptive results.

Psychological Weapons

Psychological weapons include social engineering techniques and psychological operations *(psyops)*. Psyops include deceptive strategies, which have been part of warfare in general for hundreds of years.

Sun Tzu, in his fundamental work on warfare, says that "All warfare is based on deception."[55] Deception has been described as "a contrast and rational effort ... to mislead an opponent."[56] In December 2005, it became known that the Pentagon was planning to launch a US$300 million operation to place pro-U.S. messages "in foreign media and on items such as T-shirts and bumper stickers without disclosing the U.S. government as the source."[57]

Trust is a central concept and a prerequisite for any psyops to succeed. Traditionally, trust was vested in institutions and roles; a stranger in uniform might be afforded recognition based on the trust (if any) one has in the organization they are representing, without knowing them personally. Computer networks have, for some time now, been attacked by so-called "Social Engineers" who excel in gaining and exploiting trust, and cybercrime activities such as phishing rely on victims associating mere graphics on a website with the trust they invest in their bank.

55. Sun Tzu, *Art of War*.

56. Thornton, R., *Asymmetric Warfare — Threat and Response in the Twenty-First Century*, 2007.

57. www.infowar-monitor.net/modules.php?op = modload&name = News&sid = 1302, accessed on 28 September 2006.

However, this does not represent an exhaustive list of psyops. Psyops can also target the general population by substituting the information on well-trusted news agencies' Web sites as well as public government sites with information favorable to the attackers. A good example is where the information on the Internet is misleading and does not reflect the actual situation on the ground.

Today, social networks are highly efficient tools for spreading information. The instantaneous broadcast nature of micro-blogging sites such as Twitter mean that consumers rely more on social tools for obtaining information about current events than traditional media. In the heat of the moment, fact-checking quality decreases and the probability of inserting false information into social platforms increases. Social networks are also useful in guiding public conversations; Russia's legislative elections of 2011 saw automated software posting thousands of messages on Twitter in order to drown out opposition.[58]

The problem with psyops is that they cannot be used in isolation because once the enemy stops trusting the information it receives and disregards the bogus messages posted for its attention, psyops become useless, at least for some time. Therefore, technical measures of CW should also be employed to achieve the desired effect, such as DoS and botnet attacks. That way, the enemy might not only be deceived but the information the enemy holds can be destroyed, denied, or even exploited.

Technical Weapons

There are non-subtle differences between weapons that exist in the physical realm and those that exist within the cyber realm, and the differences are useful to highlight. Bluntly put, there is no patch for an Intercontinental Ballistic Missile. To refine this further, a significant challenge facing a cyber army is that, while their attacks can occur virtually instantly, the target is able to respond as rapidly. The response may be to rollout patches for known issues, develop new patches for new vulnerabilities, employ perimeter defenses to filter out the attack traffic or simply disconnect the targeted system or network (perhaps, in the worst case scenario, even disconnect a country.)

A further challenge is the carrying of CW traffic. In the physical world, air and water provide the channels by which weapons are deployed, but in the cyber realm the path between two points is governed by a very different geography. It is a truism that in order to attack a network, an access channel extending from the attacker to the target is required. It could be a disconnected channel using flashdrives, or a highly technical and difficult operation such as the conquest of military satellites with ground-based resources or breaking into submarine cables, but the attacker must have a viable means for delivering their attack. While these complex or unreliable channels are possible, a more likely carrier for CW traffic is commercial Internet infrastructure supplied and maintained by global Internet Service Providers (ISPs), as they provide publicly accessible network links between countries around the world. In relying on commercial ISPs, attackers have the benefit of plausible deniability on the one hand, and on the other the ability to extend their reach into the commercial space of the target country, before attacking government and military targets.

58. http://www.guardian.co.uk/world/2011/dec/09/russia-putin-twitter-facebook-battles accessed on 29 February 2012.

CW attacks have the advantage that their implementation can be deployed long before any declaration of war. Whereas it is difficult to deploy physical armaments in preparation for detonating them near a target prior to a declaration of war, cyber attacks do not have the same limitation. Preparing attack launch pads either by compromising systems or by renting data center space can be performed months if not years in advance of attacks. When CW commences, the attacker is already well placed to wreak damage. A particularly effective force will compromise their target's supply chain, infusing equipment with backdoors years before they are used.

Rules of engagement present a further challenge. Traditional weapons are deployed at predetermined points in a conflict: artillery is seldom deployed when friendly troops are in the vicinity of the target, nuclear weapons may be a disproportionate response to a minor border skirmish and attacking schools or hospital without authorization may lie outside of a force's rules of engagement. Each armament has known side effects and its impact can be predicted; a commander in a physical war will understand which weapons are appropriate in each circumstance and deploy those that achieve their objectives while remaining within the constraints that are their policies and procedures. However, these norms have not been established publicly for CW, where *appropriate response* has yet to be defined. The dynamic nature of CW also means that, regardless of tools and techniques developed in the preparation phase, tools will be rapidly written during hostilities in reaction to new information or circumstances, and these could be trialed in the field while a conflict is active. Without perfect knowledge of exactly what a system controls or influences, unexpected consequences will be common in CW as the effects of an attack cannot be completely predicted.

The final significant difference between CW weapons and physical armaments is that their deterrence value is markedly different. Physical weapons demonstrate capability, which a cautious enemy will note. Developing defenses and counter-attacks against new weapons takes time in the real world, and so publicly exposing weapons capabilities can serve to avoid conflict. In the digital realm however, revealing one's weapons to an opponent simply highlights the areas they need to monitor, patch or upgrade. If an opponent provides evidence of working exploits against SoftwareX then, as a first line of defense, all of the target's machines running SoftwareX are moved behind additional layers and a plan is formulated to migrate away from SoftwareX. The defense can also perform their own investigation into SoftwareX, to determine the possible bug. By the time a conflict occurs, the revealed weapons are no longer useful. It has been shown in the commercial software exploit market that merely publishing seemingly innocuous descriptions of bugs can lead to experienced bug finders rapidly repeating the discovery without additional help. Demonstrating cyber capabilities is a confidence game in which a little skin is shown, in order to imply the strength of weapons that remain hidden. This is very susceptible to bluffing and subterfuge. With all this in mind, what do cyber weapons look like?

Previous work defined them as individual tools such as viruses, Trojans and so on. However, CW is fought at a larger scale than individual attacks, exploits and vulnerabilities. A commander on an CW battlefield is concerned with achieving objects such as disabling powergrids to support a kinetic attack on a facility. The commander firstly requires a team and infrastructure that is able to communicate and act in a distributed fashion; channeling attacks across lone routes or network links exposes a single point of failure, and attacks should be launched from a platform that is close in network terms to the target. This platform may be some distance from the command post. The weapons should be capable of working across multiple locations, and the payloads too must run in parallel and from multiple points in the network. Secondly, the commander must remain in control of attacks. For example, a worm that is unleashed against a target cannot indiscriminately attack targets on the public Internet as this would not help achieve the goal, and possibly result in collateral damage of systems unrelated to the opponent. Attacks would either be directly controlled by the commander through a command channel, or the attack would be self-limiting in terms of time or through built-in target detection. Examples of target detection are hardcoded addresses (when the reconnaissance phase was effective,) or a set of heuristics for determining at run-time whether a potential target should be attacked. This was seen in the Stuxnet attack, where the malicious code contained numerous heuristics to determine when it had finally migrated to the target SCADA installation. Until those heuristics were triggered, the program did nothing except attempt to migrate further. Lastly, a feedback loop that keeps the commander updated on whether the attack has succeeded is important. If the attack has a physical effect (for example, knocking out a powergrid), then the feedback loop would include forces on the ground. However, where the impact is virtual, then detecting attack success is not so clear cut. Consider the objective of disabling an opponent's logistics capability by preventing access to their logistics application through a deluge of traffic. Should the application become unresponsive from an attacker's perspective then it is not immediately apparent if the cause of the outage was a successful attack or due to the attack being detected and all the attacker's traffic blocked. Telemetry is vitally important.

Remember that CW is an "attack on information systems for military advantage using tactics of destruction, denial, exploitation or deception." The tactics by which the advantage is gained are determined by the weaknesses in the opponents systems, not the weapons in one's arsenal. This is important as it suggests that CW is not defined simply in terms of a set of tools; rather, the purpose or intent behind the deployment of a tactic is what defines a tactic to be part of an CW action. We shall see that so-called cyber weapons, in many circumstances, are called viruses, Trojans and the like when deployed by criminals or fraudsters. In that sense, the actual malicious components are less interesting as they are seldom unique to the field of CW and have been covered in this book already. The broader set of CW tools includes vulnerability databases, deployment tools, payloads and control consoles.

VULNERABILITY DATABASES

The vulnerability database is the result of an effort to collect information about all known security flaws in software. From the outset, it is obvious this is a massive challenge as vulnerability information is generated by thousands of sources including software vendors, vulnerability researchers and users of the software. Public efforts exist to provide identifiers for security weaknesses in software applications, such as the MITRE Corporations' Common Vulnerabilities and Exposures (CVE) project, which defines itself as "dictionary of common names (CVE Identifiers) for publicly known information security vulnerabilities."[59] The CVE contains information about a particular vulnerability in a software product, but for CW this is only part of the required information. A truly useful CW vulnerability database will also include those opposing systems that have been discovered to exhibit a particular weakness. The weaknesses are not simply software vulnerabilities; in many cases misconfigurations lead to compromise, and these are not problems with the code but snags resulting from the manner in which the system was setup.

DEPLOYMENT TOOLS

Commonly seen in commercial malware where they are known as "droppers", deployment techniques are a separate beast from the payload that executes after compromise. Deployment occurs by exploiting a vulnerability, attacking a misconfiguration, spreading misinformation, spoofing communications, collusion or coercion. Stuxnet, for example, was deployed via four previously unknown vulnerabilities in Microsoft Windows, as well as through known network-based attacks. What made Stuxnet particularly interesting is that one infection mechanism was via USB flashdisks, as the target was presumed to not have public Internet connectivity.

Development of deployment tools occupies a large portion of the preparation phase, as discovered vulnerabilities and their exploits written form the basis for deploying malicious code. A stockpile of these tools aids an CW action, especially where tools take advantage of unknown flaws in software (termed "zero day", "0day", "0-day" or "oh-day").

PAYLOADS

Merely loading malicious code onto a target does not constitute a full attack. Seldom is compromise the sole CW tactic; rather, post-compromise is where the CW tactic is implemented. Payloads consist of the post-compromise logic, and can be swapped out depending on the intended tactic. In this way, deployment and payload are separate tools but combined to form a single attack. Potential actions by malicious code are covered elsewhere in the book, here we mention a sample of possible payloads that have been seen in examples of CW.

A DoS attack is an overt example of CW, in that its effects will be plainly visible to the target; an important system will no longer be accessible or usable. DoS attacks were amongst the first malicious tactics to be labeled as actual CW maneuvers in state-on-state disputes. In 2007, Estonia suffered a massive DoS attack that lasted three weeks, and interrupted financial and governmental functions, while in a dispute with Russia.[60] Whether the attack was conducted by organs of the Russian state has never been established; however, CW does not necessitate actions are conducted only by nation states. Standards for attribution are not clearly defined, as we shall see.

The adoption of Supervisory Control and Data Acquisition (SCADA) network-connected systems for the U.S. infrastructure, such as power, water, and utilities,[61] has

59. http://cve.mitre.org/about/index.html, accessed on 10 March 2012.

60. Geers, K. (2008), *Cyberspace and the Changing Nature of Warfare*, BlackHat Asia 2008.

61. McClure, S., Scambray, J., and Kurtz, G. (2003), *Hacking Exposed: Network Security Secrets & Solutions*, 4th ed., McGraw-Hill/Osborne, 505.

made DoS attacks a lethal weapon of choice. Offline SCADA systems could have spectacular kinetic results. In 2010, a covert attack given the name Stuxnet was targeted at nuclear facilities in Iran. It succeeded in causing widespread damage by replacing control code on SCADA systems, and aimed to remain covert by feeding the operators false instrument information while the attack was underway.

CONTROL CONSOLES

In the commercial information security business, attack consoles are a known quantity. Software such as CORE IMPACT,[62] CANVAS[63] and Metasploit[64] provide interfaces that help the operator find vulnerabilities in target systems and launch exploits against those targets. The consoles ship with knowledge of hundreds of vulnerabilities, and include exploits for each one. The consoles also contain a multitude of payloads that can be attached to any exploit, that perform tasks such as account creation, command shell access or attacks against machines further in the network. An CW control console would contain the same elements as a commercial attack console, but also include the previously prepared vulnerability database as well as sport advanced telemetry to determine attack success.

Defensive Strategies

As far as prevention is concerned, experts agree that "there is no silver bullet against CW attacks."[65] In the US, defense against CW is split between two entities: the Department of Defense (DoD) is responsible for defending military resources, and the Department for Homeland Security (DHS) is responsible for protecting critical infrastructure. Purely in terms of military spending, the DoD requested $3.2 billion for cybersecurity in 2012, of which $159 million was intended for the U.S. Cyber Command (USCYBERCOM),[66] a military command who mission is to be the organization that "plans, coordinates, integrates, synchronizes, and conducts activities to: direct the operations and defense of specified Department of Defense information networks and; prepare to, and when directed, conduct full-spectrum military cyberspace operations in order to enable actions in all domains, ensure US/Allied freedom of action in cyberspace and deny the same to our adversaries."[67] From this mission statement, it is also clear that an offensive capability will be maintained. According to one military official, this was envisioned to be split approximately 85 percent defense and 15 percent offense.[68]

62. http://www.coresecurity.com/content/core-impact-overview, accessed on 10 March 2012.

63. http://immunityinc.com/products-canvas.shtml, accessed on 10 March 2012.

64. http://www.metasploit.com/, accessed on 10 March 2012.

65. Lonsdale, D. J., *The Nature of War and Information Age: Clausewitzian Future* at 140.

66. Miller, J.N., Statement to the House Committee on Armed Services, Subcommittee on Emerging Threats and Capabilities, *Hearing on the Department of Defense in Cyberspcae and U.S. Cyber Command*, March 16, 2011. Available at http://www.dod.mil/dodgc/olc/docs/testMiller03162011.pdf, accessed 11 March 2012.

67. U.S. Cyber Command Fact Sheet, http://www.defense.gov/home/features/2010/0410_cybersec/docs/CYberFactSheet%20UPDATED%20replaces%20May%2021%20Fact%20Sheet.pdf, accessed on 10 March 2012.

68. Holmes, E., "Donley Sets out Structure for Cyber Command", *Air Force Times*, February 26 2009.

Without question, the defender's job is harder than the attackers in the environment that currently exists. This is not to say it is a truism; it is certainly possible to envision a world in which uniform security is applied throughout all connected networks, however that world does not exist today. The defender's dilemma from an CW perspective has multiple facets. Apart from the oft cited statement that a defender needs to cover all avenues of attack while the attackers needs only find a single vulnerability, CW also introduces the additional difficulty of defending networks that one potentially does not control. Would an CW defense command have full access to all critical infrastructure networks? This is unlikely; rather, individual actions would have to be delegated to administrators of those networks, who best know the ins and outs of their own networks.

For the most part, the attacks listed here are preventable and detectable. The problem facing a large target entity such as a sovereign nation is to coordinate its defense of many possible individual targets. Policies and procedures must be consistent and thoroughly followed. This is a mammoth task, given the heterogeneous nature of large computing systems. CW defense calls for rapid communication between all points worthy of defense and the central defense command.

Current solutions are of an organizational nature. Many developed countries have response teams such as the Computer Emergency Response Teams (CERT), but these deal only with technicalities of attacks. Higher-level involvement from government is required to act as a line of defense for CW. The U.S. DHS has forged a link with the private and public sector in the form of the US-CERT, with the blessing of a national strategy for cyber defense, and DHS coordinates with USCYBERCOM to ensure protection across military, government and critical infrastructure networks. In the U.K., a similar role is played by the National Infrastructure Security Co-ordination Centre.

South Africa, as an example country of the developing world, does not yet have a high-level commitment to digital defense; however, there are initiatives in the pipeline to address CW issues. A number of international efforts that aim at securing the Internet and preventing attacks such as the ones mentioned here have been implemented. One such initiative is the adoption of the European Convention of Cybercrime 2001, which deals with the commercial aspects of the Internet transactions. As far as the military aspects of CW are concerned, there have been calls from a number of countries, notably Russia, that the Internet be placed under control of the United Nations.[69]

One author suggests that, while completely excluding attackers is desirable, this may not be attainable, and so proposes that "the purpose of cyberdefense is to preserve [the ability to exert military power] in the face of attack,"[70] by concentrating on desirable qualities such robustness, system integrity and confidentiality. This is achieved by architecture decisions (air-gapped networks), policy positions (centralized planning including forensic abilities, decentralized execution), strategic analysis (determining the purpose of distributed attacks) and effective operations.

69. (2003) *Russia wants the UN to take control over the Internet,*"www.witrina.ru/witrina/internet/? file_body = 20031118oon.htm, accessed on 10 May 2005.

70. Libicki, M.C., *Cyberdeterrence and Cyberwar*, Santa Monica, CA: RAND Corporation, 2009. http://www. rand.org/pubs/monographs/MG877 accessed on 29 February 2012.

Key to any cyberdefense is attribution; without identifying the source of the attack one is unable to launch counterattacks. Attribution is rarely guaranteed except when extremely simplistic markers are used. For example, using the source IP address of an attack does not imply that the owner of that addresses was aware of the attack. Botnets are typically built from thousands of vulnerable machines around the Internet and, while a machine may form part of an CW action, the owner cannot be punished militarily. Rather, the impact of the attack must be assessed in conjunction with information gleaned from other sources, in order to determine who the likely source was. Even then, the information may not be sufficient to point to state actors; industrial espionage or commercial attacks share many characteristics with CW, as we have already highlighted.

5. LEGAL ASPECTS OF CW

The fact that the Internet is, by definition, international implies that any criminal activity that occurs within its domain is almost always of an international nature.[71] The question that raises concern, however, is the degree of severity of the cyber attacks. This concern merits the following discussion.

Terrorism and Sovereignty

Today more than 110 different definitions of terrorism exist and are in use. There is consensus only on one part of the definition, and that is that the act of terrorism must "create a state of terror" in the minds of the people.[72]

The following definition of "workstation terrorism" as a variation of CW is quite suitable: "Computer terrorism is the act of destroying or of corrupting workstation systems with an aim of destabilizing a country or of applying pressure on a government,"[73] because the cyber attack's objective, *inter alia*, is to draw immediate attention by way of causing shock in the minds of a specific populace and thus diminishing that populace's faith in government.

Incidents such as hacking into energy plants, telecommunications facilities, and government Web sites cause a sense of instability in the minds of a nation's people, thereby applying pressure on the government of a particular country; therefore, these acts do qualify as terrorism and should be treated as such. Factual manifestations of war, that is, use of force and overpowering the enemy, ceased to be part of the classical definition of "war" after World War I,[74] and international writers began to pay more attention to the factual circumstances of each case to determine the status of an armed conflict. This is very significant for current purposes because it means that, depending on the scale and consequences

71. Corell (2002), www.un.org/law/counsel/english/remarks.pdf (accessed on 20 September 2002).

72. J. Dugard, International Law: A South African Perspective 149 (2nd ed. 2000).

73. Galley (1996), http://homer.span.ch/~spaw1165/infosec/sts_en/ (accessed on 20 September 2002).

74. P. Macalister-Smith, Encyclopaedia of Public International Law 1135(2000).

of a cyber attack, the latter may be seen as a fully fledged war,[75] and the same restrictions—for example, prohibition of an attack on hospitals and churches—will apply.[76]

CW may seem to be a stranger to the concepts of public international law. This, however, is not the case, for there are many similarities between CW and the notions of terrorism and war as embodied in international criminal law.

The impact of the aforesaid discussion on sovereignty is enormous. Admittedly a cornerstone of the international law, the idea of sovereignty, was officially entrenched in 1945 in article 2(1) of the United Nations (UN) Charter.[77] This being so, any CW attack, whatever form or shape it may take, will no doubt undermine the affected state's political independence, because without order there is no governance.

Furthermore, the prohibition of use of force[78] places an obligation on a state to ensure that all disputes are solved at a negotiation table and not by way of crashing of the other state's Web sites or paralyzing its telecommunications facilities, thereby obtaining a favorable outcome of a dispute under duress. Finally, these rights of nonuse of force and sovereignty are of international character and therefore "international responsibility"[79] for all cyber attacks may undermine regional or even international security.

Liability Under International Law

There are two possible routes that one could pursue to bring CW wrongdoers to justice: using the concept of "state responsibility," whereby the establishment of a material link between the state and the individual executing the attack is imperative, or acting directly against the person, who might incur individual criminal responsibility.

State Responsibility

Originally, states were the only possible actors on the international plane and therefore a substantial amount of jurisprudence has developed concerning state responsibility. There are two important aspects of state responsibility that are important for our purposes: presence of a right on the part of the state claiming to have suffered from the cyber attack and imputation of the acts of individuals to a state.

Usually one would doubt that such acts as cyber attacks, which are so closely connected to an individual, could be attributable to a state, for no state is liable for acts of individuals unless the latter acts on its behalf.[80] The situation, however, would depend on the concrete facts of each case, as even an *ex post facto* approval of students' conduct by the head of the government[81] may give rise to state responsibility. Thus, this norm of international law

75. Barkham, *Informational Warfare and International Law*, 34 Journal of International Law and Politics, Fall 2001, at 65.

76. P. Macalister-Smith, Encyclopaedia of Public International Law 1400 (2000).

77. www.unhchr.ch/pdf/UNcharter.pdf (accessed on 13 October 2002).

78. www.unhchr.ch/pdf/UNcharter.pdf (accessed on 13 October 2002).

79. *Spanish Zone of Morocco* claims 2 RIAA, 615 (1923) at 641.

80. M.N. Shaw, International Law 414 (2nd ed. 1986).

81. For example, in *Tehran Hostages Case (v.) I.C.J. Reports*, 1980 at 3, 34−35.

has not become obsolete in the technology age and can still serve states and their protection on the international level.

Attribution in the context of CW, without somebody coming forward to claim responsibility for the attack, may prove to be a difficult, if not impossible, task because to hold a state liable one would have to show that the government had effective control over the attacker but, though its conduct, failed to curtail the latter's actions directed at another state and threatens international peace and security.[82]

As a result, even though many attacks emanate from China, for example, the Chinese government will only be responsible if it supported or at least was aware of the attacker and went along with that attacker's plans. Solid forensic investigation would therefore be required before there can be any hope in attributing responsibility.[83]

Individual Liability

With the advent of a human rights culture after the Second World War, there is no doubt that individuals have become participants in international law.[84] There are, however, two qualifications to the statement: First, such participation was considered indirect in that nationals of a state are only involved in international law if they act on the particular state's behalf. Second, individuals were regarded only as beneficiaries of the protection offered by the international law, specifically through international human rights instruments.[85]

Individual criminal responsibility, however, has been a much more debated issue, for introduction of such a concept would make natural persons equal players in international law. This, however, has been done in cases of Nuremberg, the former Yugoslavia, and the Rwanda tribunals, and therefore,[86] cyber attacks committed during the time of war, such as attacks on NATO web sites in the Kosovo war, should not be difficult to accommodate.

What made it easier is the fact that in 2010, the Review Conference for the International Criminal Court introduced article *8bis* to the Rome Statute of the International Criminal Court ("ICC") which finally defined the crime of "aggression" as "the planning, preparation, initiation or execution, by a person in a position effectively to exercise control over or to direct the political or military action of a State, of an act of aggression which, by its character, gravity and scale, constitutes a manifest violation of the Charter of the United Nations".[87]

---

82. Huntley (2010) "Controlling the use of force in cyber space: the application of the law of armed conflict during a time of fundamental change in the nature of warfare" 60 Naval L. Rev. 1 2010.

83. Friesen (2009) "Resolving tomorrow's conflicts today: How new developments within the U.N. Security Council can be used to combat cyberwarfare" 58 Naval L. Rev. 89 2009.

84. J. Dugard, International Law: a South African Perspective (2nd ed. 2000), p. 1.

85. J. Dugard, International Law: a South African Perspective 1 (2nd ed. 2000), p. 234.

86. M.C. Bassiouni, International Criminal Law (2nd ed. 1999), p. 26.

87. Resolution RC/Res.6 http://www.icc-cpi.int/iccdocs/asp_docs/Resolutions/RC-Res.6-ENG.pdf accessed on 09 April 2012.

There is no doubt that use of unilateral force which threatens universal peace is prohibited in international law.[88] The difficulty in holding an individual responsible is two-fold: confirming jurisdiction of the ICC over the accused and proving the intention to commit the crime covered by the Rome Statute the ICC administers.

First, only persons who are found within the territory of the state that is a signatory to the Rome Statute or such state's nationals may be tried before the ICC. Secondly, there may be difficulties with justification of use of the same terms and application of similar concepts to acts of CW, where the latter occurs independently from a conventional war. Conventionally, CW as an act of war sounds wrong, and to consider it as such requires a conventional classification. The definition of "international crimes" serves as a useful tool that saves the situation: arguably being part of *jus cogens*,[89] crimes described by terms such as "aggression," "torture," and "against humanity" provide us with ample space to fit all the possible variations of CW without disturbing the very foundation of international law. Thus, once again there is support for the notions of individual criminal responsibility for cyber attacks in general public international law, which stand as an alternative to state responsibility.

In conclusion, it is important to note that international criminal law offers two options to an agreed state, and it is up to the latter to decide which way to go. The fact that there are no clear pronouncements on the subject by an international forum does not give a blank amnesty to actors on an international plane to abuse the apparent *lacuna*, ignore the general principles, and employ unlawful measures in retaliation.

Remedies Under International Law

In every discussion, the most interesting part is the one that answers the question: What are we going to do about it? In our case there are two main solutions or steps that a state can take in terms of international criminal law in the face of CW: employ self-defense or seek justice by bringing the responsible individual before an international forum. Both solutions, however, are premised on the assumption that the identity of the perpetrator is established.[90]

Self-Defense

States may only engage in self-defense in cases of an armed attack[91] which in itself has become a hotly debated issue.[92] This is due to recognition of obligation of nonuse of force

88. Green (2011) "Questioning the peremptory status of the prohibition of the use of force" 32 Mich. J. Int'l L. 215 2010–2011.

89. M.C. Bassiouni, International Criminal Law (2nd ed. 1999), p. 98.

90. Murphy (2011) "Mission Impossible? International law and the changing character of war" 87 Int'l L. Stud. Ser. US Naval War Col. 13 2011, (2011) Lewis "Cyberwarfare and its impact on international security" http://www.un.org/disarmament/HomePage/ODAPublications/OccasionalPapers/PDF/OP19.pdf accessed on 09 April 2012.

91. U.N.Charter art. 51.

92. Cammack (2011) "The Stuxnet worm and potential prosecution by the international criminal court under the newly defined crime of aggression" 20 Tul. J. Int'l & Comp. L. 303 2011.

in terms of Art.2(4) of the UN Charter as being not only customary international law but also *jus cogens.*[93]

Armed attack, however, can be explained away by reference to the time when the UN Charter was written, therefore accepting that other attacks may require the exercise of the right to self-defense.[94] What cannot be discarded is the requirement that this inherent right may be exercised only if it aims at extinguishing the armed attack to avoid the conclusion of it constituting a unilateral use of force.[95] Finally, a state may invoke "collective self-defense" in the cases of CW. Though possible, this type of self-defense requires, first, an unequivocal statement by a third state that it has been a victim of the attack, and second, such a state must make a request for action on its behalf.[96]

Therefore, invoking self-defense in cases of CW today, though possible,[97] might not be a plausible option, because it requires solid proof of an attack, obtained promptly and before the conclusion of such an attack,[98] which at this stage of technological advancement is quite difficult. The requirement that the attack should not be completed by the time the victim state retaliates hinges on the fact that once damage is done and the attack is finished, states are encouraged to turn to international courts and through legal debate resolve their grievances without causing more loss of life and damage to infrastructure. Since most states would deny any support of or acquiescence to the actions of its citizens in executing an attack, the more realistic court that one would turn to in pursuit of justice is the ICC.

International Criminal Court

The International Criminal Court (ICC) established by the Rome Statute of 1998 is not explicitly vested with a jurisdiction to try an individual who committed an act of terrorism. Therefore, in a narrow sense, cyber terrorism would also fall outside the competence of the ICC.

In the wide sense, however, terrorism, including cyber terrorism, could be and is seen by some authors as torture.[99] That being so, since torture is a crime against humanity, the ICC will, in fact, have a jurisdiction over cyber attacks, too.[100]

---

93. M.Dixon, Cases and Materials on International Law 570 (3rd ed., 2000).

94. P. Macalister-Smith, Encyclopaedia of Public International Law 362 (2000).

95. Military and Paramilitary Activities in and against Nicaragua *(Nic. v. U.S.A.),* www.icj-cij.org/icjwww/Icases/iNus/inus_ijudgment/inus_ijudgment_19860627.pdf (accessed on 11 October 2002).

96. M.Dixon, Cases and Materials on International Law 575 (3rd ed. 2000).

97. Barkham, *Informational Warfare and International Law,* Journal of International Law and Politics (2001), p. 80.

98. otherwise a reaction of a state would amount to reprisals, that are unlawful; see also *Nic. v. U.S.A.* case in this regard, www.icj-cij.org/icjwww/Icases/iNus/inus_ijudgment/inus_ijudgment_19860627.pdf (accessed on 11 October 2002).

99. J. Rehman, International Human Rights Law: A Practical Approach 464–465 (2002).

100. Rome Statute of the International Criminal Court of 1998 art.7, www.un.org/law/icc/statute/english/rome_statute(e).pdf (accessed on 13 October 2002).

Cyber terrorism could also be seen as crime against peace, should it take a form of fully fledged "war on the Internet," for an "aggressive war" has been proclaimed an international crime on a number of occasions.[101] Though not clearly pronounced on by the Nuremberg Trials,[102] the term "crime of aggression" is contained in the ICC Statute and therefore falls under its jurisdiction.[103]

Cyber crimes can also fall under crimes against nations, since in terms of customary international law states are obliged to punish individuals committing crimes against third states.[104] Furthermore, workstation-related attacks evolved into crimes that are universally recognized to be criminal and therefore against nations. P. Macalister-Smith, Encyclopaedia of Public International Law 876 (1992). Therefore, thanks to the absence of *travaux préparatoires* of the Rome Statute, the ICC will be able to interpret provisions of the statute to the advantage of the international community, allow prosecutions of cyber terrorists, and ensure international peace and security.

In practical terms the above will mean that a cyber attack will most probably be interpreted as part of "any weapon"[105] within the scope of the definition of "aggression" of the Rome Statute and the attacker will face the full might of the law as long as he/she is the national of the member state or finds him/herself within the physical territorial boundaries of the state that is party to the Rome Statute even though the attacker's conduct may not be enough to make the country of its nationality liable for what he/she did.[106]

Other Remedies

Probably the most effective method of dealing with CW is by way of treaties. At the time of this writing, there has been only one such convention on a truly international level, the European Convention on Cybercrime 2001.

The effectiveness of the Convention can be easily seen from the list of states that have joined and ratified it. By involving such technologically advanced countries as the United States, Japan, the United Kingdom, Canada, and Germany, the Convention can be said to have gained the status of instant customary international law,[107] as it adds *opinio juris* links to already existing practice of the states.

---

101. League of Nations Draft Treaty of Mutual Assistance of 1923, www.mazal.org/archive/imt/03/IMT03-T096.htm (accessed on 13 October 2002); Geneva Protocol for the Pacific Settlement of International Disputes 1924, www.worldcourts.com/pcij/eng/laws/law07.htm (accessed on 13 October 2002).

102. P. Macalister-Smith, Encyclopaedia of Public International Law 873–874 (1992).

103. Art.5(1)(d) of the Rome Statute of the International Criminal Court 1998, www.un.org/law/icc/statute/english/rome_statute(e).pdf (accessed on 13 October 2002).

104. P. Macalister-Smith, Encyclopaedia of Public International Law 876 (1992).

105. Article 8 *bis* 2(b) of the Rome Statute, http://www.icc-cpi.int/iccdocs/asp_docs/Resolutions/RC-Res.6-ENG.pdf acc3essed on 09 April 2012.

106. Schmitt (2011) "Cyber Operations and the *Jus in Bello*: Key Issues" 87 Int'l L. Stud. Ser. US Naval War Col. 89 2011.

107. http://conventions.coe.int/Treaty/en/Treaties/Html/185.htm (accessed on 9 October 2002).

Furthermore, the Convention also urges the member states to adopt uniform national legislation to deal with the ever-growing problem of this century[108] as well as provide a platform for solution of disputes on the international level.[109] Finally, taking the very nature of CW into consideration, "hard" international law may be the solution to possible large-scale threats in future.

The fact that remedies bring legitimacy of a rule cannot be overemphasized, for it is the remedies available to parties at the time of a conflict that play a decisive role in the escalation of the conflict to possible loss of life. By discussing the most pertinent remedies under international criminal law, the authors have shown that its old principles are still workable solutions, even for such a new development as the Internet.

Developing Countries Response

The attractiveness of looking into developing countries' response to an CW attack lies in the fact that usually these are the countries that appeal to transnational criminals due to lack of any criminal sanctions for crimes they want to commit. For purposes of this chapter, the South African legal system will be used to answer the question of how a developing country would respond to such an instance of CW.

In a 1989 "end conscription" case, South African courts defined war as a "hostile contest between nations, states or different groups within a state, carried out by force of arms against the foreign power or against an armed and organised group within the state."[110] In the 1996 *Azapo* case, the Constitutional Court, the highest court of the land, held that it had to consider international law when dealing with matters like these.[111] In the 2005 *Basson* case, the Constitutional Court further held that South African courts have jurisdiction to hear cases involving international crimes, such as war crimes and crimes against humanity.[112]

A number of legislative provisions in South Africa prohibit South African citizens from engaging, directly or indirectly, in CW activities. These Acts include the Internal Security Intimidation Act 13 of 1991 and the Regulation of Foreign Military Assistance Act 15 of 1998. The main question here is whether the South African courts would have jurisdiction to hear matters in connection therewith. A number of factors will play a role. First, if the incident takes place within the air, water, or *terra firma* space of South Africa, the court would have jurisdiction over the matter.[113]

The implementation of the Rome Statute Act will further assist the South African courts to deal with the matter because it confers jurisdiction over the citizens who commit

---

108. European Convention on Cybercrime of 2001 art. 23, http://conventions.coe.int/Treaty/en/Treaties/Html/185.htm (accessed on 9 October 2002).

109. European Convention on Cybercrime of 2001 art. 45, http://conventions.coe.int/Treaty/en/Treaties/Html/185.htm (accessed on 9 October 2002).

110. Transcription *Campaign and Another v. Minister of Defence and Another* 1989 (2) SA 180 (C).

111. *Azanian People's Organisation (AZAPO) v. Truth and Reconciliation Commission* 1996 (4) SA 671 (CC).

112. *State v. Basson* 2005, available at www.constitutionalcourt.org.za.

113. Supreme Court Act 59 of 1959 (South Africa).

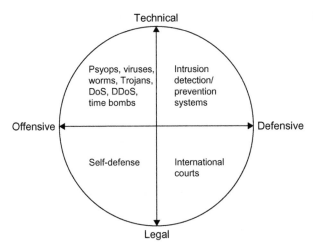

Technical

FIGURE 8.2   Holistic view of CW.

Psyops, viruses, worms, Trojans, DoS, DDoS, time bombs

Intrusion detection/ prevention systems

Offensive

Defensive

Self-defense

International courts

Legal

international crimes. It is well known that interference with the navigation of a civil air-craft, for example, is contrary to international law and is clearly prohibited in terms of the Montreal Convention.[114]

A further reason for jurisdiction is found in the 2004 Witwatersrand Local Division High Court decision of *Tsichlas v. Touch Line Media*,[115] where Acting Judge Kuny held that publication on a Web site takes place where it is accessed. In our case, should the sites in question be accessed in South Africa, the South African courts would have jurisdiction to hear the matter, provided that the courts can effectively enforce its judgment against the members of the group.

Finally, in terms of the new Electronic Communications and Transactions (ECT) Act,[116] any act or preparation taken toward the offense taking place in South Africa would confer jurisdiction over such a crime, including interference with the Internet. This means that South African courts can be approached if preparation for the crime takes place in South Africa. Needless to say, imprisonment of up to five years would be a competent sentence for each and every participant of CW, including coconspirators.[117]

6. HOLISTIC VIEW OF CYBER WARFARE

This chapter has addressed the four axes of the CW model[118] presented at the beginning of this discussion: technical, legal, offensive, and defensive. Furthermore, the specific

114. Montreal Convention of 1971.

115. *Tsichlas v. Touch Media* 2004 (2) SA 211 (W).

116. Electronic Communications and Transactions Act 25 of 2002.

117. Electronic Communication and Transaction Act 25 of 2002.

118. Supreme Court Act 59 of 1959 (South Africa).

subgroups of the axes have also been discussed. For the complete picture of CW as relevant to the discussion at hand, however, Figure 8.2 places each subgroup into its own field.[119]

7. SUMMARY

This discussion clearly demonstrated that CW is not only possible, it has already taken place and is growing internationally as a preferred way of warfare. It is clearly demonstrated that successful strategies, offensive or defensive, are dependent on taking a holistic view of the matter. Information security professionals should refrain from focusing only on the technical aspects of this area, since it is shown that legal frameworks, national as well as international, also have to be considered. The prevailing challenge for countries around the globe is to foster collaboration among lawyers, information security professionals, and technical IT professionals. They should continue striving to at least keep the registry of CW arsenal and remedies updated, which may, in turn, incite adversaries to provide us with more material for research.

Finally, let's move on to the real interactive part of this Chapter: review questions/exercises, hands-on projects, case projects and optional team case project. The answers and/or solutions by chapter can be found in the Online Instructor's Solutions Manual.

CHAPTER REVIEW QUESTIONS/EXERCISES

True/False

1. True or False? The technical side of CW deals with technical exploits on one side and offensive measures on the other.
2. True or False? It is clear that CW is all about information superiority because "the fundamental weapon and target of CW is information.".
3. True or False? In addition to training personnel and producing cyber weapons, the preparation stage also consists of a wide range of information gathering activities.
4. True or False? CW does not require the infrastructure investment that physical arms do,[120] however it requires highly trained personnel to develop cyber weapons and the process of training to the required skill levels occupies a significant portion of activities prior to hostilities breaking out.
5. True or False? The reconnaissance phase of preparation focuses on identifying government organs, industries, infrastructure, companies, organizations and individuals that are not potential targets.

---

119. Implementation of the Rome Statute of the International Criminal Court Act 27 of 2002 (South Africa).

120. Of the $707.5 billion requested for the U.S. Department of Defense 2012 budget, $159 million was earmarked for the Cyber Command.

Multiple Choice

1. What type of scanning is a common activity in the commercial security industry, where numerous scanners exist?
   A. Qualitative analysis
   B. Vulnerabilities
   C. Data storage
   D. Vulnerability
   E. DHS
2. What is an important decision in deciding on a CW strategy?
   A. Network attached storage (NAS)
   B. Risk assessment
   C. Scale
   D. Subcomponents
   E. Bait
3. What type of weapons include social engineering techniques and psychological operations (*psyops*)?
   A. Organizations
   B. Fabric
   C. Psychological
   D. Risk communication
   E. Security
4. There are _____ differences between weapons that exist in the physical realm and those that exist within the cyber realm, and the differences are useful to highlight.
   A. Cabinet-level state office
   B. Non-subtle
   C. Infrastructure failure
   D. SAN protocol
   E. Taps
5. What type of database is the result of an effort to collect information about all known security flaws in software?
   A. Irrelevant
   B. Consumer privacy protection
   C. IP storage access
   D. Vulnerability
   E. Unusable

EXERCISE

Problem

How can organizations address advanced persistent cyber threats?

Hands-On Projects

Project

How are cyber-attacks carried out?

Case Projects

Problem

What targets can be attacked?

Optional Team Case Project

Problem

What are the implications of a cyber-attack?

9

System Security

Lauren Collins

kCura Corporation

1. FOUNDATIONS OF SECURITY

Since the inception of technology, data security has revolved around cryptography. Since cryptography is only as good as the ability of a person or a program, new methods are constantly being implemented as technology becomes more sophisticated.

Differentiating Security Threats

Cipher text and secret keys are transported over the network and can be harvested for analysis, as well as impersonate a source or, worst case, cause a service denial. Thus, aiding encryption and complex distribution methods, a network needs to be secure and elegant. That is, the network should have applicable appliances that monitor and detect attacks, intelligence that discriminates between degradations/failures and attacks, and also a convention for vigorous countermeasure strategies to outmaneuver the attacker. Consequently, network security is a completely separate topic from data security.

Incident levels should be defined as low, medium, high, and catastrophic. Level 1 help-desk professionals should be equipped to handle tasks such as these. Low-severity breach examples are:

- Malware or virus-infected system that is on the local area network (LAN)
- Account credentials compromised with general rights
- Spam e-mail incidents

Medium-severity incidents should be escalated to a system administrator or engineer. These would include:

- Website destruction
- Spam impacting an entire environment's performance

- Sensitive information leak
- Account credentials compromised with administrative rights

High-severity incidents would be handled by a senior engineer, architect, manager, or director. Examples include:

- Hacking of the environment
- International, federal, or state law violations:
  1. HIPAA (Health Insurance Portability and Accountability Act)—medical field
  2. FERPA (Family Education Rights and Privacy Act)—education field
  3. Pornography
  4. Illegal download and sharing of copyright material (music, movies, software)
- Disruption of business due to malicious acts
- Breach to systems where an act is in progress of leaking confidential information and hosts need to be disconnected altogether to halt the process

Modern enterprises and their security teams need to be prepared to work with an onslaught of new, rapidly evolving menaces. From novice script writers to sophisticated hackers working for criminal organizations, if an enterprise does not have policies in place to handle threats, they will pay the price in disconcerting, expensive data breaches. An effective threat management platform is one vibrant component for any security team who deals with evolving threats from the world outside of their control. Resources must be allocated to implement such a platform, and an agenda should be put in place while also testing the program. The following are five best practices to increase effectiveness when implementing a vulnerability management program:

1. **Control notifications and alerts.** The most important thing a company can do is get a handle on threat management and ensure an IT professional is available to review and respond to a notification or alert. In order to accomplish this, one or more individuals need to have responsibility assigned to them so that everyone is aware of which point person(s) will review logs and audits on a daily basis, or in the event of an attack. It is not uncommon to see organizations assign different individuals to review different alerts consoles. Case in point: A firewall expert may review firewall changes and logs, while an applications engineer may review the logs and alerts from the Web application firewalls.
2. **Consider a holistic view.** In the domain of discovery avoidance, attackers are growing more and more cutting edge. A multichannel attack is the superficially innocuous spear where a user clicks on a link that leads to a rogue site that has been designed to look authentic. This user may then be deceived into entering sensitive data or clicking another link affecting the target machine with a bot. Once that user's sensitive information has been collected, the attacker can now attempt to log in to a system and dive deeper into the network for more valuable information. To catch multichannel attackers, alerts need to be organized in a meaningful way from all the systems into a single console where correlation rules filter activities and, when combined, creates a single, organized attack.
3. **Slash false positives.** Have you received so many email alerts that you ignore certain alerts and immediately delete them without further investigation? This author surely

has. Excessive alerts and false positives intensify the noise ratio so greatly that it can be challenging (if not impossible) to scrutinize data to find truly malicious occurrences. If an organization's administrators cannot differentiate important alert signals through all the less significant events, the system becomes useless. To reduce the number of false positives fabricated, an enterprise should first analyze the alert output of its threat-warning console and then determine if the rules can be fine-tuned to reduce the false-positive noise. Also, filtering the alerts by level of confidence may be useful so that administrators can see which alerts are more likely to be relevant. One way to lower the alert levels without losing the critical alerts would be to set the threshold levels that match normal activity on the network. For example, if a company forces all users to change the password on the same 30-day cycle, they might find that failed logins increase significantly on the day after the end of the cycle. To account for this occurrence, a rule that normally signals an alert after two failed logins could be increased to four failed logins, only on days following the password change. Those logins could also be linked to other threat indicators, such as attempts to log in using the same username from multiple IP addresses, to increase accuracy.

4. **Integrate thresholds and procedures.** As mentioned in #3, aggregating threat information into a single console gives firms threat visibility across the entire infrastructure. You want more visibility? A firm can integrate that single console view with their new, refined thresholds and procedures. That's right: Always keep the mind-set that you want to be a moving target. By treating your monitoring system the same way as your infrastructure, as the infrastructure grows please ensure that your monitoring system accommodates that growth. Rules and log aggregation tools rightfully parse through information and flag legitimate attack activity for further investigation or response. Another key to integrating effectively is to make sure engineers and admins have access to proper escalation paths, communication protocols, and approved response activities.

5. **Corroborate remediation events.** In a heated situation, one can easily overlook validating events in logs upon review. Even when performing routine maintenance such as patch management, many firms fail to close the remediation loop by validating the entries. Did the patch get loaded properly? Did it close the intended vulnerability? Without testing, an organization cannot be certain the remediation was successful and the threat exposure gap was closed. There is a threat management cycle, and it must be completed utilizing steps for validation. This may include rescanning systems to validate patches and also, by performing application and network penetration, testing to confirm that fixes or controls are blocking vulnerabilities as expected.

Hardware and Peripheral Security

Network security deals with the secure transport of data. It requires more awareness and a thorough understanding of the different types of mechanisms and attack scenarios and how they can be differentiated. A topic these days for a controversial discussion is whether to allow employees to bring your own device (BYOD) to the office. Whether it is a mobile device, a desktop or laptop, or a tablet, companies must have policies in place to address security and who owns the data on the device. Several places institute a policy where an application like ActiveSync is used, and upon an employee's termination the device(s) can be wiped of all data. That usually sounds good to the employee upon signing the consent form, but imagine losing all your contacts, music and apps, and all the data on the device. Given the breadth of end users on mobile devices and the diversity of use cases, BYOD is driving not just the need for performance upgrades but also much more fine-grained network access controls.

There is also a method for detecting signatures and how that is used to classify attacks and enhance network security. Computing platforms used in the field are intricate and require interaction between multiple hardware components (processor, chipset, memory) for their normal operation. Maintaining the security of the platforms translates to verifying that no known security exploits are present in the runtime interaction between these hardware units which can be exploited by attackers. However, given the large number of state elements in the hardware units and many control signals influencing their mutual interaction, validating the security of a commercial computing platform thoroughly can be complicated and intractable. By exemplifying challenges to correctly implement security, it is necessary to provide examples of various classes of hardware-oriented security attacks. The following are logic and tools to use:

- For the enthusiastic newbies, there are pre-made, entry-level tool packages as shown in Figure 9.1. You can diagnose your hardware without writing even one line of code. Automatically generate your device driver, and run this nifty tool on any operating system.
- Digital oscilloscopes, logic analyzers, device programmers, and spectrum analyzers are all available on eBay and are no longer out of reach for hardware hackers. Utilizing this equipment, one can take advantage of essentially the same equipment used in production engineering facilities. In Figure 9.2, a logic analyzer displays signals and program variables as they change over time.

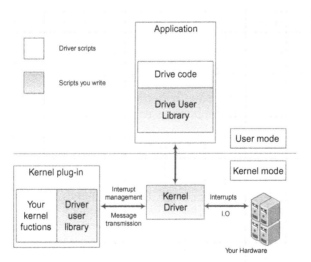

FIGURE 9.1   Architecture to access your hardware directly from the application level.

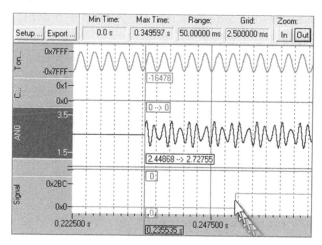

FIGURE 9.2 Signals recorded by the logic analyzer are easily configured to accurately measure signal changes and delta information, and will even allow you to zoom into the area at any point where a signal changed.

- Free tools are available that are open-source Printed Circuit Board (PCB) design tools, which include electronic design automation (EDA). These tools allow hackers to dive deep into the game without bringing a ton of years of electrical engineering to the table. Schematic captures are done interactively with an editor tool and allow one to gain insight on arrays and other miniscule passive components.

The magnificence of hardware hacking, similar to engineering design, is that rarely is there only one correct process or solution. The author's personal hardware hacking methodology consists of the following subsystems:

1. *Gather information:* Hardware hacking, much like any technology, is about gathering pertinent information from an assortment of resources. The answers include product specifications, design documents, marketing data, forums or blogs, and of course, social network sites. Social engineering techniques can be used to manipulate a human victim into divulging applicable information. Many will simply call a vendor's sales or technical engineer directly and invoke interest in a product, and will ask open-ended questions to obtain as much information as the respondent is willing to divulge.
2. *Hardware stripping:* This consists of obtaining the hardware and disassembling it to gather evidence regarding system functionality, design practices, and potential attack areas to target. The primary goal of tearing hardware down is to gain access to the circuit board, which will then allow a hacker to identify high-level subsystems, component types, and values, and in some cases, locate any antitampering mechanisms that would specifically impede physical attack or tampering. Clearly, having direct access to the circuitry allows an attacker to modify, remove, or add components.
3. *Assess external accessibility:* Any product interface that is made accessible to the outside world is an avenue of attack. Programming, debugging, or admin interfaces are of extreme interest, as it allows a hacker direct access to control the device with the same authority as a tech or engineer.
4. *Reverse engineering:* By extracting program code or data and disassembling the contents, a hacker will be able to obtain full insight into the product operation and functionality

and potentially modify, recompile, and insert the code back into the product in order to bypass security mechanisms or inject malicious behavior.

The prolific adoption of embedded systems has led to a blurring between hardware and software. Software hackers can now use their skills, tools, and techniques in an embedded environment against firmware without having to grasp hardware-specific paradigms.

The best way to close the gap between hardware and software hacking is to allow them to work together in order to achieve the desired results. The leading example will enlighten the reader as to why electronic devices used in security or financial applications cannot and should not be fully trusted without thorough analysis and stress testing.

Example

Many large cities have installed digital parking meters throughout the streets, and claim they are secure and tamper proof. While a hacker has many opportunities to attack a metering device, this example focuses on the easily accessible, external smartcard interface. By placing an uninhabited shim between the smartcard and meter, the shim was used to gain the requisite signals and the communication was then captured using an oscilloscope. (It's good to have friends with cool toys). The serial decoding function of the oscilloscope, displayed in Figure 9.3, points out the actual data bytes that were transmitted from the meter, then to the card, and finally received by the meter from the card.

Patch Management and Policies

Does anyone receive auto-generated email alerts that are excessive, false positives? Not only can it be impossible to examine all of the information, but to assert whether or not the information is truly malicious is another tedious task. Many times this author has ignored countless emails when too many false positives have occurred, which could have been a warning of potential issues. Anytime an environment changes, individuals should be attentive to editing the notifications of the environment. An example would be when

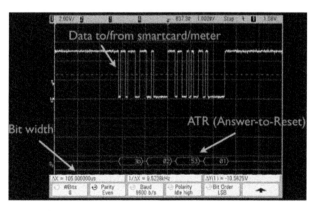

FIGURE 9.3 Oscillator output displaying the transmission between the smartcard and meter.

maintenance will be performed where five servers will be restarted multiple times for patches. The alert should be paused for these five servers in an effort to not trigger false alerts where the rest of the team is not aware of the maintenance. If the team is aware of the maintenance, this is a prime example of a false alert that is overlooked, and think through this example happening 10 times a day. Hardly anyone will pay attention to the alerts if 99.99 percent of them are false positives.

Implementing consistent, updated patches may be cost prohibitive for a company, especially for a mission-critical environment. It is necessary to maintain the integrity of an environment and the data by applying both operating system and application security patches and updates. The security team or IT manager needs to ascertain a criterion for procedures as well as an established time frame to apply patches. Windows patches may alter program functionality and capability so severely that users are unable to effectively perform their job function. For instance, some Web applications were not compatible with Internet Explorer version 9, and if updates are set to automatic, troubleshooting this issue could be quite time consuming. Unless patches have been tested in a testing environment, and were successful, there should not be any patches released to the user community. There are patch management packages that offer automation, of course, after testing has proved to be successful. Figure 9.4 depicts an example of a patch management program. Patch names are shown in the left-hand column, the next column classifies the patch, then displays whether or not the patch was installed, and shows the release date along with the arrival date.

Package management systems are charged with the task of organizing all of the packages installed on a particular system. The characteristics of architectural tasks are shown in the following checklist: An Agenda for Action for Implementing Package Architectural Tasks.

FIGURE 9.4 Patch management software is a helpful tool to track patches and whether or not the patch has been applied to a client.

AN AGENDA FOR ACTION FOR IMPLEMENTING PACKAGE ARCHITECTURAL TASKS

Please see the following package archi-tectural characteristics tasks (check all tasks completed):

_____1. Manage dependencies to ensure a package is installed with all packages required.
_____2. Group packages related to utility.
_____3. Upgrade software to latest (tested) versions from a file repository.

_____4. Apply file records to manage encapsulated files.
_____5. Verify digital signatures upon substantiation of the source packages.
_____6. Corroborate file checksums to confirm authentic, comprehensive packages.

IT admins may install and maintain software-utilizing instruments other than package management software. Dependencies will need to be managed, and additional changes may have to be assimilated into the package manager. This does not seem like a very effi-cient way to some, although having control of source code and the ability to manipulate code may be an attractive advantage. In addition to the manual process of installing patches, license codes may need to be manually activated. When dealing with large envir-onments, can you fathom typing in an activation code thousands of times? Not only is this counterproductive, but it is severely inefficient as noted in Figure 9.5.

Each hardware and software vendor may have differing frequencies for their approach to patch releases. Microsoft has "Patch Tuesday" which occurs the second Tuesday of a month. When Windows updates are set to Automatic, a computer will apply patches as

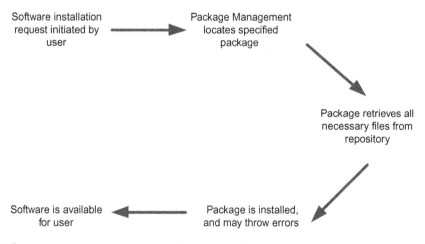

FIGURE 9.5   Cycle of a patch management software installation.

they're released. These patches may not be tested in an environment, hence the importance of setting updates to manual and having a patch management system. A good practice is to release patches once a month, and to release them roughly a week after the vendor has published the patch. Network hardware patches may not need to be applied, depending on the environment and whether or not the patch will compromise the function of the equipment. Additionally, patches may alter the command set or configuration, so be sure to back up your configuration prior to applying any patch or firmware update.

2. BASIC COUNTERMEASURES

With only 30 to 40 percent of firewall rules in use, security vulnerabilities arise due to misconfigurations. An organization may expose its network to access for which there is no business purpose.

Security Controls and Firewalls

At times, it is not an issue of data sneaking past network controls, but misconfiguration and reluctance to fix issues fearing that the business may be interrupted as changes are implemented. When a team identifies all users' network access, they are able to shape and control access based off rights and proper use. Risk is reduced by blocking unnecessary access paths prior to a security incident occurring. When a consultant is brought into a firm and shows the IT director all the paths, there are holes in the network that could be used for unauthorized access; heads roll, and a plan is soon in place to rectify the holes. Other firms are relatively weak when it comes to monitoring the data right in front of them. While many firms have the appropriate technologies, policies and awareness programs need to be in place for users and their resources. The level of awareness also needs to be known in unmanaged IP devices due to the number of vulnerabilities only increasing over time.

There are many options out there when considering a firewall for your environment. A great deal of firewalls also include other security features: unified threat management (UTM), data loss prevention (DLP), content filtering, intrusion detection and prevention services (IPS), and vulnerability management. A firewall is such a critical component of your infrastructure, and fault tolerance should not be considered optional. A network should be designed so that it is resilient enough to handle the failure of a single firewall. Most concerns with UTM are the amount of processors eaten up by the jobs being performed. With large organizations, you may find you're better off with specialty devices fulfilling each of the security functions covered by UTM. Conversely, UTMs are a great benefit for smaller companies with lower network traffic, especially where costs are concerned when selecting a bundled option.

There is a huge amount of virtual networks out there, both at company office sites and at data center facilities. Virtual firewalls are a way to maximize your security budget by consolidating multiple logical firewalls onto a single platform. Each virtual firewall has its own rules, interfaces, and configuration options that are completely independent from other virtual firewalls running in other infrastructure platforms, but in the same environment. Having this feature also adds the element that a configuration mistake will not only affect performance, but may block all traffic getting to and from the affected segment.

Whether the firewall is hardware or software based, the objective is to control whether or not traffic should be allowed in or out based on a predetermined set of rules. Imagine a security analyst parsing through hundreds pages of logs, where this would only account for 10 to 30 minutes of traffic and determining whether or not rule sets need to be altered.

Case in point: Also envision an issue arising where a complaint comes in from your company's Internet provider stating that your IP address raised a red flag and downloads of copyrighted material were performed. This Internet provider can even state the name of the movie that was downloaded. Other than the Internet provider expecting a response back describing the steps that will be taken to prevent subscriptions from downloading illegal content, internal management at this company expects actions to be taken as well. This is when a security admin will go in and parse through logs searching for the type of file that was downloaded, and if this was not already blocked it will need to be. Bit torrents may need to be blocked. However, depending on the type of work a company performs, there are many legal and necessary uses of bit torrents.

Application Security

An increasing number of organizations are questioning whether they should put a Web application firewall in front of an application, or if the code should just be fixed. Entire teams have committed to securing an application. Consultants travel all over to perform a deep dive of an application environment and suggest measures to correct loopholes. If the strategy shifted toward incorporating applications coupled with Web application firewalls, the company would be more productive integrating this plan as part of its broader application security architectures. Whether Structured Query Language (SQL) attacks or cross-site scripting was the vulnerability, a financial institution would still need about two years to patch 99 percent of the flaws in its applications. By this time, several revisions of the application will have been released, sending teams in downward spirals chasing their tails.

If you ask your customers or colleagues, there is not much collaboration between the security and development teams in an organization. The worst part is that developers are not usually motivated to address secure application development unless they are forced to in the midst of a security incident or to prove compliance initiatives. Developers are sometimes reviewed based on how much software they can build and release on time, and no one holds them accountable for the security portion. The application security challenge has become so difficult to address through development that an alternative plan relies on integrating defensive technologies like Web app firewalls, database audit and protection (DAP), and XML gateways into the infrastructure. Using Web app firewalls in conjunction with coding frameworks fits nicely into filling security functions.

Is it faster, cheaper, and more effective to use a device to shield an application from a security flaw? It may be, but meanwhile hacking strategies are also becoming more accessible, faster, free, and more attractive. Web application firewalls are an appliance, or server, that can monitor and block traffic both to and from the applications. They are common in companies such as credit-card payment firms, which have frequent code reviews. You cannot throw a piece of hardware in front of all applications and expect it to solve all your problems because it is a good idea to build your applications securely from the start.

Hardening and Minimization

The practice of safeguarding systems is to reduce the plane of exposure, also referred to as hardening. An environment where a multitude of cross-functional work is performed can increase the scale of the vulnerability surface since that plane grows larger based on the scope of work. A security engineer can reduce available trajectories of incidents by removing unnecessary software that is not related to business use, deleting usernames or logins for employees or contractors who are no longer at the firm, and also by disabling or removing unnecessary services.

Linux has so many powerful tools where a patch can be applied to the kernel and will close open network ports, integrate intrusion detection, and also assimilate intrusion prevention. While this may work for a smaller firm, the author does not recommend this solution for a robust, large environment. Exec Shield is an undertaking Red Hat began in 2002, with the goal of condensing the probability of worms or other automated remote breaches on Linux systems. After this was released, a patch was necessary that emulated a never execute (NX) bit for a CPU that lacks a native NX implementation in the hardware. This NX bit is a tool used in CPUs to isolate sections of memory that are used by either the storage of processor instructions, or code, or for storage of data. Intel and AMD now also use this architecture; however, Intel identifies this as execute disable (XD), and AMD appointed the name enhanced virus protection. An operating system with the capability to emulate and take advantage of a NX bit may prevent the heap memory and stack from being executable, and may also counteract executable memory from being writable. This facilitates the prevention of particular buffer overflow exploits from prospering, predominantly those that inject and execute code, for example, Sasser and Blaster worms. Such attacks are dependent on some portion of the memory, typically the stack, to be both executable and writable, and if it is not the stack fails.

In the realm of Wi-Fi, companies must implement tight network security controls. Device authentication is another layer of security that would not allow proximity hacking. For example, a car next door is parked in a parking lot and can easily hack onto a firm's network. Guest wireless is a common component to segregate guests off the company's network. With that being said, corporate users might be tempted to switch over to the public, guest network where there are fewer or no controls. This is where leakage may occur. Best practice would be to set up a guest network that issues only temporary credentials to allow connections. This will deter any employees from accessing and utilizing an unsecure connection, and also will not allow former guests or employees' access.

In an ideal world, all traffic would be monitored, but when a company does a cost/benefit analysis, it may seem excessive to do so. Directors make a judgment call based on the threat analysis to ascertain whether it is worth putting these controls into certain segments of the network. It is a terrible practice to have everyone on the same network, but unfortunately that is what most companies do. Whether money is not abundant enough to segment a network, or a security team is not in place to implement policies and maintain them, this is prevalent in most small and medium-sized businesses.

The best approach would be to have anomaly detection that baselines the network traffic and assesses patterns, identifying the anomalies. For the determined attacker, you need to be prepared on the host; so, you need to have it tightly secured where users do not have admin rights. Having a good anti-virus and anti-malware software platform in place is mandatory, too. Depending on the business purpose, classifying data and ultimately segregating that data is also key. The only way to access that data would be through a secured connection through Citrix or some other key/fingerprint mechanism.

In programming, minimization is the method of eradicating all unnecessary character from source code, keeping its functionality. Unnecessary characters may include comments, white space characters, new line characters, comments, and occasionally block delimiters, which are used to enhance comprehension to the code but are not required for that code to execute. In computing machine learning, a generalized model must be selected from a finite data set, with the consequent challenge of overlifting. The model may become too strongly modified to the particularities of the training set and oversimplifying new data. By balancing complexity to institute security against success to seamlessly provide data to groups across the entire firm, one can master risk minimization.

3. SUMMARY

This chapter focused on how the objective of systems security is to improve protection of information system resources. All organizational systems have some level of sensitivity and require protection as part of good management practice. The protection of a system must be documented in a systems security plan.

The purpose of the systems security plan is to provide an overview of the security requirements of the system and describe the controls in place or planned for meeting those requirements. The systems security plan also delineates the responsibilities and expected behavior of all individuals who access the system. The systems security plan should be viewed as documentation of the structured process of planning adequate, cost-effective security protection for a system. It should reflect input from various managers with responsibilities concerning the system, including information owners and the system owner. Additional information may be included in the basic plan, and the structure and format should be organized according to organizational needs.

In order for the plans to adequately reflect the protection of the resources, a senior management official must authorize a system to operate. The authorization of a system to process information, granted by a management official, provides an important quality control. By authorizing processing in a system, the manager accepts its associated risk.

Management authorization should be based on an assessment of management, operational, and technical controls. Since the systems security plan establishes and documents the security controls, it should form the basis for the authorization, supplemented by the assessment report and the plan of actions and milestones. In addition, a periodic review of controls should also contribute to future authorizations. Re-authorization should occur whenever there is a significant change in processing, but at least every three years.

Finally, let's move on to the real interactive part of this chapter: review questions/exercises, hands-on projects, case projects, and optional team case project. The answers and/or solutions by chapter can be found in the Online Instructor's Solutions Manual.

CHAPTER REVIEW QUESTIONS/EXERCISES

True/False

1. True or False? Since the inception of technology, data security revolves around cryptography.
2. True or False? Cipher text and secret keys are transported over the network and can be harvested for analysis, and furthermore to impersonate a source or, worst case, cause a service denial.
3. True or False? Network security deals with the insecure transport of data.
4. True or False? Implementing inconsistent, updated patches may be cost prohibitive for a company, especially for a mission-critical environment.
5. True or False? With only 30 to 40% of firewall rules in use, security vulnerabilities arise due to misconfigurations.

Multiple Choice

1. At times, it is not an issue of data sneaking past network controls, but _____ and reluctance to fix issues fearing that the business may be interrupted as changes are implemented.
   A. qualitative analysis
   B. vulnerabilities
   C. data storage
   D. misconfiguration
   E. DHS
2. There are many options out there when considering a _____ for your environment.
   A. firewall
   B. risk assessment
   C. scale
   D. subcomponents
   E. bait
3. There are an increasing number of organizations questioning whether they should put a (n) _____ in front of an application, or if the code should just be fixed.
   A. organizations
   B. fabric
   C. psychological
   D. Web application firewall
   E. security

4. The practice of safeguarding systems is to reduce the plane of exposure, also referred to as:
   A. cabinet-level state office
   B. nonsubtle
   C. hardening
   D. SAN protocol
   E. taps

5. The purpose of the _____ is to provide an overview of the security requirements of the system and describe the controls in place or planned for meeting those requirements?
   A. systems security plan
   B. consumer privacy protection
   C. IP storage access
   D. vulnerability
   E. unusable

EXERCISE

Problem

If continuous monitoring does not replace security authorization, why is it important?

Hands-On Projects

Project

Who should be involved in continuous monitoring activities?

Case Projects

Problem

What role does automation play in continuous monitoring?

Optional Team Case Project

Problem

What security controls should be subject to continuous monitoring?

10

Securing the Infrastructure

Lauren Collins
kCura Corporation

1. COMMUNICATION SECURITY GOALS

Since the inception of technology, data security revolves around cryptography. Because cryptography is only as good as the ability of a person or a program, new methods are constantly implemented as technology becomes more sophisticated.

Network Design and Components

Cipher text and secret keys are transported over the network and can be harvested for analysis; furthermore they can impersonate a source or, worst case, cause a service denial. Thus, to aid encryption and complex distribution methods, a network needs to be secure and elegant. That is, the network should have applicable appliances that monitor and detect attacks, intelligence that discriminates between degradations/failures and attacks, and also a convention for vigorous countermeasure strategies to outmaneuver the attacker. Consequently, network security is a completely separate topic from data security; however, the devices chosen must complement your infrastructure.

The accumulation of advances in key technologies has enabled companies to envision the implementation of an infrastructure with no limitations. Among these advances are those in materials that underlie electronic components and optical technologies, including optical fibers. Improvements in electronic integrated circuits include both the speed at which these circuits can perform their functions and the achievable complexity that allows a single chip to perform complex tasks. Advances in signal processing techniques that use electronic circuits and software to convert information and information-carrying signals into forms suitable for transport over short or long distances arrange for data to be stored, processed, and transmitted lightning fast. Such advantages have even allowed engineers and scientists to work harder and think further out to develop new technologies to follow

Cyber Security and IT Infrastructure Protection
DOI: http://dx.doi.org/10.1016/B978-0-12-416681-3.00010-0

suit on hardware and software transformations. Significant progress is required to realize and appreciate the vision of affordable media.

New algorithms and approaches complement the speed of transport networks, coupled with complex connection and session establishment and management. Total network approaches are required to resolve effective management of a cutting-edge infrastructure solution. Large costs are associated with installation and building out of fiber networks needed to provide an objective, robust network. Networks must be scalable and support multiple types of media, including coax, fiber, copper, and wireless, using both the shared media and switched approaches. Premise access must support the multiplexing of video, voice, and data sources requiring varied quality-of-service (QoS) levels and various bandwidths.

Several backbone options and avenues are available, due mostly to the era of electronic trading. These can be comprehensively separated into time division techniques and wavelength division techniques. Determining the potential of each technology would significantly contribute to a company's success, depending completely on the type of business involved. The time domain limits are determined by the speed of the electro-optic transducers, of the required buffer and memory, and of the switching and control logic required to manage the system. Additionally, high-speed regeneration technologies play a pivotal role in delivering benefits of time-division techniques to the system. Take long distances into consideration: Fiber properties such as loss and dispersion in the fiber limit the capabilities of the fiber span. Optical amplification, attenuators, and dispersion compensator devices can restore impairments induced by the fiber properties and allow the media to match the heat and light of the equipment chosen. Wavelength converters, wavelength filters, and wavelength division multipliers enable use of a greater capacity of the fiber. Optical regeneration techniques permit clock recovery and lead to full regeneration capabilities in the optical domain, avoiding unnecessary optical to electrical conversions.

Switching and Routing

Backbone networks require switches with tremendous capacity. Switches of this scale are not commercially available today, and much research, configuration, and testing must be done to make them perform a specific job. Total system throughputs of 15 terabits per second are possible with the latest and greatest equipment out there, and more is to come. A challenge for switching systems is to achieve systems that the access network can scale to either the amount of users or the amount of traffic being pumped through the network. Signaling systems for switch control must support a richer communication model than prior generations of switches. User channels can operate at any rate from a couple bits per second to a gig per second and beyond. Multipoint communication channels (one-to-many and many-to-many) are necessary for applications such as video and voice. This requires a signaling and control system that supports a multipoint call model, where a call may include multiple virtual circuits, each with its own individual characteristics. Certain applications place extreme demands on signaling systems.

Layer-specific functionality is now an important role of a switch. When ordering a switch, you now have to determine whether you only want layer 2 or whether layer 3 will be needed. Many switches have the capacity to install software to allow layer 3 capabilities;

however, some layer 3 capabilities are tied to the hardware. The author's favorite layer 3 function is IP multicast through Internet Group Multicast Protocol (IGMP) snooping. IGMP snooping with proxy reporting actively sifts IGMP packets in an effort to reduce the amount of load the router is carrying that provides the multicast. When a join leaves and heads to the next routers, routes are filtered so that the smallest number of information is transported. A switch warrants that the router has one point to contend with, no matter how many listeners are out there in the network. The router is only aware of the most recent member who joined the group. Since a switch creates the layer 1 connection, both virtually and physically, it is no longer required to have systems interconnected to the same hardware or at the same physical location.

Several switches will meet an organization's needs, and several designs are available to fit in any data center or server room. Some switches, usually just in the home or small office setting, are not rackable and can be located on a desktop or server. Rack-mounted switches are intended to be used in racked environments and can range anywhere from 1 u to an entire cabinet of 42 u (u is the measurement relating to units). A chassis switch, as seen in00000000000000000 Figure 10.1, is one that has either

FIGURE 10.1   Chassis switch.

vertical or horizontal blades that allow for hot swapping and many different, custom options. There are many switch management features:

• Bandwidth and duplex settings for circuits
• Priority settings for ports
• Simple Network Management Protocol (SNMP) configuration to monitor devices and perform health checks
• Message authentication code (MAC) filtering and port security
• Link aggregation for versions < Elastic Sky X interface (ESXi) 5, trunking for versions of ESXi > 5
• Layer 2 and Layer 3 virtual local area network (VLAN)

Switching over to routers (no pun intended), we find that when choosing a router it is important to understand the job the router should perform. Just as there are many protocols, there are many types of routing platforms to accomplish services at the edge, at the distribution layer, or at the core. An edge router operates at the edge of a multiprotocol switching network. In a (MPLS) domain, IP datagrams are forwarded, and routing information is used to determine which labels should accompany the datagram. The packets are then labelled accordingly, and the labeled packets are forwarded into the MPLS domain.

Similarly, an edge router can strip the label and forward the resulting packet over utilizing standard IP forwarding logic. Distribution routers can aggregate traffic from multiple-access routers and are not dependent on site location or geographical region. Often, distribution routers are responsible for enforcing quality of service (QoS) across a (WAN), so they may have considerable amounts of memory installed, multiple wide area network (WAN) interfaces, and extensive on-board data processing routines. These types of routers are also capable of providing connectivity to large groups of servers, whether it be file servers or additional external networks. Core routers operate on the Internet backbone at an organization to transmit lightning fast speeds and to forward IP packets just as fast. Routing also needs to be done at the core level, in some instances, and differs since edge routers have different features and sit at the edge of a network. Conversely, core routers can sit at the edge of a network if the engineer desires to build the infrastructure this way.

Ports and Protocols

Between the protocols User Datagram Protocol (UDP) and Transmission Control Protocol (TCP), there are 65,535 ports available for communication between devices. Among this impressive number are three classes of ports:

1. Well-known ports: Range from 0–1,023
2. Registered ports: Range from 1,024–49,151
3. Dynamic/Private ports: Range from 49,152–65,535

Understandably, not all of the ports listed in those three categories are secure. As a result, reference Table 10.1, which enumerates the most commonly used ports and the service/protocol that utilizes the port.

TABLE 10.1 Well-Known Port Numbers and Their Respective Service Description and Protocol.

Port	Service/Protocol
7	Echo/TCP & UDP
9	Systat/TCP & UDP
15	Netstat/TCP & UDP
20	FTP data transfer/TCP
21	FTP control/TCP
22	SSH/TCP
23	Telnet/TCP
24	Private mail/TCP & UDP
25	SMT{/TCP
39	RLP/TCP & UDP
42	ARPA/TCP & UDP
42	Windows Internet Name Service/TCP & UCP
43	WHOIS/TCP
49	TACACS/TCP & UDP
53	DNS/TCP & UDP
69	TFTP/UDP
80	HTTP/TCP
88	Kerbos/TCP & UDP
101	NIC hostname/TCP
110	POP3/TCP
115	SFTP/TCP
119	Network News Transfer Protocol/TCP
123	NTP/UDP
143	IMAP/TCP
152	Background File Transfer Protocol/TCP & UDP
156	SQL Service/TCP & UDP
161	SNMP/UDP
162	SNMPTRAP/TCP & UDP
175	VMNET/TCP
179	BGP/TCP
220	IMAP/TCP & UDP

(Continued)

TABLE 10.1 Well-Known Port Numbers and Their Respective
Service Description and Protocol. (Continued)

Port	Service/Protocol
264	Border Gateway Multicast Protocol/TCP & UDP
280	http-mgmt/TCP & UDP
389	LDAP/TCP & UDP
443	HTTPS/TCP
500	Internet Security Assoc and Key Mgmt (ISAKMP)/UDP

Ideally, when architecting a system, one should plan out the intent for the environment and should only configure the services necessary for the network to pass traffic and servers to perform their intended functions.

Table 10.1 reflects protocols that may be open by default, as well as some that are necessary for the intended purpose of the environment. When installing equipment in Section I, it is imperative that the engineer be aware of the ports that need to be open for each device or piece of software and, if needed, can be referenced in the device white paper. It is also essential to recognize the variation between the numerous types of attacks and the respective ports on which such attacks would be executed. It is necessary to monitor the ports that are open in an effort to detect protocols that may leave the network vulnerable. Running netstat on a workstation will allow one to view the ports that are running and that are open. In addition, running a local port scan will also portray which ports are exposed.

Many protocols may still be used during an installation where system administrators and users are not aware, and those may leave the network vulnerable. Simple Network Management Protocol (SNMP) and Domain Naming Service (DNS) were deployed years ago, yet still present security risks. SNMP can be utilized for monitoring the health of network equipment, servers, and other peripheral equipment. However, susceptibilities associated with the SNMP derive from use of SNMP v1. Although such vulnerabilities were raised years ago (about 10 years), exposures are still reported while utilizing the current version of SNMP. Liabilities allow for authentication evasion and execution of proprietary code when utilizing SNMP. The SNMP infrastructure has three components:

1. SNMP managed connections
2. SNMP instruments
3. SNMP network management servers

Where the devices are concerned, they load the agent, which in turn assembles information and forwards it to the management servers. Network management servers collect a substantial amount of significant network information and are possibly targets of attacks due to their use of SNMP v1, which is not secure. A community name is a point of security; however, it may be similar to a password. Usually, the community name is public and is not secure, nor is it changed, thus permitting information to leak out to invasions. Conversely, SNMP v2 uses Message Digest Version 5 (MD5) for authentication. The transmission can also be encrypted. SNMP v_3 is used across firms as the criteria; however, a number of devices are not compatible and are left to use SNMP v1 or SNMP v2.

SNMP assists spiteful users to learn too much about a system, making password speculations easier. SNMP is often disregarded when checking for vulnerabilities due to the User Datagram Protocol (UDP) ports 161 and 162. Ensure network management servers are physically secured and secured on the network layer. Consider utilizing a segregate management subnet, protecting it by using a router with an access list. Unless the service is required, it should be shut off by default. In order to defend a network infrastructure from incidents aimed at obsolete or unfamiliar ports and/or protocols, remove any unnecessary protocols while creating access-control lists to allow traffic on defined ports. This eliminates the possibility of any obscure protocols being utilized, while minimizing the danger of an incident.

Threats

Hijacking occurs when an intruder takes control of a session between a server and the client. The communication starts when a middle-man attack adds a request to the client, resulting in the client getting kicked off the session. Meanwhile, the rogue workstation talks with the server, and the attacker intercepts the source-side packets, replacing them with fresh packets that are sent over to the destination. This type of hijacking, referred to as TCP/IP hijacking, most commonly occurs during telnet and Web sessions when security is nonexistent, or lacking, and also when session timeouts are improperly configured.

During the course of a Web session, cookies are commonly used to authenticate and track users. While the authentic session is in session, an attacker may attempt to hijack a session by loading a modified cookie in the session page. Session hijacking may also ensue when a session timeout is set to be an extended period of time; this gives an attacker a chance to hijack a session. Telnet-type plaintext connections create the ideal situation for TCP hijacking. In an instance like this, when an attacker surveys the data passing in the TCP session, the attacker can take control of the user's session; this is yet another reason why it is called session hijacking. When a user is forced to authenticate prior to allowing transactions to occur, it helps to prevent hijacking attacks. Protection mechanisms include the use of unique sequence numbers (USNs) and Web session cookies. The more unique the cookies, the harder it is to crack and hijack. Additional preventative measures for this type of attack include the use of encrypted session keys and Secure Socket Layer (SSL) encryption.

Spoofing

Spoofing is a method of providing false identity information to gain unauthorized access. This can be achieved by modifying the source address of traffic or source of information. Spoofing seeks to bypass IP address filters by setting up a connection from a client and sourcing the packets with an IP address that is allowed through the filter. Blind spoofing occurs when the attacker only sends data and only makes assumptions of responses.

Informed spoofing is when the attacker can participate in a session and can monitor the bidirectional communications. Services that can be spoofed are:

1. Email
2. Web
3. File transfers
4. Caller ID

Web spoofing occurs when an attacker creates a convincing, fabricated copy of an entire Web site. The fabricated Web site will appear just as a real Web site would, and it has all the pages and links. The attacker controls the fabricated Web site so that all network traffic between the user's browser and the site goes through the attacker. In the situation for email spoofing, a spammer or virus can forge the email packet information in an email so that it appears that the email is coming from a trusted host, a friend, or even your own email. When one leaves their email address at an Internet site, or exchange email with others, a spoofer may be able to use your email address as the sender address to blast spam. File transfer spoofing involves the FTP service, and FTP is sent in clear, plain text. The data can be intercepted by an attacker. The data can then be viewed and altered prior to sending it over to the receiver. These types of attacks are intended to pull information from a network of users to accomplish a more comprehensive attack. By setting up a filter to deny traffic originating from the Internet that shows an internal network address, using the signing capabilities of certificates on servers and clients will allow Web and email services to be more secure. Using an Internet Protocol Security (IPSEC) tunnel adds more security between critical servers and their clients by preventing these types of attacks from transpiring.

Intercepting Traffic

The man in the middle attack occurs when an attacker intercepts traffic and deceives the parties at both ends into believing they are communicating with one another. An attack like this is possible due to the nature of the three-way TCP handshake process using SYNchronize (SYN) and ACKnowledge (ACK) packets. Since TCP is a connection-oriented protocol, a three-way handshake takes place when establishing a connection and when closing the session. When a session is established, the client sends a SYN request; then the server sends an ACK (sometimes referred to as SYN-ACK-ACK), completing the connection. During this process, the attacker initiates the man-in-the-middle attack by using a program that appears to be a server to the client and appears to be a client to the server. In telnet and wireless communications, this attack is common. This is a difficult attack to perform due to physical routing matters, TCP sequencing number, and speed. Since the hacker must sniff both sides of the connection simultaneously, programs have been developed to aid the attacker in order to make man in the middle easier.

If an attack is performed on an internal network, physical access to that network is mandatory. By ensuring that access to wiring closets and switches are restricted, and that they're behind locked doors, physical access becomes difficult. Once the physical segment of the network has been secured, services and resources may allow a system to be inserted into a session, so those will need to be protected. DNS can be compromised and used to redirect the initial request for service, providing an opportunity to execute the man-in-the-middle attack. DNS access needs to be restricted, allowing read-only access for anyone but administrators. By using encryption and security controls and protocols, organizations can prevent these types of attacks on their infrastructure.

Packet Capturing

Packets are captured by sniffing devices in a replay attack. Once the relevant information is extracted, packets are put back on the network. An attack such as this can be used to replay a bank transaction or other comparable types of data transfers in the hopes of replicating or changing activities, such as transfers or deposits. Protecting oneself against a replay attack will involve some type of timestamp associated with the packets, or time-valued nonrepeating serial numbers. Additionally, integrating secure protocols, such as IPSEC, prevents replays of data traffic while providing authentication and data encryption.

Denial of Service

When resources have been disrupted or services that a user would expect to have access to are compromised, they have experienced a denial-of-service attack. These types of attacks are executed by manipulating protocols and can occur without the need to be validated by the network. An attack will usually involve flooding the listening port on a machine with packets. The purpose is to make that workstation so busy processing the new connections that it cannot process legitimate service requests. Several tools are available on the Internet that will produce a denial-of-service attack. IT administrators use them daily to test connectivity and troubleshoot issues on their networks, whereas malicious users will use the tool to cause connectivity issues. Some examples of DoS attacks are:

- SYN flood—This attack takes advantage of the TCP three-way handshake. A source system will send a flood of synchronization (SYN) requests and will never send the final acknowledgment (ACK), creating partially open TCP sessions. Since the TCP stack waits before resetting the port, the attack overflows the destination workstation connection buffer, making it impossible to service requests from valid users.
- Ping flood—This attack attempts to block service or reduce activity on a host by sending ping requests directly to the target. Variations of these attacks include the ping of death, where the packet size is too large and the system is unable to handle the number of packets.
- Ping/Smurfing—This attack is based on the Internet Control Message Protocol (ICMP) echo reply function. The common name is ping, the command line tool utilized to invoke the function. The attacker sends ping packets to the broadcast address of a network, replacing the original source address in the ping packets with the source address of the target, causing a flood of traffic to be sent to the unsuspecting network device.
- Fraggle—This attack is similar to smurfing. The difference is that fraggle uses UDP rather than ICMP. The attacker sends spoofed UDP packets to broadcast addresses, just as the smurf attack does. These UDP packets are directed to port 7, echo, or port 19, Chargen. When connected to port 19, a character generator attack can be run. Refer to Table 10.1 for the commonly exploited ports.

- Land—This attack exploits a behavior in the operating systems of several versions of Windows, Unix, Mac, and Cisco IOS with respect to their TCP/IP stacks. The attacker spoofs a TCP/IP SYN packet to the victim system with the same source and destination IP address and the same source and destination ports. This confuses the system as it attempts to respond to the packet.
- Teardrop—This form of attack targets a known behavior of UDP in the TCP/IP stack of some operating systems. The Teardrop attack will send fragmented UDP packets to the target with odd offset values in subsequent packets. When the operating system attempts to rebuild the original packets from the fragments, the fragments overwrite each other, causing confusion. Since some operating systems cannot elegantly handle the error, the system will either crash or restart.

DoS attacks come in many flavors, shapes, and sizes. Take the first step to protect the firm from an attack: Understand the types of attacks and the nature in which they operate.

Distributed Denial of Service

A modest expansion of denial of service can be referred to as distributed DoS attacks. Masters are computers that run the client software, where zombies will run the software. The attacker will create a master, which in turn creates a large number of zombies, or recruits. The software that runs on the zombies can launch multiple types of attacks, such as UDP or SYN flooding on a particular target. Figure 10.2 depicts a distributed DoS attack.

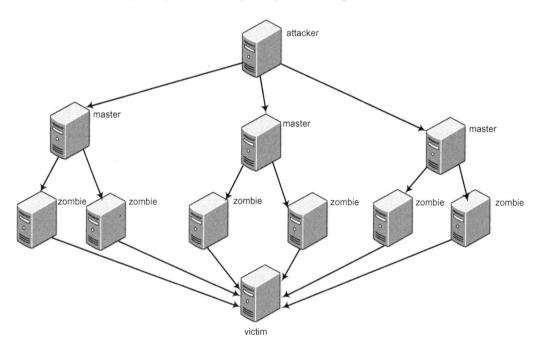

FIGURE 10.2 Distributed denial-of-service attack.

Although distributed DoS attacks usually come from the outside of the network to deny services, the impact of the attacks displayed inside the network should also be cogitated. Internal distributed DoS attacks allow disgruntled employees or malicious users to disrupt services without any outside influence or interaction. To help protect your network, set up filters on external routers to drop packets involved in these types of attacks. Also, set up an additional filter that denies traffic originating from the Internet but showing an internal IP address. By doing this, ping and some services are lost to test network connectivity, but this is where administrators should be on a separated network segment than users and would be on a segment where the filtering did not occur. If the operating system supports it, one can reduce the amount of time before the reset of an unfinished TCP connection. Doing so makes it harder to keep resources unavailable for extended periods of time.

Tip: In the case of a distributed DoS attack, it is best to get in touch with your service provider so that they can divert traffic or block traffic at a higher level.

ARP Poisoning

Every network card has a 48-bit address that is unique and hard-coded into the card. For network communications to occur, this hardware address must be associated with an IP address. Address resolution protocol (ARP), which operates at layer 2 (data link layer) of the Open System Interconnection (OSI) model, associates MAC addresses to IP addresses. ARP is a lower-layer protocol that is straightforward and consists of requests and replies without validation. However, this simplicity leads to a lack of security.

When using a protocol analyzer to look at traffic, you will see an ARP request and an ARP reply, which are the two fundamental parts of ARP communication. There are also reverse ARP (RARP) requests and RARP replies. Devices maintain an ARP table that contains a cache of the IP addresses and MAC addresses that the device has already correlated. The host device searches its ARP table to see whether there is a MAC address corresponding to the destination host IP address. When there is no matching entry, it broadcasts an ARP request to the entire network. The broadcast is seen by all systems, but only the device that has the corresponding information replies. However, devices can accept ARP replies before even requesting them. This type of entry is known as an unsolicited entry because the information was not explicitly requested.

Because ARP does not require any type of validation, as ARP requests are sent, the requesting devices believe that the incoming ARP replies are from the correct devices. This can allow a perpetrator to trick a device into thinking any IP is related to any MAC address. In addition, they can broadcast fake or spoofed ARP replies to an entire network and attack all computers. This is known as ARP poisoning. Simply worded, the attacker deceives a device on your network, poisoning its table associations of other devices.

ARP poisoning can lead to attacks such as denial of service, man in the middle, and MAC flooding. Denial of service and man in the middle were discussed earlier in this chapter. MAC flooding is an attack directed at network switches. This type of attack is successful because of the nature of the way all switches and bridges work. The amount of space allocated to store source addresses of packets is limited. When the table becomes full, the device can no longer learn new information and becomes flooded. As a result, the switch can be forced into a hub-like state that will broadcast all network traffic to every device in the network. Macof is a tool that floods the network with random MAC addresses. Switches may get stuck in open repeating mode, leaving the network traffic susceptible to sniffing. Nonintelligent switches do not check the sender's identity, thereby allowing this condition to happen.

A lesser vulnerability of ARP is port stealing. Port stealing is a man-in-the-middle attack that exploits the binding between the port and the MAC address. The principle behind port stealing is that an attacker sends numerous packets with the source IP address of the victim and the destination MAC address of the attacker. This attack applies to broadcast networks built from switches. ARP traffic operates at layer 2, the data link layer of the OSI model, and is broadcast on local subnets. ARP poisoning is limited to attacks that are local, so an intruder needs either physical access to your network or control of a device on your network. To mitigate ARP poisoning on a small network, you can use static or script-based mapping for IP addresses and ARP tables. For larger networks, utilize equipment that offers port security. By doing so, one can only permit one MAC address for each physical port on the switch. In addition, you can deploy monitoring tools or an intrusion detection system (IDS) to signal when suspicious activity occurs.

DNS Poisoning

DNS poisoning enables a perpetrator to redirect traffic by changing the IP record for a specific domain, thus permitting the attacker to send legitimate traffic anywhere he chooses. This not only sends a requestor to a different Web site, but also caches this information for a short period and distributes the attack's effect to the servers users. DNS poisoning may also be referred to as DNS cache poisoning because it affects the information that is cached.

Because all Internet requests begin with a DNS query, if the IP address is not known locally then the request is sent to a DNS server. There are two types of DNS servers: authoritative and recursive. DNS servers share information, but recursive servers maintain information in their cache. This means caching or recursive servers can answer queries for resource records even if they cannot resolve the request directly. A flaw in the resolution algorithm allows the poisoning of DNS records on a server. All an attacker has to do is delegate a false name to the domain server along with providing a false address for the server. For example, an attacker creates a hostname hackattack.gov. Next, the attacker queries your DNS server to resolve the host hackattack.gov. The DNS server resolves the name and stores the information in its cache. Until the zone expiration, any further requests for hackattack.gov do not result in lookups but are answered by the server from its cache. It is now possible for the attacker to set your DNS server as the authoritative server for the zone with the domain registrar. If the attacker conducts malicious activity, the attacker can make it appear that your DNS server is being used for those malicious activities.

DNS poisoning can result in many different implications. Domain name servers can be used for distributed DoS attacks. Malware can be downloaded to an unsuspecting user's computer from the rogue site, and all future requests by that computer will be redirected to the fake IP address. This could be used to build an effective botnet. This method of poisoning could also allow for cross-site scripting exploits, especially since Web 2.0 capabilities allow content to be pulled from multiple Web sites simultaneously.

To minimize the effects of DNS poisoning, check the DNS setup if you are hosting your own DNS. Be sure the DNS server is not open-recursive. An open-recursive DNS server responds to any lookup request, without checking where the request originated. Disable recursive access for other networks to resolve names that are not in your zone files. Also, use different servers for authoritative and recursive lookups and require that cached information is discarded except from the com servers and the root servers. As far as users are concerned, educate them. However, it is becoming increasingly difficult to spot an issue by watching the address bar on an Internet browser. Therefore, operating system vendors are adding more protection by notifying the user that a program is attempting to change the system's settings, thus preventing the DNS cache from being poisoned.

2. ATTACKS AND COUNTERMEASURES

To secure a network, a firewall can be successfully implemented and utilized whether it is software or hardware based. The purpose of a firewall is to control the incoming and outgoing traffic by analyzing packets and determining whether or not a rule set will allow the traffic in or not.

Network Firewall

In Figure 10.3, the firewall is protecting the network, rather than leaving it directly exposed to the Internet. The firewall will sit in conjunction with a network device and will serve as a gateway between two networks.

Firewalls inspect all traffic routed between two networks to determine whether or not that traffic meets predetermined criteria. If it does, the traffic is allowed through and routed to the appropriate destination. Otherwise, the traffic is blocked. Firewalls can also manage public access to private network resources, such as host applications. Hard drive space on firewalls is becoming increasingly important since log entries can grow to be

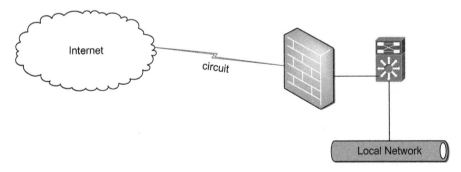

FIGURE 10.3   A firewall is placed between the outside world and the internal local network components.

terabytes of data, depending on the amount of traffic on your network. Consider your logging setup to log every attempt to enter into and exit the network. When half the company is surfing the Internet during their lunch time, one can fathom how large the log files can grow to be. Firewalls can also filter packets specific to network types and is known as protocol filtering. Since the decision to forward or reject traffic is dependent on the protocol used, a user attempting to access a server via HTTP, FTP, or telnet will either be allowed or denied based not only on their access to the server, but also on whether the firewall allows specific protocol access to that target server.

Firewalls use two approaches: Allow all traffic unless said traffic meets a certain criteria or deny all traffic unless it meets a certain criteria. Additionally, firewalls can fit into four categories: packet filters, circuit-level gateways, application-level gateways, and stateful multilayer inspection firewalls. Packet filtering firewalls sit at the Network Layer, or the IP layer of the TCP/IP Layer. Depending on the packet criteria, the firewall can drop the packet, forward it, or send a message to the initiator. Rules can include source and destination IP address, source and destination port number, and protocol used. The advantage of packet filtering firewalls is that they are affordable and have no impact on network performance. If a higher level firewall is used, packet filtering rules will not add any overhead to the network traffic. A lower level firewall will not support many other features that an organization may desire, such as network address translation (NAT). NAT is used in many different types of companies, whether it is a trading firm or a law firm. Understanding private and public IP addressing is the first step in translating network addresses. Your internal network will communicate with internal IPs; however, if you have a client that needs to access a server on your network, giving them the internal IP on your network will not allow them access unless they're on your virtual private network (VPN). So, translating that IP to a public IP will allow the user to access that internal server, but the firewall is the tool that gives the user outside access by translating the IP. Additionally, the firewall needs to know that 66.55.44.123 is a public IP that belongs to internal IP 10.10.10.100. How will the user access the server? If a user wants to RDP to 10.10.10.100, the firewall must give RDP access to that server. Specific ports and protocols are allowed at the firewall level, too. When implementing a firewall, one must consider the following measures:

- Determine the access denial methodology: Most recommend denying all access by default right at the start. That would have a gateway that routes no traffic and is a brick wall with no doors in it. If you prefer a solid, secure environment, this is the first step, and then you can allow access from here.
- Determine inbound access: If all of your Internet traffic originates on the LAN, a NAT router will block all inbound traffic that is not in response to requests originating from within the LAN. As mentioned in the preceding example, only the external IP address is given to a client. The internal IP addresses of hosts behind the firewall are never revealed to the outside world, which makes intrusion difficult. Most hosts are nonpublic IPs, so it would make it difficult unless the attacker was on the internal network; however, it is the best practice. Packets coming in from the Internet in response to requests from local hosts are addressed to dynamically allocate port

numbers on the public side of the NAT router. These numbers change rapidly, making it nearly impossible for an intruder to make assumptions of which port number they could use. You may also want to determine which criteria can be used when a packet originates from the Internet and whether or not to allow it into the LAN. The more rigorous the rules, the more secure your network will be. Ideally, you'll know which public IP addresses on the Internet originate inbound traffic, and by limiting inbound traffic to packets originating from specific hosts, you decrease the likelihood of hostile intrusion. Going further, earlier protocols were mentioned, and limiting communication-based off-protocol sets like HTTP or FTP adds greater security.

- Determine outbound access: When users only need access to the Internet, a proxy server may provide enough security, with access granted based off user rights. This type of firewall can be a great deal to manage since it requires manual configuration of each Web browser on every machine. Outbound protocol filtering can also be transparently achieved with packet filtering and no sacrifice on security. If you are using NAT without inbound mapping or traffic originating from the Internet, then it is possible to allow users access to all services on the Internet without compromising security. Consequently, there is a risk of employees acting irresponsibly through email or external hosts, but that is a management or HR issue and not IT.

Proxies

Proxy servers are capable of functioning on dedicated hardware or as software on a utility server. It acts as a transitional point of communication between two clients attempting to reach out to other servers. For example, if a client connects to a proxy server, requesting some file or connection, the proxy server will assess the request in an effort to simplify and regulate the intricacy of the communication, as shown in Figure 10.4.

Proxies can perform just as a firewall would by handling connection requests for packets coming into an application and by blocking any other packets. A proxy server can be thought of as a gateway from Network A to a certain network application, while acting as a proxy for the user on the network. When an administrator properly designs the function of a proxy, it is much more difficult for an outside attacker to access the internal network. However, an attacker may utilize a highly available system and use it as a proxy for their

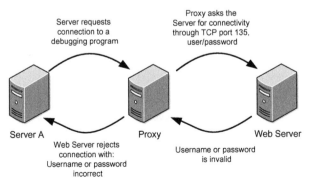

Server requests connection to a debugging program

Proxy asks the Server for connectivity through TCP port 135, user/password

Server A

Web Server rejects connection with: Username or password incorrect

Proxy

Username or password is invalid

Web Server

FIGURE 10.4 Communication between two servers connecting through a proxy, the third server.

selfish means. This allows the proxy to deceive other machines, forcing them to think the proxy is safe and on their network, or their proxy. Utilizing internal, private IP addresses adds another layer for security; conversely, hackers could spoof the IP's attempt to gain access and transmit packets to a network.

Proxy servers have become prevalent in the gaming community since real-time, Internet gaming surfaced. Considering how many kids and adults are into gaming, the network for real-time streaming multiplayer gaming requires a low-latency proxy server-network topology. Client-server or peer-to-peer topologies provide a variety of positive aspects and can be applied intricately, leading to their high acquiescence for computer gaming. Both models also have many disadvantages, which results in weak QoS and constrains robust gaming architectures where there are a high amount of users. As soon as the player numbers increase, client-server and peer-to-peer topologies do not scale well. Additionally, the server in a client-server framework forms a single point of failure for the entire session. While the peer-to-peer method eradicates the problem of a single point of failure, a hacked client can cheat, since acquiesced game updates are not filtered by a server instance and concealed information becomes readily available to the player.

Architecting a proxy server setup, stemming from a peer-to-peer server-network, is shown in Figure 10.5. Utilizing several interconnected proxy servers for a one-user gaming session shows each proxy server having a full view of the comprehensive game architecture. Each client communicates with a single proxy, sending user selections and obtaining updates of the game status.

Proxy servers process user actions and forward them to other proxies, manipulating multicast at the IP or application level to synchronize the disseminated game state. With regard

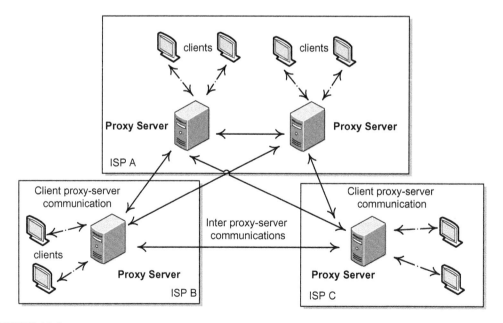

FIGURE 10.5   One session using the proxy server model.

to low-latency Internet-centered sessions, proxy servers need to be disbursed among different Internet service providers (ISPs), such that each client will connect to a proxy at its local ISP. Through testing, the author has set up the servers manually; however, testing proves that a dynamic setup of proxies falls in line with user demand and quick response times. Rather than replicating a gaming world, one could partition the approach across servers, compelling clients to exchange servers depending on their region. This approach may work well to accommodate slower flow of traffic, but it cannot be applied to the low-latency, graphic-intensive world. Pauses are annoying for users, as are noticeable server changes. Because the proxy has a wide spectrum to view the game state, best practices avoid a proxy server-network to attempt multiple reconnects during one session.

To manage replication utilizing proxy servers in a gaming infrastructure, ensure that the architecture is scalable, responsive, and consistent, simulating large amounts of data. Although trade-offs may be involved, implementing strong consistency patterns will increase the amount of inter-proxy communication. For example, proxies would order changes of the game state using timestamps or a physical clock mechanism. This would delay the transmission of acknowledgments of user actions to clients, thus reducing the responsiveness of the game. Talk about detrimental; especially when you've stood in line for 18 hours outside of the store, and now you're competing with 500,000 other users during the first hour of the game. A scalable, distributed model with real-time performance can only be achieved if all the servers do not talk to each other simultaneously; nonetheless, servers must be able to share the same data at all times. To implement this architecture, only allow one process to alter specific parts of replicated data (shown in Figure 10.6). Changes must be propagated to other processes, certifying the reliability of the replicated state immediately as the message arrives. The process in Figure 10.6 can be described by following these steps: (1) user actions are transferred from clients; (2) the server checks to see if the input is authorized to block cheating before changing the state; (3) consistency for the

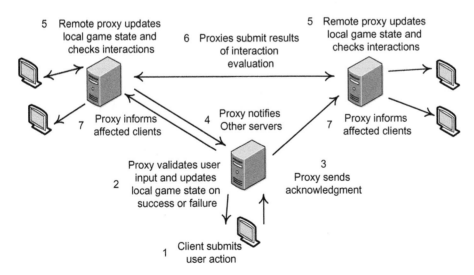

FIGURE 10.6 A user performing a single action—acknowledging and forwarding an action.

altered part of the game state is guaranteed, and the clients receive acknowledgments for movement commands in a short amount of time; (4) informs proxies about updating position values; (5) update local copies consequently; (6)in the case of interactions, notified proxies also check whether local clients are affected, and if local clients are affected, the proxy updates the game state of its local client and informs other servers; and (7) for all state updates received from other proxy servers, each proxy evaluates which local clients are affected and informs them. The architecture presented allows for management of a distributed state, with efficient synchronization of the game state in conjunction with fast acknowledgment of user actions.

3. SUMMARY

This chapter focused on how security is presented to protect the infrastructure. Smart grid cybersecurity must address not only deliberate attacks, such as from disgruntled employees, industrial espionage, and terrorists, but also inadvertent compromises of the information infrastructure due to user errors, equipment failures, and natural disasters.

Infrastructure Security Tasks Checklist

The primary intent of this chapter is to increase your awareness of specific technologies that secure the foundation of your infrastructure. Although this part of the chapter is called a checklist, each of the tasks in the checklist (An Agenda for Action for Implementing Infrastructure Security Tasks) requires so much elaboration that it is easy to lose the thread of organization. The guiding structure is to first summarize the major types of security vulnerabilities and mitigation techniques in general, and then traverse the OSI communication reference model layers (previously discussed) while discussing specific security considerations.

AN AGENDA FOR ACTION FOR IMPLEMENTING INFRASTRUCTURE SECURITY TASKS

Please see the following infrastructure security tasks (check all tasks completed):

Infrastructure security tasks are designed to thwart several types of threats:

_____1. Unauthorized traffic types going where they should not go (unauthorized access and denial of service).

_____2. Authorized traffic types using more bandwidth or other resources than they should (denial of service).

_____3. Unauthorized devices mimicking authorized devices (violating integrity).

_____4. Unauthorized devices intercepting communications intended for other devices (violating privacy).

At the infrastructure level, these threats are thwarted by:

_____5. Securing the routers and switches themselves so that they continue to perform their packet/frame forwarding and filtering functions.

_____6. Keeping unauthorized devices from being in the communication path by using filters and security mitigation features at different layers of the protocol stack and protecting against frame forgery and spoofing attempts to bypass the filters.

Filters that operate at most layers of the protocol stack under various feature names are appropriate at the following points in the network:

_____7. Ingress directly on hosts, servers, or endpoint devices (considered separately under host hardening, as opposed to infrastructure security features). (*Note:* This is distinct from filters that you can apply on Ethernet switches or other networking gear.)

_____8. Ingress Ethernet ports in wiring closet switches, where traffic first enters a network.

_____9. IP subnet boundaries where traffic crosses between VLANs.

_____10. Boundaries between network segments that are in different administrative domains

The following protocols that form the core of IP network functionality are critical components to consider as candidates for spoofing attacks:

_____11. Ethernet frame headers that contain source/destination link layer addresses.

_____12. IP packet headers that contain source/destination network layer addresses.

_____13. Address Resolution Protocol (ARP), which binds permanent Ethernet hardware addresses to configuration-specific IP logical addresses.

_____14. Dynamic Host Configuration Protocol (DHCP), which automatically assigns IP addresses to devices.

_____15. Domain Name Service (DNS), which maps human-readable names to IP addresses.

_____16. Hot Standby Router Protocol (HSRP), which provides a single virtual Ethernet hardware address and IP address for a group of routers that provide redundant default gateway services.

_____17. IEEE 802.1d Spanning Tree Protocol (STP), which controls the layer 2 Ethernet frame forwarding behavior in a switched Ethernet LAN or metropolitan area network (MAN).

_____18. IEEE 802.1q Ethernet trunk interfaces, which let a single physical Ethernet port share multiple VLANs.

_____19. Virtual Trunking Protocol (VTP) and other control protocols, which switch use to exchange VLAN configuration information.

_____20. Routing protocols that control the layer 3 packet forwarding behavior in a network.

This chapter also addressed the critical cybersecurity needs in the areas of encryption key management, security requirements, testing criteria for remote upgrades, and privacy recommendations for third-party data usage. The chapter also provided foundational cybersecurity guidance, outreach, and foster collaborations in the cross-cutting issue of cybersecurity in the smart grid. Remember that a system is only as secure as its most vulnerable path, and it is difficult (if not impossible) to build a secure voice solution if the infrastructure foundation is insecure.

Finally, let's move on to the real interactive part of this chapter: review questions/exercises, hands-on projects, case projects, and optional team case project. The answers and/or solutions by chapter can be found in the Online Instructor's Solutions Manual.

CHAPTER REVIEW QUESTIONS/EXERCISES

True/False

1. True or False? Since the inception of technology, data security revolves around cryptography.
2. True or False? Cipher text and secret keys are transported over the network, and can be harvested for analysis, and furthermore to impersonate a source or, in a worst case, cause a service acceptance.
3. True or False? Backbone networks require switches with tremendous capacity.
4. True or False? Between the UDP and TCP protocols, there are 5,535 ports available for communication between devices.
5. True or False? Hijacking occurs when an intruder takes control of a session between a server and the port.

Multiple Choice

1. What is a method of providing false identity information to gain unauthorized access?
   A. Qualitative analysis
   B. Vulnerabilities
   C. Spoofing
   D. Misconfiguration
   E. DHS
2. What attack occurs when an attacker intercepts traffic and deceives the parties at both ends into believing they are communicating with one another?
   A. Firewall
   B. Risk assessment
   C. Scale
   D. Man in the middle
   E. Bait
3. What are captured by sniffing devices in a replay attack?
   A. Organizations
   B. Fabric

   C. Packets
   D. Web application firewall
   E. Security
4. When resources have been disrupted or services are compromised that a user would expect to have access to, they have experienced a:
   A. cabinet-level state office
   B. denial-of-service attack
   C. hardening
   D. SAN protocol
   E. taps
5. A modest expansion of denial of service can be referred to as:
   A. systems security plan
   B. consumer privacy protection
   C. IP storage access
   D. vulnerability
   E. distributed denial of service attacks

EXERCISE

Problem

Which Ethernet ports require 802.1x authentication?

Hands-On Projects

Project

What 802.1x authentication mechanism should one use?

Case Projects

Problem

Do all clients support 802.1x?

Optional Team Case Project

Problem

Does 802.1x have security vulnerabilities?

11

Access Controls

Lauren Collins

kCura Corporation

1. INFRASTRUCTURE WEAKNESSES: DAC, MAC, AND RBAC

The dichotomy between types of companies and implementing layers of security led to the use of three types of access control mechanisms: discretionary access control, mandatory access control, and role-based access control.

Discretionary Access Control

Discretionary access control (DAC), also known as file permissions, is the access control in Unix and Linux systems. Whenever you have seen the syntax drwxr-xs-x, it is the ugo abbreviation for owner, group, and other permissions in the directory listing. Ugo is the abbreviation for user access, group access, and other system user's access, respectively. These file permissions are set to allow or deny access to members of their own group, or any other groups. Modification of file, directory, and devices are achieved using the chmod command. Tables 11.1 and 11.2 illustrate the syntax to assign or remove permissions. Permissions can be assigned using the character format:

```
Chmod [ugoa] [ + − = ] [rwxXst] fileORdirectoryName
```

In DAC, usually the resource owner will control who access resources. Everyone has administered a system in which they decide to give full rights to everyone so that it is less to manage. The issue with this approach is that users are allowed not only to read, write, and execute files, but also to delete any files they have access to. This author has so often seen system files deleted in error by users, or simply by the user's lack of knowledge. This is an instance where DAC could be seen as a disadvantage, or less advantageous.

TABLE 11.1 Notation to Add, Remove Access, and how to Explicitly Assign Access.

+	add access
−	remove access
=	access explicitly assigned

TABLE 11.2 Notation for File Permissions.

r	Permission to read file
	Permission to read a directory (also requires '*x*')
w	Permission to delete or modify a file
	Permission to delete or modify files in a directory
x	Permission to execute a file/script
	Permission to read a directory (also requires '*r*')
s	Set user or group ID on execution
u	Permissions granted to the user who owns the file
t	Set sticky bit. Execute file/script as a user root for regular user

Mandatory Access Control

Mandatory access control (MAC) regulates user process access to resources based on an organizational security policy. This particular policy is a collection of rules that specify what types of access are allowed on a system. System policy is associated with MAC comparably to how firewall rules are associated with firewalls. Security-enhanced Linux (SELinux) is a Linux kernel implementation of a supple MAC mechanism called type enforcement. These policies restrict users and processes to the minimal amount of privilege required to perform tasks. Type enforcement uses a type identifier and assigns it to every user and object; these authorizations are defined in a SELinux policy.

The SELinux implementation of MAC exercises a type of enforcement mechanism that necessitates every subject and object be assigned an identifier. We will use the terms *subject* and *object* for this example. Consider the subject as a user or a process, and the object as a file or a process. Characteristically, a subject cannot access an object unless the type identifier assigned to the subject is authorized to access the object. The default policy is to deny all access that is not specifically allowed. Authorization is determined by rules defined in the SELinux policy. The following is an example of rule-granting access:

```
allow httpd_t httpd_sys_content_t : file (ioctol read getattr lock);
```

where the subject http daemon is assigned the type identifier of httpd_t and is granted permissions ioctol, read, gettattr, and lock for any file object assigned in the type identifier httpd_sys_content_t. Basically, the http daemon is allowed to read a rule that is assigned the type identifier httpsd_sys_content_t. This is a simpler rule; there are thousands of rules, varying in complexity. There are also many types of identifiers for use with subjects and objects. SELinux adds type enforcement to standard Linux distributions. To access an object, the user must have both the appropriate file permissions (DAC) and the correct SELinux access. ELinux security context covers three capacities:

1. The user
2. The role
3. The type identifier

By running the ls command with the -Z switch, conventional file information is displayed along with the security context for each element in the subdirectory. See the following example, where the security context for the index.html file encompasses user_u as the user, object_r as the role, and httpd_sys_content_t as the type identifier:

```
[web_admin@localhost html]$ ls -Z index.html
-rw-r--r-- web_admin web_admin user_u:object_r:httpd_sys_content_t index.html
```

Role-Based Access Control

Role-based access control (RBAC) is a method whereby only authorized users can gain access to an environment and the sessions contained in the environment, as shown in Figure 11.1. Some refer to RBAC as role-based security due to the roles an organization creates to assign permissions to users, who perform specific functions, and such users acquire their roles and rights when their account is created. In Active Directory, either the users are in a department that assigns rights by department or the users have customized access based off their role to perform a job function. Referring to the model in Figure 11.1, use the following conventions:

• Subject (S)—person or agent
• Role (R)—job function
• Permission (P)—authorization to access a resource or utility

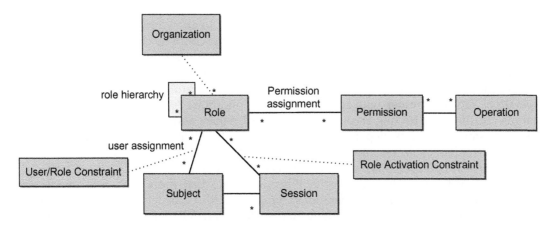

FIGURE 11.1   Role-based access control model that restricts environment access to authorized users.

- Session (SE)—mapping, including S, R, and/or P
- Subject Assignment (SA)
- Permission Agent (PA)
- Partial Instructional Role Hierarchy (RH)— $\geq$ (where $x \geq y$ requires x to inherit permissions of y)
  1. Subjects are allowed multiple roles.
  2. Roles are allowed to contain multiple subjects.
  3. Roles are allowed to assign multiple permissions.
  4. Permissions can be allocated to multiple roles.
  5. Operations can be allocated to multiple permissions.
  6. Permissions can be allocated many operations.

Whereas a constraint positions a provisional rule on the possibility of inherited permissions from contrasting rules; it can thus be utilized to attain applicable partitions of duties. As such, a user should not be permitted to both create a login or to empower such an account creation. RBAC is comprised of three principal guidelines:

1. Role assignment: A subject can implement permission once the subject has been designated or has allocated a role.
2. Role authorization: A subject's dynamic role requires permission for the subject. Refer to rule 1, above, which warrants users only inherit roles for which they are sanctioned.
3. Permission authorization: A subject can employ permission merely if the permission is approved for the subject's functional role. Refer to rules 1 and 2; rule 3 confirms users can only carry out permissions for which they are allowed.

Several additional controls can be applied on top of the former three rules, and roles can be combined in a hierarchy where higher level roles consider permissions retained by subroles. In larger organizations, typically those with over 500 users, administrators tend to combine MAC or DAC.

As previously mentioned, RBAC can be referred to as an adaptable secure access control. RBAC diverges from access control lists (ACLs) in that it appoints permissions to exclusive operations for users to perform their job functions, rather than to low-level data objects. Let's say an access control list could be utilized to allow or deny write access to a certain file system, but it is unable to dictate how that file could be changed.

As an example, in financial systems, an operation may seek to create a new trading account or to create a new database for a particular trading product. The assignment of the permission to perform a particular operation is meaningful in this instance, since the operations are so granular with meaning to an application. You would not want college interns creating new trading accounts utilizing real money and would prefer that only an administrator of the risk department had those rights. Even concerning trading limits, imagine if traders could go into the application and raise their trading limits themselves. Risk controls are put into place to protect assets and rights.

RBAC is well suited to separate liabilities, ensuring that more than two people are involved in authorizing critical operations. Integrating RBAC benefits access control policies and aids the IT infrastructure where Active Directory, SQL Server, and any other proprietary applications are concerned.

Logical Access Controls

Logical access controls tools are used for credentials, validation, authorization, and accountability in an infrastructure and the systems within. These components enforce access control measures for systems, applications, processes, and information. This type of access control can also be embedded inside an application, operating system, database, or infrastructure administrative system. Physical access control is a mechanical form and can be thought of physical access to a room with a key. The line is often unclear whether or not an element can be considered physical or logical access control. Physical access is controlled by software, the chip on an access card and an electric lock grant access through software. Thus, physical access should be considered a logical access control. A benefit of having logical access controlled centrally in a system allows for a user's physical access permissions to be instantaneously revoked or amended. For example, when an employee is fired, his or her badge access can be disabled, as can the employee's multiple system access accounts. Persons in possession of the proper access card, the appropriate security level, and in some cases a pin are granted entry to a room once the credentials are checked against a database.

Physical Access Controls

Physical access control is a mechanical form and can be thought of physical access to a room with a key. The line is often unclear whether or not an element can be considered a physical or a logical access control. When physical access is controlled by software, the chip on an access card and an electric lock grants access through software (see checklist: An Agenda for Action for Evaluating Authentication and Access Control Software Products), which should be considered a logical access control. That being said, incorporating biometrics adds another layer to gain entry into a room. This is considered a physical access control. Identity authentication is based on a person's physical characteristics. The most common physical access controls are used at hospitals, police stations, government offices, data centers, and any area that contains sensitive equipment and/or data.

AN AGENDA FOR ACTION FOR EVALUATING AUTHENTICATION AND ACCESS CONTROL SOFTWARE PRODUCTS

Before one starts evaluating authentication and access control software products, they'll need to answer several questions about the technology; as well as the organization's specific needs (check all tasks completed):

_____ 1. **What needs to be protected?** The type and level of protection required depends on the assets you'll be safeguarding. After all, national security secrets need more extensive (and costly) protection

---

than a public domain data collection. This is an important matter you will need to discuss with a security professional.

2. **Which type of authentication is best?** There are four basic ways of authenticating users: asking for something only the authorized user knows (such as a password), testing for the presence of something only the authorized user has (like a smart card), obtaining some nonforgeable biological or behavioral measurement of the user (like a fingerprint), or determining that the user is located at a place where only the authorized user can enter. The best (and most effective) solutions require a combination of two or more authentication methods.

3. **Is the software compatible with existing systems and devices?** The solution must be compatible with current operating systems and applications. Compatibility is a particularly big concern with biometric systems, since existing hardware and applications often must be adapted and/or reprogrammed to work with these tools.

4. **Does it offer an acceptable trade-off between security and convenience?** Organizations must balance the value of the information being protected with the authentication and access control software's ease of use. Solutions that are difficult to use may protect systems, but only at the expense of user convenience and productivity.

5. **How easy is it to upgrade and expand the software?** You'll want a product that you can use for many years. Over that time span, it will need to be upgraded to accommodate new security practices and technologies.

6. **Will the software work with other types of solutions, such as antifraud and user behavior-monitoring technologies?** These days, access control is often a part of a multifaceted enterprise security initiative. It's important to know if the software you're looking at plays well with others.

7. **What are the product's management features?** Authentication and access control software products are notoriously difficult to set up and maintain. Look for management features that are straightforward and easy to understand.

8. **Has the software ever been defeated? If so, how?** If the product has ever been hacked, you'll want to know what steps the vendor has taken to make its technology more secure.

9. How much does the software cost? Don't look at the license fee alone. The total product cost includes acquisition, customization, deployment, management, user training, extra hardware, productivity impact, and maintenance. Ask vendors for detailed statements, policies, and prices for each of these factors.

A significant element surrounding physical access controls as opposed to conventional security solutions is its capacity to capture multifaceted and detailed images of physical traits, encode such traits in files, and evaluate sets of data within seconds. Homeowners are now considering this layer of security since loved ones and belongings are sacred, and this layer of security is not possible to forge. Physical access controls not only enhance security but also allow for efficiency, only requiring one form of authentication, a physical trait (fingerprint, retina, palm of hand). This eliminates the risk of a card being stolen or a PIN being hacked.

2. STRENGTHENING THE INFRASTRUCTURE: AUTHENTICATION SYSTEMS

Authentication might involve confirming the identity of a person or software program (see checklist: An Agenda for Action for Evaluating Authentication and Access Control Software Products). The introduction to this chapter mentioned three categories authentication may fall under. Whether it is knowledge specific to a user, a piece of information the user has, or the position the user is in, each of them aims to verify the user's identity. Each authentication factor covers a range of elements used to authenticate or verify a person's identity prior to being granted access. Examples include a computer approving a transaction request, electronically signing a document or other work product, administrators granting authority to users with management approval, and a chain of authority that must be established to keep the controls in place and consistent. Security investigations have determined that the standard for verification must include components from at least two factors, and preferably three. Three authentication factors are as follows:

1. *Ownership factors*: something tangible the user has (ID card, security token, software token, phone or cell phone)
2. *Knowledge factors*: a piece of information the user knows (password, pass phrase, PIN, or a challenge response, such as a security question only the user knows the answer to)
3. *Physical factors*: a physical trait of an individual (fingerprint, retinal pattern, signature, voice, or another biometrical identifier)

A common example of a two-factor authentication is when one uses his or her ATM card and has to enter a PIN. Some organizations not only require a username and password to authenticate to the VPN, but also give employees a token with a random set of numbers that change every 30 seconds. The author has visited multiple data center facilities, and while some differ in their choice of the second authentication factor, all data centers require two-factor authentication. While one data center may require use of a badge and your pointer finger fingerprint, others may use a PIN along with a biometric hand scan. Additionally, a handful of facilities include a third factor for authentication, a mantrap. The mantrap screens the person's height, weight, facial features, and retina. These facilities institute higher security standards and are generally financial or governmental collocation sites.

Kerberos and CHAP

Kerberos is a secure method for authenticating a request for a service in a network. Kerberos was developed in the Athena Project at the Massachusetts Institute of Technology (MIT). Based on the name of the Needham-Schroeder protocol, Kerberos is named after a three-headed dog who guarded the gates of Hades in Greek mythology. Kerberos lets a user request an encrypted "ticket" from an authentication process that can then be used to request a particular service from a server. The user's password does not have to pass through the network. MIT offers a download for both the client and server versions of Kerberos, or you can buy a copy.

One weakness is that Kerberos requires the continuous availability of a central server. Knock out the Kerberos server and no one can log in. This problem can be mitigated by using multiple Kerberos servers. The technology is also sensitive to clock settings and won't work properly unless the clocks of the involved hosts are synchronized. Default configuration requires that clock times be no more than 10 minutes apart. Additionally, the administration of the protocol is not standardized and differs between server implementations. And since the secret keys for all users are stored on the central server, a compromise of that server will jeopardize all users' secret keys.

Big data is a hot subject these days, and without question an increasing number of enterprise information security teams are going to be asked about the security-related ramifications of big data projects. There are many issues to look into, but here are a few ideas to make the big data environment more secure during architecture and implementation phases:

1. Create data controls as close to the data as possible, since much of this data isn't "owned" by the security team. The risk of having big data traversing your network is that you have large amounts of confidential data—such as credit-card data, Social Security numbers, and personally identifiable information (PII)—residing in new places and being used in new ways. Also, you're usually not going to see terabytes of data siphoned from an organization, but you should be concerned about the search for patterns to find the content in these databases. Keep the security as close to the data as possible and don't rely on firewalls, IPS, DLP, or other systems to protect the data.
2. Verify that sensitive fields are indeed protected by using encryption so that when the data is analyzed, manipulated, or sent to other areas of the organization, you're limiting risk of exposure. All sensitive information needs to be encrypted once you have control over it.
3. After you've made the move to encrypt data, the next logical step is to concern yourself with key management. There are a few new ways to perform key management, including creating keys on an as-needed basis so you don't have to store them.
4. In Hadoop designs, review the Hadoop Distributed File System (HDFS) permissions of the cluster and verify that all access to HDFS is authenticated. When first implemented, Hadoop frameworks were notoriously bad at performing authentication of users and services. This allows users to impersonate as a user the cluster services themselves. You can be authenticated to the Hadoop framework using Kerberos, which can be used with HDFS access tokens to authenticate to the name node.

TABLE 11.3   Authentication Scheme used by CHAP Packets.

				CHAP Packets		
Description	1 Byte	1 Byte	2 Bytes	1 Byte	Variable	Variable
Challenge	Code = 1	ID	Length	Response length	Challenge value	Name
Response	Code = 2	ID	Length	Response length	Response value	Name
Success	Code = 3	ID	Length		Message	
Failure	Code = 4	ID	Length		Message	

Challenge-Handshake Authentication Protocol (CHAP) is an authentication scheme used by Point-to-Point Protocol (PPP) hosts to authorize the identity of remote users and clients. CHAP occasionally validates the identity of the client by using a three-way handshake. This occurs simultaneously as the initial link is established, and can take place randomly at any time. Substantiation is based on a shared secret—for example, the user or client's password. Steps in the CHAP authentication scheme are as follows (reference Table 11.3):

1. Once the link has been established, the authenticator sends a "challenge" message to the peer.
2. The peer then responds with a determined value using a one-way hash function on the challenge and the secret combined.
3. The authenticator checks the response against the expected answer, or calculation of the expected hash value. If the values match, the authenticator acknowledges the authentication. If it does not match, the connection is terminated.

Randomly, the Authenticator Sends Another Challenge to the Peer and Repeats the Steps Mentioned Above

The ID chosen for the random challenge is also used in the corresponding response, success, and failure packets. A new challenge with a new ID must be different from the last challenge with another ID. If the success or failure is lost, the same response can be sent again and will trigger the same success or failure indication. For MD5 as hash, the response value is MD5(ID||secret||challenge), the MD5 for the concatenation of ID, secret, and challenge.

Wireless Security Access Controls

The IT Department has just been notified that the company wishes to allow personnel to access the company network from personal devices. A common approach to achieve this is to create separately named networks, (SSIDs), and corresponding VLANs inside your wired network. Segregating VLANs will separate the traffic between the other network traffic. Public wireless can be placed on a separate VLAN rather than private wireless, and there could also be a Mobile Wireless VLAN added to separate laptop wireless traffic from mobile devices.

However, you still want network access protection and a secure and simple way for key personnel to register their own devices for secure access to a private wireless network. Ask your wireless vendor if it sells a visitor management feature or a registration portal capable of walking personal devices through authorization and Wi-Fi provisioning. Another method for network access protection and wireless access control could be using a Mobile Device Manager (MDM) to drive these tasks.

WPA2-Personal requires every device to supply a Pre-Shared Key (PSK) derived from a passphrase. For example, devices on your trading floor might be required to supply the same random string of 20 characters known only to your IT department and configured during deployment. This method is often combined with MAC address filtering, so that only known devices with the right PSK are granted access. However, MAC address filters are easily bypassed, as are PSKs that are too short or too easy to guess. WPA2-Enterprise requires every device to complete an 802.1X log-on process that can support various authentication methods. For example, each device on your trading floor might be required to prove its identity with a unique digital certificate. Alternatively, each device might be required to supply a unique username and password configured during deployment and known only to your IT department. With this Wi-Fi access control method, you will be able to tell which individual machines are logged on. When used with certificates, WPA2-Enterprise is less vulnerable to password sharing and reuse, which are common problems when employees know a valid username/password or PSK and simply configure those into personal devices.

3. SUMMARY

Although only the most commonly used access mechanisms are discussed in this chapter, many extensions, combinations, and different mechanisms are possible. Trade-offs and limitations are involved with all mechanisms and access control designs, so it is the user's responsibility to determine the best-fit access control mechanisms that work for their business functions and requirements.

Also included in this chapter are the most commonly used access control policies. Since access control policies are targeted to specific access control requirements, unlike access control mechanisms, specific limitations cannot be inherently associated with them. And like access control mechanisms, it is up to the users to select the best policies for their needs. In addition to the limitations and issues, quality biometrics depends not only on the consideration of administration cost, but also on the flexibility of the mechanism helping the user in assessing or selecting among access control systems.

Finally, let's move on to the real interactive part of this chapter: review questions/exercises, hands-on projects, case projects, and optional team case project. The answers and/or solutions by chapter can be found in the Online Instructor's Solutions Manual.

CHAPTER REVIEW QUESTIONS/EXERCISES

True/False

1. True or False? The dichotomy between types of companies and implementing layers of security led to the use of three types of access control mechanisms: denial of access control, mandatory access control, and role-based access control.
2. True or False? Discretionary access control (DAC), also known as file permissions, is the access control in Unix and Windows systems.
3. True or False? Mandatory access control (MAC) regulates user process access to resources based on an organizational security policy.
4. True or False? Role-based access control (RBAC) is a method whereby only authorized users can lose access to an environment and the sessions contained in the environment.
5. True or False? Role-based access controls tools are used for credentials, validation, authorization, and accountability in an infrastructure and the systems within.

Multiple Choice

1. What is a mechanical form and can be thought of as physical access to a room with a key?
   A. Qualitative analysis
   B. Vulnerabilities
   C. Spoofing
   D. Physical access control
   E. DHS
2. What might involve confirming the identity of a person or software program?
   A. Firewall
   B. Risk assessment
   C. Scale
   D. Authentication
   E. Bait
3. What is a secure method for authenticating a request for a service in a network?
   A. Organizations
   B. Fabric
   C. Kerberos
   D. Web application firewall
   E. Security
4. What requires every device to supply a Pre-Shared Key (PSK) derived from a passphrase?
   A. Cabinet-level state office
   B. Denial-of-service attack
   C. WPA2-Personal
   D. SAN protocol
   E. Taps

5. What is an authentication scheme used by Point-to-Point Protocol (PPP) hosts to authorize the identity of remote users and clients?
   A. Systems security plan
   B. Consumer privacy protection
   C. IP storage access
   D. Vulnerability
   E. Challenge-Handshake Authentication Protocol (CHAP)

EXERCISE

Problem

Which type of authentication is best?

Hands-On Projects

Project

Is the access control and authentication software compatible with existing systems and devices?

Case Projects

Problem

Does access control and authentication software offer an acceptable trade-off between security and convenience?

Optional Team Case Project

Problem

How easy is it to upgrade and expand access control and authentication software?

Assessments and Audits

Lauren Collins

kCura Corporation

1. ASSESSING VULNERABILITIES AND RISK: PENETRATION TESTING AND VULNERABILITY ASSESSMENTS

Penetration testing usually occurs in the compliance sphere, both in the semantics we use to describe technical points like "regulating deployments" and in the language technology vendors employ to describe those implementations. Compliance, however, is intolerant when it comes to accuracy in writing, and elusive inconsistencies in words can mean the difference between compliance and noncompliance. Erratic interpretations of conditions can lead to incongruous control selection, vague or unsuitable management responses, misrepresentation of controls to auditors, and many other problems. These differences can result in the very violations we are striving to avoid by integrating assessments prior to audits occurring. Penetration tests are valuable for multiple reasons:

- To identify vulnerabilities that may be evasive or impractical to detect with automated network or application vulnerability scanning software
- To identify high-risk vulnerabilities resulting from an amalgamation of lower risk vulnerabilities exploited in a noteworthy sequence
- To regulate the viability of a particular set of attack vectors
- To assess the magnitude of potential business and operational impacts of successful incidents
- To test the ability of network defenders to successfully detect and counter incidents

Multiple techniques can be used to conduct a penetration test; the variance is the volume of knowledge of the implementation factors pertaining to the system undergoing testing. Black box testing assumes no prior familiarity with the testing environment. A tester lays out the scenario and gathers information about the infrastructure prior to formulating an analysis. Black box testing can become exponentially expensive as time goes on. Not only is it labor intensive, but it is also taxing on the network and could cause noticeable slowness due to

Cyber Security and IT Infrastructure Protection
DOI: http://dx.doi.org/10.1016/B978-0-12-416681-3.00012-4

scanning. White box testing specifies all the information necessary: source code, IP addressing schemes, network diagrams, and any other pertinent information that is available. Believe it or not, gray box testing is also out there. Gray box testing depends on the type of test one can administer; which is entirely based on the extent of the information available.

Vulnerability assessments and penetration tests are habitually exercised interchangeably among technical associates, auditors, and controllers. The misconception is that a penetration test and a vulnerability assessment are notably different exercises. As a result, it is necessary for compliance professionals to become educated on the differences of each in an effort to ensure they are appropriately satiating compliance intentions that the controls perform in an approach they would expect and that they are correctly demonstrating controlled deployments to peers. At a high level, a vulnerability assessment is any interest aimed at research and subsequently at detailed prospective attack points (the vulnerabilities) within a given set of data. In a corporate information technology context, it usually embraces an attentive study of information systems (applications, systems, network devices, etc.) in order to identify concerns that compromise the security of that environment. Potential concerns may include omission of patching, unprotected configurations, and weak passwords.

Vulnerability assessments can be conventional, or they can focus on a more meticulous level of the technology stack, such as an application-level vulnerability assessment. Best practice is to incorporate practical scanning manners, such as running an automated vulnerability scan to query the scope of systems and devices. The next step would be to run a report on the security issues that might be present. The point of the action is to specify as many potential issues as possible that may negatively impact the environment's security. A vulnerability assessment will contain an automated scan of the environment using a proprietary scanning tool. Furthermore, both types of activities can include vulnerability scoring and prioritization. In the case of a vulnerability assessment, the purpose is to provide information about the qualified severity level and remediation priority for the located issues. The penetration test, on the other hand, is designed to avoid providing attackers with information that gives them ideas on prolific attack opportunities.

From a regulatory compliance stance, the range of a vulnerability assessment or a penetration test will depend on the specific control objective you wish to meet. Since these conditions are sometimes used interchangeably, compliance specialists may find it necessary to ask some key questions rather than assume that a technical process or control implementation includes particular characteristics. Questions to ascertain if a vendor or partner is referring to vulnerability assessments or penetration testing include the following:

- Will the test include a vulnerability list, an activity report, or something else?
- What is the process output or report format?
- Will testers attempt to gain access to control sensitive resources?
- Is there a manual component, or is there just automated scanning?

By making invalid assumptions, you may not be receiving the controls and processes you hoped for. This could lead to more trouble than you had anticipated. Make sure you understand what the partners or vendors mean when they are discussing vulnerability assessments and penetration testing. Ask questions.

Port Scanning and Password Cracking

Port scanning is one of the most popular techniques a hacker can use to discover services that can be compromised. For instance, a port scanner will send a TCP SYN request to the host (or range of hosts) set to scan. Ping sweeps are also an option when attempting to define which hosts are available before starting the TCP port scans. Most port scanners only scan TCP ports by default, and some will have UDP by default as well. Some software packages will perform the discovery and auditing of your systems and network, or if you're really good and know your way around the command line on a switch, you can navigate around a network quickly to locate and there are free open-source programs as well. Network Mapper (NMAP), an open-source license, will allow scanning of UDP packets and is shown in Figure 12.1. Other common programs that can be used, other than NMAP, are SuperScan and NetScan. A scan will probe the accessible hosts for up to 65,535 viable TCP and UDP ports. You can select specific ports you'd like to scan in order to return fewer results, and also filter to view the services available. Port scans provide the following information from accessible hosts on the network:

- Network address of the hosts discovered
- Services and/or applications the hosts are running

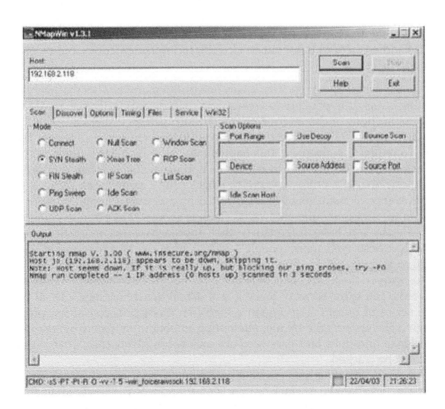

FIGURE 12.1   Network Mapper (NMAP), a utility used for scanning ports.

- Hosts that are operational and reachable on the network

For your initial scan, it is recommended that you scan all ports from 1 to 65,535. There are many options to get as granular as you want. For instance, a scan can be performed on only well-known ports, or a scan may only involve a certain range of ports specific to your system. If the scanner is unable to find hosts that you are certain would show up, ICMP may be blocked. Once you have concluded what hosts are available and which ports are open, more sophisticate scans can be run to verify that the ports are open and that the tool is not reporting a false positive:

- *UDP Scan* is a basic UDP scan that looks for any open UDP ports on the host. This option is used to see what is running and determine whether or not Intrusion Detection Systems (IDS), firewalls, or other logging devices log the connection.
- *Connect* is a basic TCP scan that looks for any open TCP ports on the host. This scan is used to see what is running and determine whether or not IDS, firewalls, or other logging devices log the connection.
- *SYN Stealth* is a scan that initiates a half-open TCP connection, with the host potentially dodging IDS systems and logging. This option is a great scan for testing IDS systems, firewalls, and other logging devices.
- *FIN Stealth, Xmas Tree and Null* are scans that allow you to get creative by sending odd-shaped packets to the network hosts in order to see how the hosts respond. These scans basically alter the flags in the TCP headers of each packet, which allows you to test how each host handles them to point out weak TCP/IP implementations and patches that may need to be applied.

In Chapter 60, denial-of-service attack was one of the many attacks that were described. When running scans, it is possible to create your own denial-of-dervice attack and potentially crash applications or the entire network. Unfortunately, if there is a host on the network with a weak TCP/IP stack, there is no way to prevent your scan from becoming a DoS attack. To reduce the chance of this happening, use slow NMAP timing options when running scans. Refer to Figure 12.1 to see all the options available when running scans.

Password cracking is a process whereby a hacker or a system can retrieve passwords from records that have been stored or transmitted by a system. A popular tactic, and most common, is to try and guess the password. There is always the option to change the password and to state you have forgotten it; that approach works more than most would assume and has destroyed many people's virtual lives. In an organization, it is always more secure to assign a user a new password rather than allow them to answer a set of questions to recover their forgotten password. Although only administrators can assign new passwords, the extra security layer is a must. When reflecting how all of us have answered a series of questions to regain a forgotten password, consider a program running through a file system, file by file, attempting to obtain the record where the answers to your challenge questions and password are makes complete sense. That is exactly how a password can be cracked.

Encryption is a common process that individuals and organizations practice, and although it may take longer to crack, an encrypted password is easily attainable. If MD5 or SHA1 hash is used to encrypt a string of characters, that encrypted password is then a string of characters that is stored in the database. Rainbow tables of encrypted hashes contain all possible uses of a password, and such tools are available for free downloads. When comparing the rainbow tables and the target hashes, newer computers have a powerful enough processor and graphics card to achieve quantifiable results quickly. Graphic processing units (GPUs) were designed to do supercomputing where high-end math calculations can be done quickly in electronic trading and password cracking. GPUs are much faster than CPUs at calculating predefined tasks and comprise faster memory and wider input/output (I/O) channels to facilitate rapid computations.

There are several ways to limit the effectiveness of the powerful tools available to hackers. Salted hashes are a randomly generated piece of information that is added to the data prior to running it through the hashing process. A salt is arbitrarily generated information that is added to the data before running through the hashing process. Now the encrypted value cannot be cracked using rainbow tables, and the salt will have to be stored in encrypted databases utilizing a different salt for each password. A hacker would have to decrypt the database as well as each password and its record. Two-factor authentication is another technique organizations can use to intensify security measures. This is a form of security that will add greater security, even in the event a hashed password has been breached.

OVAL and CVE

Open Vulnerability and Assessment Language (OVAL) is the standard for determining vulnerability and configuration issues on systems. OVAL is an open community that was created by MITRE, and it is where knowledge can be shared and the content stored may be accessible to the public in an effort to standardize security efforts and how to assess and report systems and their states. OVAL utilitizes a three-step system assessment:

1. Represent system information.
2. Articulate detailed machine states and report the results of the assessment.
3. Supply organizations with precise, stable, and actionable evidence to improve security.

Here is a case where OVAL could be useful: An organization designed their security procedures, protocols, and policies surrounding the Cisco products that were in their infrastructure. Three companies were acquired, and each of the three companies had hardware other than Cisco. Any vulnerability that was found prior to the acquisition and was corrected will no longer be valid once this other hardware is integrated into the infrastructure. Scanning your territory with three or four tools will now yield completely different results, making it more complex and prove that customized needs will have to be developed for the new assessment tool. Vendors, partners, and various other contributors will report the state of their systems, and this data should be referenced anytime your environment changes. The need for open standardization is clear in an example like this, and the process is represented in Figure 12.2.

Through public analysis, direct vendor support, and community contributions, OVAL provides vulnerability content that is reliable and verifiable. OVAL uses the robustness of XML to create a standard language for defining, assessing, and reporting vulnerabilities and configurations. Providing this vulnerability scanning content for the IT industry to

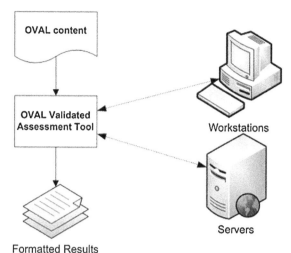

FIGURE 12.2   The assessment process of OVAL.

TABLE 12.1   Repositories Available Within OVAL.

Repository	Platform	Content
MITRE	Any platform	Open community based support for configuration and vulnerability information
Red Hat	Red Hat Enterprise Linux	Vulnerability content
NIST SCAP	Any platform	SCAP related

collaborate and share technical details allows administrators and engineers to rapidly determine which systems are vulnerable and to rectify those vulnerabilities. And when there is a bug or a false positive, the community is astute to share fixes through use of publicly accessible repositories.

So, where do you go to get this content? There are tools that ship with vulnerability checks and receive regular content updates, or one of the OVAL repositories can assist. Table 12.1 represents the repository and its corresponding platform and content.

New repositories are added to OVAL's Web site after they have been created and verified. If you are assessing systems for use with the U.S. federal government, the NIST SCAP repository is your area of interest. Microsoft Security Guides, DISA Security Technical Implementation Guides, and Federal Desktop Core Configuration guides have been developed for assessing the systems established on current federal and vendor systems. Whether you are assessing the impact of the latest vulnerability or checking for federal compliance, the substantial public environment of OVAL developers and contributors will provide useful information to you and your infrastructure.

Common Vulnerabilities and Exposures (CVE) provides reference for information security vulnerability and exposures. MITRE assigns a CVE identifier to every vulnerability or exposure. A CVE is used to track vulnerability through different pieces of software, as a single CVE can affect multiple software packages and multiple vendors. The vulnerability is defined as a mistake in the software which may be directly oppressed by an attacker to compromise a system, and an exposure as a fault that could be used as an opportunity to launch an attack. CVE efforts include:

- Vulnerability Management
- Patch Management
- Vulnerability Alerting
- Intrusion Detection
- Security Content Automation Protocol (SCAP)
- National Vulnerability Database (NVD)
- US-CERT Bulletins
- CVE Numbering Authorities (CNAs)

When working with a common identifier, administrators and engineers find it less difficult to share data across separate databases, tools, and services. This data is not only easily accessible but can be integrated with ease. Unless a report comes up stating there is a bug, you're good to go. CVE is free and available for anyone who is interested in correlating data between diverse vulnerability or security tools, repositories, and services. Anyone could search or download CVE, copy it, redistribute it, reference it, and analyze it, provided you do not modify CVE itself. Companies are allowed to add links and pages to CVE's Web sites, products, publications, or other capacities. CVE Identifiers, or CVE names, are exclusive and collective identifiers for publicly known information. CVE-2001-0731 references a bug on how Google indexed a file without an external link. A CVE Identifier can be in the form of one of the following:

- Identifier number ("CVE-2001-0731")
- Description of the security vulnerability or exposure
- Any pertinent references (vulnerability reports and advisories or an OVAL-ID)

Using CVEs to identify vulnerabilities and exposures in your organization will allow for accurate and obtainable information from a vast selection of CVE information sources. CVE can help you make informed decisions and determine which of the capabilities are appropriate for your particular needs. Another plus is having the ability to create a suite of interoperable security tools and capabilities available as a translation mechanism.

2. RISK MANAGEMENT: QUANTITATIVE RISK MEASUREMENTS

By focusing on implementing best practices in your environment, you will be able to accomplish the following tasks:

- *Real-time alert configuration*: Data centers have become the core of a business, acting as an operations center. Managing logs is a significant step, and it is equally important to access and monitor alerts.

- *Proactive protection of the environment*: Log management tools and baseline analysis assist an organization to be proactive in their security methodology. Catching holes in security or issues existing, engineers can make a significant difference in time and money. Patching a server is an easy task, but when it is overlooked patch after patch, a vulnerability exists.
- *Incident containment*: When an unauthorized event occurs in an infrastructure, logs that are set up correctly can alert engineers and pinpoint the exact location quickly. If an engineer can see where the issue resides in a timely manner, that network or server can be isolated to prevent further damage.
- *Creation of an audit trail for forensics analysis*: When an intrusion is suspected or data loss has occurred, a rockstar audit trail will allow forensic data engineers to retrace the steps taken by someone who has entered the environment and correlate that data into usable information.
- *Creation of online documentation as the environment evolves*: IT must keep an activity log, tracking all logs across all the environments. Understanding the various systems and how they're performing allows engineers to shape the infrastructure as the business needs change.

Establishing a Baseline

Two types of alerts should be logged: faults that are generated by the system and the applications running on it, and faults or errors reported by the system's users. Fault logging and analysis is often the only way of finding out what is unsuitable about a system or application. The analysis of fault logs can be used to identify trends that may indicate deeper issues, such as defective hardware or a lack of competence or training for system administrators or users. All operating systems and many applications, such as database software, provide event logging and basic alerting faculties. This logging functionality should be configured to log all faults and send alerts if the error threshold is above an acceptable, defined threshold. Fault logging and analysis is often the only way to find out what is wrong with a system or an application. Documentation is key when defining which faults to record or report, who is responsible to investigate the faults, and an expected resolution time.

Since data center environments continue to grow, it has become more evident that administrators need to properly manage logs. Checking in on servers, firewalls, appliances, and switching gear event logs will assist IT to do more than simply check for reactive issues. If the process is managed and kept accurate, engineers can create a proactive environment that is capable of spotting and controlling issues before they even arise. Logs can also help an environment plan for the future. Network logs can show engineers where they are lacking and how they can competently plan for growth.

Auditing and Logging

Many devices that provide protection to the infrastructure within networks allow the ability to log events and take actions based on those events. This application system and monitoring provide details both on what has happened to the device and on what is happening in real time. It provides security against lapses in perimeter and application defenses by alerting an administrator about issues, so that defensive measures can be enacted prior to any damage taking place. Without monitoring, an organization does not stand a chance of ascertaining whether a live application is under attack or if it has been compromised.

Business critical applications, processes handling valuable or sensitive information, previously compromised or abused systems, and those systems connected to third parties, all require active monitoring. Whenever suspicious behavior or critical events arise, an alert will be generated and must be acted on. Risk assessments must be done to determine logging levels and which actions are projected from a specified set of alerts. Logging and auditing work together, ensuring that users are only performing the activities they are authorized to perform. This data also plays a key role in preventing, spotting, tracking, and stopping unwanted or inappropriate activities. The levels of alerts, log reviews, and monitoring are an additional necessary component, and at least the following will need to be logged:

- Date, time, and other crucial events
- User ID or IP address
- Successful connections and failed attempts to access systems, data, or applications
- Files, servers, and networks accessed
- Changes to configurations
- Consumption of system utilities
- Exceptions and other security-related events, such as triggered alarms
- Activation of protection systems (intrusion detection systems and malware).

When these types of data are collected, that data will assist in access control monitoring and can provide audit trails when an incident is being investigated. Usually, logs are covered by some form of regulation of how many days it should be kept in case they are needed for an investigation. Employees need to be made aware of any firm monitoring policy activities on the network. Log files are a great source of information, but they serve absolutely no purpose if no one monitors them. When a firm purchases and deploys a solution, the product will not provide security unless the information is collected and analyzed on a regular basis. Some procedures require that the results be reviewed regularly to identify possible security threats and incidents. Each company differs in its processes based on the operations and content, and on how attractive that data may be.

Reviewing Policy Settings

Small networks can generate large amounts of information if the log settings are not optimal. Although log analyzers could automate the auditing and analysis of logs, storage for logs may be another challenge. This type of automated feedback frees up your resources, and your engineer can work to refine the log levels or parse through alerts of accurate threats. Recognizing true threats will help reduce the number of false positives. Eliminating false positives, while maintaining strict controls, is next to impossible. New threats and changes in the network infrastructure are ever changing and will likely affect the effectiveness of existing rule sets. Analyzing logs can provide a basis for focused security awareness training, reduced network misuse, and stronger policy enforcement.

Administrators have powerful access, and their activity should also be recorded and checked. A system restart may be prompted to correct serious errors, and those restarts may not be recorded if an administrator disables the alarm. Administrators' actions should be logged, noting start and finish times, who was involved and at what capacity, and what actions were taken. The name of the individual recording the information also should be recorded, along with the date and time. An organization with an internal audit team needs to maintain these records.

3. SUMMARY

An information security assessment and audit is the process of determining how effectively an entity being assessed (host, system, network, procedure, person—known as the assessment object) meets specific security objectives. Three types of assessment and audit methods can be used to accomplish this—testing, examination, and interviewing. *Testing* is the process of exercising one or more assessment and audit objects under specified conditions to compare actual and expected behaviors. *Examination* is the process of checking, inspecting, reviewing, observing, studying, or analyzing one or more assessment and audit objects to facilitate understanding, achieve clarification, or obtain evidence. *Interviewing* is the process of conducting discussions with individuals or groups within an organization to facilitate under-standing, achieve clarification, or identify the location of evidence. Assessment and audit results are used to support the determination of security control effectiveness over time.

This chapter presents the basic technical aspects of conducting information security assessments and audits. It presents technical testing and examination methods and techniques that an organization might use as part of an assessment and audit, and it offers insights to assessors on their execution and the potential impact they may have on systems and networks. For an assessment and audit to be successful and have a positive impact on the security posture of a system (and ultimately the entire organization), elements beyond the execution of testing and examination must support the technical process. Suggestions for these activities (including a robust planning process, root cause analysis, and tailored reporting) are also presented in this chapter (see checklist: An Agenda for Action for Implementing Information Security Assessments and Audits).

AN AGENDA FOR ACTION FOR IMPLEMENTING INFORMATION SECURITY ASSESSMENTS AND AUDITS

The processes and technical recommen-dations presented in this chapter enable organizations to (check all tasks completed):

_____1. Develop information security assessment and audit policy, methodology, and individual roles

and responsibilities related to the technical aspects of assessment and audits.

_____2. Accurately plan for a technical information security assessment and audit by providing guidance

---

on determining which systems to assess and the approach for assessment and audit, addressing logistical considerations, developing an assessment and audit plan, and ensuring legal and policy considerations are addressed.

_____3. Safely and effectively execute a technical information security assessment and audit using methods and techniques, and respond to any incidents that may occur during the assessment and audit.

_____4. Appropriately handle technical data (collection, storage, transmission, and destruction) throughout the assessment and audit process.

_____5. Conduct analysis and reporting to translate technical findings into risk mitigation actions that will improve the organization's security posture.

_____6. Establish an information security assessment and audit policy. This identifies the organization's requirements for executing assessments and audits, and provides accountability for the appropriate individuals to ensure assessments and audits are conducted in accordance with these requirements. Topics that an assessment and audit policy should address include the organizational requirements with which assessments and audits must comply; roles and responsibilities; adherence to an established assessment and audit methodology; assessment and audit frequency; and, documentation requirements.

_____7. Implement a repeatable and documented assessment and audit methodology. This provides consistency and structure to assessments and audits; expedites the transition of new assessment and audit staff; and addresses resource constraints associated with assessments and audits. Using such a methodology enables organizations to maximize the value of assessments and audits while minimizing possible risks introduced by certain technical assessment and audit techniques. These risks can range from not gathering sufficient information on the organization's security posture for fear of impacting system functionality to affecting the system or network availability by executing techniques without the proper safeguards in place. Processes that minimize risk caused by certain assessment and audit techniques include using skilled assessors and auditors, developing comprehensive assessment plans, logging assessor and auditor activities, performing testing off-hours, and conducting tests on duplicates of production systems (development systems). Organizations need to determine the level of risk they are willing to accept for each assessment and audit, and tailor their approaches accordingly.

_____8. Determine the objectives of each security assessment and audit, and tailor the approach accordingly. Security assessments and audits have specific objectives, acceptable levels of risk, and available resources. Because no individual technique provides a comprehensive picture of an organization's security when executed alone, organizations should use a combination of techniques. This also helps organizations to limit risk and resource usage.

_____9. Analyze findings, and develop risk mitigation techniques to address weaknesses. To ensure that security assessments and audits provide their ultimate value, organizations should conduct root cause analysis upon completion of an assessment and audits to enable the translation of findings into actionable mitigation techniques. These results may indicate that organizations should address not only technical weaknesses, but weaknesses in organizational processes and procedures as well.

The information presented in this chapter is intended to be used for a variety of assessment and audit purposes. For example, some assessments and audits focus on verifying that a particular security control (or controls) meets requirements, while others are intended to identify, validate, and assess a system's exploitable security weaknesses. Assessments and audits are also performed to increase an organization's ability to maintain a proactive computer network defense. Assessments and audits are not meant to take the place of implementing security controls and maintaining system security.

Finally, let's move on to the real interactive part of this chapter: review questions/exercises, hands-on projects, case projects, and optional team case project. The answers and/or solutions by chapter can be found in the Online Instructor's Solutions Manual.

CHAPTER REVIEW QUESTIONS/EXERCISES

True/False

1. True or False? Penetration testing usually occurs in the compliance sphere, both in the semantics we use to describe technical points like "regulating deployments" and in the language technology vendors use to describe those implementations.

2. True or False? Port scanning is one of the most popular techniques a hacker can use to discover services that can be compromised.

3. True or False? Open Vulnerability and Assessment Language (OVAL) is not the standard for determining vulnerability and configuration issues on systems.

4. True or False? Two types of alerts should be logged: faults that are generated by the system and the applications running on it, and faults or errors reported by the system's users.

5. True or False? Since data center environments continue to grow, it has become more evident that administrators need to properly manage logs.

Multiple Choice

1. Many devices that provide protection to the infrastructure within networks, allow the ability to _____ events, and take actions based on those events.
   A. qualitative analysis
   B. vulnerabilities
   C. log
   D. physical access control
   E. DHS

2. Business critical applications, processes handling valuable or sensitive information, previously compromised or abused systems, and those systems connected to third parties, all require:
   A. firewall
   B. risk assessment
   C. scale
   D. authentication
   E. active monitoring

3. What are usually covered by some form of regulation of how many days they should be kept in case they are needed for an investigation?
   A. Organizations
   B. Fabric
   C. Kerberos
   D. Logs
   E. Security

4. What can generate large amounts of information if the log settings are not optimal?
   A. Cabinet-level state office
   B. Denial-of-service attack
   C. WPA2-Personal
   D. Small networks
   E. Taps

5. Who has powerful access, where their activity should be recorded and checked?
   A. Systems security plan
   B. Consumer privacy protection
   C. Administrators
   D. Vulnerability
   E. Challenge-Handshake Authentication Protocol (CHAP)

EXERCISE

Problem

Why are risk assessment and risk management relevant to information security?

Hands-On Projects

Project

How is risk assessment related to ISO/IEC 27001 (BS 7799)?

Case Projects

Problem

Does ISO/IEC 27001 (BS 7799) define the methodology for risk assessment?

Optional Team Case Project

Problem

After implementation, must the organization reassess risks?

Fundamentals of Cryptography

Scott R. Ellis, EnCE, RCA, RCIA

kCura Corporation

1. ASSURING PRIVACY WITH ENCRYPTION

Encryption provides a secure layer, at the storage byte level, under which information can be secured from prying eyes (see checklist: An Agenda for Action for Implementing Encryption and Other Information Security Functions). Data, or "plaintext" as it is called in cryptography, is rendered into cipher text through a ciphering process. Most importantly, encryption protects stored data. Files such as database data files, spreadsheets, documents, and reports can contain critical information—information which, if lost, could cause damage to:

- Sales generation
- Operations
- Reputation
- Competitive advantage
- Individuals
- Market capabilities
- Finances

AN AGENDA FOR ACTION FOR IMPLEMENTING ENCRYPTION AND OTHER INFORMATION SECURITY FUNCTIONS

Encryption implementation recommendations presented in this chapter enable organizations to ask the following questions (check all tasks completed):

_____1. Does your product perform "cryptography," or otherwise contain any parts or components that are capable of performing any

---

of the following "information security" functions?

_____a. encryption

_____b. decryption only (no encryption)

_____c. key management/public key infrastructure (PKI)

_____d. authentication (password protection, digital signatures)

_____e. copy protection

_____f. anti-virus protection

_____g. other (please explain):

_____

_____h. NONE/NOT APPLICABLE

_____2. For items with encryption, decryption, and/or key management functions (1.a, 1.b, 1.c above):

     _____a. What symmetric algorithms and key lengths (56-bit DES, 112 / 168-bit Triple-DES, 128 /

256-bit AES/Rijndael) are implemented or supported?

_____b. What asymmetric algorithms and key lengths (512-bit RSA / Diffie-Hellman, 1024 / 2048-bit RSA/Diffie-Hellman) are implemented or supported?

_____c. What encryption protocols (SSL, SSH, IPSEC, or PKCS standards) are implemented or supported?

_____d. What type of data is encrypted?

_____3. For products that contain an "encryption component," can this encryption component be easily used by another product, or else accessed/re-transferred by the end user for cryptographic use?

Ultimately, the loss of enough data, especially were it due to incompetence, could be a business-ending event. Inadvertent disclosure of data, especially personally identifiable data, can mean financial liabilities and the need for restitution to injured parties.

Ensuring that files are encrypted in storage, everywhere, allows the files to be protected in the event of a breach of physical security. Should a hacker gain access to a system, database encryption will prevent her from accessing the database files. Whole-disk encryption will prevent her from accessing drive shares and pulling excel spreadsheets.

The past decade has seen additional liabilities and exposures of sensitive data in the form of lost backup tapes, lost laptops, and recycled computers that were not destroyed, encrypted, or wiped. After a third-party courier service lost a box of backup tapes, Bank of New York Mellon Corp. officials implemented a policy to encrypt data on all storage devices. Furthermore, they said they would limit the type and amount of confidential client data stored on tape backups. It took two losses of unencrypted data before the policy was launched.

Unfortunately, far too many companies wait for disaster to strike before they begin to think about all of the things they really need to do to ensure, or at least substantially mitigate, their risk of data loss. There are three primary reasons why industry executives are reticent to implement encryption:

1. The cost of doing it—the complexity of setting it up
2. Their feeling that it can't happen to them
3. The fear of data loss due to key loss—an inability to decrypt the data

The cost of implementing an encryption policy pales in comparison to the cost of a data loss due to a breach, or due to release of data simply because Joe Smith left his laptop on the train. In an interesting, real-life situation, the author of this chapter did, in fact, once find a small box of hard drives in a bag on a train. The drives were labeled backup01, backup02, and backup03. Fortunately, the box had a CDW Computer Centers, Inc. shipping label that identified a client number. After reaching out to a friend at the computer company on the label, who contacted the owner (a large university library), a reunion was arranged. The kindness and responsibility of strangers cannot serve, however, as a failsafe. If anything, the loss of ALL the backup data was narrowly averted. According to the library executive, the backup drives held *everything*. She also promised that the policy would be changing immediately.

Encryption also introduces an additional level of difficulty in the event of corruption. Certain segments of the drive, if they become corrupted, can make retrieval of the data more challenging. This necessitates the storage, offsite, of secure, unencrypted backups. This may seem contrary to the purpose of this chapter, but consider that:

a. The data must be delivered to the unencrypted DR site *encrypted*.
b. Access to the unencrypted backup site should be manned access only with biometric access controls and no Internet or network connectivity.
c. As physical security and controls *increase*, the need for encryption *decreases*.

Such a high level of security allows the data to be under a much higher degree of control than the data in production data centers. A regular program of data movement, refreshing, and redundancy checks should be in place to ensure against data corruption. Placing data on a disk is no guarantee that two years later (if the disk has sat idle) the data will be coherent. Data can become corrupt just sitting on a disk.

Organizations should consider and design a program that understands and includes recipient and sender environments, and ensures that data encryption and decryption are as seamless and unintrusive as possible. In Figure 13.1, a clock-face approach to security balances the need for physical security against the need for encryption. Observe how, as the network segment approaches the 12th hour, everything is encrypted.

This model only inserts five categories of devices and activities. Each "hour" could conceivably have its own protocols. The analogy of "hour" is used by this author simply to explain and set forth this model as one plausible way of making it easier to think about security, and thus categorize applications based on the activity or on the type of encryption required.

Physical Versus Logical Security

In this clock-face model, the level of physical security decreases the need for encryption security. Physical and data security are applicable to each of the items shown in this

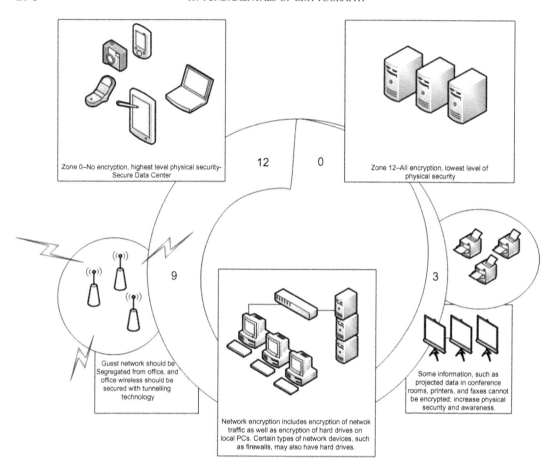

FIGURE 13.1 In a clock-face model, the most physically secure enterprise segments are at the zero hour, with the possibility of imminent attack or loss increasing up to the 12th hour. Note that the crescent line indicates increasing risk of loss, as well as a decrease in physical security.

diagram. For some items, such as digital cameras, security can get complicated. GPS locators and remote wiping are available for many personal devices, but digital cameras, for example, do not have any sort of a mechanism for encrypting their memory cards.

Consider ranking things in order of "Needs no encryption" to "Must be encrypted." As mentioned previously, the security requirement for encryption decreases as physical security increases. For example, a computer, sealed in cement and sunk to the bottom of the Mariana trench needs not be encrypted. Cell phones and laptops, on the other hand, should be. Create a panel of advisors to assist with the ranking. Depending on the workplace and the industry, the threat level of various areas could vary. *Moving items from one position on the clock face to a lower number effectively diminishes the immediate need for encryption. This can be accomplished by increasing physical security.* For example, whether a PC in an office is more deserving of encryption than a data center that is hooked into the Internet and has lots of virtual traffic through it may be dependent on other factors. Increasing the security in the office may effectively reduce the need for encryption to a level beneath that of the data center.

Deciding which area is *more likely to be attacked first* requires some decision making—decisions that may, down the road, turn out to be wrong. Planning the implementation requires a *healthy* imagination, not a paranoid one. Too much paranoia can bog down the project, but a healthy dose of possible, real-life scenarios and a little imagination can make planning both enjoyable and effective. See the sidebar, Using Imagination to Effectively Plan, for an example scenario cooked up by the author with one of his coauthors.

As shown in Figure 13.1, devices can (generally) be ordered by Highest Concern for Encryption and least physical security to Least Concern for Encryption and highest physical security:

- Cell phones, PDAs, memory sticks, USB drives, tablets
- Data Center Web farm (financial data)
- Office PCs
- BackOffice Data Center
- Printers and Fax
- DR site (of course, in a failover, encryption protocols should be activated)
- Data Vault

Most organizations will need to take into account their own strategy. This allows for deployment of a planned implementation of encryption in an orderly and risk-biased way.

The Confidentiality, Integrity, and Availability (CIA) Model and Beyond

CIA, or confidentiality, integrity, and availability, is a model for establishing security and risk. It dovetails into the clock-face model presented herein in that CIA provides the litmus tests needed for assessing *into which* zone things must be placed.

IMAGINATION ALLOWS ACCURATE RANKING

One way of ranking is to imagine that a hacker is actually employed (unbeknownst to you) in your organization. One afternoon, after a particularly strange day of slowness in the network that you finally have been able to trace, you've narrowed it down to a group of three people: Justin Smirks, Nate Doomer, and Scotty Potomac.[1] You mention it to HR, who immediately panics, and later in the afternoon you learn (from an email) that Justin, Nate, and Scott were all fired, simultaneously, and they are really angry about it, and uttered some threats on their way out. "I'll get you, my pretty!" they hear Justin shouting as they drag Justin out kicking and screaming. Scott escapes security, grabs his backpack, crashes through the 23rd floor plate glass window with fist

1. All persons listed in this sidebar are fictional. Any resemblance to any persons, living or dead, is purely noncoincidentally intentional.

shaking in the air, and base jumps out to safety. Nate snarls, laughs, and vanishes in a puff of smoke, with an evil, lingering laugh, echoing through the corridors.

What are you going to do first (besides change your pants because you assume that Scott is "in" and did his damage on the way down, before his parachute finished opening)? In order of importance, would you say (very generally speaking) that it is more important to have disk encryption on the back-office systems or on the PCs? What is the highest priority?

It takes a special kind of mind to examine an organization and architect a solution that will decrease the vulnerable surface area of a system. Such a plan includes intrusion detection, prevention, firewall policy, and encryption, holistically. Unfortunately, the challenges of creating a comprehensive encryption strategy are daunting. To achieve affective encryption, it must be both seamless and the default action. There are three types of encryption that are well known:

1. Secret Key Cryptography (SKC): A single key decrypts and encrypts data.
2. Public Key Cryptography (PKC): A user's public key is used to encrypt data, and a private key is used to decrypt.
3. Hash Functions: A mathematical formula transforms the data to a set length of characters. For example, an MD5 hash reduces large blocks of information to a single, 128 bit, hexadecimal string.

Figure 13.2 demonstrates one example of how they are used and implemented in industry. Type 3 encryption is generally an augmentation of 1 and 2, used to send keys, to verify identity, and to ensure losslessness of information. By hashing a file before and after it is received, sender and recipient are then able to agree that they have the same file.

Users should be aware of the zones, what data lies within them, and the required encryption protocols. Auditors should check new processes, place them within the zones, and ensure compliance. If a new application happens to fail one of the tests, but passes another, move the application into a different zone until it can be made compliant. Zone 4 is "zone exceptions."

Step 1: Identify Areas of Risk:

1. The location of any personally identifiable information. This information takes priority.
2. Laptops, PDAs, any portable computers or systems, and remote workers that work with the data in item 1.
3. Email and other information transport communications.
4. Instant messages might be plaintext sent across the network and may be stored locally as well.
5. Vulnerable server drives and application communications.
6. Backups.

Step 2: Organize

Many organizations have very disparate legacy applications. Get organized—knowing the location, method of transport, and types of applications is critical. Understand where data is housed, how it gets transferred to other organizations, how employees generate and store data and where. Mapping out the ins and outs of how data gets generated and how it flows will both assist in understanding the overall security topology of the network and identify areas that should be encrypted. The end state

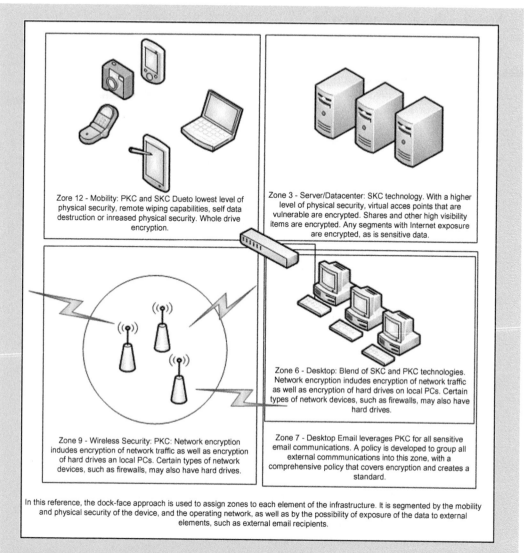

FIGURE 13.2 A sample of enterprise encryption. In this diagram, PKC and SKC forms of encryption are layered across the network in a zoned model of encryption.[2]

may be that ALL information should be encrypted, and it may be that only some small amount of data should be encrypted.

Ultimately, the following steps will assist in implementing and enterprise encryption strategy.

2. The diagram in Figure 13.2 represents the author's viewpoint of how encryption *might* be deployed across a network that he just imagined in his head. The purpose of this is to create a model, a framework of sorts, that can be copied and adjusted as needed. It is meant to start a conversation, not end one.

Step 3: Choose Cryptography Applications—Develop an Implementation Plan

All aspects of encryption that are planned for deployment should be fully understood. For example, using public key infrastructure (PKI) encryption gives users of the Internet the ability to exchange private data, securely, through the use of a public and private key pair that both recipient and sender share through a mutually agreed upon, trusted authority. Without this man-in-the middle trust factor, the process will not work. Essentially, the authority provides assignment and revocation of digital certificates that identify individuals and organizations. See the sidebar, How PKI Encryption Works, for more details on asymmetric key operations. The vendor selection team should have a great understanding.

Developing a strategy of encryption should be treated as a major project. From the outset, things like planning and compliance teams should be established. IT should be involved as well, and all access controls should be audited. Creating an encryption program makes sense, but only if the access controls system is tight. What good is an encrypted disk if the intruder can simply log in and see the unencrypted data right there? Additionally, the National Institute for Science and Technology (NIST) cryptographic toolkit provides standards and guidance over a wide range of the technology used in cryptography. Any vendors should be familiar with these standards and ensure compliance with them.

The final plan should be endorsed by management, and should be communicated to staff. It should include consequences for noncompliance. This plan should also mesh well with data destruction and retention policies.

Step 4: Implement Encryption Protocols

Sadly, no single "enterprise encryption" solution exists. Many vendors offer products A–Z that can be deployed and integrated together in a piecemeal solution, but this sort of hodgepodge approach can also be defined and planned by an experienced project manager. Such a plan will consider possible regulatory compliance requirements as well.

Step 5: Periodic Audits

Periodic audits will help ensure compliance. Conduct them as needed or as things change in significant ways. Maintenance of zone plans and software security measures should be frequent. All documentation should be kept up to date.

Confidentiality

To the degree that some information must be made available only to a certain group of people, this determines the level of restriction needed. Unauthorized access to information must be prevented. In areas of the network where information transmissions are uncontrolled and breach the perimeter, encryption of confidential data must occur.

This is especially true of wireless networks. Frequently, wireless networks are set up with weak, flawed, or no security.

HOW PKI ENCRYPTION WORKS

In this scenario of message encryption, as shown in Figure 13.3, the infrastructure relies on the use of a public key to encrypt any message sent. This is called public key cryptography. Traditionally, cryptography relies on a secret key used for both encryption and decryption. The most serious flaw of this method is that the secret key can be uncovered, discovered, or stolen.

A public key cryptography approach has a higher level of trust because, on the Internet, the transmission of a private key could be intercepted. So, the public key infrastructure is the preferred approach on the Internet. (The private key system is sometimes known as symmetric cryptography and the public key system as asymmetric cryptography.)

A public key infrastructure requires the following components:

- The certificate authority (CA) that performs the following functions:
  - Issues and verifies digital certificate that includes the public key
- A registration authority (RA):
  - Provides verification for the certificate authority
  - Issues the digital certificate to a requestor
- Storage directories to house the certificates and public keys.
- A system of certificate management.

In public key cryptography, when someone uses the service, a public and private key are simultaneously created using the

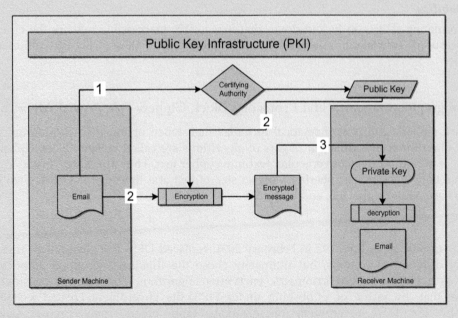

FIGURE 13.3 Step 1: The email requests the public key for the targeted recipient. Step 2: The email message is encrypted using the public key. Step 3: The email is unencrypted using the private key.

same algorithm, such as the Rivest-Shamir-Adleman (RSA) algorithm. The certificate authority creates the key.

Subsequently, the private key is sent only to the requesting party. Then, the public key is made available in a common storage location as defined above. The private key remains private.

The private key is then used to decrypt information that has been encrypted by someone else using your public key. People using the public key system can find another user's public key in a central repository and use it to encrypt information that they are sending to them. Users then decrypt the message using their private key. In fact, a message encrypted using a public key can only be decrypted in this fashion.

A number of services, such as RSA, Verisign, and PGP, are all examples of companies in this vertical. Each of them provides PKI services.

Integrity

Information should never be transmitted in ways that may disturb the integrity of the files or data. Unauthorized personnel should not be able to destroy or alter data. Hash values for files should be stored and transmitted with the file and accessed programmatically for validation.

Availability

Information that is so locked down that it is nearly inaccessible reduces the efficiency of operations. Information should be readily accessible to those who are authorized to view it.

Cryptographic Standards and Protocols: Block Ciphers—Approved Algorithms

Block ciphers utilize mathematical formulas that, when operated in cryptography, are called algorithms, and different flavors of algorithms are called ciphers. Block ciphers are a type of algorithm that converts plaintext into cypher text. They are called "block" ciphers because they work by enciphering a preset size of text at a time. Three well-known block ciphers are AES, Triple DES, and Skipjack.

AES

AES, published in FIPS 197 in February 2001, replaced DES. The government reviewed several different algorithms, but ultimately chose the Rijndael encryption algorithm to serve as a FIPS-approved symmetric encryption algorithm. The primary consideration here is that, by virtue of publishing under FIPS, the government created a standard whereby the U.S. government organizations (and others) may protect sensitive information.

Federal agencies also review the Office of Management and Budget (OMB) guidance, which suggests that AES is a standard that will be secure for 20 to 30 years. Furthermore, the OMB guidance warns agencies that the loss of cryptographic keys presents a risk to the availability of information needed to accomplish critical mission tasks and objectives.[3]

In today's world of extremely complex communication systems, the need for a full understanding of security, which includes a detailed understanding of the business itself first, has never been more apparent. The ability to protect and secure information depends entirely on the ability of those doing the protecting to understand the business. It cannot be solely dependent on the mathematical strengths of the encryption algorithm or the ability of someone to classify certain information. Likewise, you cannot count on the classification of the material to always be an accurate predictor of which encryption algorithm to use. Flexibility MUST be built into the system. There MUST be a way for the governing organization to stop, look, and listen. Many factors must be considered in choosing an algorithm and process for encryption, and these factors may, of course, change over time. An inflexible policy risks failure. The following factors are most relevant:

- How well the implementation of the algorithm will perform in specific software, firmware, or hardware configurations;
- The ability to develop a functional key management system, or of the algorithm to mesh with an existing solution;
- The fragility of the of the information to be protected; and/or
- Any requirements to interoperate, globally, where encryption algorithm restrictions may exist.

Considered in total, these requirements demand the implementation of a flexible implementation and policy that mixes the best of breed software with best practices derived from the individual business requirements.[4]

2. SUMMARY

Ultimately, the best encryption protocol would be completely seamless, effective, and transparent. A seamless encryption utility would provide, across the enterprise, a single-console approach to management. Phones, PDAs, hard drives, servers, network communications, and the like, all could be added to the encryption layer with the drag of a mouse. An effective algorithm is one that is not just unbreakable in the near foreseeable future, but rather, is simply unbreakable. A transparent system would provide encryption services without any observation by the user. They would not know, nor would they have reason to know, that their emails are encrypted using PKC technology. Unfortunately, modern information technology has not been able to provide any sort of all-encompassing program for managing secure communications. In the meantime, it is up to information technologists to cobble together a best of breed solution that protects and secures information simultaneously.

3. http://csrc.nist.gov/drivers/documents/ombencryption-guidance.pdf.

4. Additional information regarding the use of AES can be found in CNSS Policy No. 15, Fact Sheet No. 1 National Policy on the Use of the AES to Protect National Security Systems and National Security Information, June 2003.

Finally, let's move on to the real interactive part of this chapter: review questions/exercises, hands-on projects, case projects, and optional team case project. The answers and/or solutions by chapter can be found in the Online Instructor's Solutions Manual.

CHAPTER REVIEW QUESTIONS/EXERCISES

True/False

1. True or False? Encryption provides an insecure layer, at the storage byte level, under which information can be secured from prying eyes.
2. True or False? Ultimately, the gain of enough data, especially were it due to incompetence, could be a business-ending event.
3. True or False? Ensuring that files are encrypted in storage everywhere allows the files to be protected in the event of a breach of physical security.
4. True or False? The cost of implementing an encryption policy pales in comparison to the cost of a data loss due to a breach or to release of data simply because Joe Smith left his laptop on the train. In an interesting, real-life situation, the author of this chapter did, in fact, once find a small box of hard drives in a bag on a train.
5. True or False? Encryption also introduces additional levels of difficulty in the event of corruption.

Multiple Choice

1. The data must be delivered to the following unencrypted DR site:
   A. Qualitative analysis
   B. Vulnerabilities
   C. Log
   D. Encrypted
   E. DHS
2. Which unencrypted backup site should be manned accessed with only biometric access controls and no Internet or network connectivity?
   A. Firewall
   B. Risk assessment
   C. Scale
   D. Access
   E. Active monitoring
3. As physical security and controls *increase*, the need for encryption does which one of the following:
   A. Organizations
   B. Fabric
   C. Decreases
   D. Logs
   E. Security

4. Who or what should consider and design a program that understands and includes recipient and sender environments, and ensures that data encryption and decryption are as seamless and unintrusive as possible?
   A. Organizations
   B. Denial-of-service attack
   C. WPA2-Personal
   D. Small networks
   E. Taps
5. Deciding which area is *more likely to be attacked first* requires some _____ decisions that may, down the road, turn out to be wrong.
   A. Systems security plan
   B. Consumer privacy protection
   C. Administrators
   D. Decision making
   E. Challenge-Handshake Authentication Protocol (CHAP)

EXERCISE

Problem

What are the cryptographic module specification types?

Hands-On Projects

Project

What is cryptographic key management?

Case Projects

Problem

What types of self-tests must the cryptographic module perform?

Optional Team Case Project

Problem

What is the minimum information required in a cryptographic module security policy?

14

Satellite Cyber Attack Search and Destroy

Jeffrey Bardin
Treadstone 71 LLC

In the movie *Enemy of the State*, satellites play a vital role in making the viewer believe in the ultimate power of the National Security Agency (NSA). Satellites are repurposed and moved around the sky in moments. They peer down from the heavens tracking the hero's movements, able to determine tiepin logos and license plate expiration dates. Viewers are made to believe that satellites are God-like, roving the atmosphere, seeing everything we do. The NSA does employ satellites for signals and other intelligence; however, it is the National Reconnaissance Office (NRO) that normally owns and operates U.S. spy satellites. The closest Hollywood has come to reality in spy satellites was during the movie *Patriot Games* when Harrison Ford had to look at images through a microscope trying to ascertain the identity, much less the gender of people in the photographs. Grainy images with shadows that look like other images is more in line with reality.

When thinking of satellites, thoughts often drift to Hollywood's images and the surveillance aspects of their capabilities. However, satellites play many roles in society. They provide methods for communication and remote sensing of critical infrastructures, deliver global positioning systems for navigation, keep us occupied with broadband for entertainment, and support mechanisms for videoconferencing and telemedicine. We never see them, but they are essential components in daily human activity. According to the Satellite Industry Association, nearly 37% of all operational satellites are used for business communications. Civil communications accounts for 11%, military communications for 9%, military and surveillance 9%, navigation 8%, remote sensing 9%, and meteorological 4%. The Satellite Industry Association also maintains information on world satellite industry revenue. Satellite growth increased significantly between 2005 and 2011 at an average of 11% per year in growth. The Satellite Industry Association states that satellite services continue to represent the single largest industry sector driven by satellite-TV growth at around 10%

Cyber Security and IT Infrastructure Protection
DOI: http://dx.doi.org/10.1016/B978-0-12-416681-3.00014-8

[1]. Space launch industry and satellite manufacturing revenues reflect a history of aggre-gate growth by yearly fluctuation, while ground equipment revenue growth reflects slight but relatively consistent year-on-year consumer and network equipment sales. It is safe to say that satellites play a prominent role in everyday life.

Very Small Aperture Terminals (VSATs) are prevalent in everyday lives. They consist of a parabolic dish and associated hardware and software. The purpose is to send and receive (uplink and downlink) signals via a satellite. They dot the landscape on homes, recreational vehicles, and boats. Human reliance on satellites is growing at an exponential rate. As with any growing commercial opportunity, security is less than the primary con-cern. Economics drives the opportunity.

1. HACKS, INTERFERENCE, AND JAMMING

April of 2007 started a series of issues with satellites. Tamil rebels in Sri Lanka were accused of hacking the Intelsat satellite positioned over the Indian Ocean for communicat-ing propaganda [2]. Intelsat responded, indicating this to be a case of signal piracy (not hacking) that would not be tolerated. In a response to the Intelsat press release, the Tamil Tiger rebels indicated that they were not accessing the satellite illegally and that therefore no signal piracy had occurred. The rebels intimated a relationship with the service pro-vider for the satellite but would provide no further explanation [3].

In 2007, the media reported that NASA satellite Landsat-7 used for ground mapping was hacked, experiencing 12 minutes of interference [4]. The same article goes on to state that in 2008, another NASA satellite, Terra AM-1 was hacked for 2 minutes in June and for 9 minutes in October. The problem with the articles and subsequent follow on by the media as well as the NASA Office of Inspector General is the depiction that the satellites were hacked. These two events were not cyber-related events but events characterized by the interference and jamming of radio signals in order to disrupt satellite send and receive transmissions. The point to be made here is that this had nothing to do with cyber security but rather with traditional satellite communication protocols using radio transmissions.

Recently, there have been writings on the Internet of the potential for hacking NASA satellites to access the Curiosity land rover on Mars. Although this is pure speculation, much discussion has occurred due to the subject. The initial topic focused on the pushing of updates to change Curiosity's payload. The idea would be to intercept or to a play man-in-the-middle attack against communications between satellites and the rover. Although highly unlikely, the impact would be significant should such an activity occur. It highlights a renewed focus on satellites as objects for disruption of command, control, communications, and computers. The Jet Propulsion Laboratory (JPL) in Pasadena, California, houses the scientists, engineers, specialists, and mission control center for Curiosity. NASA missions employ a highly compartmentalized framework for computer systems tied to the mission. They are self-contained systems located in self-contained buildings running variations of operating systems or operating systems created specifically for the mission at hand, operated by personnel vetted on several levels. Once a configura-tion of the operating system, firmware, or other related software is proven to work per the specifications of the designers and engineers, the configuration is locked down as a module ready for execution. It is highly unlikely that a hack or intercept of the encoded transmission between JPL mission control in Pasadena and the Curiosity rover on Mars could occur. Such an unlikely occurrence would have an enormous impact on the mission. But the mission of discovering life on another planet is hardly a target for exploitation that a foreign intelligence service would undertake. It is more likely that a foreign intelligence service would target earth-born operations.

In October 2011, Creech Air Force Base was the subject of a malware attack on the Predator and Reaper drones. It was reported that a keystroke logger infected the ground control stations for drones operating in the Afghanistan theater. The malware proved to be a resilient strain that continued to reoccur after multiple system cleanings. The malware was most likely created by a foreign nation-state intent on learning as much information as possible about the United States' drone activities. What was not stated in the press is the fact that the 30th Reconnaissance Squadron of the United States Air Force operates out of Creech AFB. This is significant since this squadron operates the RQ-170 Sentinel UAV. The same UAV captured by Iran a mere two months after the keystroke logger event at Creech AFB. In what could be termed a coincidence, Iran stated that its Army's electronic warfare unity had downed an RQ-170 violating Iranian airspace by overriding the UAV's controls. An Iranian engineer later stated that Iran used GPS coordinate spoofing, fooling the UAV into thinking it was landing at an air base in Afghanistan. The Iranian engineer further claimed that it was quite easy to exploit the navigational weakness in the drone system. It is possible that signal jamming of the encrypted channels used by the military forced the UAV to revert to a communications failover process that used unencrypted methods to communicate [5]. Once the failover took place, Iranian engineers were able to manipulate the drone GPS. If the Iranian claim of control override is true, the keystroke logging event at Creech AFB takes on new meaning for cyber security surrounding ground control stations for satellite-based weapons systems. Unsubstantiated claims of Russian or Chinese intelligence services actually executing the keystroke logger and subsequently the downing of the RQ-170 become a potential premise that should be explored further. It demonstrates the need for improved cyber security measures for each component of the satellite command and control ecosystem. It also demonstrates that traditional cyber security countermeasures are not sufficient to prevent penetration or malware infection, or both. In most cases, ground control stations are air-gapped from other networks. Air gapping is a method of security control that delivers network compartmentalization, keeping all networks and devices not required to operate, manage, monitor, and/or control a sensitive system entirely separate. This is usually accompanied by stringent rules related to the use of removable media. It has been intimated that infected nonauthorized hardware was attached to the air-gapped system, providing for the infection of the target ground control stations. Malware of this type with a keystroke logger payload is used for cyber intelligence collection for later disposition and cyber countermeasures to be deployed by the initiating entity. The ability for the malware to communicate data collection efforts back to a collection hub also requires additional review since the methods of cyber security detection are often devised to keep perpetrators out, and not to prevent them from leaving as an additional level of security. It is interesting to note that a 2002 GAO report specifically warned of spoofing as a content-oriented threat for commercial satellites and the unauthorized modification or deliberate corruption of network information, services, and databases, including malicious software implanted into computer systems referencing ground control stations as a target [6]. Just under 10 years later, we have experienced exactly what the GAO warned against.

In June 2012, a group of researchers at the University of Texas at Austin used the spoofing method described by the Iranians to hack the GPS system of a drone. This demonstrates the viability of the claim and presents another issue for concern: Adversaries have the ability to both commandeer and use the drones as flying missiles whether armed or not. The cost to spoof the drone was reported to be in the range of £700 or about $1100. This ratio of cost to the potential impact is a cornerstone of asymmetric warfare exhibited by Al-Qa'eda on 9/11. Questions over what security controls were or were not in place continue as U.S. military authorities maintain a tight lid on the exact problems and remediation methods employed since the downing of the RQ-170. Additional rumors surfaced that Iran overrode the RQ-170 self-destruct capabilities, while others have claimed no such capabilities exist on the drone.

A few years ago, a $29 program called SkyGrabber (as shown in Figure 14.1) made the news. SkyGrabber allowed interception of packet radio service from a laptop connected to a small satellite. Insurgents in Iraq (as shown in Figure 14.2) were using and training others to use the SkyGrabber software to intercept satellite and small drones communications used to scout positions of enemies prior to special forces or military activities in that particular area. Insurgents were able to intercept these communications with the $29 program largely because of lack of security over the communications between satellite and drone. This flaw was actually well known by the designers of the system. They did not apply the appropriate security controls because applying encryption to the process slowed the communications down to the point where they thought it was not effective. Regardless

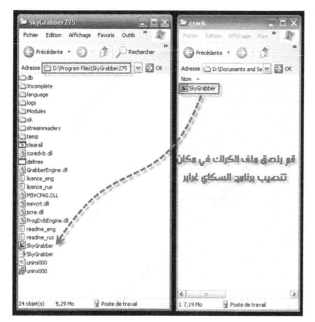

FIGURE 14.1   Jihadist use of SkyGrabber.

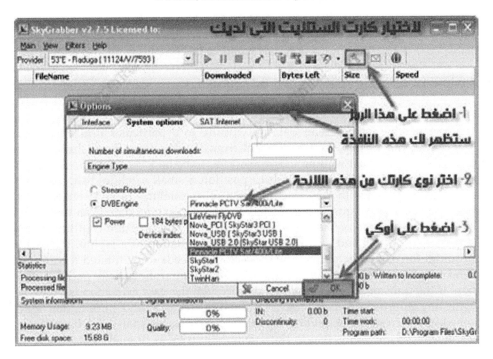

FIGURE 14.2   SkyGrabber.

of their decision, insurgents intercepted this information for quite some time before being discovered. SkyGrabber uses what is called general packet radio service or GPRS. GPRS is a nonvoice service that is added to networks over 2.5- to 3-gigabit wireless communications. Consumers know this as 3 G or 4 G speeds [7]. The service uses IP transmissions to its advantage. Because Internet Protocol (IP) traffic is made of packets, the network does not need to have continuous data transmission. Each channel is divided eight timeslots, with a maximum data transmission of 13.4 kb per second. One of these timeslots is used for control, and normal allocation reserves two slots for voice traffic as well. Asymmetric traffic (more downloads and uploads) dictates the distribution of the remaining timeslots.

Requests are sent via the LAN connection, while responses are received from the satellite; since requests are usually small and responses are large, a narrowband connection is quite enough for requests. At the same time, responses were received at a high rate of 4 MB per second, which makes working with the Internet comfortable. If there is no encryption, it is open for interception. When the activity of the insurgents using SkyGrabber was made public, many pundits and even cyber security professionals called this interception hacking. What needs to be understood is that this was not a hack since there was in fact, nothing to hack. Without encryption, the communication mechanism is open for interception. Hacking refers to the reconfiguring or reprogramming of the system to function in ways not facilitated by the owner, administrator, or designer. The term has several related meanings in the information technology industry. A hack may refer to a clever quick fix to a computer program problem or to what may be perceived to be a clumsy solution to a problem. The terms *hack* and *hacking* are also used to refer to a modi-fication of the programmer device to give the user access to features that were otherwise unavailable such as to do-it-yourself circuit bending [8]. It is from this usage that the term *hacking* is often incorrectly used to refer to more nefarious criminal uses such as identity theft, credit-card fraud, or other actions categorized as computer crime. Since there is a distinction between security breaking and hacking, a better term for security breaking would be *cracking* [8]. As we already know, responses are received from the satellite. However, the satellite cannot send data specifically to a particular user and so instead sends data to all dishes that receive a signal from it. Therefore, if you have the proper equipment, the signal is just waiting in the airwaves to be had.

As already surmised, it is not enough to position a small satellite dish, and that dish will also receive a signal with the same data that other satellites receive. The satellite dish may get the signal, but the question remains as to how to extract data from the intercepted signal. That is the purpose of the SkyGrabber program. The program captures what other satellite dishes download and saves the captured information to a laptop. Internet access is not required for this interception. The satellite dish needs to be rotated toward the pro-vider, and the SkyGrabber program, with some configuration, will perform the data extraction. If the transmission is encrypted or encoded, the data extraction is prevented.

As with any information technology, information security and information assurance need to be built in from the beginning. Cyber security professionals have been stating this for years. Regardless, it seems that in the satellite industry as in many others, information security controls will not be built in until such time as a painful breach has occurred. This has been the standard mode of operation for designers, developers, and engineers for years.

Identifying Threats

In 1998 when Presidential Decision Directive 63 was originally issued, satellites were not included in the nation's critical infrastructures. This was seen as a significant oversight in the satellite industry. The General Accounting Office (GAO) report in 2002 referenced issues concerning security around satellites and covered several different areas concerning security. The GAO report covered secure data links and communication ground stations. The report also discussed issues surrounding the use of satellites that have certain security controls especially established to enhance the availability of the satellite. Since the release of that report in 2002, much has been done to bolster the security of satellites. Satellites consist of ground station tracking and control links, which are referred to as a tracking telemetry and control (TT&C) links and data links and satellites. The GAO report exam-ined unintentional threats to commercial satellite systems and divided the threats into three different areas:

1. Ground-based threats
2. Space-based threats
3. Interference-oriented threats [6]

Examples of the ground-based threat could be naturally occurring ones such as acts of God, earthquakes, hurricanes, tornadoes, and floods. Space-based threats could be related to solar activity, different temperature variations, and different types of space debris as more countries launch satellites. Interference-oriented threats to commercial satellite systems focus more on information technology. This deals with unintentional or intentional human interference caused by terrestrial and space-based wireless systems or computer systems intended to cause harm. The interference- and content-oriented threats that are intentional threaten commercial satellite systems with malicious software, denial-of-service attacks, distributed denial-of-service attacks, service moving data interception, and potential man-in-the-middle attack methods. This includes the jamming of communications between ground stations and satellite systems. Over the years, the United States government has worked to ensure the confidentiality, integrity, and availability of satellite systems, although the focus on security is limited based on risk. The likelihood of such an attack has not been high, although attacks are increasing each year as more attention is given to satellites. Since the attacks have not been of paramount concern, satellites related to cyber security controls have been limited in scope and function. It is probable that security controls will increase directly with the increase of threats and validated exploitation.

Communicating with Satellites

There are several methods for communicating with satellites. Many commercial satellites use baseband signals, a method that allows for only one car on the road at a time so to speak. Only one transmission either from the ground station to the satellite or from the satellite to the ground station can occur at a time. Direct broadcast satellites (DBS) is common to consumers. DBS is used by vendors such as DISH and DirecTV. DBS transmissions use various methods to secure the data transfer:

- Basic Interoperable Scrambling System, usually known as BISS, is a satellite signal scrambling system developed by the European Broadcasting Union and a consortium of hardware manufacturers. Prior to its development, "ad-hoc" or "Occasional Use" satellite news feeds were transmitted either using proprietary encryption methods (PowerVu) or without any encryption. Unencrypted satellite feeds allowed anyone with the correct equipment to view the program material.
- PowerVu is a conditional access system for digital television developed by Scientific Atlanta [1]. It is used for professional broadcasting, notably by Retevision, Bloomberg Television, Discovery Channel, AFRTS, and American Forces Network. PowerVu is also used by cable companies to prevent viewing by unauthorized viewers. PowerVu has decoders that decode signals from certain satellites for cable distribution services. These decoders can also be used just like the FTA (Free-To-Air) satellite receivers if properly configured. PowerVu is considered highly secure since it uses a complicated system to authorize each PowerVu receiver and trace its history of ownership and usage. Most PowerVu users are professional cable or satellite companies, using the service and equipment for signal redistribution, because regular users cannot afford it. On March 10, 2010, the hacker called Colibri published after previous work done in 2005 a cryptanalysis of a PowerVU system implementation. The hacker described a flawed design that can be used to gain access to the encryption keys and ultimately decrypt the transmitted content.

- DigiCipher 2, or simply DCII, is a proprietary standard format of digital signal transmission and encryption with MPEG-2 signal video compression used on many communications satellite television and audio signals. The DCII standard was originally developed in 1997 by General Instrument, which is now the Home and Network Mobility division of Motorola [9]. The original attempt for a North American digital signal encryption and compression standard was DigiCipher 1, which was used most notably in the now-defunct PrimeStar medium-power direct broadcast satellite (DBS) system during the early 1990s. The DCII standard predates wide acceptance of DVB-based digital terrestrial television compression (although not cable or satellite DVB) and therefore is incompatible with the DVB standard [9]. The primary difference between DigiCipher 2 and DVB lies in how each standard handles SI, or System Information. DigiCipher 2 also relies on the fact that its signals must be understood in terms of a virtual channel number in addition to the DCII signal's downlink frequency, whereas DVB signals have no virtual channel number [9]. Approximately 70% of newer first-generation digital cable networks in North America use the 4DTV/DigiCipher 2 format. The use of DCII is most prevalent in North American digital cable television set top boxes. DCII is also used on Motorola's 4DTV digital satellite television tuner and Shaw Direct's DBS receiver [9].

Scrambling and de-scrambling equipment for cable and satellite televisions has been the norm for over 30 years. The solutions have evolved over the years to more advanced solutions for DBS.

There are other encryption methods for DBS such as the use of smart cards allowing a single user to access television shows based on the smart card, receiver hardware, and associated software that securely and accurately identifies the users and their individual subscriptions. This is truly commonplace in the commercial market. Advances have been made to incorporate the Advanced Encryption Standard (AES) in satellite transport networks, providing much greater security using encryption keys. Regardless of the security solution in use, the intent is to protect pay-TV signals enforcing subscription-based access to available programs.

Improving Cyber Security

According to a 2009 report from IGI Global as written by Marlyn Kemper Littman titled "Satellite Network Security," satellite transmissions are subject to lengthy delays, low bandwidth, and high bit-error rates that adversely affect real-time, interactive applications such as videoconferences and lead to data corruption, performance degradation, and cyber incursions [10]. Littman goes on to say that multiple layers of security covering all aspects of the satellite's ecosystem is needed to adequately protect satellite networks. This includes policies and legislation requiring minimum necessary security protocols and standards. The Defense Information Systems Network (DISN) Satellite Transmission Services Global (DSTS-G) Performance Work Statement states that:

> DODD 8581.1E requires that commercial satellites used by the Department of Defense employ NSA-approved cryptography to encrypt and authenticate commands to the satellite if supporting Mission

Assurance Category (MAC) I or II missions as defined in DoD Directive 8500.1. While NSA approved cryptography is preferred for satellites supporting MAC III missions, cryptography commensurate with commercial best practices is acceptable for encrypting and authenticating commands to satellites that only support MAC III missions.

The change in cryptography requirements is for commercial interoperability with DOD satellite systems. These changes went into effect in 2005 and represent a shift to encrypt using the latest technologies transmitted over higher bandwidth, using mission-specific data networks. The change also calls for continued modifications to the security environment as new threats appear and new solutions are available. The cryptography requirements directly align to the Satellite Internet Protocol Security or SatIPSec initiative from 2004. This protocol provides for encrypted transmissions using a standard symmetric method that clearly identifies the sender and receiver. SatIPSec used in conjunction with the Satellite-Reliable Multicast Transport Protocol (SAT-RMTP), which provides secure transmission methods for audio and video files, enhances the satellite ecosystem security posture.

There are several areas for improvement in satellite cyber security. As with many commercial ventures, the sharing of information is limited due to the potential for leaking intellectual property or proprietary processes, procedures, and methods. The information and cyber security industry is rife with examples of limited information sharing. Most companies are remiss to share information on breaches due to the potential embarrassment public awareness could bring. What is missed is the opportunity to share remediation strategies and information on the attacker. This actionable intelligence could prevent other organizations from suffering the same fate. Methods of remediation that are successful should be shared across the satellite industry and within federal and state governments. The opportunity to share effective security practices could vastly improve satellite cyber defenses. Information sharing coupled with the appropriate education and awareness-raising efforts for the satellite industry is an effective method of propagating actionable intelligence.

Until recently, organizations did not agree on what represented an attack. The underlying issue is the use of a common taxonomy relative to satellite security. Incorporating already defined words, phrases, and concepts from the information security community can and will speed up the adoption of and integration of a common book of knowledge (CBK) surrounding satellite cyber security. Just as Web sites and applications on the Internet are subject to continuous probes, scans, denial of service, and distributed denial-of-service activity, the satellite industry faces continuous intentional interference and jamming. The satellite industry could learn how to adopt methods of interference and jamming prevention by incorporating proven principles and methods achieved over years of parallel activity on the Internet. Additionally, organizations managing satellites need to distinguish between advertent and inadvertent events and events that are intentional and unintentional. The data points gathered by the scores of government and commercial satellite organizations worldwide could be organized into information that is analyzed for links, tendencies, and trends to help devices' ever-changing defenses to transmission penetration and jamming. The underlying premise is information sharing for the benefit of nonhostile entities to improve their defensive, preventive, and even predictive countermeasures through intelligence analysis of satellite-specific data points using proven methods in cyber security. An organization such as the National Council of Information Sharing and Analysis Centers (ISAC) could sponsor or propose an ISAC specific to the satellite industry adopting proven methods across the member ISACs to assist in information-sharing activities. The Communications ISAC could further expand into the satellite industry with very specific goals, emphasizing sharing information used to mitigate and prevent typical satellite-related impacts to confidentiality, integrity, and availability.

Many members of the cyber security industry may overlook the physical security aspects of satellite security. Like any centralized management function, satellite monitoring and maintenance is performed from a ground location. Data centers require hardened perimeters and multiple layers of redundancy. Satellite ground controls stations require the same level of attention to security detail. These facilities should have standardized CCTV and access control methods. Security guards performing 24×7 monitoring and response and employee training and awareness programs must be in place. Many ground control stations are not equipped to withstand electromagnetic plus radiological fallout, or instances of force majeure. They lack what many in the information technology industry would term standard requirements for availability. Furthermore, many ground control stations are within proximity of public areas, providing potentially easy access for those with malicious intent. Standards for the continuity of operations for ground control stations should include conditioned and generated power, as well as backup locations in varied geographic locations with an inventory of equipment available in case of an incident. Ground control centers should also practice disaster recovery and business continuity through regularly scheduled exercises. The points mentioned herein are standard functions of an information technology data center that can and should be applied to the satellite industry. All ground control stations should have centralized and backup network operations, security operations, and satellite operations centers integrated into a cohesive monitoring and data-sharing environment.

Several "anti" solutions should be tested and embedded in each satellite's ecosystem based on risk. Sensitive or military satellites should be required to consistently and continually provide antijamming, antispoofing and antitampering capabilities that can be monitored by the ground control station. Ground control stations need to be outfitted with prevention-based cyber security solutions that either prevent or detect penetrations, prevent malware and data exfiltration, and monitor, record, and analyze malware characteristics.

Another concept for all U.S.-based satellites is the use of all appropriate satellites to act as a sensor while in orbit. The idea is for each satellite to share information on surveilled targets after agreeing to install a government payload or sensor that provides a space-based surveillance and warning network. This concept borrows from cyber security technologies using sensors to monitor network activity across government or commercial entities. The government could offer some type of concession or support to the commercial organization in exchange for carrying the nonintrusive payload.

Although many of the recommendations are already a regular occurrence in military satellite systems, commercial systems do not necessarily require the same level of security or scrutiny. Regardless, recent interference and jamming of satellite-controlled device under the military's purview and the penetration of malware of ground control stations indicate a need for increased attention to security whether it is cyber or of a more traditional need. A call for all satellite ecosystems to undergo assessment and authorization procedures as defined in the Federal Information Security Management Act (FISMA) and as detailed on the DoD Information Assurance Certification and Accreditation Process (DIACAP) may be warranted based on the role satellites play in critical infrastructures. The use of DIACAP and DSTS-G can help drive cyber security framework standardization for satellites (see checklist: An Agenda for Action for Implementing Cyber Security Framework Standardization Methods for Satellites). They can help drive mitigation measures using onboard satellite radio frequency encryption systems.

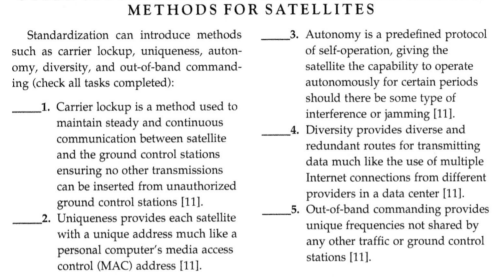

AN AGENDA FOR ACTION FOR IMPLEMENTING CYBER SECURITY FRAMEWORK STANDARDIZATION METHODS FOR SATELLITES

Standardization can introduce methods such as carrier lockup, uniqueness, autonomy, diversity, and out-of-band commanding (check all tasks completed):

_____1. Carrier lockup is a method used to maintain steady and continuous communication between satellite and the ground control stations ensuring no other transmissions can be inserted from unauthorized ground control stations [11].

_____2. Uniqueness provides each satellite with a unique address much like a personal computer's media access control (MAC) address [11].

_____3. Autonomy is a predefined protocol of self-operation, giving the satellite the capability to operate autonomously for certain periods should there be some type of interference or jamming [11].

_____4. Diversity provides diverse and redundant routes for transmitting data much like the use of multiple Internet connections from different providers in a data center [11].

_____5. Out-of-band commanding provides unique frequencies not shared by any other traffic or ground control stations [11].

When it comes to ground-based network operations centers (NOC) and security operations centers (SOC), traditional cyber security standards and controls apply for both physical and virtual measures. Much the same applies to interference. Interference in the satellite ecosystem comes from several sources such as human error, other satellite interference, terrestrial interference, equipment failure, and intentional interference and jamming [11].

The satellite industry continues to take steps to mitigate and deliver countermeasures to the various types of interference. Use of various types of shielding, filters, and regular training and awareness can help reducemost types of interference. Intentional or purposeful interference (PI) is not remediated through these measures. The satellite industry has created an information technology mirror process and procedure called the Purposeful Interference Response Team or PIRT. Many of the same methods, processes, and procedures used in a computer emergency response team (CERT) program have been adopted for use in the PIRT.Root cause analysis of PIRT incidents is shared back into the process and out to satellite owners to ensure effective security practices and countermeasures are shared across the industry. Communications and transmission security measures are employed using standards such as those defined by the National Institutes of Standards and Technology (NIST) and its Federal Information Process Standard (FIPS) 140−2.

As the satellite industry continues its move toward traditional information technology-type hybrid networks, satellites will be subjected to the same types of IT vulnerabilities that ground-based systems suffer today. The issues associated with this migration are apparent, but so too are the solutions. Cyber security standards, processes, procedures, and methods are available without the need for creating them anew. Regardless, their application is required in the design phase of the satellite ecosystem in order to be fully effective. Onboard IT systems provide greater features and real-time modifications, but they also introduce traditional IT vulnerabilities and exploits if not managed properly.

2. SUMMARY

Contrary to what is portrayed in Hollywood, satellites cannot be immediately retasked, nor can they see and hear everything humans do. Satellites have progressed substantially over the years, providing society with cell phone services, pay-TV solutions, hand-held global position systems, GPS for automobiles, motorcycles, and boats, telemedicine, and law enforcement. Satellites play roles in society that are now commonplace. The ubiquitous nature of satellites combined with advances in computing power and capabilities is a double-edged sword for satellite ecosystems. The last several years have seen a parallel increase in satellite deployments and efforts to purposefully interfere with satellites, jam satellite transmissions, and penetrate components of the satellite ecosystem with malicious code. In many cases, radio frequency interference and jamming has been confused as hacking. This may change in time as satellites increase the use of onboard computer capabilities with remote updating needs and patching requirements, much like land-based information technology systems. Foreign intelligence services continue to target U.S. satellite ecosystems in particular, with ground control stations as the least path of resistance method of penetration for traditional computer hacking and malware distribution. Once penetrated, the malware can perform various tasks based on its payload. To date, the payload has been intelligence gathering. Future penetrations could result in cyber sabotage or terrorist activities, resulting in the loss of life and disruptions to critical infrastructures.

The need to build cyber security into satellite ecosystems can remediate risk at inception. The risk-based approach, heavily reported to be the best method of cyber security posture management, could in fact be nothing more than a step in developing a cyber security life cycle—a life cycle that could mature appreciably by transparently embedding cyber security into every facet of every process, procedure, method, and component of the satellite ecosystem.

Finally, let's move on to the real interactive part of this chapter: review questions/exercises, hands-on projects, case projects, and optional team case project. The answers and/or solutions by chapter can be found in the Online Instructor's Solutions Manual.

CHAPTER REVIEW QUESTIONS/EXERCISES

True/False

1. True or False? Very Small Aperture Terminals (VSATs) are prevalent in everyday lives.
2. True or False? Recently, there have been writings on the Internet of the potential for hacking NASA satellites to access the Curiosity land rover on Venus.
3. True or False? In October of 2011, Wright Patterson Air Force Base was the subject of a malware attack on the Predator and Reaper drones.
4. True or False? In June of 2012, a group of researchers at the University of Texas at Austin used the spoofing method described by the Iranians to hack the stealth system of a drone.
5. True or False? A few years ago, a $29 program called SkyGrabber made the news. The program allowed interception of packet radio service from a laptop connected to a large satellite.

Multiple Choice

1. Examples of the _____ could be those that are naturally occurring such as acts of God, earthquakes, hurricanes, tornadoes, and floods.
   A. reputation
   B. Internet filters
   C. ground-based threat
   D. encrypted
   E. content-control software
2. There are several methods for communicating with satellites. Many commercial satellites use _____, a method that allows for only one car on the road at a time so to speak?
   A. opinity
   B. Web content filtering
   C. scale
   D. baseband signals
   E. active monitoring
3. What is a satellite signal scrambling system developed by the European Broadcasting Union and a consortium of hardware manufacturers?
   A. Basic Interoperable Scrambling System (BISS)
   B. Rapleaf
   C. Worms
   D. Content
   E. Security

4. What is a conditional access system for digital television developed by Scientific Atlanta?
   A. PowerVu
   B. Denial-of-service attack
   C. Venyo
   D. Port traffic
   E. Taps
5. What is a proprietary standard format of digital signal transmission and encryption with MPEG-2 signal video compression used on many communications satellite television and audio signals?
   A. Systems security plan
   B. DigiCipher 2 (DCII)
   C. Denying service
   D. Decision making
   E. URL lists

EXERCISE

Problem

A GAO report examined unintentional threats to commercial satellite systems. The report broke the threats into three different areas. What were those areas?

Hands-On Projects

Project

Please explain in explicit detail the Basic Interoperable Scrambling System.

Case Projects

Problem

Please explain PowerVu in explicit detail.

Optional Team Case Project

Problem

Please explain DigiCipher 2 in explicit detail.

References

[1] C. David, State of the Satellite Industry, Washington, DC, November 13, 2006.
[2] D. Morrill, Hack a satellite while it is in orbit. <http://it.toolbox.com/blogs/managing-infosec/hack-a-satellite-while-it-is-in-orbit-15690>, April 13, 2007.

[3] Sri Lankan rebels deny illegal use of US satellite. <http://www.radioaustralia.net.au/international/2007-04-13/sri-lankan-rebels-deny-illegal-use-of-us-satellite/721866>, April 2007.

[4] C. Franzen, Report: Chinese military suspected in hacks of U.S. government satellites. <http://idealab.talkingpointsmemo.com/2011/10/report-chinese-military-suspected-in-hacks-of-us-government-satellites.php>, October 27, 2011.

[5] N. Owano, RQ-170 drone's ambush facts spilled by Iranian engineer. <http://phys.org/news/2011-12-rq-drone-ambush-facts-iranian.html>, December 17, 2011.

[6] Office, United States General Accounting. Critical Infrastructure Protection Commercial Satellite Security Should Be More Fully Addressed. Washington, United States GAO, 2002.

[7] What is meant by gprs connection?. <http://answers.yahoo.com/question/index?qid = 20060828085726 AAKiqNr>, 9 1, 2006.

[8] Free Engineering Seminar PPT Slides DOC. <http://www.urslides.com/> February 10, 2012.

[9] DigiCipher 2. <http://mp3umax.org/?p = DigiCipher_2>, January 1, 2012.

[10] M.K. Littman, Satellite Network Security. Fort Lauderdale, Nova Southeastern Unniversity, USA, 2009.

[11] Committee, President's National Security Telecommunications Advisory. NSTAC Report to the President on Commercial Satellite Communications Mission Assurance. Washington, DC, NSTAC, 2009.

Advanced Data Encryption

Pramod Pandya
CSU Fullerton

1. MATHEMATICAL CONCEPTS REVIEWED

In this section we introduce the necessary mathematics of cryptography: Integer and Modular Arithmetic, Fermat's Theorem [1]:

Euler's Phi-Function $\phi(n)$

Euler's totient function finds the number of integers that are both smaller than n and coprime to n:

1. $\phi(1) = 0$
2. $\phi(p) = p-1$ if p is a prime
3. $\phi(m \times n) = \phi(n) \times \phi(m)$ if m, and n are coprime
4. $\phi(p^e) = p^e - p^{e-1}$ if p is a prime

Examples:

$$\phi(2) = 1; \phi(3) = 2; \phi(4) = 2; \phi(5) = 4; \phi(6) = 2; \phi(7) = 6; \phi(8) = 4$$

Fermat's Little Theorem

In the 1970s, the creators of digital signatures and public-key cryptography realized that the framework for their research was already laid out in the body of work by Fermat and Euler. Generation of a key in public-key cryptography, involves an exponentiation modulo in a given modulus:

$$a \equiv b \pmod{m} \text{ then } a^e \equiv b^e \pmod{m} \text{ for any positive integer } e$$
$$a^{e+d} \equiv a^e \cdot a^d \pmod{m}$$
$$(ab)^e \equiv a^e \cdot b^e \pmod{m}$$
$$(a^d)^e \equiv a^{de} \pmod{m}$$

Cyber Security and IT Infrastructure Protection
DOI: http://dx.doi.org/10.1016/B978-0-12-416681-3.00015-X

Theorem: Let p be a prime number:

1. If a is coprime to p, then $a^{p-1} \equiv 1 \pmod{p}$
2. $a^P \equiv a \pmod{p}$ for any integer a

Theorem: Let p and q be distinct primes:

1. If a is coprime to pq, then

$$a^{k(p-1)(q-1)} \equiv 1 \pmod{pq}, k \text{ is any integer}$$

2. For any integer a,

$$a^{k(p-1)(q-1)+1} \equiv a \pmod{pq}, \ k \text{ is any positive integer}$$

Discrete Logarithm

In this section we will deal with multiplicative group $G = <Z_{n*}, \ x>$. The order of a finite group is the number of elements in the group G. Let us take an example of a group,

$$G = <Z_{21*}, \ x>$$

$\phi(21) = \phi(3) \times \phi(7) = 2 \times 6 = 12$, that is, 12 elements in the group, and each is coprime to 21.

$$\{1, 2, 4, 5, 8, 10, 11, 13, 16, 17, 19, 20\}$$

The order of an element, ord(a), is the smallest integer i such that

$$a^i \equiv e \pmod{n}, \text{where } e = 1.$$

Find the order of all elements in $G = <Z_{10*}, \ x>$

$\phi(10) = \phi(2) \times \phi(5) = 1 \times 4 = 4$
$\{1, 3, 7, 9\}$

Primitive Roots

In the multiplicative group $G = <Z_{n*}, \ x>$, when the order of an element is the same as $\phi(n)$, then that element is called the primitive root of the group.
$G = <Z_{8*}, \ x>$ has no primitive roots. The order of this group is, $\phi(8) = 4$

$$Z_{8*} = \{1, 3, 5, 7\}$$

1, 2, 4 each divide the order of the group which is 4:

$$1^1 \equiv 1 \pmod{8} \qquad \rightarrow \text{ord}(1) = 1$$
$$3^1 \equiv 3 \pmod{8}; \ 3^2 \equiv 1 \pmod{8} \quad \rightarrow \text{ord}(3) = 2$$
$$5^1 \equiv 5 \pmod{8}; \ 5^2 \equiv 1 \pmod{8} \quad \rightarrow \text{ord}(5) = 2$$
$$7^1 \equiv 7 \pmod{8}; \ 7^2 \equiv 1 \pmod{8} \quad \rightarrow \text{ord}(7) = 2$$

In the example above, none of the elements have an order of 4; hence this group has no primitive roots. The group $G = <Z_{n^*}, x>$ has primitive roots only if n is 2, 4, p^t, or $2p^t$, where p is an odd prime not including 2 and t is an integer.

If the group $G = <Z_{n^*}, x>$ has any primitive roots, the number of primitive roots is $\phi(\phi(n))$. If a group, $G = <Z_{n^*}, x>$ has primitive roots, then it is cyclic, and each of its primitive root is a generator of the whole group.

Group $G = <Z_{10^*}, x>$ has two primitive roots because $\phi(10) = 4$, and $\phi(\phi(10)) = 2$. These two primitive roots are {3, 7}:

$$3^1 \bmod 10 = 3 \; 3^2 \bmod 10 = 9 \; 3^3 \bmod 10 = 7 \; 3^4 \bmod 10 = 1$$
$$7^1 \bmod 10 = 7 \; 7^2 \bmod 10 = 9 \; 7^3 \bmod 10 = 3 \; 7^4 \bmod 10 = 1$$

Group, $G = <Z_{p^*}, x>$ is always cyclic.
The group $G = <Z_{p^*}, x>$ has the following properties:

1. Its elements are from 1 to (p − 1) inclusive.
2. It always has primitive roots.
3. It is cyclic, and its elements can be generated using g where x is an integer from 1 to $\phi(n) = p - 1$.
4. The primitive roots can be used as the base of logarithm—discrete logarithm.

Modern encryption algorithms such as DES, AES, RSA, and ElGammal to name a few are based on algebraic structures such as Group Theory and Field Theory as well as Number Theory. We will begin with a set S, with finite number of elements, and a binary operation (*) defined between any two elements of the set:

$$*:S \times S \rightarrow S$$

that is, if a and $b \in S$, then $a^*b \in S$. This is important, for it implies that the set is closed under the binary operation. We have seen that the message space is finite, and we want to make sure that any algebraic operation on the message space satisfies the closure property. Hence, we want to treat the message space as a finite set of elements. We will remind the reader that messages that get encrypted must be finally decrypted by the received party; thus encryption algorithm must run in polynomial time. Furthermore, the algorithm must have the property that it be reversible to recover the original message. The goal of encryption is to confuse and diffuse the hacker such that it would make it almost impossible for the hacker to break the encrypted message. Therefore, encryption must consist of finite number substitutions and transpositions. The algebraic structure, Classical Group, facilitates the coding of the encryption algorithm. Next we give some relevant definitions and examples before we proceed to introduce the essential concept of a Galois Field, which is central to formulation of the Rijndael algorithm used in the Advanced Encryption Standard (AES).

Definition Group

A group (G, •) is a finite set G together with an operation • satisfying the following conditions:

1. Closure: $\forall$ a, $b \in G$, then $(a \bullet b) \in G$
2. Associatively: $\forall$ a, b, $c \in G$, then $a \bullet (b \bullet c) = (a \bullet b) \bullet c$

3. Existence of Identity: $\exists$ a unique element $e \in G$ such that $\forall\ a \in G$: $a \bullet e = e \bullet a$
4. $\forall a \in G$: $\exists\ a^{-1} \in G$: $a^{-1}a = a^{-1} \bullet a = e$

Definition of Finite and Infinite Groups (Order of a Group)

A group G is said to be finite if the number of elements in the set G is finite. Otherwise, the group is infinite.

Definition of Abelian Group

A group G is abelian if for all a, b$\in$G, $a \bullet b = b \bullet a$

The reader should note that in a group, the elements in the set do not have to be a number or objects: They can be mappings, functions, or rules.

Examples of a Group

The set of integers Z is a group under addition ($+$); that is, (Z, $+$) is a group with identity e $=$ 0, and the inverse of an element a is ($-$a). This is an additive abelian group, but infinite.

Nonzero elements of Q (rationals), R (reals), and C (complex) form a group under multiplication, with the identity element e $=$ 1, and a^{-1} being the multiplicative inverse. For any n $\geq$ 1, the set of integers modulo n forms a finite additive group of n elements:

$G = <Z_n, + >$ is an abelian group.

The set of Z_{n*} with multiplication operator, $G = <Z_{n*}, x>$ is also an abelian group. The set Z_{n*}, is a subset of Z_n and includes only integers in Z_n that have a unique multiplicative inverse:

$$Z_{13} = \{0, 1, 2, 3, 4, 5, 6, 7, 8, 9, 10, 11, 12\}$$
$$Z_{13*} = \{1, 2, 3, 4, 5, 6, 7, 8, 9, 10, 11, 12\}$$

Definition Subgroup

A subgroup of a group G is a nonempty subset H of G, which itself is a group under the same operations as that of G. We denote that H is a subgroup of G as H$\subseteq$G, and H$\subset$G is a proper subgroup of G if the set H$\neq$G. Examples of Subgroups:

Under addition, Z$\subseteq$Q$\subseteq$R$\subseteq$C.

$H = <Z_{10}, + >$ is a proper subgroup of $G = <Z_{12}, + >$

Definition of Cyclic Group

A group G is said to be cyclic if there exists an element a$\in$G such that for any b$\in$G, and i $\geq$ 0, $b = a^i$. Element a is called a generator of G. The group $G = <Z_{10*}, x>$ is a cyclic group with generators g $=$ 3 and g $=$ 7:

$$Z_{10*} = \{1, 3, 7, 9\}$$

The group $G = <Z_6, + >$ is a cyclic group with generators g $=$ 1 and g $=$ 5:

$$Z_6 = \{0, 1, 2, 3, 4, 5\}$$

Rings

Let R be a nonempty set with two binary operations: addition (+) and multiplication (*).

Then R is called a ring if the following axioms are met:

1. Under addition, R is an abelian group with zero as the additive identity.
2. Under multiplication, R satisfies the closure, associative, and identity axiom. 1 is the multiplicative identity, and that $1 \neq 0$.
3. For every a, and b that belongs to R, $a \bullet b = b \bullet a$.
4. For every a, b, and c that belongs to R, then $a \bullet (b + c) = a \bullet b + a \bullet c$

Examples

Z, Q, R, and C are all rings under addition and multiplication. For any $n > 0$, Z_n is a ring under addition and multiplication modulo n with 0 as identity under addition, 1 under multiplication.

Definition Field

If the nonzero elements of a ring form a group under multiplication, then the ring is called a field.

Examples

Q, R, and C are all fields under addition and multiplication, with 0 and 1 as identity under addition and multiplication.

[Note that Z under integer addition and multiplication is not a field because any non-zero element does not have a multiplicative inverse in Z.]

Finite Fields GF(2^n)

Construction of finite fields and computations in finite fields are based on polynomial computations. Finite fields play a significant role in cryptography and cryptographic protocols such as the Diffie and Hellman key exchange protocol, ElGamal cryptosystems, and Advanced Encryption Standard (AES):

For a prime number p, the quotient Z/p (or F_p) is a finite field with p number of elements. For any positive integer q, $GF(q) = F_q$

We define A to be algebraic structure such as a ring or a group or a field.

Definition

A polynomial over A is an expression of the form:

$$f(x) = \sum_{i=0}^{n} a_i x^n$$

where, n is a nonnegative integer, the coefficient $a_i \in A$, $0 \leq i \leq n$, and $x \notin A$.

Definition

A polynomial $f \in A[x]$ is said to be irreducible in $A[x]$ if f has a positive degree and $f = gh$ for some $g, h \in A[x]$ implies that either g or h is a constant polynomial. The reader should be aware that a given polynomial can be reducible over one structure, but irreducible over another.

Definition

Let f, g, q, and $r \in A[x]$ with $g \neq 0$. Then we say that r is remainder of f divided by g:

$$r \equiv f(\bmod\ g)$$

The set of remainders of all the polynomials in $A[x](\bmod\ g)$ denoted as $A[x]_g$.

Theorem

Let F be a field and f be a non-zero polynomial in $F[x]$. Then $F[x]_f$ is a ring, and is a field iff f is irreducible over F.

Theorem

Let F be field of p elements and f be irreducible polynomial over F. Then the number of elements in the field $F[x]_f$ is p^n.

For every prime p and every positive integer n there exist a finite field of p^n number of elements. For any prime number p, Z_p is a finite field under addition and multiplication modulo p, with 0 and 1 as the identity under addition and multiplication.

Z_p is an additive ring and nonzero elements of Z_p, denoted by Z_{p^*} form a multiplicative group. Galois Field, $GF(p^n)$ is a finite field with number of elements p^n, where p is a prime number and n is a positive integer.

Example

Integer representation of Finite Field (Rijnadel) element. Polynomial $f(x) = x^8 + x^4 + x^3 + x + 1$ is irreducible over F_2.

The set of all polynomials $(\bmod\ f)$ over F_2 forms a field of 2^8 elements; they are all polynomials over F_2 of degree less than 8. So any element in the field $F_2[x]_f$

$$b_7 x^7 + b_6 x^6 + b_5 x^5 + b_4 x^4 + b_3 x^3 + b_2 x^2 + b_1 x^1 + b_0$$

where, $b_7, b_6, b_5, b_4, b_3, b_2, b_1, b_0 \in F_2$ Thus any element in this field can represent a 8-bit binary number.

Data inside a computer is organized in bytes (8 bits) and is processed using Boolean logic; that is, bits are manipulated using binary operation addition and multiplication. These binary operations are implemented using the logical operator XOR, or in the language of finite fields, GF(2). Since the extended ASCII defines 8-bit per byte, an 8-bit byte has a natural representation using a polynomial of degree 8. Polynomial addition would be mod 2, and multiplication would be mod polynomial degree 8. Of course this polynomial degree 8 would have to be irreducible. Hence the Galois Field $GF(2^8)$ would be the most natural tool to implement the encryption algorithm. Furthermore, this would provide a close algebraic formulation. Consider polynomials over GF(2) with $p = 2$ and $n = 1$:

$$1, \ x, \ x + 1, \ x^2 + x + 1, \ x^2 + 1, \ x^3 + 1$$

Polynomials with negative coefficients, -1 is the same as $+1$ in GF(2). Obviously, the number of such polynomials is infinite. In algebraic operations of addition and multiplication, the coefficients are added and multiplied according to the rules that apply to GF(2). The set of such polynomials forms a ring.

Modular Polynomial Arithmetic over GF(2)

The Galois Field $GF(2^3)$: Construct this field with eight elements that can be represented by polynomials of the form:

$$ax^2 + bx + c \text{ where } a, b, c \in GF(2) = \{0, \ 1\}$$

Two choices for a, b, c gives $2 \times 2 \times 2 = 8$ polynomials of the form:

$$ax^2 + bx + c \in GF_2[x]$$

What is our choice of the irreducible polynomials for this field?

$$(x^3 + x^2 + x + 1), \ (x^3 + x^2 + 1), \ (x^3 + x^2 + x), \ (x^3 + x + 1), \ (x^3 + x^2)$$

These two polynomials have no factors: $(x^3 + x^2 + 1)$, $(x^3 + x + 1)$. So we choose polynomial $(x^3 + x + 1)$. Hence all polynomial arithmetic multiplication and division is carried out with respect to $(x^3 + x + 1)$. The eight polynomials that belong to $GF(2^3)$:

$$\{0, \ 1, \ x, \ x^2, \ 1 + x, \ 1 + x^2, \ x + x^2, \ 1 + x + x^2\}$$

You will observe that $GF(8) = \{0,1,2,3,4,5,6,7\}$ is not a field, since every element (excluding zero) does not have a multiplicative inverse such as $\{2, 4, 6)$ (mod 8).

Using a Generator to Represent the Elements of GF(2ⁿ)

It is particularly convenient to represent the elements of a Galois Field with the help of a generator element. If α is a generator element, then every element of $GF(2^n)$, except for the 0 element, can be written down as some power of α. A generator is obtained from the irreducible polynomial that was used to construct a finite field. If $f(\alpha)$ is the irreducible polynomial used, then α is that element that satisfies the equation $f(\alpha) = 0$. You do not actually solve this equation for its roots since an irreducible polynomial cannot have actual roots in the field GF(2). Consider the case of $GF(2^3)$ defined with the irreducible polynomial $x^3 + x + 1$. The generator α is that element which satisfies $\alpha^3 + \alpha + 1 = 0$:

Suppose α is a root in $GF(2^3)$ of the polynomial $p(x) = 1 + x + x^3$

that is, $p(\alpha) = 0$, then $\alpha^3 = -\alpha - 1 \ (mod \ 2) = \alpha + 1$

$$\alpha^4 = \alpha(\alpha + 1) = \alpha^2 + \alpha$$
$$\alpha^5 = \alpha^4.\alpha = (\alpha^2 + \alpha)\alpha = \alpha^3 + \alpha^2 = (\alpha^2 + \alpha + 1)$$
$$\alpha^6 = \alpha^5.\alpha = \alpha.(\alpha^2 + \alpha + 1) = (\alpha^2 + 1)$$
$$\alpha^7 = (\alpha^2 + 1).\alpha = (2\alpha + 1) = 1$$

All powers of α generate nonzero elements of GF_8.

We will now consider all polynomials defined over GF(2), modulo the irreducible polynomial $x^3 + x + 1$. When an algebraic operation (polynomial multiplication) results in a polynomial whose degree equals or exceeds that of the irreducible polynomial, we will take for our result the remainder modulo the irreducible polynomial. For example,

$$(x^2 + x + 1) * (x^2 + 1) \bmod (x^3 + x + 1)$$
$$= (x^4 + x^3 + x^2) + (x^2 + x + 1) \bmod (x^3 + x + 1)$$
$$= (x^4 + x^3 + x + 1) \bmod (x^3 + x + 1)$$
$$= -x^2 + x$$
$$= x^2 + x$$

Recall that $1 + 1 = 0$ in GF(2). With multiplications modulo $(x^3 + x + 1)$, we have only the following eight polynomials in the set of polynomials over GF(2):

$$\{0, 1, x, x + 1, x^2, x^2 + 1, x^2 + x, x^2 + x + 1\}$$

We will refer to this set as $GF(2^3)$ where the power of 2 is the degree of the modulus polynomial. The eight elements of Z_8 are to be integers modulo 8. Similarly, $GF(2^3)$ maps all of the polynomials over GF(2) to the eight polynomials shown above. But you will note that the crucial difference between $GF(2^3)$ and 2^3: $GF(2^3)$ is a field, whereas Z_8 is NOT.

GF(2³) is a Finite Field

We know that $GF(2^3)$ is an Abelian group because the operation of polynomial addition satisfies all of the requirements on a group operator and because polynomial addition is commutative. $GF(2^3)$ is also a commutative ring because polynomial multiplication is a distributive over polynomial addition. $GF(2^3)$ is a finite field because it is a finite set and because it contains a unique multiplicative inverse for every nonzero element.

$GF(2^n)$ is a finite field for every n. To find all the polynomials in $GF(2^n)$, we need an irreducible polynomial of degree n. In general, $GF(p^n)$ is a finite field for any prime p. The elements of $GF(p^n)$ are polynomials over GF(p) (which is the same as the set of residues Z_p). Next we show how the multiplicative inverse of a polynomial is calculated using the Extended Euclidean Algorithm:

Multiplicative inverse of $(x^2 + x + 1)$ in $F_2[x]/(x^4 + x + 1)$ is $(x^2 + x)$
$(x^2 + x)(x^2 + x + 1) = 1 \bmod(x^4 + x + 1)$
Multiplicative inverse of $(x^6 + x + 1)$ in $F_2[x]/(x^8 + x^4 + x^3 + x + 1)$ is
$(x^6 + x^5 + x^2 + x + 1)$
$(x^6 + x + 1)(x^6 + x^5 + x^2 + x + 1) = 1 \bmod (x^8 + x^4 + x^3 + x + 1)$ [1][2]

2. THE RSA CRYPTOSYSTEM

Now that we have reviewed the necessary mathematical preliminaries, we will focus on the subject matter of Asymmetric Cryptography, which uses a public and a private key to encrypt and decrypt the plaintext. If Alice wants to send plaintext to Bob, then she will use Bob's public key, which is advertised by Bob, to encrypt the plaintext, and then send it to Bob via an insecured channel. Bob would decrypt the data using his private key, which is known to him only. Of course, this would appear to be an ideal replacement for Symmetric-key cipher, but it is much slower since it has to encrypt each byte; hence it is useful in message authentication and communicating the secret key. See the following Key Generation Algorithm:

1. Select two prime numbers p and q such that $p \neq q$.
2. Construct $m = p \times q$.
3. Set up a commutative ring $R = <Z_m, +, x>$ which is public since m is made public.
4. Set up a multiplicative group $G = <Z^*_{\phi(m)}, x>$ which is used to generate public and private keys. This group is hidden from the public since $\phi(m)$ is kept hidden.
5. $\phi(m) = (p - 1)(q - 1)$
6. Choose an integer e such that $1 < e < \phi(m)$ and e is coprime to $\phi(m)$.
7. Compute the secret exponent d such that, $1 < d < \phi(m)$ and that $ed \equiv 1 \pmod{\phi(m)}$.
8. The public key is "e" and the private key is "d".
9. The value of p, q, and $\phi(m)$ are kept private.

Encryption:

1. Alice obtains Bob's public key (m, e).
2. The plaintext x is treated as a number to lie in the range $1 < x < m - 1$.
3. The ciphertext corresponding to x is $y = x^e \pmod{m}$.
4. Send the ciphertext y to Bob.

Decryption:

1. Bob uses his private key (m, d).
2. Computes the $x = y^d \pmod{m}$.

Why RSA works

$$y^d \equiv (x^e \bmod m)^d$$
$$\equiv (x^{ed}) \bmod m$$
$$d \cdot e = 1 + km = 1 + k(p - 1)(q - 1)$$
$$y^d \equiv x^{ed} \equiv x^{1+k(p-1)(q-1)} \equiv x \pmod{m}$$

Example:
Choose $p = 7$ and $q = 11$, then $m = p \times q = 7 \times 11 = 77$
$R = <Z_{77}, +, x>$ and $\phi(77) = \phi(7)\phi(11) = 6 \times 10 = 60$
The corresponding multiplicative group $G = <Z^*_{60}, x>$
Choose $e = 13$ and $d = 37$ from Z^*_{60} such that $e \times d \equiv 1 \pmod{60}$
Plaintext $= 5$ $y = x^e \pmod{m} = 5^{13} \pmod{77} = 26$
$x = y^d \pmod{m} = 26^{37} \pmod{77} = 5$

Note: 384-bit primes or larger are deemed sufficient to use RSA securely. The prime number $e = 2^{16} + 1$ is often used in modern RSA implementations.

Factorization Attack

The RSA algorithm relies on the fact that p and q are the distinct prime numbers; and, must be kept secret, even though m = p x q is made public. So if n is an extremely large number, then the problem reduces to finding the factors that make up the number n, which is known as the factorization attack. If the middle man, Eve, can factor n correctly, then she guesses correctly p, q, and ϕ(m). Remind yourselves that if the public key e is public, then Eve has to compute the multiplicative inverse of e:

$$d \equiv e^{-1} \ (\text{mod } m)$$

So if the modulus m is chosen to be 1024 bits long, then it would take considerable time to break the RSA system unless an efficient factorization algorithm could be found [1][2].

Chosen-Ciphertext Attack

Z_n is a set of all positive integers from 0 to (n − 1).
Z_n^* is a set all integers such that gcd(n,a) = 1, where $a \in Z_n^*$.

$$Z_n^* \subset Z_n$$

Φ(n) calculates the number of elements in Z_n^* that are smaller than n and coprime to n.

$$\Phi(21) = \Phi(3) \times \Phi(7) = 2 \times 6 = 12$$

Therefore the number of integers in $\in Z_{21}{}^*$ is 12.

$$Z_{21}^* = \{1, 2, 4, 5, 8, 10, 11, 13, 16, 17, 19, 20\}, \text{ each of which is coprime to } 21$$

$$Z_{14}^* = \{1, 3, 5, 9, 11, 13\}, \text{ each of which is coprime to } 14$$

$$\Phi(14) = \Phi(2) \times \Phi(7) = 1 \times 6 = 6 \text{ number of integers in } Z_{14}^*$$

Example:
Choose p = 3 and q = 7, then m = 3 × 7 = 21,
Encryption and decryption take place in the ring, $R = \ <Z_{21}, \ +, x>$.

$$\Phi(21) = \Phi(2) \ \Phi \ (6) = 12$$

Key-Generation Group, $G = \ <Z_{12}^*, x>$

$$\Phi(12) = \Phi(4)\Phi(3) = 2 \times 2 = 4 \text{ number in } Z_{12}^*$$

$$Z_{12}^* = \{1, 5, 7, 11\}$$

Alice encrypts the message P using the public key e of Bob and sends the encrypted message C to Bob:

$$C = P^e \ \text{mod } m$$

Eve the middle man intercepts the message and manipulates the message before forwarding to Bob:

1. Eve chooses a random integer $X \in Z_m{}^*$ (since m is public).
2. Eve calculates $Y = C \times X^e \pmod{m}$.
3. Bob receives Y from Eve, and he decrypts Y using his private key d.
4. $Z = Y^d \pmod{m}$.
5. Eve can easily discover the plaintext P as follows:

$Z = Y^d \pmod{m} = [C \times X^e]^d \pmod{m} = [C^d \times X^{ed}] \pmod{m} = [C^d \times X] \pmod{m}$

Hence $Z = [P \times X] \pmod{m}$

Eve, using the Extended Euclidean Algorithm, can then compute the multiplicative inverse of X and thus obtain P:

$P = Z \times X^{-1} \pmod{m}$

The eth Roots Problem

Given:

1. a composite number n, the product of two prime numbers p and q
2. an integer $e \geq 3$
3. gcd $(e, \Phi(n)) = 1$
4. an integer $c \in Z_{12}^*$
5. Find an integer m such that $m^e \equiv c \bmod n$[1,2].

Discrete Logarithm Problem

Discrete logarithms are perhaps simplest to understand in the group Z_{p^*}, where p is the prime number. Let g be the generator of Z_{p^*}; then the discrete logarithm problem reduces to computing a, given $(g, p, g^a \bmod p)$ for a randomly chosen $a < (p - 1)$.

If we want to find the *kth* power of one of the numbers in this group, we can do so by finding its kth power as an integer and then finding the remainder after division by p. This process is called *discrete exponentiation*. For example, consider Z_{23^*}

To compute 3^4 in this group, we first compute $3^4 = 81$, and then we divide 81 by 23, obtaining a remainder of 12. Thus $3^4 = 12$ in the group Z_{23^*}

Discrete logarithm is just the inverse operation. For example, take the equation $3^k \equiv 12$ (mod 23) for k. As shown above $k = 4$ is a solution, but it is not the only solution. Since $3^{22} \equiv 1 \pmod{23}$, it also follows that if *n* is an integer then $3^{4+22n} \equiv 12 \times 1^n \equiv 12 \pmod{23}$. Hence the equation has infinitely many solutions of the form $4 + 22n$. Since 22 is the smallest positive integer *m* satisfying $3^m \equiv 1 \pmod{23}$, that is, 22 is the order of 3 in Z_{23^*}, these are all solutions. Equivalently, the solution can be expressed as $k \equiv 4 \pmod{22}$ [1].

In designing public-key cryptosystems, two problems dominate the designs: the integer factorization problem and the discrete logarithm problem. Large instances of these problems are still intractable today.

Discrete logarithms have a natural extension into the realm of elliptic curves and hyperelliptic curves. And Elliptic ElGamal has proved to be a strong cryptosystem using elliptic curves and discrete logarithms. In the next part of the chapter, we will take a look at the discrete logarithm problem and discuss its application to cryptography.

Discrete Logarithm Problem (DLP)

The discrete logarithm problem in group G, given some generator α of a cyclic subgroup G^* of G and an element $\beta \in G^*$, is to find the element x, $0 \le x \le (p-2)$, such that $\alpha^x = \beta$. The most frequently used cryptosystem utilizing the DLP is ElGamal; we give an elliptic curve variant of ElGamal below [1–3]. For example:

ElGamal Cryptosystem:

Alice wants to talk secretly with Bob.

Setting up: Sometime in the past, Bob has created his keys in the following way:

1. Bob chooses a random large prime p and a generator α of the multiplicative group Z_p^*.
2. Bob chooses a random integer a where $1 \le a \le (p-2)$.
3. Bob computes α^a mod p.
4. The triple $e_B = (p, \alpha, \alpha^a)$ is the public key, and d_B (p, α, a) is the private key.

    Alice obtains Bob's public key from some public key server.

Encryption: Alice wants to encrypt a plaintext M with the cipher $e_B = (e, d, n)$. She starts by choosing a random integer k where $1 \le k \le (p-2)$ and then encrypting the plaintext M into the cipher-text C:

$$E_{K_B}(M) = C = (\gamma, \delta) = (\alpha^k, M * (\alpha^a)^k \bmod p)$$

Alice then sends Bob the encrypted message C.

Decryption: Bob then decrypts the cipher-text $C = (\gamma, \delta)$ with the cipher $d_B = (e, d, n)$ in the following manner:

$$D_{K_B}(C) = M = (\gamma^{-\alpha}) * \delta \bmod p$$

Lattice-based Cryptography—NTRU

An n-dimensional lattice (see Figure 15.1) is generated using n-linearly independent vectors:

$v_1, \ldots, v_n \varepsilon R^n$; these vectors are known as the basis of the lattice. There are infinite numbers of such bases that can generate the same lattice.

$$L(v_1, \ldots, v_n) = \left\{ \sum_{i=1}^{n} \alpha_i v_i | \alpha_i \varepsilon Z \right\}$$

In group theory, a lattice in R^n is a discrete subgroup of R^n which spans the real vector space R^n. A lattice is the symmetry group of discrete translational symmetry in n directions. Two NP-hard problems related to lattices are the shortest vector problem (SVP) and the closest vector problem (CVP; see Figure 15.2). Given an arbitrary basis for a lattice, find the SVP in the lattice or find the CVP to an arbitrary nonlattice vector. In both the quantum and classical computational problems, these problems are hard to solve for high-dimensional lattices (see Figure 15.3). There are a number of lattice-based cryptographic schemes, but the NTRU-based cryptographic algorithm appears to be most practical [4,5].

What is a Lattice?   FIGURE 15.1   Definition of Lattice.

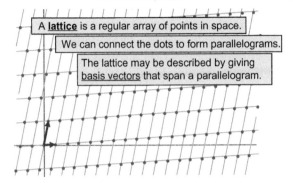

What is the Closest Vector Problem?   FIGURE 15.2   Closest vector problem (CVP).

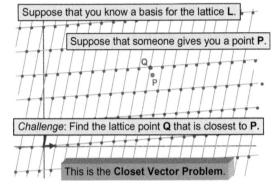

Why Is That A Hard Problem?   FIGURE 15.3   The hard closest vector problem.

For lattices in the plane, you're right, it's very easy.
It's not even very hard in dimension 3, or 4, or 5.
However, the Closest Vector Problem is **very hard** in
high dimension, say in dimension 500.

NTRU Cryptosystem

NTRU is not based on factorization or discrete logarithmic problems. Rather, it is a lattice-based alternative to RSA and ECC and is based on the shortest vector problem in a lattice. NTRU was founded in 1996 by three mathematicians: Jeffrey Hoffstein, Joseph H. Silverman, and Jill Pipher. Later on with the addition of yet another member, Daniel Lieman, to the team, NTRU Cryptosystems was incorporated in Boston. NTRU Cryptosystems was acquired by Security Innovation in 2009.

The NTRU cryptosystem was introduced at the rump session of Crypto'96 and was later published in the proceedings of the ANTS-III conference. NTRU is a ring-based public-key cryptosystem and is therefore quite different from the group-based cryptosystems whose security relies on the integer factorization problem or the discrete logarithm problem. This extra structure can be exploited to obtain a very fast cryptosystem: To encrypt/decrypt a message block of length N, NTRU only requires $O(N^2)$ time, whereas the group-based schemes require $O(N^3)$ time. Furthermore, NTRU also has a very short key size of $O(N)$ and very low memory requirements, which makes it ideal for constrained devices such as smart cards.

Truncated Polynomial Rings

Consider a polynomial of degree $(N - 1)$ having integer coefficients:

$$a = a_0 + a_1 X + a_2 X^2 + a_3 X^3 + a_4 X^4 \ldots \ldots \ldots \ldots + a_{(N-1)} X^{(N-1)}$$

The set of all such polynomials is denoted by R. The arithmetic on the polynomials in R is as follows. Consider two polynomials a and b:

$$a + b = (a_0 + b_0) + (a_1 + b_1)X + \ldots \ldots + (a_{(N-1)} + b_{(N-1)})X^{(N-1)}$$

Suppose $N = 3$ and $a = 2 - X + 3X^2$, $b = 1 + 2X - X^2$

$$a + b = 3 + X + 2X^2 a * b = (2 - X + 3X^2) * (1 + 2X = X^2) = 2 + 4X - 2X^2 - X - 2X^2 + X^3 + 3X^2 + 6X^3 - 3X^4$$

$N = 3$; hence the polynomial cannot have powers of X more than 2, so we have to truncate powers of X higher than 2 with the following rules:

$$X^4 \text{ by } X$$

$$X^3 \text{ by } X^0 = 1$$

Hence,

$$a * b = 2 + 4X - 2X^2 - X - 2X^2 + 1 + 3X^2 + 6 - 3X = (9 - X^2)$$

The distributive law also holds for the polynomials

$$a * (b + c) = a * b + a * c$$

The inclusion of the above law makes the algebraic structure of polynomials into a ring, the Ring of Truncated Polynomials. This ring R is isomorphic to the quotient ring, $Z[X]/(X^{(N-1)})$.

Inverses in Truncated Polynomial Ring

The inverse modulo q of a polynomial a is a polynomial a^{-1} with the property:

$$a * a^{-1} = 1 (mod\ q)$$

Example:

$$N = 7, \quad \text{and} \quad q = 11$$

$$a = 3 + 2X^2 - 3X^4 + X^6$$

then,

$$a^{-1} = 2 + 4X + 2X^2 + 4X^3 - 4X^4 + 2X^5 - 2X^6 = (3 + 2X^2 - 3X^4 + X^6) * (2 + 4X + 2X^2 + 4X^3$$
$$- 4X^4 + 2X^5 - 2X^6) = -10 + 22X - 22X^3 + 22X^6 = 1(\text{mod } 11)$$

NTRU Parameters and Keys

N—a polynomial in the ring R with degree N − 1, with N being a prime number:

Q—a large modulus to which the coefficient is reduced
P—a small modulus to which each coefficient is reduced
q and p are coprime
f—a polynomial that is a private key
g—a polynomial that is used to generate the public key h from f
    NOTE: g (secret) is discarded later on.
H—a polynomial that is a public key
r—a random binding polynomial (discarded later on, but kept secret.
D—coefficient.

Key Generation

Consider a truncated polynomial ring with a degree at most N − 1:

$$a_0 + a_1 X + a_2 X^2 \ldots \ldots a_{N-1} X^{(N-1)}$$

1 Choose two small polynomials f and g in the ring R; polynomial f must have an inverse.
2 The inverse of f modulo q and the inverse of f modulo p are computed.
3 $F_q = f^{-1}(\text{mod } q)$ and $F_p = f^{-1}(\text{mod } p)$
4 $f*F_q = 1(\text{mod } q)$ and $f*F_p = 1(\text{mod } p)$
5 Compute $h = p*(F_q*g)$ mod q.
6 Alice's private key: a pair of polynomials f and F_p
7 Alice's public key: the polynomial h
    Public parameters (N, p, q, d) = (7, 3, 41, 2).

Alice chooses: $f(x) = X^6 - X^4 + X^3 + X^2 - 1$

$$g(x) = X^6 + X^4 - X^2 - X$$

$$F_q(x) = f^{-1}(X) - 1(mod\ q) = 8X^6 + 26X^5 + 31X^4 + 21X^3 + 40X^2 + 2X + 37\ (mod\ 41)$$

Private Key

$$F_p(x) = f^{-1}(X) - 1(mod\ q) = X^6 + 2X^5 + X^3 + X^2 + X + 1\ (mod\ 3)$$

Public Key

$$h(x) = p * (F_q) * g(mod\ q) = 20X^6 + 40X^5 + 2X^4 + 38X^3 + 8X^2 + 26X + 30\ (mod\ 41)$$

NTRU Encryption

Alice has a message to transmit:

1. Puts the message in the form of polynomial m whose coefficient is chosen modulo p between $-p/2$ and $p/2$ (centered lift).
2. Randomly chooses another small polynomial r (to obscure the message).
3. Computes the encrypted message:

$$e = r * h + m(modulo\ q)$$

Example of NTRU Encryption

Alice decides to send Bob the message:

$$m(X) = -X^5 + X^3 + X^2 - X^1 + 1$$

using the random key $r(x) = X^6 - X^5 + X^1 - 1$

$$e = r * h + m\ (modulo\ q)$$

$$e(x) \equiv 31X^6 + 19X^5 + 4X^4 + 2X^3 + 40X^2 + 3X + 25\ (mod\ 41)$$

$$(N, p, q, d) = (7, 3, 41, 2)$$

NTRU Decryption

Bob receives a message e from Alice and would like to decrypt it.
Using his private polynomial f, he computes a polynomial

$$A = f * e(mod\ q).$$

Bob needs to choose coefficients that lie in an interval of length q. He computes the polynomial $b = a(mod\ p)$. Bob reduces each of the coefficients of a modulo p. Bob uses the other private polynomial F_p to compute $c = F_p*b(modulo\ p)$, which is the original message of Alice.

Example of NTRU Decryption

$$a = f * e(\text{mod } q)$$

Bob computes $a \equiv X^6 + 10X^5 + 33X^4 + 40X^3 + 40X^2 + X + 40 \pmod{41}$
Bob then center lifts modulo q to obtain

$$b = a(\text{mod } p) = X^6 + 10X^5 - 8X^4 - X^3 - X^2 + X - 1 \pmod{3}$$

Bob reduces a(x) modulo p and computes

$$c = F_p(x) * b(x) \equiv 2X^5 + X^3 + X^2 + 2X + 1 \pmod{3}$$

Center lifting modulo p retrieves Alice's plaintext

$$m(x) = -X^5 + X^3 + X^2 - X^1 + 1$$

$$(N, p, q, d) = (7, 3, 41, 2)$$

Why Does NTRU Work?

$$a = f * e(\text{mod } q) = f * (r * h + m) \ (\text{mod } q) = f * (r * pF_q * g + m)(\text{mod } q) = pr * g + f * m(\text{mod } q)$$

$$b = a = f * m(\text{mod } p)$$

$$c = F_p * b = F_p * f * m = m(\text{mod } p)$$

NTRU167≡ECC112≡RSA512
NTRU263≡ECC168≡RSA1024
NTRU503≡ECC196≡RSA2048

TABLE 15.1   NTRU Parameters.

Security Level	N	q	p
Moderate	167	128	3
Standard	251	128	3
High	347	128	3
Highest	503	256	3

Source: www.ntru.com

Underlying every public-key cryptosystem lurks an extremely difficult mathematical problem waiting to be solved. There is no direct proof that breaking a cryptosystem is equivalent to solving the mathematical problem. Below we list the public-key cryptosystem and the corresponding mathematical problem.

RSA   Integer Factorization Problem
Diffe-Hellman   Discrete Logarithm Problem in F_q^*
Elliptic Curve   Discrete Logarithm Problem on an
Cryptography   Elliptic Curve
Lattices   SVP and CVP

3. SUMMARY

In this chapter, we reviewed aspects of advanced data encryption security: number theory, group theory, and finite fields relevant to public-key cryptography, as well as advanced data encryption security features (see checklist: An Agenda for Action for Implementing Advanced Data Encryption Security Features). The security of public-key cryptography is determined by what is known as the discrete logarithm problem (DLP), and we gave an example of DLP based on the elliptic curve. In the final section of this chapter, we presented public-key cryptography based on lattice theory—known as the NTRU cryptosystem.

Finally, let's move on to the real interactive part of this chapter: review questions/exercises, hands-on projects, case projects, and optional team case project. The answers and/or solutions by chapter can be found in the Online Instructor's Solutions Manual.

AN AGENDA FOR ACTION FOR IMPLEMENTING ADVANCED DATA ENCRYPTION SECURITY FEATURES

Please see the following advanced data encryption security features checklist that needs to be implemented in your organization (check all tasks completed):

Core Advanced Data Encryption Security Functionality

_____1. Hard Drive Encryption.
_____2. Saved Files.
_____3. Temporary Files.
_____4. Page Files.
_____5. Deleted Files.
_____6. Secure File Deletion.
_____7. Registry or Operating System Boot Files.
_____8. Unused Sectors.
_____9. Hidden Partitions.
_____10. Hibernation Mode.
_____11. Logout/Lockout.
_____12. Nonmagnetic Drives.
_____13. Removable Drives.
_____14. Data Recovery by Administrator.

Conformance to Protocol Standards

_____15. Password Management/Recovery (Admin).
_____16. PKI Authentication.
_____17. Multifactor Authentication.
_____18. Revocation of Access.

PKI Standards

_____19. X.509 Certificates.

_____**20.** LDAP Repository.
_____**21.** Certificate Revocation.
_____**22.** Cryptographic Algorithms.

Cryptographic Standards

Encryption Algorithms
_____**23.** Advanced Encryption Standard (AES).
_____**24.** Triple-Data Encryption Standard (3DES).

Key Establishment Algorithms

_____**25.** Rivest, Shamir, Adleman (RSA).
_____**26.** Other algorithms based on exponentiation of finite fields.
_____**27.** Key Exchange Algorithm (KEA).
_____**28.** Elliptic Curve algorithms.

Digital Signature Algorithms

_____**29.** RSA.
_____**30.** Digital Signature Algorithm (DSA).
_____**31.** Other algorithms based on exponentiation of finite fields.
_____**32.** Elliptic Curve Digital Signature Algorithm (ECDSA).

Hashing Algorithms

_____**33.** SHA-1.
_____**34.** SHA-224.
_____**35.** SHA-256.
_____**36.** SHA-384.
_____**37.** SHA-512.

Assurance Standards

_____**38.** FIPS 140-1.
_____**39.** FIPS 140-2.

Cryptographic Algorithm Validation Program

_____**40.** Cryptographic Module Validated.

Configurability

_____**41.** Changeable Default Values.
_____**42.** Multiple Users.
_____**43.** Different User Access Rights.
_____**44.** Transaction Logging.
_____**45.** Log Integrity.
_____**46.** Log Centralization.
_____**47.** Security Alerts.

Usability

_____**48.** Configuration by Users.
_____**49.** Authentication by Users.
_____**50.** Interruptions during Initial Encryption Process.
_____**51.** Computer use during Initial Encryption Process.
_____**52.** Software/Hardware Compatibility.
_____**53.** Maintenance by Administrators.
_____**54.** Administrator Recovery.
_____**55.** Third Party Recovery.

Manageability

_____**56.** Central Management.
_____**57.** Remote Management.
_____**58.** Unattended Reboot.
_____**59.** Authentication of Management Traffic.
_____**60.** Encryption of Management Traffic.

Scalability

_____**61.** Degree of Scalability.

CHAPTER REVIEW QUESTIONS/EXERCISES

True/False

1. True or False? Generation of a key in public-key cryptography involves exponentiation modulo a given modulus.
2. True or False? The order of a finite group is the number of elements in the group H.
3. True or False? In the multiplicative group, $H = <Z_{n^*}, x>$; when the order of an element is the same as $\phi(n)$, then that element is called the primitive root of the group.
4. True or False? A group H is said to be finite if the number of elements in the set H is finite.
5. True or False? The set of integers Z is a group under addition $(+)$; that is $(Z, +)$ is a group with identity $e = 0$, and inverse of an element a is $(-a)$.

Multiple Choice

1. A subgroup of a group G is a nonempty subset H of G, which itself is a group under the same operations as that of:
   A. R
   B. I
   C. N
   D. E
   E. G
2. What group is said to be cyclic if there exists an element $a \in G$ such that for any $b \in G$, and $i \geq 0$, $b = a^i$?
   A. O
   B. W
   C. S
   D. G
   E. A
3. Let _____ be a nonempty set with two binary operations addition $(+)$, and multiplication $(*)$.
   A. R
   B. I
   C. W
   D. C
   E. S
4. If the nonzero elements of a ring form a group under multiplication, then the ring is called a:
   A. field
   B. denial-of-service attack
   C. venyo
   D. port traffic
   E. taps

5. Construction of finite fields and computations in finite fields are based on:
   A. systems security plan
   B. polynomial computations
   C. denying service
   D. decision making
   E. URL lists

EXERCISE

Problem

How does advanced data encryption work?

Hands-On Projects

Project

What is a key?

Case Projects

Problem

What is the difference between public and private keys?

Optional Team Case Project

Problem

Which types of data can be encrypted.

References

[1] W. Mao, Modern Cryptography, Theory & Practice, Prentice Hall, 2004.
[2] B.A. Forouzan, Cryptography and Network Security, McGraw-Hill, 2008.
[3] P.L. Jensen, Hyperelliptic Curves and Their Application to Cryptography, University of Copenhagen, 2004.
[4] J. Hoffstein, D. Lieman, J. Pipher, J. Silverman, "NTRU": A Public Key Cyrptosystem, NTRU Cryptosystems, Inc. <www.ntru.com>.
[5] J. Hoffstein, J. Pipher, J. Silverman, NTRU—A Ring Based Public Key Cryptosystem.

Index

Note: Page numbers followed by "*f*", "*t*" and "*b*" refers to figures, tables and boxes, respectively.

Printed and bound by CPI Group (UK) Ltd, Croydon, CR0 4YY

03/10/2024

01040324-0014